Deconstruction and the Interests of Theory

Oklahoma Project for Discourse and Theory

OKLAHOMA PROJECT FOR DISCOURSE AND THEORY

SERIES EDITORS

Robert Con Davis, University of Oklahoma
Ronald Schleifer, University of Oklahoma

ADVISORY BOARD

Deconstruction and the Interests of Theory

by Christopher Norris

University of Oklahoma Press : Norman and London

By Christopher Norris

Deconstruction: Theory and Practice (New York, 1982)
Shostakovich: The Man and His Music (New York, 1983)
The Deconstructive Turn: Essays in the Rhetoric of Philosophy (New York, 1984)
(Editor) *Orwell: Views from the Left* (Topsfield, Mass., 1984)
The Contest of Faculties: Deconstruction, Philosophy, and Theory (New York, 1985)
Deconstruction and the Interests of Theory (Norman, 1989)

For Alison, Clare and Jenny

Library of Congress Cataloging-in-Publication Data

Norris, Christopher.
  Deconstruction and the interests of theory.
  (Oklahoma project for discourse and theory ; v. 4)
  Includes index.
  1. Deconstruction.   2. Criticism.   I. Title.
II. Series.
PN98.D43N59 1989   801'.95   88-40546
ISBN: 0–8061–2208–0 (cloth)
ISBN: 0–8061–2388–5 (paperback)

Deconstruction and the Interests of Theory is Volume 4 in the Oklahoma Project for Discourse and Theory.

Contents

Acknowledgments

During the period (roughly the past four years) over which these essays were written I read a good deal, talked to many people, and visited quite a number of university departments, in Britain and overseas. I won't even try to acknowledge all the debts thus incurred, except by singling out the names that came to mind most often as I read the book through in typescript. My thanks therefore to Andrew and Kate Belsey, Carol Bretman, Simon Critchley, Terence Hawkes, Kathy Kerr, Karen McDonaugh, Nigel Mapp, Duncan Salkeld, Peter Sedgwick, David Skilton, Rob Stradling and Ian Whitehouse in Cardiff; to Seymour Chatman, Art Quinn and Susan Shahzade in Berkeley, California; to Jacques Derrida whose writings and personal generosity have been a constant source of inspiration; to Andrew Benjamin, Tom Docherty, Joe Margolis and Dan Latimer for numerous helpful suggestions along the way; and to all those participants at seminars in Berkeley, Santa Cruz, Oregon, Christchurch, Passau, Warsaw, Antwerp, Copenhagen and elsewhere who offered various comments and criticisms. Most of all I want to thank Alison, Clare and Jenny for putting up with my much too frequent trips away from home and late-flowering romance with the word-processor. This book is dedicated to them by way of very partial recompense.

Some chapters or parts thereof were previously published as articles or reviews in *Paragraph, Journal of Law and Society, New Formations, Comparative Literature, Diacritics, The Southern Review* (Adelaide), *Southern Humanities Review* and *London Review of Books*. 'Post-Structuralist Shakespeare' first appeared in *Alternative Shakespeares*, John Drakakis (ed.), London, Methuen (1985), and 'Pope Among the Formalists' in Christopher Norris and Richard Machin (eds), *Post-Structuralist Readings of English Poetry*, Cambridge, Cambridge University Press (1987). I should like to thank the editors and publishers concerned for their permission to reprint this material.

Cardiff
May 1988

Series Editors' Foreword

In *Deconstruction and the Interests of Theory*, Christopher Norris continues his long-standing meditation on contemporary forms of discourse theory – on philosophy, literary studies, and, most intensely, on deconstruction. Norris has consistently attempted to understand the difficulties of contemporary discourse, especially the philosophy of Jacques Derrida, in relation to the largest intellectual movements of our time. For this reason, the meanings of *interest* in this book are manifold. Like Kierkegaard's definition of "interest" (*inter esse*, meaning both "in between" and "a matter of concern"), Norris's idea of the interests of contemporary theory ranges across disciplines and evinces a great concern for the proliferation of contemporary understandings of discourse. Norris's concern is apparent in all the essays collected here, and their range – from Shakespeare and Alexander Pope to music criticism, deconstruction, and analytical philosophy – reinforces the sense Norris offers of being in the midst of great intellectual movement and ferment.

Deconstruction and the Interests of Theory, however, also opens a third sense of "interest," which Kierkegaard neglects, a sense that is simultaneously political and moral. In the *Politics*, Aristotle articulates both this idea of "interest" and the kind of politico-ethical concern with it that Norris articulates in this book. Aristotle distinguishes between "two sorts of wealth-getting": household management and retail trade. The former, he says, is necessary and honorable,

> while that which consists in exchange is justly censured; for it is unnatural, and a mode by which men gain from one another. The most hated sort, and with the greatest reason, is usury, which makes a gain out of money itself, and not from the natural object of it. For money was intended to be used in exchange, but not to increase at interest. And this term interest, which means birth of money from money, is applied to the breeding of money because the offspring resembles the parent. Wherefore of all modes of getting wealth this is the most unnatural.

The great concern of *Deconstruction and the Interests of Theory* is precisely this kind of "breeding" that Aristotle describes: the multiplying of applications of literary theory to other disciplines, such as philosophy, history, and law, in which extensions of discursive analyses raise troubling political and ethical issues.

In other words, Norris attempts to situate contemporary theory within a framework that will allow the wide range of "interests", both positive and negative, generated by that theory to make themselves clear. This allows him to read disparate texts closely as an occasion for exploring the ethical and political consequences of deconstruction. In so doing, he articulates questions about contemporary discourse theory that are, we believe, among the most important issues facing literary and cultural studies today. Moreover, the essay format allows Norris to combine close examination of local texts and issues with an ethics of broad (discursive) understanding to present the various senses of interest we have mentioned: a wide-ranging concern that examines the proliferation of "critical" theories with an eye toward their disciplinary, political, and ethical consequences.

Within this overall concern can be heard, as a continual counterpoint, a rereading and rethinking of Paul de Man's work. Norris does not re-situate de Man within the context of the recently discovered Belgium papers, but he does re-situate de Man's "way of recasting ethical issues in a rhetorical, linguistic, or tropological register." In so doing, Norris follows one side of de Man's theoretical interests – and he does so in an explicit attempt to demonstrate the powerful *disinterested* intelligence of de Man's austere deconstruction – by focusing on the "imperialistic" aspect of theory, the ease with which it "colonizes" other disciplines, and the political and ethical questions such ease occasions.

Behind de Man in this volume, however, is the more cheerful and more self-consciously "interested" science of Jacques Derrida, which, finally, is less a recasting of ethics into rhetoric than a presentation of an ethics of rhetoric, an ear for hearing, as Norris says, the risks of writing and of interpretation. Norris notes "the risk that goes along with entrusting one's words to the ear of the other," but he also notes "the need to reject any too quick or evasive retreat into a rhetoric of textual freeplay or 'undecidability.'" In this Derridean meditation in *Deconstruction and the Interests of Theory*, Norris is testing – in the true manner of an *essai* – the caveat Aristotle made toward the "unnatural" breeding of interest and at the same time expressing his concern for the proliferation of a mode of "critical" analysis that seems to effect very little.

In other words, these more or less "freestanding" readings delimit a mode of *interested* reading across their various focuses. As such, they – and this collection as a whole – define a moment in contemporary theory in which an ethical assessment of the significance of discourse in the last two decades, with all the great interest it has generated, can be made. Such assessment is the aim of all the books in the Oklahoma Project for Discourse and Theory, and we are very pleased to welcome Christopher Norris's book to this series.

ROBERT CON DAVIS
RONALD SCHLEIFER

Norman, Oklahoma

Introduction: on the uses and abuses of literary theory

These essays cover a wide range of topics, from Shakespeare and Pope to musical criticism, deconstruction, the 'ethics of reading' and issues in current analytical philosophy. They are united by a general concern with the uses of theory and — more specifically — the way that certain 'advanced' forms of literary-critical thinking have been extended to other disciplines, often (as I argue) with untoward effects. This colonizing drive has resulted in a loss of argumentative rigour, a blurring of distinctions between logic and rhetoric, and a generalized notion of 'intertextuality' which reduces all language to a mere play of ungrounded narrative or figural representations. In so doing, it has lent support to a fashionable form of relativist doctrine which would have it that 'truth' is nothing more than a product of existing consensus beliefs, a value that holds good only in relation to this or that set of knowledge-constitutive interests. Any attempt to criticize such interests — whether on historical, political or philosophic grounds — would then appear simply a delusive endeavour, a throwback to that old 'foundationalist' belief in reason, truth and valid argument which has now (so it is argued) lost all its power to convince or persuade.

This attitude has various names in the currency of contemporary critical debate. One is neo-pragmatism, a position defended most persuasively by the philosopher Richard Rorty[1] and the literary theorist Stanley Fish (who has also, more recently, turned his attention to issues in the field of law and jurisprudence).[2] Another is 'postmodernism', or at least that version of postmodernist thought which rejects all forms of enlightenment critique, regarding them as so many ruses in the service of an outworn rationalist epistemology. Thus Jean-François Lyotard argues that we are now living in a post-philosophical culture, an epoch that has witnessed the final collapse of those old 'meta-narratives', or myths of self-legitimizing knowledge, that sought some grounding for reason and truth outside the range of currently acceptable beliefs.[3] Knowledge must henceforth be conceived in purely performative terms, as a capacity to bring about desired effects through the strategic deployment of discursive interventions whose only claim to 'truth' is their pragmatic yield in securing this or that short-term benefit. And for Jean Baudrillard likewise, we have now lived on into a postmodern epoch where there is simply no distinguishing between 'truth' or 'reality' on the one hand, and on the other those various forms of mass-media simulation which pass themselves off for the genuine article.[4] What we take as reality just *is* a product of the superinduced illusions, fantasies, images and forms of manipulative cultural feedback that constitute our knowledge of the world. In fact such language no longer makes sense, since to talk of 'simulation' or 'illusion' is implicitly to fall back into the old habit of thought (whether Platonist, Kantian, Marxist or whatever) that equates truth with the capacity to transcend mere *doxa*, belief, ideology, rhetoric, false conscious-ness or other such benighted states. For Baudrillard (like Lyotard) this is just one more melancholy symptom of the fact that so few intellec-tuals have yet caught up with the current (postmodern) rules of the game.

Deconstruction is often taken for another form of this will to under-mine truth and reason by way of a thoroughgoing 'textualist' critique that reduces such values to so many ultimately groundless metaphors and fictions. Thus Rorty reads Derrida as a useful ally in his own neo-pragmatist campaign, while writers on postmodernism tend to treat his work as pretty much equivalent, in its aims and effects, to that programme of wholesale 'delegitimization' carried on by Lyotard and Baudrillard. I think this is a highly misleading idea, the result of a failure to read or comprehend what is actually there, not only in Derrida's texts but in those of other thinkers (like Paul de Man) who resist such treatment on principled grounds. The following essays are therefore intended to rescue deconstruction — and 'literary theory' in general — from the various forms of misunderstanding that would blunt its genuinely critical edge. They also examine the effects of importing such ideas into adjacent disciplines like law, philosophy and historiography. These disciplines might indeed benefit from a knowledge of developments in recent literary theory, but they have everything to lose — as I shall argue — from the kind of pan-textualist pseudo-theory that would treat them as so many 'kinds of writing' devoid of all rational or truth-telling warrant.

I think we might start from some of Paul de Man's remarks on the 'resistance to theory' in literary studies.[5] This resistance doesn't only come from outside in the form of institutional prejudice or refusal to acknowledge new ways of reading and thinking. There is also a resistance internal to theory itself, a point at which texts have a habit of *not* turning out to mean what one expects them to mean according to this or that set of theoretical assumptions. This is why de Man so admired the best of the 'old' American New Critics. Certainly they were apt to raise local insights into a wholesale ontology of language and form, a rhetoric of 'irony', 'paradox' or whatever that supposedly defined the very nature of poetic meaning. But they were also — some of them — such fine close-readers that often their perceptions went completely against what they wanted to say and registered something quite different — maybe an odd turn of phrase or discrepant detail that called their whole approach in question.[6] De Man thought this the best possible way of teaching poetry, or for that matter any kind of text. That is to say, one needs theory to avoid reading stupidly, accepting language at face value, which is always the value placed on it by commonsense belief or ideology. In de Man this takes the form of a heightened attention to rhetoric and the way that rhetorical tropes can undermine the logic or the grammar of straightforward assertion. For theories of this sort are equally capable of turning into ironcast critical systems, as one already sees happening in certain quarters of the American deconstruction industry. So there also had to be this 'internal' resistance to theory, one that held out against system and method, that continued to cultivate the virtues of analytical close-reading, but also found room for theoretical reflection when it came to diagnosing the sources of that same resistance.

I think this might help to locate some real problems with theory as currently taught at undergraduate and graduate levels. Too often it is a matter of running through the various systems on offer, presenting them as so many self-contained options and leaving the students to apply one or other as best they can. This turns the whole business into a kind of intellectual supermarket where the main object is to pick the most radical theory going, expound its claims from the nearest secondary source, and then show briefly that you know how to work it by pulling the appropriate levers. The trouble is that all these theories (Marxist, feminist, post-structuralist or whatever) work perfectly well with just about any kind of text so long as they are applied at this level of abstract generality. Any resistance that the text might put up — any sign of its not responding ideally to the chosen method of approach — is rendered invisible by a whole new set of stubborn theoretical preconceptions. A brief glance at the current journals is enough to bear this out. It is not so much the canon that has changed as the variety of methods, theories and approaches that now have something like canonical status. For every poem or novel in the Great Tradition there must be by now at least one reading that treats it from, say, a Freudian–Lacanian, or a New Historicist, or a Marxist post-structuralist, or a Derridean or a feminist–psychoanalytic standpoint. Some of these readings are inventive, resourceful and convincing. Others are so remote from the text as scarcely to be 'readings' at all. Very often, even with the best of them, there is an overriding need to prove the theory right at all costs and a corresponding lack of that internal resistance — a resistance 'specific to theory itself' — that de Man locates in the rhetorical aspect of language.

The most typical feature of so-called 'literary' deconstruction is its tendency to fasten onto well-worn themes like the self-reflexive character of texts, the way that mimetic illusion is undone by the play of figural language, and the specular regress (or *mise-en-abyme*) that results from a reading always on the look-out for signs of metaphorical slippage.[7] Again, this is more or less guaranteed to work with just about any fictional text, since we know (after all) that novels aren't *really* windows on reality, that language can't provide an unmediated access to the world, that realism is in some sense a product of signifying codes and conventions . . . and so forth. Of course this gives room for displays of ingenuity in showing how the argument applies just as much to novels in the great realist tradition as to postmodern texts that positively flaunt their anti-mimetic character.[8] Still there is something odd about the repeated demonstration, carried off each time with an air of triumphant discovery. On the other hand there seems little point in deconstructing postmodernists like Borges, Barthelme or Calvino, writers who effectively manage to pre-empt just about everything the critic might want to say. In the end such readings most often invite the Johnsonian riposte that nobody in their right mind ever *actually* confused fictive with real-life experience, or succeeded so far in suspending disbelief that all such distinctions dropped away. One problem with literary deconstruction is that it tends to come up with sophisticated reasons for believing what we always knew. Often this produces an uncomfortable sense that the theory is working all right, but that it couldn't really fail to work, given the basic absurdity of the beliefs it sets out to deconstruct. Again, it is the lack of any possible resistance from the text — any obstacle to theory on its otherwise triumphal progress — that renders such arguments decidedly suspect.

Perhaps this is simply to re-state the familiar point that American deconstruction has been largely transformed from a philosophical activity into a branch of literary criticism. As a result, its procedures have been loosened up, foregoing the kind of consequential argument and analytic rigour that one finds in Derrida's essays on Plato, Kant, Hegel or Husserl, and becoming much more a species of elaborate verbal gymnastics. Of course it may be argued that such criticisms are beside the point, since Derrida has shown (hasn't he?) that there is really no difference between 'philosophy' and 'literature'; that all philosophical concepts come down to metaphors in the end; and that therefore we had much better drop such deluded categorical distinctions and read all texts with an eye to their covert structures of figural meaning. In fact this ignores the many passages, especially in *Margins of Philosophy*, where Derrida says just the opposite. If indeed it is true that the texts of philosophy are littered with with dead or forgotten metaphors — if the very word 'concept', along with others like 'theory' or 'idea', are ultimately tropes whose origin we have repressed, as Nietzsche argued, through the will-to-power that masquerades as philosophic truth — then equally it is the case that our very notions of metaphor, of literature and of figural as opposed to literal language are notions that have always been produced and worked over by the discourse of philosophic reason.[9] Derrida is far from endorsing Richard Rorty's proposal that we should drop the idea of 'philosophy' as a discipline with its own particular interests, modes of argument, conceptual prehistory etc., and henceforth treat it as just one 'kind of writing' among others, on a level with poetry, literary criticism and the human sciences at large.[10] In fact his recent essays have laid increasing stress on this need to conserve what is specific to philosophy, namely its engagement with ethical, political and epistemological issues that cannot be reduced *tout court* to the level of an undifferentiated textual 'freeplay'.[11]

This does have a bearing on the practical question of how best to teach 'theory' at undergraduate and graduate levels. One thing that is happening in many British universities is a gradual interpenetration of the disciplines, such that (for instance) people from departments of literature are offering courses to students of philosophy, history or the social sciences. The benefits of this arrangement are obvious enough. There is good reason to think that the old institutional boundaries no longer correspond to what is going on at the cutting edge of those disciplines. Thus students of philosophy might gain from some knowledge of current developments in literary theory (more specifically, from a reading of Derrida or de Man), and historians from a course in narrative poetics, perhaps starting out with Hayden White's *Tropics of Discourse* and then moving on to a detailed rhetorical analysis of texts in the manner that White proposes.[12] Or again, there are many points of contact between literary theory and the interests of modern jurisprudence, including such basic issues as the interpretation of case-law precedent, the role (if any) of framers' intentions in fixing the scope and proper meaning of documents and the whole vexed question of how far law can be treated — as the legal formalists believed — as a self-contained system of axiomatic rules and principles, ideally immune from the pressure of social and political interests.[13] In each of these disciplines — philosophy, history and law — there are already signs of a challenge being mounted on terms that derive from literary theory, especially from the current post-structuralist critique of language, ideology and representation. So far it has happened mainly in American universities, where the credit system gives students more freedom to opt for courses outside their chosen major discipline. But the same broad trend is observable in Britain, and no doubt in other countries as it becomes steadily more difficult — more obviously an artificial exercise — to pretend that these disciplines truly exist as so many self-enclosed realms of special expertise.

Now of course I wouldn't want to deny the value and desirability of such interdisciplinary contacts. In straightforward practical terms — as a matter of showing how 'literary studies' can earn their keep at a time of economic cutbacks, cost-effectiveness as the universal yardstick and widespread scepticism as regards the humane or civilizing role of the arts — it is obviously useful to strike up relations on as many fronts as possible. If these seem merely opportunist arguments, there is also the mutual benefit to be had from the exchange of ideas across intellectual borderlines, and the testing of assumptions in a spirit of open-minded dialogue. Besides, many teachers can attest to the feelings of professional bad conscience that result from continuing to profess a discipline — English Literature — whose ideological history has now been so thoroughly exposed to view, and whose reliance on a set of largely unargued and self-promoting values they can demonstrate easily enough in books and articles, but not when it comes to the business of day-to-day seminar teaching.[14] Much better to give up that old, isolationist stance and replace it with a range of demystified alternatives: reception-theory, narrative poetics, discourse-studies, 'New Historicism' and the like. At least these are eminently teachable skills, of use across a range of contiguous disciplines and carrying none of the obscurantist overtones that dogged the inheritance of English Studies from Arnold to Leavis and beyond.

But there are, as I have suggested, certain dangers in the move to colonize other disciplines in the name of an all-embracing literary theory. One is the tendency to reduce those disciplines to the level of a generalized 'intertextuality' that takes no account of their specific problems, their conceptual pre-history and characteristic modes of argument. The result — as seen most clearly in neo-pragmatist appropriations of Derrida's work — is to encourage a levelling consensus view of language, truth and reason which deprives theory of its critical force by arguing that all such claims come down to a species of rhetorical imposition. This is no doubt why Derrida has insisted more emphatically in his recent writing that any deconstruction of philosophic truth-claims must at some point go by way of a meticulous and detailed close-reading of texts in the modern, post-Kantian enlightenment tradition.[15] The same applies to those current attempts to extend literary theory into the domain of history, jurisprudence or the social sciences in general. For the result may be not so much a salutary questioning of ideas, arguments and values ordinarily taken for granted, as a means of evading the forms of self-criticism that those disciplines have evolved in the process of examining their own distinctive truth-claims. Once again, I am not suggesting that people should stick to their appointed professional spheres and reject any interdisciplinary overtures that might threaten the existing intellectual division of labour. On the other hand there is nothing to be gained — indeed much to be lost — by a wholesale undoing of histories of thought which have laboured long and hard to separate truth from the various currencies of true-seeming fiction and consensus-belief.

'I find it bizarre', Stanley Fish writes in a recent essay, 'that so many people today think that by extending the techniques of literary analysis to government proclamations or diplomatic communiqués or advertising copy you make criticism more political or more aware of its implication in extra-institutional matters; all you do (and it is nothing to sneer at) is expand the scope of the institution's activity, plant the flag of literary studies on more and more territory.'[16] I find it equally bizarre (not to say ironic) that this argument should come from a thinker like Fish, one who has pushed the neo-pragmatist case 'against theory' to the point of denying that criticism can do anything to challenge the consensual meanings and beliefs embodied in a given 'interpretive community'.[17] In Chapter 5 I shall be looking more closely at Fish's arguments and their political implications. For the moment his case can be summarized roughly as follows: (1) that all interpretation, whether in literature, law, philosophy or the human sciences at large, takes place within some such communal enterprise;

(2) that this includes any theory, however radical, that sets out to criticize the terms of that consensus; and (3) that theorists must therefore be deluded if they think to advance any counter-hegemonic or strong revisionist argument that would somehow lay claim to an independent standpoint. This applies both to positive theorists, those who adopt a value-laden rhetoric of rights, first principles, ethical absolutes or whatever, against which to measure the supposed short-comings of a present-day consensus, and negative theorists, those like the Marxists and deconstructors who think to expose the mystified character of current consensual norms by pointing out the symptoms of strain, contradiction or aporia that characterize various kinds of discourse. To Fish, such claims are simply incoherent, since in order to achieve any kind of acceptance — that is, to carry weight with readers, critics, members of the relevant professional or cultural community — they *must* in the end be construed in terms of some pre-given cultural consensus. This is why Fish is quite happy with the notion of expanding the scope of literary studies into law, politics and other such fields, just so long as critics don't then delude themselves that this can make their writing more 'political', or better placed to challenge the current institutional status quo. Indeed, his own work is a striking example of what might be called 'travelling anti-theory' — that is, the kind of all-purpose pragmatist argument that can be used to discredit oppositional thinking in law, criticism or any other field where professional interests are in play.[18]

All the same it is hard to deny that some current uses of theory do make an easy target for Fish's techniques of knock-down argument. The reason — as I have said — is that they operate with a massively generalized notion of rhetoric or intertextuality which reduces all writings to a dead level of suasive or performative effect. This is why de Man, in his later essays, insists on preserving the distinction between logic, grammar and rhetoric, no matter how complex (or ultimately undecidable) their relation in any given case. For otherwise there is no possibility of tensions developing, of the text putting up the kind of localized resistance to preconceived methods or meanings that then offers a hold for critical understanding. Thus, in de Man's words, 'reading is an argument . . . because it has to go against the grain of what one would expect to happen in the name of what has to happen'.[19] It is only at these points of unexpected resistance — moments when the text disrupts any form of settled, consensual belief — that reading can escape what Fish conceives as the closed circle of interpretive foreknowledge. Any theory that doesn't make allowance for such possibilities, that reduces all meaning to a play of intertextual codes and conventions, or all truth to a product of ideological vested interests, will end up as one more handy confirmation of Fish's neo-pragmatist views.[20]

These arguments have an added urgency in the present political climate. After all, we in Britain are living through a period when it is especially vital to maintain a due sense of the difference between fact and fiction, historical truth and the various kinds of state-sponsored myth that currently pass for truth. It is not a good time to be telling students that history is only what counts as such according to some present consensus-view, and that finally it all comes down to a struggle for power between various, more or less plausible narrative fictions. The fact that many people currently believe what they are told to believe — that such distinctions may indeed become desperately blurred — makes it all the more important not to go along with this last-ditch relativist argument. The issue is posed most starkly with regard to sensitive periods like the 1930s, where a great effort is now under way to pretend that left-wing 'pacifists' and appeasers were somehow responsible for Hitler's rise to power, that the left did nothing to oppose Fascism (ignoring minor episodes like the Spanish Civil War) and that only conservatives — then as now — had the wisdom to press for rearmament and a firm foreign policy stance. This latter line of argument has to pass clean over such resistant bits of evidence as Chamberlain, Munich and the widespread opposition to war with Hitler among bankers, industrialists and conservative politicians who hoped to make common cause with the Nazis in a coming anti-Soviet front. Such distortions played a significant role in Tory propaganda during the run-up to the 1987 General Election. They are more or less taken for granted across a broad section of the popular press, and will no doubt find their way into the school history textbooks if the government manages to push through its latest 'core curriculum' proposals. Indeed there might come a time when this is the established consensus-view and when any opposition is marginalized to the point of becoming totally invisible. But it would still be a massively *falsified* consensus, brought about by the misreading or manipulative use of evidence, the suppression of crucial facts and the creation of a certain selective amnesia in those whose memory might otherwise go far enough back.

I think that these reflections should at least give pause to proponents of a sceptical historiography that regards truth as entirely a product of rhetorical or narrative contrivance. Of course this is not to suggest that the facts in any given case can be simply read off from the documents, or established in a straightforward positivist way without recourse to interpretative frameworks of any kind. Nor is it to deny that a reading of Foucault, Hayden White or other theorists of a relativizing bent may help to sharpen the student's awareness of those contests that are always being fought out over the interpretation of historical texts. But there is a great difference between this sort of lesson in the critical reading of evidence and the other form of wholesale Nietzschean scepticism which would render such lessons ultimately useless. What students need to know — by way of counterbalancing the current post-structuralist wisdom — is that there are strong arguments on philosophical, methodological and other grounds for rejecting such a desperate conclusion. These include various ways in which the criteria or truth-conditions for historical discourse differ from those that we normally apply to fictional texts. (Causal factors, chronological constraints, ascriptions of agency and question of material circumstance are among the more obvious topics that would need to be taken into account.)[21] There is, to say the least, something premature and suspect about any treatment of historical texts that fastens exclusively on their narrative or tropological aspects while ignoring these other constitutive dimensions.

The same applies to law, or those current forms of radical jurisprudence (like the Critical Legal Studies movement) that often make use of deconstructionist thinking in order to point up the blind-spots, conflicts and antinomies that plague the discourse of received legal wisdom.[22] Their work has focused mainly on procedural issues and questions in the realm of judicial review, especially in the context of American law, where debate often turns on clauses of the written Constitution which are framed in such a vague or indeterminate manner as to lend support to widely differing interpretations. Thus the theorists are agreed in rejecting any version of the formalist view which holds law to be a system of neutral precepts and principles, possessed of its own self-validating logic and untainted by political interests. Such beliefs they regard as mere legitimizing ruses in the service of an authoritarian discourse which smuggles in all manner of prejudicial values under cover of its own, self-serving objectivist rhetoric. The main object of the Critical Legal Theorists is to show how this discourse in fact gives rise to various disabling contradictions, notably the fact/value antinomy, the problematic distinction between 'private' and 'public' domains (especially as it bears on contract law) and the problems that arise in establishing the scope and limits of legal doctrine.[23] These latter apply both to case-law precedent, in so far as any choice of 'relevant' pre-history involves a whole series of interpretative judgments as to meaning, context, historical conditions, present-day circumstances etc., and equally to statute-law provisions since here also debate runs high between 'constructionists' who claim to respect framers' intentions, sceptics who deny that this is either possible or desirable, and others of various political persuasion who think that we can best make sense of what the framers had in mind from a standpoint of enlightened present-day wisdom. On the strength of such arguments the theorists go on to denounce the appearance of a settled consensus that enables mainstream (liberal) jurisprudence to think of 'hard cases' as a special category, a deviant sub-class whose problematic features can always be clarified by treating them in light of more straightforward, every-day rules and precedents.

So one can see why deconstruction has come to exert such a potent influence on the Critical Legal Studies movement. To begin with, it provides a whole set of useful strategies for inverting or undoing commonplace distinctions, for example those between fact and value, the 'letter' and the 'spirit' of the law, perspicuous cases and those that require some degree of interpretative insight. More specifically, it offers a sophisticated means of making the point that all legal discourse is performative in character, i.e. designed to secure assent through its rhetorical power to convince or persuade, even in the case of statute-law provisions whose language appears to be purely constative, or to specify its own meaning and terms of application without giving rise to such interpretative vagaries. De Man has some powerful arguments to this effect in his essay on Rousseau's *Social Contract*, a reading that pursues the antinomies of law to the point where they reveal a fundamental divergence beween the logic, the grammar and the rhetoric of legal texts. In de Man's words:

> no law is a law unless it applies to particular individuals. It cannot be left hanging in the air, in the abstraction of its generality. Only by thus refer-ring it back to particular praxis can the *justice* of the law be tested, exactly as the *justesse* of any statement can only be tested by referential verifiability . . . It turns out, however, that the 'law of the text' is too devious to allow for such a simple relationship between model and example, and the theory of politics inevitably turns into the history, the allegory of its own inability to achieve the status of a science . . . The text can be considered as the theoretical description of the State, considered as a contractual and legal model, but also as the disintegration of this same model as soon as it is put in motion. And as the contract is both statutory and operative, it will have to be considered from this double perspective.[24]

Such a reading has large implications for a project like Critical Legal Studies, one that sets out precisely to analyze the unspoken assump-tions, the conflicts and aporias of mainstream legal discourse. But with de Man the argument proceeds by way of detailed close-reading and a refusal simply to let go of the distinction between logic, grammar and rhetoric, as if thereby to discredit the whole enterprise of legal theory. It is their tendency to fall back on this undiffer-entiated notion of rhetoric that leaves the delegitimizers open to the charge of intellectual and moral nihilism, and which also exposes them to Fish's line of knock-down polemical response. For if it is indeed the case, as they argue, that all legal discourse — all talk about 'theories' and 'principles' — comes down to a species of disguised apologetics for the current institutional status quo, then this must apply equally to their own line of talk, whatever its radical preten-sions. This is why — to recall the cryptic sentence of de Man — reading becomes 'an argument' to the extent that it goes 'against the grain of what one would expect to happen in the name of what has to happen'. Otherwise there is no way of avoiding the pragmatist upshot, along with its inherently conservative implications.

I shall take up these questions again in Chapter 5, where my topic is precisely the misreading of deconstruction by some exponents of Critical Legal Studies. Here I am more concerned to establish their bearing on the present situation in British legal politics, with a government prepared to invoke quite unprecedented powers in pursuit of its own, self-justified aims and objectives. 'Unprecedented' in modern times, that is, since such practices were common enough before the establishment of parliamentary democracy in its present constitutional form. One example is the use of Royal Prerogative as a means of circumventing likely opposition in cases where the interests of 'national security' supposedly justify such measures. Royal Prerogative is defined as 'the residue of discretionary power left at any moment in the hands of the Crown, whether such power be in fact exercised by the Queen herself or by her ministers'.[25] Until recently the general opinion was that this power had been more or less relinquished, except for certain well-defined procedural purposes; that it lingered in the text-books only as a kind of quaint technicality, left over from the days of absolute monarchy when the law of the land was ultimately a matter of sovereign will. Thus 'the conventional view of the Royal Prerogative is that, following the Glorious Revolution of 1688, it was made subject to parliamentary control; and our constitution, based on parliamentary government under rule of law, dates from that time.[26] But in fact it has been used by the present government on a number of occasions, always with some pretext involving 'national security' or interests of state that are taken to transcend any possible objections in law. The first such use was in January, 1984 and had to do with the ban on union membership among civil servants engaged with surveillance and intelligence work at the Cheltenham communications centre. More recent cases have involved decisions not to prosecute members of the police or security forces who have killed suspected terrorists, allegedly unarmed and without being given due warning. In one such case Sir John Donaldson, Master of the Rolls, delivered himself of the notable opinion that when officers of the law commit 'illegal' acts they can always be protected from criminal prosecution by invoking special prerogative.

If accepted, such arguments would totally undermine the most basic principle of any constitutional democracy, the doctrine that requires a separation of powers between the executive, legislative and judicial branches. It would amount to a vote of no confidence in parliament and the courts, an admission that 'interests of state' as interpreted by the government — or by those highly placed judges who share the government's view — must always override the appeal to established constitutional or legal precepts. And it is far from clear how limits could be placed on the exercise of these same prerogative powers. Since 1979 they have been called upon to push through items of controversial legislation in the areas of trade-union reform, local government reorganization, official secrets and the freedom of the press to engage in discussion of these and related matters. Increasingly, it seems, the courts can be relied on to implement policy decisions arrived at by a government whose parliamentary majority enables them to carry such measures after minimal debate, or otherwise — in more 'sensitive' cases — to bypass debate altogether and fall back on prerogative powers. Or it may be that a High Court decision is overturned when the case goes to appeal, and then upheld by the Law Lords who reject the grounds of appeal and reinstate the original verdict. Most often, as in recent controversial cases, at the end of the day this process has resulted in the endorsement of government policy.

There is no doubt that deconstruction has a part to play in understanding how law becomes subject to these forms of distorting political pressure. One could take a lead from de Man's reading of the

Social Contract, especially those passages where he draws out the antinomies of legal discourse, the tensions that develop between law as a language of purportedly timeless, universal justice and law as a matter of specific application to the case in hand. As he describes it, this predicament extends to every kind of language since there is always a point at which the signifying structure — the repetitive and quasi-automatic 'grammar' of meaning — exceeds any particular act of reference. This is what Derrida terms the 'iterability' of speech-acts, their capacity for being grafted, taken out of context, used across a vast and potentially infinite range of situations, such that no normative logic of meaning can possibly set limits to their proper usage.[27] According to de Man it is in the discourse of law that such effects have the greatest political consequence. 'Just as no law can ever be written unless one suspends any consideration of applicability to a particular entity including, of course, oneself, grammatical logic can function only if its referential consequences are disregarded.'[28] That is to say, the authority of law depends on its claim to exist outside and above all particular interests, all private and political involvements that would compromise the claims of absolute justice. Language itself lends credence to those claims in so far as it enables law to be encoded in a 'grammar' of formalized statutes and maxims that take on a kind of autonomous, self-acting force. But it is precisely this aspect of legal discourse that dissociates justice from real human interests, and which creates all manner of mischievous perversions in the Rousseauist contractual model. For this process can always be enlisted on the side of a populist rhetoric that equates the absolute authority of law with the voice of the people as expressed in a language of mystified collective will. De Man goes on to cite passages from the *Social Contract* that show very clearly how this comes about; how the legislative process may reach its 'highest point' when it succeeds in creating an effect of metaphorical substitution such that 'each citizen can act only through the others', and 'the acquired power of the whole' (in Rousseau's words) 'is equal or superior to the sum of natural forces of all individuals'.[29] For it then becomes possible for those speaking in the name of 'the people' to impose their will through a rhetoric of the public good, 'national security', interests of state or whatever, a rhetoric that exploits precisely those mechanisms of language that enable law to establish its authority in the first place.

It is not hard to see how such a reading might apply to the use of Royal Prerogative as a means of circumventing parliamentary and democratic process. In fact de Man's model has far-reaching implications for any project, like Critical Legal Studies, that sets out to question received or controversial aspects of legislative practice. But this exercise will lack any purpose, as I have argued, if it doesn't maintain some grounds for distinguishing between rightful and abusive instances of law, those that respect constitutional procedures and those that involve some form of unwarranted pretextual imposition. De Man is not directly concerned with such issues in the province of applied legal theory. But he does maintain the essential distinction between logic, grammar and rhetoric, the latter most often turning out to problematize the very terms of this model, but only as the upshot of meticulous close-reading and a rigorous sequence of argument. Otherwise there can be no grounds for criticism, no normative standpoint from which to comprehend the distortions, perversions or exploitative uses of legal power. This is why the deconstructive critique of law has to go beyond rhetorical analysis as such to an account of the knowledge-constitutive interests that define the tradition of liberal jurisprudence. In the end one cannot separate these questions of interpretative theory from the various substantive philosophical convictions that underwrite the discourse of legal reason.

Thus any criticism of a government for making illegitimate use of Royal Prerogative will have to take account of how such moves contravene the most basic principles of modern parliamentary democracy, principles that embody a certain, highly specific set of beliefs about freedom, justice and the status of the individual subject before the law. And these beliefs have a grounding in the discourse of enlightened reason, the idea (most forcefully defended by Kant) that justice and truth are best served by removing all sources of absolute, coercive power and respecting the faculties of critical judgment that rightfully belong to rational agents.[30] Thus in matters of law, as in ethics, religion and philosophy, there is a duty that devolves upon the thinking subject *not* to take beliefs on trust from some higher authority, but to question their validity and assent to them only in so far as they square with the dictates of reason, conscience and truth. This enlightenment philosophy has not fared well at the hands of post-structuralists and other present-day demythologizing thinkers. It is often reduced (as by Foucault) to a mere passing episode in the history of thought, a 'fold' in the order of language and representation that gave rise to man, the transcendental subject of his own self-engendering and delusive discourse.[31] But such arguments make no attempt to engage with the specific complexities of Kantian thought. They take for granted that wholesale reduction of reason to a play of rhetorical 'discourses' or codes which renders criticism powerless in the face of neo-pragmatist adepts like Fish. And nowhere could this effect be more damaging than in the discipline of legal studies. For here the Kantian assumptions go deep, both historically (by virtue of their common point of origin with the basic tenets of liberal justice and constitutional law) and philosophically (in so far as they provide the only basis for enlightened critique of existing practices). To regard them as just one transient episode in the order of shifting discursive regimes is effectively to jettison the very possibility of thinking constructively *within and against* that same tradition.

I have argued that current ideas in literary theory provide at best a partial and at worst an actively misleading model for the conduct of other disciplines. They lend support to a fashionable relativist trend which undermines critical reason, treats history as simply a collection of narratives or fictions, and renounces any claim to distinguish between truth and the various currencies of true-seeming ideological belief. This has come about partly through a narrow conception of 'critical theory', one that derives almost entirely from French post-structuralist sources and shows small interest in the other, post-Kantian tradition of thought taken up by philosophers like Adorno and Habermas. For it is here that the claims of critical reason have received their most persistent and vigorous defence in the face of various irrationalist or relativist creeds.

In Habermas this takes the form of a 'transcendental pragmatics', a large-scale attempt to preserve what is essential in the Kantian enlightenment tradition while acknowledging the force of current anti-foundationalist arguments. Hence his appeal to the normative criterion of an 'ideal speech-situation', one in which the discourse of various parties would no longer be subject to the pressures, distortions and misunderstandings that result from the unequal distribution of knowledge and power in present-day society.[32] Although it exists necessarily as a kind of utopian projection, this ideal is implicit — so Habermas argues — in each and every act of communicative utterance, each attempt to make our own meaning clear or to understand what others are saying. It is Kantian in so far as it rejects the idea — common to all forms of neo-pragmatist thinking — that truth can be only a matter of consensus values, or what is currently 'good in the way of belief'. For if this were the case, then thought would be incapable of attaining any kind of critical perspective, any standpoint that questioned received ideas in the name of some better, more adequate understanding.

One need only look to the current wave of right-wing revisionist historiography to see how those assumptions are the first target of counter-enlightenment thought. Thus Jonathan Clark sets out to demolish what he takes as the old, creaky meta-narrative that underwrites Whiggish or liberal–progressive accounts of British history. He rejects (among other things) the belief that constitutional reform came about through a struggle against older conceptions of divine right or Royal Prerogative; the idea of 1688 as marking a decisive turning-point in the progress of social–democratic institutions; and the whole 'adversarial' concept of history as a field of contending forces where interests of a broadly progressive, enlightened or emancipatory character were pitched against residual forms of the old regime.[33] Equally suspect, in Clark's view, is any use of the word 'revolution' to describe events like those of the middle- or late-seventeenth century, events which can then be made to fit in with the 'teleological' reading of history as an onward march towards present-day notions of democracy, justice and reason. *Rebellion*, not revolution, is Clark's preferred term for what he sees as merely localized symptoms of unrest against a background of largely unchanging assent to the existence of sovereign powers and a rigidly stratified social order. This change of usage helps us to appreciate 'that many conflicts (like the Civil War or 1688) can better be described as reactions against innovations, a deeply rooted resistance to undesired change'.[34] For indeed, as Clark points out, the word 'revolution' has itself undergone a revolution of meaning over the past two centuries, before which time it was taken to signifying the end to some disruptive episode and the return full-circle to a previous, more settled and orderly dispensation.

So Clark's main object in proposing this terminological shift is to free historical discourse from the various accretions of Whiggish ideology built into its currently prevailing meta-narrative stance. Even the concept of 'rebellion' needs rescuing, he writes, since

> we often take a revolution to be a successful rebellion; and by 'revolution' we now understand, in addition to the political aspects, a fundamental challenge to the legitimacy of social structures, including patterns of hierarchy or stratification, and titles to economic ownership or control . . . So to distinguish these two explanatory categories helps us to disengage ourselves from the assumption that revolutions are always 'forward-looking', that they embody the progressive aspirations of 'rising' social classes to speed up developments being impeded by the 'forces of reaction'. [Clark, 1986, p. 4]

In pursuit of this aim Clark offers a wholesale revisionist account of the entire period from 1640, through the Restoration and Hanoverian settlement, to the Industrial Revolution (which term he thinks highly misleading but uses as a matter of convenience) and the history of nineteenth-century socio-political change. In so far as a consensus exists on these topics it is one that he finds so deeply infected by the liberal or, worse still, the Marxist malaise that its assumptions need refuting point by point. At each stage he argues that the so-called 'forces of reaction' were in fact always dominant; that any changes towards greater participant democracy or constitutional reform were short-term adjustments only; and therefore that historians go badly wrong when they overrate the importance of such episodes and ignore the more profound continuities that emerge if one abandons this false perspective. The opposing schools can be categorized roughly as 'old hat' (Whiggish), 'old guard' (Marxist) and 'class of 68' (self-explanatory). What they share is a set of stubborn preconceptions about progress, enlightenment and the proper ends of historical understanding that have, as Clark believes, exerted a regular distorting influence on their powers of scholarly judgment.

His revisionist account of the period in question can be summarized briefly as follows. The events of 1641 and 1688 were *not* 'revolutions' in the sense of that term proposed by liberal or left-wing historians. They had little to do with the clash of opposing social forces, the rise of a disaffected merchant or 'middle-class' interest, the assertion of parliamentary powers against Royal Prerogative, or any of those 'underlying' socio-economic causes that had hitherto been called upon by way of explanation. Rather, they were short-term responses to specific kinds of grievance, most often brought about by some shift in the perceived relationship between Crown, Church and State. The result in each case was *not* (so Clark argues) to advance a stage toward the overthrow of Absolute Monarchy or the concept of Divine

Right, but to find some new, more effective form of working compromise that would keep those institutions firmly in place. So there remained a close link between monarchy and the legitimizing power of established religion, a link that not only survived 1688 but was in fact powerfully reinforced by the Hanoverian claim to represent the true authority of Church and State as against the now discredited Jacobite interest. Thus nothing much had changed over the past fifty years bar the advent of a so-called 'Lockean consensus' which in fact merely offered a new apologia for the status quo ante, and otherwise exists only as a product of wishful-thinking subsequent historians. 'The effective absolutism of the King was actually strengthened by the fiction of the King-in-Parliament within the Clarendonian constitution as implemented after 1660. Consequently, 1688–9 did not resolve the issue of sovereignty in favour of the representative principle, nor did it liquidate the monarch. William III was no puppet. The mixture was as before' (Clark, op. cit., p. 132). And the same goes for the 'Industrial Revolution', an event which never happened, according to Clark, or at least one whose origins, date and character remain largely undefined. In short, 'the Industrial Revolution was an historical category, not an event. We may doubt whether it was even a *process*, if by that we are to understand a single, unified and thematically coherent development' (Clark, op. cit., p. 39). In which case the historian had much better recognize that this, like other such putative 'revolutions', has no reality outside the Whiggish meta-narrative that interprets everything as lending support to its own providentialist thesis.

What Clark wants to do is effect a great shift in the discursive terrain of modern historiography, such that the opposing viewpoints (old-hat liberal or old-guard Marxist) no longer make any kind of sense. At times he is quite disarmingly frank about these tactical or polemical aims. Thus he presents the whole issue very often in terms of a generation-gap or war of ideas between his own (revisionist) colleagues and the defenders of an old orthodoxy. Furthermore, he concedes that 'genres of scholarship do fall into desuetude for reasons not wholly indicative of their intellectual merits', and that changes in the currency of authorized knowledge may have much to do with shifts of intellectual fashion or changes in the climate of political belief. 'For reasons of which we are only now becoming aware, [this] fate may now be overtaking the characteristic idioms of some of the schools of thought discussed here: less denounced as false, more neglected as slightly quaint (Clark, op. cit., p. 43). In fact his whole strategy is to speed up this process by ridiculing the positions he thinks are 'old hat' and representing their exponents as so many sadly superannuated figures who have not yet managed to grasp the new rules of the game.

To this extent Clark could be seen as endorsing the current postmodernist or Foucauldian view that history is always a 'history of the present', a discursive domain whose contours are shaped by prevailing social or political interests. Thus his work has two revisionist stories to tell, the first mainly occupied with events between 1640 and

1832, the other with the fortunes of modern historiography in the wake of the 'electoral shock' of 1979. Up till then there existed a broad left–liberal consensus in history, economics and political science, a nexus of Fabian and Keynesian ideas which more or less commanded the field. But since 1979 that consensus has collapsed, and along with it the claims to serious attention of all those thinkers who have remained under its spell. In the words of Kenneth Burgin, cited approvingly by Clark: 'it would be easy to list a succession of books by men who have been left like stranded whales by the ebb of the Keynesian tide . . . Too many existing political scientists belong to the generation of 1968 — a provenance that almost disqualifies them from comment on late 20th century politics' (Clark, op. cit., p. 20). As Clark sees it this same condition applies to historical scholarship, since 'truth' at any given time — or within any given community of knowledge — can only be determined according to the currently prevailing consensus.

Now clearly there is a sense in which this all goes to confirm what Foucault, Hayden White and others have argued: namely, that history is a field of competing rhetorical or narrative strategies, a plural discourse which can always produce any number of alternative accounts. But it might be well to question this relativist line if it lends itself so readily to the purposes of right-wing revisionist historians like Clark. For the result of such thinking is not only to efface the distinction between fact and fable but to undermine the very concept of historical reason as aimed toward a better, more enlightened or accountable version of significant events. Clark sees nothing but error and delusion in the idea that episodes like 1640 and 1688 might be interpreted as stages in the growth toward this kind of questioning, critical awareness. Thus he assembles passages from the work of 'old-guard' historians in order to demonstrate the supposed absurdity of this way of thinking.

> Educated men had been taught 'to think for themselves: they could not easily accept the dictates of kings and bishops'. 'Competing religious ideologies shattered the unquestioning and habit-forming faith of the past.' Orthodox theology and patrician social authority equals dogma produces bigotry demands unthinking acceptance or rational dissent: such was the pattern of prejudice which had hamstrung the scholarship of the Hanoverian era also. [Clark, op. cit., p. 104]

His point is to ridicule the very idea that reason — or the power of critical thought — can effect transformations of a social or political order which historians are then called upon to interpret through a similar exercise of rational intelligence. Clark's whole revisionist approach is premised on the argument that no such understanding can ever come about; that historical events, like historical interpretations, arise in response to short-term pressures of circumstance and then disappear just as quickly when the times change. In which case historians can only be deluded if they try to make sense of the past on assumptions that derive from an outworn mythology of reason, progress and enlightened secular critique. For such beliefs line up all too readily with the notion of people 'thinking for themselves', and of history as offering intelligible evidence of the way this process worked itself out in socio-political terms. Hence Clark's argument that the old coerceive powers of religion and monarchy never really lost their grip; that Divine Right lingered on in all but name; and that therefore we had much better recognize these deep continuities and drop all talk of 'revolutions' and suchlike chimerical events.

It is not hard to see how this position might square with other current forms of right-wing revisionist thinking. Thus for instance one could take it as offering support — historical warrant — for the government's revival of Royal Prerogative as a means of enforcing its policy interests through the courts while avoiding any kind of parliamentary or public opposition. My point is that 'critical theory' in the current post-structuralist mode cannot engage with such issues because it has effectively renounced any claim to distinguish between reason and rhetoric, knowledge and power, judgments arrived at through a process of uncoerced, rational debate and judgments resting on prejudice, dogma or the exercise of unchecked authority. What is needed is an openness to other kinds of theory that have held out against this relativizing drift on account of its conservative implications. They include (as I have argued) the Frankfurt tradition of *Ideologiekritik*, especially that modified version of it — the theory of communicative action — which Habermas deploys by way of contesting present-day irrationalist trends.[35] There is also much to be gained from a reading of those deconstructionist texts that abjure the pleasures of unlimited 'freeplay' for the sake of advancing a cogent critical argument. But these issues in the sphere of textual under-standing cannot be divorced from substantive questions of politics, ethics and right reason. Any attempt to counter the revisionists on their own historical ground will need to do more than offer some alternative rhetoric or some preferable story that highlights different episodes. It will have to make good the basic claim — basic, that is, to all forms of genuinely critical thinking — that truth is not a product of consensus–belief but the upshot of an ongoing rational debate where consensus values should always be subject to question.

References

1. See for instance Richard Rorty, *Consequences of Pragmatism*, Minneapolis, University of Minnesota Press (1982).
2. See Stanley Fish, 'Working on the Chain Gang: interpretation in the law and in literary criticism', *Critical Inquiry*, IX, (1982/3), pp. 201–16 and 'Dennis Martinez and the Uses of Theory', *Yale Law Journal*, Vol. XCVI (1987), pp. 1773–1800.
3. Jean-Francois Lyotard, *The Postmodern Condition: a report on knowledge*, Geoff Bennington and Brian Massumi (trans.), Minneapolis, University of Minnesota Press, (1984).
4. See for instance Jean Baudrillard, *The Mirror of Production*, Mark Poster

(trans.), St Louis, Telos Press, (1975) and *For a Critique of the Political Economy of the Sign*, Charles Levin (trans.), St Louis, Telos Press, (1981).

5. See especially the essays collected in Paul de Man, *The Resistance to Theory*, Minneapolis, University of Minnesota Press, (1986).

6. See de Man, 'The Return to Philology', in *The Resistance to Theory* (op. cit.), pp. 21–6.

7. For a powerfully argued critique of this tendency among exponents of 'literary' deconstruction, see Rodolphe Gasché, *The Tain of the Mirror*, Cambridge, Mass., Harvard University Press, (1986).

8. Some striking examples may be found in J. Hillis Miller, *Fiction and Repetition: seven English novels*, Oxford, Basil Blackwell, (1982).

9. See Jacques Derrida, 'White Mythology: metaphor in the text of philosophy', in *Margins Of Philosophy*, trans. Alan Bass, Chicago, University of Chicago Press, (1982), pp. 202–71.

10. Richard Rorty, 'Philosophy as a Kind of Writing', in *Consequences Of Pragmatism* (op. cit.), pp. 90–109 and 'Deconstruction and Circumvention', *Critical Inquiry*, Vol. XI (1984), pp. 1–23.

11. See especially Derrida, 'The Principle of Reason: the university in the eyes of its pupils', *Diacritics*, Vol. XIX, No. 2 (1983), pp. 3–20.

12. Hayden White, *Tropics Of Discourse*, Baltimore, Johns Hopkins University Press, (1978).

13. For suggested reading on law, literary theory and the Critical Legal Studies movement, see Chapter 5, Notes.

14. A problem remarked on by several contributors to Peter Widdowson (ed.), *Re-Reading English*, London, Methuen, (1982).

15. See especially Jacques Derrida, 'The Principle of Reason' (op. cit.) and 'The Age of Hegel', in *Glyph*, Vol. I, new series, University of Minnesota Press, (1986), pp. 3–43.

16. Stanley Fish, 'Driving from the Letter: truth and indeterminacy in Milton's *Areopagitica*', in Mary Nyquist and Margaret W. Ferguson (eds), *Re-Membering Milton*, London, Methuen, (1987), pp. 234–54; 249–50.

17. See Fish, *Is There A Text In This Class? The Authority of Interpretive Communities*, Cambridge, Mass., Harvard University Press, (1980).

18. This line of argument is discussed and criticized from various points of view in W.J.T. Mitchell (ed.), *Against Theory: literary theory and the new pragmatism*, Chicago, University of Chicago Press, (1985).

19. Paul de Man, Foreword to Carol Jacobs, *The Dissimulating Harmony*, Baltimore, Johns Hopkins University Press, (1979), pp. vii–xii; p. xi.

20. See for instance Stanley Fish, 'Dennis Martinez and the Uses of Theory' (op. cit.) and 'Critical Legal Studies, Unger and Milton', *Raritan*, Vol. VII, No. 2 (1987), pp. 1–20.

21. These arguments receive a cogent exposition in Maurice Mandelbaum, *Philosophy, History and the Sciences: selected critical essays*, Baltimore, Johns Hopkins University Press, (1984).

22. See Peter Fitzpatrick and Alan Hunt (eds), *Critical Legal Studies*, Oxford, Basil Blackwell, (1987); David Kairys (ed.), *The Politics of Law: a progressive critique*, New York, Pantheon Books, (1982); Mark Kelman, *A Guide to Critical Legal Studies*, Cambridge, Mass., Harvard University Press, (1987); Roberto M. Unger, *The Critical Legal Studies Movement*, Cambridge, Mass., Harvard University Press, (1986).

23. See especially Clare Dalton, 'An Essay in the Deconstruction of Contract Doctrine', *Yale Law Journal*, XCIV (1984), pp. 997–1114.

24. Paul de Man, 'Promises (*Social Contract*)', in *Allegories Of Reading: figural language in Rousseau, Nietzsche, Rilke, and Proust*, New Haven, Yale

University Press, (1979), pp. 246–77; 269–71.

25. As defined by the jurist Albert Dicey; cited by Patrick McAuslan, 'The Royal Prerogative as a Threat to the Rule of Law', *The Independent*, 27 January 1988, p. 18.
26. Ibid., p. 18.
27. Jacques Derrida, 'Signature Event Context', *Glyph*, Vol. I (1977), pp. 172–97.
28. De Man, 'Promises' (op. cit.), p. 269.
29. Ibid., p. 271.
30. In this connection see Immanuel Kant, *The Conflict of the Faculties*, Mary J. Gregor (trans. and ed.), New York, Abaris Books, (1979).
31. See Michel Foucault, *The Order of Things: an archeology of the human sciences*, New York, Vintage, (1973).
32. See especially Jürgen Habermas, *Knowledge and Human Interests*, Jeremy J. Shapiro (trans.), 2nd edn. London, Heinemann, (1978); *Communication and the Evolution of Society*, Thomas McCarthy (trans.), London, Heinemann, (1979).
33. J.C.D. Clark, *Revolution And Rebellion: state and society in England in the seventeenth and eighteenth centuries*, Cambridge, Cambridge University Press, (1986). This volume is a more polemical treatment of issues first raised in Clark's *English Society 1688–1832: ideology, social structure and political practice during the Ancien Regime*, Cambridge, Cambridge University Press, (1985).
34. Clark, *Revolution And Rebellion* (op. cit.), p. 4.
35. See especially Jürgen Habermas, *The Philosophical Discourse of Modernity: twelve lectures*, Frederick Lawrence (trans.), Cambridge, Polity Press, (1987). Gillian Rose pursues a broadly similar line of argument in her book *Dialectic Of Nihilism: post-structuralism and law*, Oxford, Basil Blackwell, (1984).

1 Utopian deconstruction: Ernest Bloch, Paul de Man and the politics of music

The signs are that Marxist criticism is at present undergoing one of its periodic shifts of theoretical vision. What is at stake is a widespread revaluation of utopian or visionary thought as it bears upon the Marxist project of historical understanding. This amounts to a questioning of the received view that utopian reverie was a kind of infantile disorder, an escape from the problems and exigencies of materialist critique into a realm of unanchored speculation where thinking encountered no resistance to its wildest dreams. This attitude was supposedly warranted by Marx's scattered allusions to utopian mystics and ideologues like Saint Simon, Fourier and Robert Owen. It was also based on a decidedly selective reading of Engels's *Communism: scientific and utopian* (1880), where the argument for Marxist 'science' in fact goes along with a qualified respect for the genuine emancipatory impulses embodied in utopian thought.

Fredric Jameson's book *The Political Unconscious* (1981) sets out to reclaim a positive or future-orientated version of Marxist hermeneutic, a philosophy of principled utopian faith to set against the purely demystifying drive of so much recent theoretical work.[1] He is even willing to enlist various patristic, theological and other-worldly schemes of interpretative thought, provided these can be effectively co-opted into a master-narrative whose ultimate terms are secular and Marxist. Thus Jameson argues for a reappropriation of the traditional four 'levels' of exegesis — the literal, moral, allegorical and anagogical — as stages on the path to an enriched understanding of Marxist hermeneutic method. History remains, in Jameson's words, the 'untranscendable horizon' of thought, the point toward which all meanings converge in the quest for some ultimate 'totalizing' grasp. Dialectical materialism is the only standpoint from which these various partial narratives and perspectives can at last be seen as composing a history that makes sense of them in adequately complex and non-reductive terms. Otherwise Marxism is always in danger of imposing a monological scheme of understanding, either through some variant of the crude base/superstructure model, or — as in Althusser's case — by reducing consciousness, history, culture and subjective agency to mere effects of a dominant structural complex whose workings can only appear under the aspect of detached theoretical knowledge.[2]

Jameson's ideas are expressly indebted to the greatest of modern utopian thinkers, the German Marxist and visionary philosopher Ernst Bloch. There is a well-known passage from one of Marx's letters that Bloch was fond of quoting, and that indicates something of his own close but ambivalent relationship to Marxist thought.

> So our slogan must be: reform of consciousness, not through dogma, but through the analysis of that mystical consciousness which has not yet become clear to itself. It will then turn out that the world has long dreamt of that of which it had only to have a clear idea to possess it really. It will turn out that it is not a question of any conceptual rupture between past and future, but rather of the *completion* of the thoughts of the past.[3]

This passage is remarkable for the fact that it prefigures all the major themes of Bloch's utopian thinking. It is also of interest, in light of what I have said so far, for rejecting the idea of revolutionary change as a rupture with past ways of thought, or as striving to achieve, in Althusserian terms, a decisive 'epistemological break' that marks the transition from lived ideology to genuine theoretical knowledge. One can read Bloch's work as a sustained, indeed lifelong effect to give substance to the kind of alternative vision held out by these comments of Marx. That they strike a note distinctly alien to most subsequent versions of Marxist thought is a fact to which Bloch's life-history and the debates around his work bear eloquent witness.

Up to now it has been difficult for the monoglot English reader to obtain more than a hazy impression of Bloch's enormously ambitious and wide-ranging work. Apart from Jameson's pioneering chapter in *Marxism And Form* (1971), the main source was through Bloch's various debates and polemics with other Marxist thinkers, notably Adorno, Lukacs and Brecht.[4] The sheer bulk of his writings, as well as their charged poetic style and resistance to orderly exposition, have so far conspired against his entering the mainstream of Western Marxist debate. However, this situation has now begun to change with the appearance of two major texts in English translation. One is Bloch's *magnum opus*, *The Principle of Hope*, a three-volume work which ranges over the entire compass of his thinking, from the politics of popular culture and everyday life to philosophy, religion, aesthetics, psychoanalysis and every sphere of thought where Bloch detects the latent signs of an as-yet unrealized utopian potential.[5] The other is a collection of essays *On the Philosophy of Music* which brings together work from his early 'expressionist' period with pieces written much later when Bloch's thinking had undergone a shift towards more overtly Marxist concepts and categories.[6] Between them, these volumes make it possible at last for the English reader to grasp the full extent of Bloch's innovatory thinking.

In what follows, I shall concentrate on those aspects of his work most directly concerned with music in its political or utopian-redemptive aspect. For Bloch, as for others before him in the German philosophical tradition — notably Schopenhauer and Nietzsche — music was at once the most humanly revealing form of art and the form most resistant to description or analysis in conceptual terms. But this was no reason, he argued, for retreating into an attitude of mystical irrationalism which denied music any kind of cognitive import, or (conversely) for adopting the formalist standpoint which reduced it to a play of purely abstract structures and relationships devoid of expressive content. If musical aesthetics had hitherto tended to vaccillate between these extremes, it was not so much by reason of some ultimate deadlock in the nature of thinking about music, but more an indication of the limits placed upon thought by its present confinement to a narrowly rationalist logic and a subject-object dualism incapable of transcending such antinomies. Bloch sees an example of this limiting perspective in the way that Bach's music has been praised alternately for its qualities of 'pure', mathematical structure and its power to move emotions by a kind of affective contagion quite beyond reach of analysis. 'Utterly wrong though the romanticizing which occurred in Mendelssohn's rendering of Bach is, equally an understanding of Bach cannot be achieved by mere dead dismissal of romanticism, as if nothing remained after it but reified form.[7]

Here Bloch concurs with Adorno's argument in the polemical essay 'Bach defended against his devotees'.[8] Critics and performers who celebrate Bach in the name of 'absolute music' are in fact submitting their judgment to those forces of inhuman abstraction and reification which mark the latest stage of capitalist social relations. 'This "new objectivity" in relation to Bach reproduces with a supposedly positive significance the judgment which was common half a century after Bach's death and which in fact submerged him as the greatest musician' (*Principle of Hope*, p. 1064). And such excesses always lead to a swing in the opposite direction, in this case toward a style of sentimentalized performance which lacks any feeling for structure or form. Thus 'a poorly overcome romanticism took revenge by again introducing expressive interpretation, but now not even in the Mendelssohnian style but in the style of the sentimental bower' (ibid., p. 1065). This reception–history is for Bloch symptomatic of everything that presently stands in the way of an adequate musical response. It reflects the kind of bad dialectic, the shuttling back and forth between extremes of 'objective' and 'subjective' response, which leaves its mark on every thought and perception in an age of commodified cultural experience. Bloch would no doubt have found this judgment amply confirmed had he lived to witness the present-day obsession with 'authenticity' in musical performance. Such ideas can only be deluded, he would argue, in so far as they substitute a dead, monumentalized concept of tradition for the living, evolving, dialectical process of change which has come between us and the cultural products of an earlier age. The jargon of authenticity is in fact nothing more than a kind of self-defeating nostalgia, a harking-back to ideas and practices that are falsified as soon as one sets them up as absolute, ahistorical values.

For Bloch, the only way to transcend such reified notions is by a new kind of listening, one that effectively opens the path toward a state of redeemed utopian promise. This 'surplus' of future-orientated meaning was ungraspable, he thought, within the terms handed down by Western philosophical tradition. Certainly music had figured at various points in this tradition as a kind of qualitative touchstone, a name for whatever surpassed or eluded the powers of abstract conceptualization. For Schophenhauer especially, music gave access to a realm of primordial experience — the Will in its all ceaseless strivings and desires — which the other arts (painting, architecture, poetry) could only express at a certain distance of formal representation. Thus music was the truth to which philosophy aspired but which could never reach the point of articulate understanding since language itself, and philosophical language in particular, dealt only in concepts or abstract figures of thought. There is a deeper ambivalence about Schopenhauer's attitude to music, since he commits himself to the following contradictory propositions: (1) that the highest point of human wisdom and felicity is to achieve detachment from the restless activity of Will, this state to be arrived at through a kind of self-disciplined contemplative repose, much akin to the Nirvana of Buddhist teaching; (2) that music most directly embodies the unconscious, inarticulate strivings of Will; and (3) despite this, that music is the highest form of art since it dispenses with the various intermediary concepts and representations which characterize other kinds of aesthetic experience. All three propositions are integral to his thinking, but there is no way of squaring their plainly contradictory entailments.

This problem has been recognized by Schopenhauer's commentators, even the more sympathetic among them, who treat it as a curious logical flaw in his otherwise intensely single-minded philosophy.[10] For Bloch, on the other hand, it is a sign of Schopenhauer's failure to grasp the utopian or forward-looking element in music, its appeal not to a realm of archaic, instinctual desire that precedes articulate thought, but to that which lies beyond the aporias of self-conscious reason and which draws thinking on toward the promise of transcending all such antinomies. Schopenhauer can conceive of no ultimate good save that which comes of escaping the Will, putting away all objects of desire and thus enjoying that long-awaited 'sabbath' from the penal servitude of instinct when 'the wheel of Ixion stands still' and the mind achieves a state of perfected stoical indifference. But what then of music, the experience of which — as Bloch says, paraphrasing Schopenhauer — 'speaks of the exclusive essence itself, weal and woe only, the universal Will and that alone as the most serious and the most real thing of all we can find'? (*PM*, p. 127). This desperate conclusion is forced upon Schopenhauer by his identification of 'reality' with the dark, destructive, self-preying nature of human instinct, and his total disbelief in the redemptive power of history, politics or secular reason. By renouncing all hope in the future, by ignoring the utopian dimension of music and hearing it only as a record of archaic struggles and defeats, Schopenhauer condemns his own philosophy to self-contradiction and ultimate nihilist despair.

Bloch's can be seen as the affirmative counterpart to Schopenhauer's gloomy metaphysics of will and representation. He concurs in treating music as the source of primordial truths that can as yet find no voice in philosophy or the other arts. This power he attributes to music's peculiarly inward character, its capacity to call out feelings and responses that have hitherto existed only in confused or inchoate form, but which now find expression in the realm of ordered sound. Such is the capacity for 'visionary listening' (*Hellhören*) that can work to transfigure the very conditions of human sensuous awareness. What music embodies in potential form is 'a figuring-out *in fonte hominum et rerum* that is utopian and fermenting, in an area of intensity that is open only to music' (*PM*, p. 228). For music provides the most striking intimation of that always conditional future state when subject and object, mind and nature might yet be reconciled beyond their present, divided condition. Like Schopenhauer again, he contrasts this inwardness of musical experience with the external, phenomenal or visual character pertaining to other artforms. Of course this is not so obviously the case with poetry or literary language. But in so far as these partake of *representation* — of that which, according to Schopenhauer, exists only at a certain remove from the primordial experience of Will — they are likewise to be thought of as mediated forms of expression which lack the sheer intensity of musical experience.

This is not to say that Bloch in any sense devalues literature, or sets up the kind of rigid hierarchical system that one finds in Schopenhauer's theory of art. Indeed, some of his most powerful writing in *The Principle Of Hope* is devoted to Goethe's *Faust* and other such works where the impulse of utopian thought is expressed through images of secularized mystical experience or Promethean overreaching. But it is in music that his thinking finds its elective homeground, a domain where the subject–object relation takes on a peculiarly charged and prophetic character. This is why its meaning eludes any theory based on notions of 'absolute form', or of structural relations, numerical proportions and so forth as the ultimate constituents of music. Such ideas are *theoretical* in the root sense, going back to the Greek terms for seeing, contemplation and other essentially visual metaphors raised into concepts of purely intellectual knowledge. As Jacques Derrida reminds us, these sublimated figures so permeate the discourse of Western philosophy that it is impossible to escape their influence.[11] But we can, according to Bloch, at least imagine an alternative realm of experience, one which points beyond the kind of static ontology enforced by these visual analogues, and which thus opens up a more active, transformative grasp of the subject–object dialectic.

Music is, for a deeper reason than was hitherto evident, the latest of the arts, succeeding visuality and belonging to the formally eccentric philosophy of inwardness, its ethics and metaphysics . . . This means objectivity penetrating to the core of the listener instead of the savant, instead of mere form-analysis . . . Both the existence and the concept of music are only attained in conjunction with a new object–theory, with the metaphysics of divination and utopia. [*PM*, pp. 130–1].

Thus music holds out the promise of a radical transformation, not only in our habits of aesthetic response but in every sphere of thought — ethics and politics included — where the relation between knower and known is a field potentially open for creative reimagining.

Of course there are problems in coming to terms with any philosophy which stakes its faith on such a leap outside all past and present categories of thought. The difficulty is posed most acutely by Bloch's attempts to explain the 'dialectic of nature' in terms of an envisaged utopian overcoming of the subject–object dualism. This might seem to place him in dangerous proximity to that current of vulgar Marxist materialism which naïvely conflates the dialectical process of thought with the antagonistic forces (or so-called 'contradictions') of external nature. In fact Bloch is everywhere alert to such confusions, and regards them as determined in part by the inadequate heritage of formal, post-Aristotelian logic, and in part by the pitiless divorce between subject and object imposed by an alien, dissociated sense of how thinking relates to the world of sensuous experience. His reiterated *noch nicht* ('not yet') is therefore both a kind of logical shifter — designed to bring about a qualitative change in the order of classical logic — and a means toward imagining the ultimate transcendence of man's alienation from nature. (In this respect Bloch comes close to the position adopted by the early Lukacs in *History and Class-Consciousness*, although their paths diverged sharply when Lukacs came to repudiate his own 'idealist' leanings in the name of Stalinist orthodoxy.) Yet this transcendence can only be achieved through a veritable leap of faith, since Bloch's arguments depend absolutely on a speculative concept of nature and a logic (as some would say, a pseudo-logic) whose potential is as yet unrealized by existing forms of thought.

These problems are addressed by Wayne Hudson in the only full-length study of Bloch yet to appear in English. If it is not possible, as Hudson says, 'to extract much emancipatory potential from the dialectical process of nature in its present form', then there is always the risk that this process will be 'arbitrarily transferred to history, despite the fact that in history, unlike nature, a subjective factor has emerged with conscious purposes'.[12] In a sense this criticism undoubtedly hits the mark. One could cite from almost every page of Bloch's writing sentences which metaphorically double back and forth between images of natural growth and development on the one hand, and figures of utopian–redemptive promise on the other. Very often they strike an apocalyptic tone which does indeed suggest that these metaphors are carrying a burden of meaning that resists articulation in more prosaic terms, and that might appear largely nonsensical if so treated. The following passage may stand as a fairly representative instance:

> Only the musical note, that enigma of sensuousness, is sufficiently unencumbered by the world yet phenomenal enough to the last to return — like the *metaphysical* word — as a final material factor in the fulfilment of mystical self-perception, spread purely upon the golden sub-soil of the receptive human potentiality. [*PM* p. 120].

Such writing is clearly open to the charge that it works by assimilating nature — or a certain quasi-dialectical image of nature — to a language shot through with metaphors of human purpose, activity and conscious striving for change. To this extent it bears out Hudson's argument that Bloch is in danger of collapsing ontological distinctions, treating history as a kind of organic process, and thus producing a mystified account of those social and material forces that shape human existence.

One response to this charge might be that Bloch is after all attempting nothing less than a full-scale revision of the concepts and categories that have hitherto governed what counts as 'rational' argument. This takes him back to the heritage of German metaphysical and speculative thought, to those philosophers (Kant, Fichte, Schelling and Hegel) in whose work there unfolds a dialectical debate on the relationship between subject and object, knower and known. It also leads to his revisionist account of those ancient, medieval and renaissance thinkers whom Bloch regards as having opened up a space for utopian divination. In his late work *Experimentum Mundi* (1975), he explores the lineage of an 'Aristotelian left' which worked to convert the 'immaterial forms' of a Platonizing Greek philosophy into an 'active form-laden matter', a realist doctrine which nonetheless rejected any notion of the real as fixed in terms of its self-same present attributes.[13] For Aristotle, reality is not exhausted by giving an account of what offers itself to immediate knowledge and perception. It must also include an aspect of future possibility, a dimension wherein things are latently other than they seem, and where knowledge takes on a forward-looking modality adequate to this sense of the capacity for change possessed by objects in the natural world. Aristotle's potentialist metaphysics was largely lost to view through the subsequent growth of more narrowly empirical philosophies of mind and nature. But its promise was maintained by those heterodox thinkers — notably Avicenna and Averroës — who continued to develop a kind of utopian materialism, one that held out against the reification of matter as inert substance, and the consequent reduction of knowledge itself to a passive contemplation of external forms. Even where this tradition led into byways of mystical and pantheist thought — as with Bruno and renaissance neo-Platonism — there was still, Bloch argues, a materialist subtext of unrealized hopes and desires which might yet be reclaimed by a Marxism open to such heterogeneous sources.

But there remains a real problem with any such use of organicist or naturalizing images and metaphors. This problem takes on a political edge when one considers the role played by such analogies in the history of aesthetics, and especially of musical aesthetics, in the wake of German romanticism. For Schopenhauer, as we have seen, music gave access to a realm of experience beyond words or concepts, a realm of ultimate truth, to be sure, but of a truth which could never find expression in articulate form. For Nietzsche as well, music holds out the promise of a knowledge beyond mere conceptual reason, a knowledge forgotten since the time of Socrates, when Greek tragic drama entered its period of decline and philosophy — in the shape of Socratic dialectic — asserted its claims to rational mastery.[14] Nietzsche is very firm in rejecting what he sees as the world-weary quietism and escapist ethos of Schopenhauer's thinking. Music — and specifically Wagner's music — brings with it a force of creative renewal which will make of nineteenth-century German culture a second epoch of world-historical achievement, one in which the two great opposing impulses — the Dionysian and Apollonian — will again be interlocked in the kind of titanic struggle that engenders great works of art. Up to now, Nietzsche argued, this vital energy had been lost through the predominance of the Apollonian principle, of everything that belonged on the side of form, self-discipline, abstraction and rational control. Hence the conventional view of Greek culture promulgated by scholars like Winckelmann, the notion that its highest attainments consisted in the 'classical' ideals of harmony, grace, perfected balance and proportion. What was lost to sight through this civilizing process was precisely the repressed Dionysian element, the dark side of irrational energies and drives which could scarcely be contained by that other, form-giving principle.

Such is the pseudo-historical myth of origins that animates the argument of Nietzsche's early tract, *The Birth of Tragedy from the Spirit of Music*.[15] It seeks to transform the very nature of thought and perception by asking us to hear, in Wagner's music, the signs of a new aesthetic dispensation that would overcome all forms of conceptual abstraction, including the subject–object antinony that had plagued the discourse of philosophy from Socrates to Kant. In this respect Nietzsche is simply pushing to its extreme that high-romantic faith in the synthesizing powers of creative imagination that typifies the work of philosopher–critics like Goethe and Coleridge. Aesthetics takes over the burden of achieving what cannot be achieved by any form of theoretical reason, namely that union of sensuous experience with concepts of pure understanding which had figured, since Kant at least, as the main preoccupation of philosophy. Kant himself had claimed to resolve this problem in some notoriously obscure passages where he appeals to the 'productive imagination' as a faculty that somehow manages to synthesize the forms of *a priori* knowledge (for instance, our concepts of causality, time and space) with the concrete data of phenomenal experience which alone give substance to those concepts.[16] Otherwise thinking would soon become lost in the toils of metaphysical abstraction, in those airy regions of speculative paradox which Kant describes under the heading 'Paralogisms of Pure Reason'. And this would lead inevitably to the dead-end of epistemological scepticism, the despair of discovering any valid or necessary link between concepts and phenomena. Hence his dictum that 'concepts without intuitions are empty; intuitions without concepts are blind'. But this claim is made good at crucial points in Kant's argument (including the 'Transcendental Aesthetic' that lays out his groundwork for the *Critique of Pure Reason*) in terms that derive, more or less obliquely, from the discourse on art and the modalities of aesthetic experience that would occupy Kant in the Third *Critique*.[17]

So it was that such questions were installed at the heart of subsequent (post-Kantian) philosophy of mind and knowledge. In Hegel, Schopenhauer and Nietzsche, aesthetics comes to play an increasingly central role, as the emphasis shifts from a critical account of reason, its constitutive powers and limits, to a kind of expressionist philosophizing that tries to make sense — narrative or mythical sense — of the various forms and manifestations of human creative activity. Two themes in particular emerge in the course of this development: the pre-eminence of music as the highest realm of aesthetic experience, and the superiority of symbol over allegory in terms of artistic beauty and truth.[18] These assumptions went together to the extent that language in its symbolic mode was treated, like music, as a means of overcoming the otherwise insurmountable split between thought and perception, subject and object, concepts and sensuous intuitions. If literature henceforth aspired to the condition of music, then it did so in the shape of a symbolist aesthetic which dreamed that language might at least momentarily transcend these hateful antinomies, thus managing to reconcile the world of phenomenal perception with the realm of conceptual understanding. And this remains the belief of those modern interpreters for whom the Romantic ideal of 'unmediated vision' retains its considerable seductive power. In the words of M.H. Abrams, 'the best Romantic meditations on a landscape . . . all manifest a transaction between subject and object in which the thought incorporates and makes explicit what was already implicit in the outer scene'.[19] Such moments can only come about through the power of language to fuse organically with nature and the objects of sensory perception, so that meaning is experienced as somehow consubstantial with the images, memories or natural forms which evoke these visionary states of mind. The relation between signifier and signified is no longer conceived (in Saussurian terms) as a arbitrary link, one that exists solely as a product of linguistic and social convention. Rather, it is thought of as a constant struggle to transcend that unfortunate condition, to achieve a kind of hypostatic union between thought, language and reality where all such distinctions would at last fall away.

Paul de Man's classic essay 'The Rhetoric of Temporality' sets out to deconstruct this high-romantic dream of origins, truth and presence. De Man mounts a case against the symbolist aesthetic which draws attention to the blind-spots of argument that recur in the various programmatic statements put forward by its past and present-day adherents. Such thinking is a potent source of ideological mystification, a habit of thought that persistently ignores or represses those aspects of language that resist assimilation to an order of transcendent, ahistorical truth. It does so primarily by masking the temporal aspect of all interpretation, the fact that knowledge can never achieve such a moment of ecstatic visionary inwardness with nature. In the criticism of neo-Romantic theorists like Abrams it is made to seem at times as if 'imagination did away with analogy altogether . . . and replaced it with a genuine and working monism. "Nature is made thought and thought nature" [Abrams writes] both by their sustained interaction and by their seamless metaphoric continuity.'' '[20] But such ideas are undermined by a reading that shows how the symbolist aesthetic cannot in the end make good its claims; how language itself undoes the illusion that mind and nature might ever attain this kind of idealized organic relation. For it always turns out, according to de Man, that the passages in question depend for their effect on tropes and devices which stubbornly resist this will to aesthetic transcendence. Chief among these is the figure of allegory, treated condescendingly by critics and philosophers like Goethe, Coleridge and Hegel. For allegory works precisely by insisting on the arbitrary character of signs, the lack of any natural or quasi-natural bond between signifier and signified. To interpret a text allegorically is to read it as an artificial construct whose meaning unfolds in a narrative or temporal dimension, and where signs point back to no ultimate source in the nature of 'organic' or phenomenal perception.

Thus allegory serves as a powerful demystifying trope, one that resists the truth-claims vested in romantic or symbolist conceptions of art. In these latter, 'the valorization of symbol at the expense of allegory' can be seen to coincide with 'the growth of an aesthetics that refuses to distinguish between experience and the representation of experience'.[21] This can never be the case with allegorical modes of understanding, marked as they are by a constant awareness of the gap that opens up, as soon as we begin to interpret, between subject and object, nature and language, the desire for a purely self-originating source of meaning and the knowledge that no such source can be found. Thus 'the prevalence of allegory always corresponds to the unveiling of an authentically temporal destiny . . . [and] this unveiling takes place in a subject that has sought refuge against the impact of time in a natural world to which, in truth, it bears no resemblance'.[22] In this relatively early (1971) essay, de Man has nothing explicit to say about the political or ideological values that attach to these opposing conceptualizations of language. But his later work brought a sharper awareness of the ways in which aesthetic ideology worked to mystify the relationship between history, language and the processes of critical thought. For it was, he argued, precisely by construing that relationship in terms of an organic or quasi-natural principle that various forms of post-Kantian aesthetics had managed to avoid any rigorous reflection on the historicity or temporal predicament of all understanding. And in the case of allegory, conversely, it is the material resistance that language puts up — the discrepancies between what a text actually *says* and what a mainstream, traditional or conformist reading would predictably have it mean — that opens a space for political or counter-hegemonic readings.

Hence de Man's claim that such textual complications in some sense 'generate history', a claim that is all too easily misread as a species of mystifying 'textualist' rhetoric designed to head off any serious thought about the relationship between literature, politics and history. In an essay on Rousseau's *Social Contract* he even goes so far as to assert that 'the political destiny of man is structured like and derived from a linguistic model that exists independently of nature and independently of the subject'. And yet, the passage goes on, 'contrary to what one might think, this enforces the inevitably political nature, or more correctly, the "politicality" (since one could hardly speak of "nature" in this case) of all forms of human language, and especially of rhetorically self-conscious or literary language'.[24] For it is language that works to promote the various forms of ideological misrecognition, forms whose common feature is the habit of confusing the cultural–linguistic with the natural–phenomenal realm. But it is language also that provides a model for deconstructing that conservative mystique, for showing how organic or naturalizing metaphors begin to break down and how history effectively reasserts its hold at the point where understanding is forced to recognize its own temporal condition. This conflict of interests is sharpened and intensified when language has to bear — as it does in all versions of aesthetic ideology — a weight of significance tied up with its presumed capacity to articulate the claims of sensuous cognition with those of conceptual understanding. 'What gives the aesthetic its power and hence its practical, political impact, is its intimate link with knowledge, the epistemological implications that are always in play when the aesthetic appears over the horizon of discourse.[25]

This excursion into the province of literary theory may help us to grasp what is at stake when Bloch insists that the meaning of music can only be grasped in allegorical terms. For there is, as we have seen, a strong countervailing tradition of post-romantic thought, one that treats music as the highest form of art on account of its unique expressive power, its capacity to fuse the phenomenal sound-world of sensuous experience with a sense of some ultimate significance beyond the grasp of mere reason. When literature seeks to emulate this condition, it does so in forms — like that of lyric poetry — where language seems closest to the lived actualities of sensuous experience, where the sound (in Pope's phrase) is supposedly 'an echo to the sense', and where subjectivity is felt to exist in a peculiarly intimate relation to the objects of outward, phenomenal experience. As the language of symbolism takes precedence over that of allegory, so the lyric achieves absolute pride of place in a scale of hierarchical values which tends to demote those other, more extended or narrative forms where language cannot possibly achieve this degree of aesthetic formalization.

Michael Sprinker has addressed this topic in a book that seeks to articulate the claims of deconstruction with those of Marxist ideological critique.[26] He shows just how close was the perceived relationship between music, lyric poetry and those versions of the symbolist aesthetic that found their way into literary criticism through the precepts and practice of poets like Gerard Manley Hopkins, writers who determined to break with the conventional forms of their day and achieve a more 'musical', sensuous or immediate quality of language and style. To their way of thinking, 'lyric poetry not only aspires to the condition of music, it offers instances (in meter and in its various phonic devices) of genuine musicality'.[27] But what Sprinker finds in his reading of a Hopkins sonnet is evidence that language resists this kind of ultimate musicalization; that meaning cannot in the end be assimilated to the order of phenomenal perception, since language turns out to signify in ways that exceed and complicate the presumed correspondence between sound, sense and the realm of sensuous experience. The standard exegetical line with Hopkins is to argue that the poetry achieves such correspondence to a quite remarkable degree, and can thus be said to manifest God's presence in the world through a kind of literalized incarnationist metaphor. 'Nothing is more familiar . . . than [this] claim for the aesthetic unity of a work based upon the congruence of the work's phonic and semantic features.'[28] But in fact, as Sprinker shows, such readings are highly selective, ignoring those dissonant details of sound and sense that cannot be reduced to such a preconceived order of aesthetic harmonization. When read deconstructively, with an eye to such details, the poetry can appear to suggest just the opposite: that language is not so much an 'organic' phenomenon as a field of conflicting rhetorical forces where unity is achieved only through a naturalized habit of reading that ignores these signs of internal disruption. Like de Man, Sprinker locates the source of this delusion in a form of deep-laid 'aesthetic ideology' that blinds critics to the various ways in which language inevitably fails to 'harmonize' with the world of phenomenal cognition. It is precisely in so far as it encourages such forms of aesthetic mystification that music comes to occupy its privileged place in post-symbolist aesthetic theory.

This is why Bloch in the end asserts his distance from the potent ideology inscribed in such forms of organicist thinking. 'Nothing in his [Schopenhauer's] account is more obscure than "the ineffably inward nature of music", and nothing is more incomprehensible than "the profound wisdom it contains as a language which reason does not understand", but which Schopenhauer still claims to have fully decoded' (*PM*, p. 220). Such notions are at odds with his own belief that music is not a 'natural' phenomenon, or at least not one whose nature could ever be theorized in terms borrowed from the realm of perceptual experience. They are regressive in the sense that they betray the listener back into a world of inchoate sensations, emotions and fantasies where thought — as in Schopenhauer — becomes the mere plaything of archaic instinctual drives. In Wagnerian opera Bloch hears something like a full-scale programmatic realization of Schopenhauer's aesthetic creed. Only rarely is this music 'attuned to a signal of liberation that would break Nature's spell . . . Nearly all Wagner's creatures are at home in the volcanic world of impulse, in the Schopenhauerian Will, acting and talking from within this natural dream-state' (*PM*, p. 222). As Bloch understands it, this confinement to a realm of dark, destructive, elemental passions is a price that is inevitably paid for the identification of music with nature, and of nature in turn with those inhuman forces that exist beyond hope of redemptive change.

So Bloch's utopianism doesn't at all imply that the history of music as we have known it so far has been a progress toward ever more refined or humanly adequate means of expression. Such ideas are just a version of the shallow optimism which equates the utopian element in music with the signs of mere technical advance, like Wagner's exploitation of hitherto unknown harmonic and chromatic resources. It is thus bound up with that same aesthetic ideology which identifies the ultimate meaning of music with its power to evoke ideas directly through sensuous intuitions, without (as in the case of other art-forms) any detour by way of mere words, concepts or mediating representations. Bloch never ceases to denounce the idea that musical progress can be read off as so many stages on the path to some ultimate fulfilment that had always, so to speak, been latent in its nature as an organically evolving language. On the contrary, as he writes: 'social trends have been reflected and expressed in the sound-material, far beyond the unchanging physical facts . . . No other art is conditioned by social factors as much as the purportedly self-acting, self-sufficient art of music; historical materialism, with the accent on "historical", abounds here' (*PM*, p. 200).

Organicist ideas of music tend to go along with evolutionist accounts of musical history, both being governed by the same basic metaphor, one that traces the development of forms and expressive styles through a process of quasi-natural growth and fruition. This metaphor is particularly prevalent in treatments of the German line of succession from Bach, through Beethoven to Brahms, Wagner, Mahler and Schoenberg. Often it is presented in terms of a struggle for legitimacy, a debate as to where exactly the line runs, or which composers are the rightful heirs. Thus loyalties divided over the rival merits of claimants like Brahms and Wagner, the one representing a development primarily in formal or structural terms, the other seen as extending the harmonic resources of musical language to a point of extreme chromaticism that was always latent, just waiting to be realized, in earlier stages of the same evolution. Hence Schoenberg's polemical essay 'Brahms the Progressive', intended both to rescue Brahms from the misconceived devotions of his more conservative admirers, and to establish the claims of his own (Schoenberg's) music as deriving simultaneously from Wagner and Brahms, and thus carrying on the high destiny of German musical tradition.[29]

This argument is connected with Schoenberg's attempt to establish the legitimacy of atonal and twelve-tone music by deriving its harmonic innovations from the very nature of the sound-material that composers had to work with. If such music encountered widespread resistance, it was only because it reached out into more remote regions of the overtone series, renouncing the desire for home-keys and familiar tonal centres that continued to exert a regressive hold upon listeners trained in the old expectations. Thus Schoenberg's defence takes the form of an appeal to nature as the ground of all musical experience, the source of phenomenal perceptions whose validity is beyond all doubt, since they correspond to what is actually given in the sound-world of music itself.[30] His own passage from a post-Wagnerian chromaticism, through atonality to twelve-tone technique can thus be presented as the outcome of a dynamic process set in motion by the very nature of music, but finding its highest, most evolved forms in the great tradition of German composers from Bach to Schoenberg. One can trace the emergence of this organicist doctrine through the various theories and critical approaches devised by nineteenth-century commentators in the effort to make sense of music that defied analysis on the older, more conventional terms.[31] It took hold at about the same time that post-Kantian philosophers and literary theorists were elaborating an aesthetics of the symbol that likewise claimed to reconcile concepts with sensuous intuitions, or to provide a bridge between the natural world and the realm of articulate thought. Indeed, the two developments are closely allied, since they both locate the ultimate value of aesthetic experience in the power of art to reconcile otherwise disparate orders of experience. History itself can then be viewed in a providential light, as the process whereby certain languages, artforms and cultural modes of expression evolve toward a state of organic unity in which consciousness discovers its authentic relationship to nature. And it is, as we have seen, very often in connection with music — or with various images and metaphors drawn from the realm of musical experience — that this aesthetic ideology achieves its most seductive and plausible form.

Bloch holds out against all versions of this organicist creed, whether applied to individual works of art or to the history through which these works come into being. 'A rudimentary musical theme', he writes, 'however well chosen, sharply delineated and productive of movement, is no acorn from which . . . the forest of the symphony will grow' (*PM*, pp. 108–9). His reason for resisting such analogies is that they carry along with them an inbuilt tendency to treat the work as something closed, finished, possessed of its own self-determining principle and thus incapable of taking on a new significance. When this same aesthetic ideology is extended from art to history itself — as occurs in the discourse of late romantic criticism — then history is likewise immobilized, reduced to an outcome of natural forces whose origin is thrown far back into a mythical past. Bloch is implacably opposed to such ideas, and for much the same reason that Walter Benjamin offers in his 'Theses on the Philosophy of History'. Benjamin rejects any notion of future time as continuous or homogeneous with our knowledge of past events. 'Historicism' and 'universal history' are the characteristic forms of this Hegelian drive to assimilate the future to a kind of organic temporality where nothing can possibly come as a shock to our settled beliefs and expectations. For Benjamin, on the contrary, 'history is the subject of a structure whose site is not empty, homogeneous time, but time filled by the presence of the now'.[32] And again: 'to articulate the past historically does not mean to recognize it "the way it really was". It means to seize hold of a memory as it flashes up at a moment of danger [which] affects both the content of the tradition and its receivers.'[33] Superficially there might seem little enough resemblance between Bloch's utopian outlook and Benjamin's dark-hued meditations. But in fact Bloch perceives quite as clearly as Benjamin the risk that any hope stored up in past meanings and memories will be repossessed by the forces of cultural inertia; that tradition will assert its hold once again as a weapon of those with the power to dictate what shall count as authentic history. One major form in which this power stands revealed is the notion of history as an organic process, a providence whose meaning unfolds through time in a series of exemplary figures, meanings or events.

In musical terms, this leads to the idea of Wagner as in some sense fulfilling the destiny prefigured in earlier composers like Bach, Mozart and Beethoven. Bloch very firmly rejects this idea, asserting that Beethoven 'is as superior to Wagner as Kant is to Hegel, and as the restless *a priori* in man is to any kind of prematurely fulfilled objectivism' (*PM*, p. 35). These analogies, though presented in cryptic form, will I think stand up to a good deal of conceptual unpacking. Wagner's music is Hegelian in the sense that it seeks to transcend all antinomies through an ultimate merging of mind and nature, subject and object in a realm where no such distinctions any longer obtain. In Beethoven, conversely, the will to transcendence is encountered in a restless, dynamic form which precludes such a false or premature sense that this state has actually been achieved. Again we can turn to de Man — especially his late essays on Kant — for a better grasp of how these issues in the province of philosophy connect with Bloch's understanding of music. De Man brings out very clearly the ways in which Kant is forced back upon allegorical or figural modes of explanation at exactly those points where his argument is most concerned with questions of epistemological and ethical truth.[34] Kant's very desire not to be seduced into forms of premature identification — as between the realms of phenomenal cognition, understanding and practical (ethical) reason — obliges him to resort to such figural strategies despite his repeated warnings elsewhere against what he sees as their seductive and misleading nature.[35]

This is not the place to rehearse de Man's arguments in detail. But their upshot can be summarized as follows: that allegory is the one authentic mode of reading in so far as it acknowledges the inevitable failure of all attempts to make meaning coincide with the realm of intuition or phenomenal self-evidence. To read allegorically is always to recognize that understanding is a temporal process, one that takes place not on the instant of punctual, self-present perception but through a constant anticipatory awareness of what is lacking in the present. Thus 'allegory designates primarily a distance in relation to its own origin, and, renouncing the nostalgia and the desire to coincide, it establishes its language in the void of this temporal difference.[36] For de Man, as indeed for Bloch, it is only by accepting this condition of deferred interpretative grasp that thought can hold out against the delusive promise of fully achieved understanding. This is why notions of 'organic form', however refined or elaborate, always tend to seek their ultimate grounding in a principle of order which denies or suppresses the restless, utopian, forward-looking character of musical experience. Such ideas cannot account for the meaning of music, 'any more than logic and a theory of categories account for metaphysics'. They treat the formal element as something implicitly there from the outset, given as part of the work's thematic material, and subject to development only in so far as that material contains *in nuce* every detail of its own unfolding. Whereas in Bloch, 'the theme is not found at the start but overlies it like an *a priori* that is working from a distance' (*PM* p. 108). And this means that any analysis of musical form based on notions of organic unity or self-contained thematic development will be closed to whatever potential the work may possess for renewing our perceptions through repeated acts of creative listening. What then takes hold is 'the same fatalism and occasionalism, the same transfer of "efficient cause" to the first principle alone as applies in all other reactionary Romantic systems' (*PM*, p. 129). In its place Bloch proposes something more like a Aristotelian teleology, one that treats music in terms of its 'final cause', the end toward which everything strives in the effort to realize its full potential.

It is in Beethoven especially that Bloch discovers this resistance to preconceived ideas of what does or should constitute musical form. He takes the first movement of the 'Eroica' symphony as an instance of how such ideas break down when confronted with music that everywhere exceeds their explanatory grasp. Thus

> the question of sonata design is primarily focused . . . on the problem of the new, unsuspected, productive element, the dissipating, mutually overriding and self-surmounting sequence of events in the development section . . . He is under no binding obligation toward either an individual theme or even to all the initial themes. He can restrict himself to mere thematic fragments of motifs, can even depart from the guiding thread of tonality . . . provided that after all his divagations he does reestablish the surrendered key, the secret and, in the end, triumphantly emerging end-cause of the entire harmonization. [*PM*, p. 108]

This passage gives a fair impression of Bloch's style, his use of open-ended syntactic patterns and phrase-structures which gather momentum from point to point, and thus prevent the reader from resting content with what has been said so far. It is a style, once again, that enacts *allegorically* the distance between musical meaning and verbal description, in this case by deferring the moment of ultimate grasp through a sequence of fragmentary hints and suggestions that cannot be reduced to any straightforward sense of thematic coherence. Thus Bloch rejects any appeal to 'programmatic' elements as such, even in a case like the *'Eroica''s* first movement, where the extra-musical associations are particularly hard to ignore. For 'the dictatorship of the programme' leads, as he argues, to 'an almost entirely unmusical line of reasoning', one that produces an essentially fixed, pre-conditioned habit of response, and thus ignores what is going on from moment to moment as the music reworks and transfigures its thematic material.

He is equally opposed to any kind of analytical criticism which seeks to articulate musical structure in terms of some quasi-mathematical ideal or rule-governed formal procedure. The fallacy here is the assumption, going back at least to Pythagoras, that music is the sensuous embodiment of laws, ratios and harmonic proportions which exist in nature — as witnessed by phenomena like the overtone series — but whose true character can be best be divined from their kinship with pure mathematics. Again, this may remind us of Schoenberg's attempt to deduce the predestined historical emergence of twelve-tone composition from its supposed grounding in the realm of phenomenal perception. Bloch's main objections to this whole way of thinking are to be found in his 1925 essay 'On the Mathematical and Dialectical Character of Music'. Here he rejects every version of the analogy between music and mathematics, pointing out that wherever such thinking has prevailed it has also tended to arrest musical history by laying down laws of harmonic proportion that supposedly reflect a natural, immutable order of things. One example is the Pythagorean ban on intervals of the third and sixth, felt to represent a destabilizing force within the quaternary system of harmonic–numerical consonance, and hence proscribed as a matter of ethical as well as musical decorum. 'Mathematics remains the key to Nature, but it can never be the key to history and to those self-informings by the non-identical and the asymmetrical which number was devised to counter, and for whose gradual objectification the human spirit ultimately produced great music' (*PM*, p. 169). It is precisely where music takes a heretical turn, where it outruns all the laws of harmonic good form, of preconceived symmetry and structural proportion, that it becomes open to this transformation by a process whose character is *historical* through and through, and not subject to any such formal-transcendental laws. 'It was only the need of polyphonic song, which did not worry about mathematics, that resorted to the forbidden third, thereby attaining the major chord, that cornerstone of all harmonic development' (*PM*, p. 185). And such changes come about, not in answer to some principle of historical inevitability, but through music's responsiveness to new configurations of social and historical hope.

It should be clear by now that Bloch's utopian outlook is not to be confused with the kind of wishful thinking which treats every setback on the road to enlightenment as a mere local aberration. In fact it is more akin to Benjamin's sense of future time as momentarily prefigured in the present, as offering itself to a redemptive vision that must seize its opportunity on the instant if everything is not to fall back under the sway of cultural inertia and reaction. But it is Adorno, not Benjamin, who provides the most obvious point of departure for assessing how far Bloch's philosophy stands up to the rigours of negative critique. For Adorno, the very notion of affirmative culture — of art as an index to the liberating power of human creativity — had to be renounced in the light of such evidence as modern history afforded. Hence the relentlessly self-denying character of Adorno's thought, his insistence that the only kind of truth now available is that which unmasks the delusive truth-claims of all aesthetic ideologies and other such falsely positive systems of thought.[37] Since Schiller, philosophy had held out the notion of art as a healing or reconciling power, a realm of experience where the conflicts and antinomies of alienated consciousness could at last find an image of perfect fulfilment in the 'free play' of human creativity, of sensuous cognitions in a state of ideally harmonious reciprocal balance. This ideal had once possessed a genuine emancipatory force, as in works like *Fidelio* or the Ninth Symphony, music where the ethos of liberal humanism found expression not only in dramatic terms, but in every detail of the work's dynamic tonality and structural form. But this moment had passed irrevocably, Adorno thought, with the advent of a modern 'culture-industry' which had taken over these musical resources, adapting them to the needs of passive consumption and utterly negating their original redemptive character. Henceforth they could only be heard as hollow gestures, as a language whose apparent spontaneity, vigour and force were in fact mere symptoms of cultural regression, of a music that recycled past styles and forms in a mode of more or less unwitting self-parody. The best that philosophy could do in face of this massive reification was to denounce all forms of commodified culture, maintain an intransigently negative attitude, and thus keep faith with the critical spirit that had once found authentic expression in the works of an earlier, more hopeful epoch.

Schoenberg's music served Adorno as a measure of what art might yet achieve in this implacably critical or deconstructive mode. That is to say, it expressed the alien reality of modern social conditions by refusing all forms of aesthetic transcendence, by extending a tight compositional control over every aspect of structure and style, and thus giving the lie to notions of art as a source of compensatory freedoms untouched by the grim truth of historical events. In Adorno's words,

The total rationality of music is its total organization. By means of organization, liberated music seeks to reconstitute the lost totality — the lost power and the responsible binding force of Beethoven. Music succeeds in so doing only at the cost of its freedom, and thereby it fails. Beethoven reproduced the meaning of tonality out of subjective freedom. The new ordering of twelve-note technique virtually extinguishes the subject.[38]

Thus Schoenberg's very 'failure', the fact that his music cannot make good the Beethovenian promise, is also — paradoxically — the source of its ultimate value and truth. Max Weber had described the process of increasing 'rationalization' that marked the development of music in a culture long subjected to the order of bourgeois social relations, to the work ethic and its forms of instrumental or means–end reasoning.[39] For Adorno, this process arrives at its most advanced point in the serialist claim to derive all the parameters of a musical work from some single generative source (the tone-row) whose permutations would then account for every aspect of its style and form. Such music 'fails' in so far as it defeats its own object, negates the very impulse of 'subjective freedom' and thus falls prey to an extreme form of reification which reflects the worst, the most inhuman aspects of present-day rationalized existence. But it also succeeds — and for just that reason — in exposing those conditions, forcing them to the point of manifest self-defeat, and thus closing off the various seductive escape-routes provided by music in its other, less taxing contemporary forms.

For Adorno, philosophical thinking is subject to the same necessity, compelled to keep faith with the values of enlightened reason but always in the knowledge that those values have been falsified, turned to inhuman or destructive ends, by the advent of a social order founded on eminently 'rational' means of surveillance and control. Hence Adorno's 'negative dialectics', a relentlessly self-critical habit of thought which interrogates its own procedures at every stage, resisting any kind of residual attachment to method or system. 'The life of the mind only attains its truth when discovering itself in desolation. The mind is not this power as a positive which turns away from a negative . . . it is this power only when looking the negative in the face, dwelling upon it.'[40] This is not Adorno but Hegel, or rather it is Adorno quoting Hegel very pointedly against himself, against that version of Hegelian dialectic that identifies the present (for Hegel, Christianity and the Prussian nation–state) with a final overcoming of all antinomies. For Adorno, on the contrary, any suggestion that thinking might *presently* achieve such a state is at best mere utopian reverie, and at worst a delusion complicit with the forces that work to produce this predicament of chronic bad faith. As Fredric Jameson writes in his commentary on Adorno: 'the very mark of the modern experience of the world is that precisely such identity is impossible, and that the primacy of the subject is an illusion, that subject and outside world can never find such ultimate identity or atonement under present historical circumstances'.[41] Philosophy, like music, is confronted with this ultimate choice: *either* the pleasure that comes of regressing to an earlier, more 'positive' phase of cultural history, *or* the sad wisdom (Adorno's 'melancholy science') that results from perceiving how impossible it is for thought to maintain this deluded stance.

It might seem from all this that Adorno and Bloch are worlds apart in their attitude to music and music's role in the critique of existing social realities. Indeed their personal dealings were marked by a persistent habit of reserve, on Adorno's side at least, which suggests a deep measure of intellectual difference. But there is also a sense in which Bloch and Adorno were complementary thinkers, coming at the same basic problems and conflicts from opposed but not wholly incompatible points of view. In David Drew's words, 'the disillusionment Adorno pursues and cherishes so ardently belongs within the dark circle at the foot of Bloch's lighthouse, and is far removed from any modish cynicism'.[42] Indeed one can pick out many passages from Adorno that explicitly require some utopian dimension to complete and give purpose to the labours of negative thought. 'Without hope', Adorno writes, 'the idea of truth would be scarcely even thinkable, and it is the cardinal untruth, having recognised existence to be bad, to present it as truth simply because it has been recognised.'[43] This sentence could well have been taken from one of Bloch's meditations on the false positivity of present, self-evident fact, the way that our perceptions are hemmed in and distorted by the belief that what exists is the sole reality available to thought.

This underlying kinship is yet more evident when Adorno appeals to Kant's articulation of the faculties — of reason in its pure and practical forms with aesthetic judgment — to bring out their reciprocal involvement one with another. The passage needs quoting at length, since it is couched in that highly aphoristic but rigorously consequent style that Adorno adopted in order to head off the temptations of premature systematizing thought.

> Is not indeed the simplest perception shaped by fear of the thing perceived, or desire for it? It is true that the objective meaning of knowledge has, with the objectification of the world, become progressively detached from the underlying impulses; it is equally true that knowledge breaks down where its effort of objectification remains under the sway of desire. But if the impulses are not at once preserved and surpassed in the thought which has escaped their sway, then there will be no knowledge at all, and the thought that murders the wish that fathered it will be overtaken by the revenge of stupidity . . . [This] leads directly to a depreciation of the synthetic apperception which, according to Kant, cannot be divorced from 'reproduction in imagination', from recollection.[44]

This is why aesthetic judgment plays such crucial role in the Kantian theory of knowledge and perception. For it is, as we have seen, by way of the aesthetic that concepts join up with sensuous intuitions, thus providing a bridge between *a priori* knowledge and experience of the phenomenal world. Adorno like de Man thinks this an unattainable or strictly utopian ideal, one that gives rise to a sequence of unstable and shifting relations where subject and object can never perfectly coincide. Thus when Kant speaks of the 'productive imagination', he connects it always with this temporal dimension where thought comes up against the limits of its static concepts and categories. This is the point, in de Man's reading, where Kantian critique takes on a distinctly allegorical aspect, a meaning that is deferred through the various figures, tropes and analogical examples to which Kant resorts in the course of his argument. For Adorno as well, there can be no moment of 'synthetic apperception' — no means of reconciling concepts with sensuous intuitions — that doesn't involve some appeal to desire, imagination and the future as a realm of as yet unrealized possibility.

So it is wrong to assume that Bloch and Adorno are straight-forwardly antagonistic thinkers, the one espousing a redemptive metaphysics of hope and secular salvation, the other renouncing all such beliefs in a grim determination not to be deceived by tokens of false promise. Among the many passages of Adorno that belie this reading, one in particular — from the closing paragraph of *Mimima Moralia* — stands out for its clear statement of the need for negative thinking not to lose sight of its positive, utopian counterpart.

> The only philosophy which can be responsibly practised in the face of despair is the attempt to contemplate all things as they would appear from the standpoint of redemption . . . . Perspectives must be fashioned that displace and estrange the world, reveal it to be, with its rifts and crevices, as indigent and distorted as it will appear one day in the messianic light.[45]

While the passage alludes more overtly to Benjamin, it also opens the way — as David Drew remarks — to a reading of Adorno's and Bloch's work that would treat them as paradoxically kindred thinkers, engaged in the same redemptive enterprise, though starting out from very different premises. For on Bloch's side also, any hope of attaining an authentically utopian perspective is dependent on thought's having first made the passage through a 'labour of the negative', an undeceiving process that leaves us the more acutely aware of our present, limited powers of perception. Thus 'nobody has as yet heard Mozart, Beethoven or Bach as they are really calling, designating and teaching . . . this objective-indeterminate element in music is the (temporary) defect of its qualities' (*PM*, pp. 207–8). If Adorno's negativity cannot in the end do without a countervailing impulse of hope, then equally it is the case that Bloch's utopian outlook would collapse into mere facile optimism were it not for this chastening awareness of the obstacles — the pressures of social and historical circumstance — that stand in its path.

The same applies to de Man's practice of deconstructive reading, on the face of it a wholly negative practice, in so far as it works to undo or to problematize everything we commonly take for granted about language, experience and the nature of human understanding. Music is important for de Man because it has served as a source of that potent aesthetic ideology which locates the redemptive capacity of art in its promise of transcending the conflict between sensuous and intellectual realms of experience. But in fact, de Man argues, this promise has always turned out to be delusory, not least in those thinkers (like Rousseau) who have expressly treated music as a 'natural' language of emotions, a language that is (or that ought to be) untouched by the decadent, corrupting influence of latter-day civilized life.[46] Thus Rousseau praises the Italian music of his time for its unforced, spontaneous character, the fact that it remains close to those sources of vitality and warmth that issue directly in melody and the singing line. He attacks contemporary French composers like Rameau for their practice of elaborate harmonization and their use of an 'advanced' contrapuntal style which leads them to lose touch with those same elemental passions and desires. Melody is good because it belongs to that stage of human existence when the passions can still find authentic voice and there is no need, as yet, for the resort to mere artifice and stylized convention. Harmony is bad because it goes along with all those other concomitants of modern 'civilized' life — social inequality, delegated power, civil and political institutions, distinctions of class or rank on an unjust, arbitrary basis — which Rousseau denounces in the 'advanced' democracies of his day.

So his treatment of music is precisely analogous to Rousseau's thinking on matters of ethical, social and political concern. 'Man was born free, but is everywhere in chains', the freedom identified with a lost state of natural grace which has long since been overtaken by these melancholy symptoms of latter-day decline. And this also applies to language, since speech had its origin (so Rousseau asserts) in the same elemental passions and desires which produced spontaneous melody. In this original condition, language was a kind of primitive speech–song which expressed human sentiments simply and directly without any detour through arbitrary signs and conventions. For there was, as yet, no need for people to disguise and dissimulate their meaning, to adopt such forms of linguistic subterfuge by way of exerting power over others. To speak was necessarily to mean what one said, since language gave access to the speaker's innermost thoughts and sentiments, in a context of ideally reciprocal exchange where no advantage could possibly accrue from lies, hypocrisy or pretence. Here again progress has taken its toll by requiring a different, more sophisticated kind of language, one that is able to articulate abstract ideas, and to convey them not, as was once the case, through an intimate face-to-face communion of souls, but through forms of elaborated social code devoid of authentic meaning. Thus language, like music, registers the impact of a civilizing process which in truth is nothing of the kind; a process that alienates man from nature, language from the expression of genuine feeling and society from those ties of communal trust and understanding which alone provide the basis — so Rousseau believes — for a state of harmonious coexistence.

De Man's main argument is that Rousseau is too canny, too rhetorically self-aware to be wholly taken in by this seductive myth of origins. That is, he may *declare* quite explicitly that language is authentic only where it approximates to a kind of pre-articulate speech–song; that culture supervenes upon nature as a kind of progressive catastrophe, a history of absolute loss and decline; and that only by returning to a pure state of nature can mankind escape from this sorry predicament. But what emerges in the course of de Man's reading is a subtext of unsettling rhetorical implications, passages where Rousseau is constrained to state just the opposite of his overt or express intentions. Thus language turns out to be strictly inconceivable except on the basis of arbitrary signs, codes and socialized conventions which cannot have existed in that first, happy state. Rousseau's argument again comes up against the limits of intelligibility when he tries to give substance to the claim that mankind once enjoyed a 'natural' form of organic communal life, at a time when culture had not yet obtruded its alien codes and customs. For there is simply no conceiving of society except in terms of a differential system that must always to some extent — even in 'primitive' cultures — rest upon distinctions of class, gender, kinship and other such socially imposed categories. Rousseau is in this sense a proto-structuralist *malgré lui*, obliged to acknowledge — implicitly at least — that language and society can only exist in separation from the state of nature, or only in so far as they exhibit all the signs of cultural organization. Any 'language' that lacked the identifying marks of structural relationship and difference would in fact not be language at all, but merely a string of articulate sounds with some possible emotive significance. Similarly, any 'culture' or 'society' that hadn't yet developed to the stage of hierarchical structures, kinship-systems and so forth, would for that very reason elude all possible terms of description or analysis.

Now de Man's point is that Rousseau himself deconstructs the Rousseauist myth of origins, or — more precisely — that his text provides all the requisite materials for its own deconstructive reading. It is the mainstream interpreters who, with their confident knowledge of his meaning and intentions, read with an eye only to those passages or levels of explicit statement that serve to confirm their stubborn preconceptions. In so doing, they are blinded to rhetorical complexities which in fact — so de Man argues — can be seen to undo that naïve mystique of origins, presence and naturalized meaning that supposedly lies at the heart of Rousseau's philosophy. It is here that the instance of music plays a crucial role in de Man's argument. For it is usually taken as read by the commentators that Rousseau's thinking on this topic follows the familiar pattern; that he associates authentic musical expression with a language of strongly emotive and sensuous appeal that speaks directly to the heart by virtue of precisely those qualities. From which it follows that music must enter upon the road to decadence as soon as it acquires the 'civilized' graces of harmony, counterpoint, elaborate structure and all the other signs of its present, unnatural condition. Indeed Rousseau says just that in a number of passages that leave little room for a contrary or deconstructive reading. But he also says the following (as cited by de Man):

In a harmonic system, a given sound is nothing by natural right. It is neither tonic, nor dominant, harmonic or fundamental. All these properties exist as relationships only and since the entire system can vary from bass to treble, each sound changes in rank and place as the system changes in degree.[47]

Nor does this apply to one system only — the 'harmonic' — as opposed to some other, more natural language of music that would operate in terms of melody alone and thus escape the bad necessity imposed by the decadent turn toward harmony. For Rousseau is equally clear on the point that melody without harmony is unthinkable; that there is always an implicit harmonic dimension to even the simplest melodic idea, since otherwise we would hear it as simply a series of disconnected notes, lacking any sense of cadence or musical shape. Thus Rousseau is brought round *by the logic of his own argument* to concede that music is not, after all, a natural language of the emotions, a language whose meaning coincides at every point with the nature of its humanly expressive sound material. Rather, it is a 'system' of tonal relationships that belongs entirely to the history of musical styles, genres, forms and conventions, and which cannot be grasped except in terms of the structural properties that make such a system possible. Rousseau very often states just the opposite, but his statements are just as often undone by the clear implications of his own more consequent thinking.

For de Man, this ambivalence in Rousseau's philosophy of music is an index to the tensions that emerge everywhere in his writing. In each case there is a conflict between Rousseau's desire to discover some authentic, natural point of origin beyond the bad effects of civilized life, and his forced recognition that no such discovery is possible; that language, art and society were *always already* caught up in that process of decline, no matter how far one tries to push back toward a lost age of communal innocence and grace. This conflict is nowhere more evident (so de Man argues) than in Rousseau's reflections on the phenomenology of musical perception.

> On the one hand, music is condemned to exist always as a moment, as a persistently frustrated intent towards meaning; on the other hand, this very frustration prevents it from remaining within the moment. Musical signs are unable to coincide: their dynamics are always oriented toward the future of their repetition, never toward the consonance of their simultaneity. Even the potential harmony of the single sound, *à l'unisson*, has to spread itself out into a pattern of successive repetition; considered as a musical sign, the sound is in fact the melody of its potential repetition.[48]

Music thus serves as the single most striking instance of de Man's general thesis: that whenever Rousseau seeks to articulate his philosophy of nature and origins, he must always have recourse to a language that implicitly calls such thinking into question. 'Music is the diachronic version of the pattern of non-coincidence within the moment.'[49] For this pattern is repeated in language itself, where meaning can never be consistently reduced to an order of pure, self-present, phenomenal sense.

What then emerges in the reading of Rousseau's texts is an allegory of music's failure to achieve that wished-for natural state, since neither in music itself nor in the language that purportedly emulates music can any such condition be realized. As we have seen, de Man thinks of allegory primarily in terms of its demystifying power, its capacity to keep us always in mind of the gap that opens up between nature and language, phenomenal cognition and linguistic meaning. Music has very often served the purposes of aesthetic ideology by maintaining the delusory promise of a language that would finally transcend this condition, overcoming the ontological gulf between signs and sensuous intuitions. But this promise has just as often been accompanied by a deeply conservative mystique that assimilates music to the world of natural processes and forms, and which thus cuts it off from any intelligible relationship to history, politics and cultural change. This argument finds ample confirmation in subsequent versions of the Rousseauist myth, where often the theme of a return to nature takes on a decidedly conservative toning. It is then used — by ideologues like Burke — not to criticize some existing state of society, but to argue that such criticism is pointless and misguided, since national cultures evolve through a process of 'organic' growth and development which cannot be influenced (except for the worse) by any mere spirit of reformist zeal. This shift in the political currency of Rousseauist ideas is very evident in the later writings of Coleridge, and thereafter in a line of conservative culture-critics whose chief modern spokesman is T.S. Eliot.[50] And one major source of such thinking — as de Man makes clear — is that mode of aesthetic ideology which identifies language in its highest, most expressive forms with a principle of nature that can then be extended to organicist metaphors of history and social evolution. 'What we call ideology is precisely the confusion of linguistic with natural reality, of reference with phenomenalism.' From which it follows, according to de Man, that 'more than any other mode of enquiry . . . the linguistics of literariness is a powerful and indispensable tool in the unmasking of ideological aberrations, as well as a determining factor in accounting for their occurrence'.[51]

We can now begin to see why Bloch insists so strongly that music is not a 'natural' artform, at least in any sense that could justify the notion that its meaning derives from its phenomenal or sensory–acoustic nature. Hence his opposition to Schopenhauer's aesthetic, where music takes precedence over the other arts only on account of its supposedly inhabiting a realm of primeval, undifferentiated Will, a realm where mere intellect has no place and we experience nature as a flux of inchoate desires, instincts and sensations. Hence also his rejection of the opposite fallacy, that which equates the expressive power of music with the laws of mathematical proportion and harmony. 'Whereas music as a mood remains buried within the soul and seems the most chthonian of the arts, so-called *musica mathematica* becomes wholly Uranian and steps off into heaven' (*PM*, p. 210). For Bloch, as indeed for de Man, music is allegorical through and through, since its significance can never be grasped once and for all in an act of fulfilled, self-present perception. Otherwise, as he remarks, 'music would never have gone beyond descending fifths'. Just as melody unfolds through a temporal process, a sequence of intervals whose character is essentially mobile or propulsive, so musical works take on their significance through time, in a history of successive re-encounters whose meaning can never be exhausted. 'Any number of human tensions are added to the tension of the fifth to create a more complicated cadence and thus the history of music' (*PM*, p. 200). Bloch goes on to elaborate this point in a passage that resembles some of de Man's formulations, transposed into a language of explicitly utopian character. 'Melody's most remarkable attribute — the fact that in each of its notes, the immediate following one is latently audible — lies in human anticipation and hence in expression, which is now above all a humanized expression' (*PM*, p. 200). This can only come about, Bloch argues, in so far as music (or our thinking about music) breaks with the kind of regressive appeal exerted by the spell of nature.

These beliefs were put to the test in Bloch's collaboration with Otto Klemperer on a 1929 Vienna production of *The Flying Dutchman*. This caused a great scandal at the time and was later to mark them both down as cultural bolsheviks and enemies of National Socialism.[52] The production followed closely on performances of *Mahagonny* and *The Threepenny Opera*, and it made extensive use of Brechtian techniques to undermine the sanctified aura of Wagnerian music–drama. Bloch's contribution was a programmatic essay — 'The Rescue of Wagner through Surrealistic Penny Dreadfuls' — which argued for the vitalizing power of popular culture, the intimations of a better world that could be glimpsed even in 'debased' modern forms like the comic strip, sentimental romance, advertisements and adventure stories.[53] The reactions were predictable: it seemed, as David Drew nicely comments, that 'Bayreuth was about to be stormed by Peachum and his beggars'. But what lay behind this staging of the *Dutchman* was a practical experiment in redemptive hermeneutics, a version of Bloch's own ambivalent responses to Wagner. The hold of tradition could only be broken through a new kind of listening, one that denied itself the pleasures of a passive abandonment to nature's spell, and which understood music as the active prefiguring of forces and tensions beyond the grasp of any merely 'authentic' performing style. It is a theme that Bloch takes up in his essay 'Paradoxes and the Pastorale in Wagner's Music'. Where Wagner transcends the Schopenhauerian ethos, it is by virtue of his momentarily escaping the realm of blind passion or instinctual Will, and transforming this atavistic impulse into a music pregnant with future possibilities. At such moments 'Wagner gives resonance its full due, like a vibration *ante rem* which continues to give out figured sound *in re*, not to say *post rem datam*; a sound-figure through which it takes up objects of nature and seeks through art to raise them to a higher power (*PM*, p. 181).

This might seem utterly remote from what we learn of the Klemperer production, with its aim of 'rescuing' Wagner from the Wagner-cult by exposing his music to all manner of parody and down-market pastiche. In fact there is a similar principle at work: namely, the belief that present conditions block and distort our ways of perceiving, so that for now at least the only way forward is to deconstruct the values, mythologies and forms of sanctified false consciousness that pass themselves off as 'natural' habits of response. It is here that Bloch's philosophy makes common cause with that strain of rigorously negative thinking espoused by theorists like Adorno and de Man. To keep faith with music's utopian potential may require an effort of demystification that appears superficially far removed from any hopeful or affirmative standpoint. But it is precisely this undeceiving 'labour of the negative' — this testing of hope through a hard-won knowledge of everything that presently conspires against it — which marks the difference between Bloch's way of thinking and other, more naïve utopian creeds. Again, it is Adorno who provides the most fitting commentary when he writes that 'in the end hope, wrested from reality by negating it, is the only form in which truth appears'.[54]

References

The first three paragraphs of this essay are based on ideas and formulations from an earlier article: Norris, 'Marxist or Utopian?: the philosophy of Ernst Bloch', *Literature and History*, Vol. IX, No. 2 (1983), pp. 240–5.

1. Fredric Jameson, *The Political Unconscious: narrative as a socially symbolic act*, London, Methuen, (1981).
2. See especially Louis Althusser, *For Marx*, Ben Brewster (trans.), London, Allen Lane, (1969).
3. Marx, letter to Alfred Ruge, collected in Siegfried Kröner (ed.) *Die Frühschriften*, Stuttgart, Alfred Kröner, (1979), p. 171; cited by Bloch in *The Principle of Hope, Vol. I*, Neville Plaice, Stephen Plaice and Paul Knight (trans.), Oxford, Basil Blackwell, (1987), pp. 155–6.
4. Fredric Jameson, *Marxism and Form* Princeton, NJ, Princeton University Press, (1971), pp. 116–59.
5. Bloch, *The Principle of Hope* (op. cit.).
6. Bloch, *Essays on the Philosophy of Music*, Peter Palmer (trans.), Cambridge, Cambridge University Press, (1985). All further references given in the text by initials *PM* and page number.
7. Bloch, *The Principle of Hope*, p. 1064.
8. Theodor W. Adorno, 'Bach Defended Against his Devotees', in *Prisms*, S. and S. Weber (trans.), London, Neville Spearman, (1967).
9. Arthur Schopenhauer, *The World as Will and Representation, Vols. I and II*, New York, Dover, (1958). See also Schopenhauer, *Parerga and Paralipomena: short philosophical essays*, London, Oxford University Press, (1974).
10. See for instance Brian Magee, *The Philosophy of Schopenhauer*, London, Oxford University Press, (1983).
11. See Jacques Derrida, 'White Mythology: metaphor in the text of philosophy', in *Margins of Philosophy*, Alan Bass (trans.), Chicago, University of Chicago Press, (1982), pp. 207–71.
12. Wayne Hudson, *The Marxist Philosophy of Ernst Bloch*, London, Macmillan, (1982).
13. Bloch, *Experimentum Mundi*, Frankfurt, Suhrkamp Verlag, (1975).
14. Friedrich Nietzsche, *The Birth of Tragedy* and *The Case of Wagner*, Walter Kaufmann (trans.), New York, Vintage Books, (1967).

15. On the relationship between music, myth and ideology in Nietzsche, see especially Paul de Man, *Allegories of Reading*, New Haven, Yale University Press, (1979), pp. 79–102 and Michael Sprinker, *Imaginary Relations: aesthetics and ideology in the theory of historical materialism*, London, Verso, (1987).

16. See Immanuel Kant, *Critique of Pure Reason*, F. Max Müller (trans.), New York, Macmillan (1922), p. 116.

17. On the relation between Kantian aesthetics and epistemology, see Paul de Man, 'Phenomenality and Materiality in Kant', in Gary Shapiro and Alan Sica (eds), *Hermeneutics: questions and prospects*, Amherst, University of Massachusetts Press, (1984), pp. 121–44.

18. See Paul de Man, 'The Rhetoric of Blindness: Jacques Derrida's reading of Rousseau', in *Blindness and Insight: essays in the rhetoric of contemporary criticism*, London, Methuen, (1983), pp. 102–42.

19. Cited by de Man in his essay 'The Rhetoric of Temporality', in *Blindness and Insight* (op. cit.), pp. 187–228; p. 185.

20. Ibid., p. 195.

21. Ibid., p. 188.

22. Ibid., p. 206.

23. See especially the essays collected in de Man, *The Resistance to Theory*, Minneapolis, University of Minnesota Press, (1986).

24. de Man, *Allegories of Reading* (op. cit.), p. 156.

25. de Man, 'Aesthetic Formalization: Kleist's *Über das Marionettentheater*, in *The Rhetoric of Romanticism*, New York, Columbia University Press, (1984), pp. 264–5.

26. Sprinker, *Imaginary Relations* (op. cit.).

27. Ibid., p. 62.

28. Ibid., p. 63.

29. See Arnold Schoenberg, 'Brahms the Progressive', in *Style and Idea*, Dika Newlin (trans.), London, Faber, (1975).

30. Thus Schoenberg: 'even those who have so far believed in me will not want to acknowledge the necessary nature of this development . . . I am being forced in this direction . . . I am obeying an inner compulsion which is stronger than any upbringing' (cited by Charles Rosen, *Schoenberg*, London, Fontana, (1975), p. 15. Rosen's comments on this passage are worth quoting at length in the present context of argument.

> In his justification, Schoenberg brings forward the classic dichotomy of nature and civilization . . . In this notorious pair, the rights are traditionally on the side of nature — and, indeed, Schoenberg's critics were to accuse him of violating the natural laws of music, of substituting a purely artificial system for one that [accorded with] the laws of physics . . . If the dichotomy can so easily be stood on its head, it should lead us to be suspicious of the opposition. A great deal of nonsense has been written about the relation of music to the laws of acoustics . . . but the irresistible force of history — Schoenberg's 'inner compulsion' — ought not to inspire any greater confidence. [Rosen, p. 15]

These remarks have an obvious bearing on music's role as a privileged source of those organicist models and metaphors that characterize aesthetic ideology.

31. On this and related questions, see Jacques Attali, *Noise: the political economy of music*, Brian Massumi (trans.), Minneapolis, University of

Minnesota Press, (1985); Alan Durant, *Conditions of Music*, London, Macmillan, (1984); Joseph Kerman, *Musicology*, London, Fontana, (1985); Richard Leppert and Susan McClary (eds), *Music and Society: the politics of composition, performance and reception*, Cambridge, Cambridge University Press, (1987); Susan McClary, 'Pitches, Expression, Ideology: an exercise in mediation', *Enclitic*, Vol. VII (1983), pp. 76–86; Richard Norton, *Tonality in Western Culture*, Philadelphia and London, University of Pennsylvania Press, (1984); Kingsley Price (ed.), *On Criticizing Music: five philosophical perspectives*, Baltimore, Johns Hopkins University Press, (1981); John Shepperd *et al.* (eds) *Whose Music? a sociology of musical languages*, London, Latimer, (1978) and Rose Rosengard Subotnik, 'The Role of Ideology in the Study of Western Music', *Journal of Musicology*, Vol. II (1983), pp. 1–12.

32. Walter Benjamin, 'Theses on the Philosophy of History', in *Illuminations*, Harry Zohn (trans.), London, Fontana, (1970), pp. 255–66.

33. Ibid., p. 257.

34. See de Man, 'Phenomenality and Materiality in Kant' (op. cit.) and 'The Epistemology of Metaphor', in *Critical Inquiry*, Vol. V (1978), pp. 13–30.

35. For Kant's warning against the confusions created by uncontrolled figural language, see especially Section 59 of the *Critique of Judgment*, J.C. Meredith (trans.), London, Oxford University Press, (1978). As de Man points out, Kant's language here is itself replete with metaphors, analogies and question-begging tropes which must at least throw doubt on philosophy's power to regulate its own discourse.

36. de Man, 'The Rhetoric of Temporality' (op. cit.), p. 207.

37. See especially T.W. Adorno, *Negative Dialectics*, E.B. Ashton (trans.), London, Routledge & Kegan Paul, (1973); *Aesthetic Theory*, C. Lenhardt (trans.), London, Routledge, (1984) and *Philosophy of Modern Music*, Anne G. Mitchell and Wesley V. Blomster (trans.), London, Sheed and Ward, (1973).

38. Adorno, *Philosophy of Modern Music* (op. cit.), p. 69.

39. Max Weber, *The Rational and Social Foundations of Music*, Don Martindale, Johannes Riedel and Gertrude Neuwirth (trans.), Carbondale, University of Illinois Press, (1958).

40. Cited by Adorno, *Minima Moralia*, E.F.N. Jephcott (trans.), London, New Left Books, (1974), p. 16.

41. Jameson, *Marxism and Form* (op. cit.), p. 42.

42. David Drew, 'Introduction' to Bloch, *Essays on the Philosophy of Music* (op. cit.), p. xlii.

43. Adorno, *Minima Moralia* (op. cit.), p. 98.

44. Ibid., p. 122.

45. Ibid., p. 247.

46. See de Man 'The Rhetoric of Blindness', in *Blindness and Insight* (op. cit.), pp. 102–41. De Man provides his own translation of passages from Rousseau, *Essai sur l'origine des langues*, Paris, Bibliothèque du Graphe, (1817).

47. Rousseau, op. cit., p. 536, cited by de Man in 'The Rhetoric of Blindness', p. 128.

48. Ibid., p. 129.

49. Ibid., p. 129.

50. See especially T.S. Eliot, *Notes Towards the Definition of Culture*, London, Faber, (1948).

51. de Man, *The Resistance to Theory* (op. cit.), p. 11.

52. On the background to this event and on Bloch's association with

Klemperer, see Peter Heyworth, *Otto Klemperer: his life and times,* Vol. I, Cambridge, Cambridge University Press, (1983).

53. These themes are also taken up in Bloch, *The Principle of Hope* (op. cit.), especially the section of *Vol. I* entitled 'Wishful Images in the Mirror: display, fairytale, travel, film, theatre' (pp. 337–447).

54. Adorno, *Minima Moralia* (op. cit.), p. 98.

2 Reading Donald Davidson: truth, meaning and right interpretation

The writings of Donald Davidson have generated widespread discussion among Anglo-American analytical philosophers and, more recently, literary theorists.[1] The reasons for this interest are by no means uniform, but they tend to divide along fairly predictable lines. Of the two possible readings of Davidson, one seems to me a very definite *mis*reading that goes clean against the logic and significance of his work. The other (I shall argue) is the more authentically Davidsonian reading, though it doesn't fit at all with currently fashionable ideas about language, meaning and representation. That the work of one thinker should support — or at least appear to support — two such diametrically opposed interpretations is indeed a curious phenomenon, and all the more so in view of Davidson's commitment to a truth-conditional theory of interpretative reason. In fact it might be argued by proponents of the rival (post-structuralist or pragmatist) view that the very existence of uncertainties like this lends support to their case for regarding Davidson's talk of truth as holding good only relative to a certain culture-specific set of ideas and assumptions. His work would then serve as a nice illustration of the fact that even 'mainstream' analytical philosophy has at last come round to their way of thinking, i.e. the view of 'truth' as an essentially contested concept, produced by the various discourses of power/knowledge that compete for cultural hegemony.

It will help if we adopt a simplifyng shorthand to distinguish these two viewpoints. 'Davidson I' is the philosopher who asserts that some notion of truth — or what it means to make a truthful statement — is simply indispensable to all our thinking about language, logic and the nature of human understanding.[2] Otherwise, he argues, we would lack any basis for deciding between rival interpretative claims, or indeed for making sense of language at the level of day-to-day communicative grasp. That is to say, the attitude of holding-true is a kind of logical primitive, a notion presupposed by every form of linguistic inference, even in cases (like fictional language or metaphor) where this standard has no very obvious bearing. For without it we would be forced back upon an attitude of wholesale cultural relativism, the idea that languages or texts only signify according to their own inbuilt codes and conventions, so that meaning must ultimately lie beyond the grasp of any speaker not brought up in the same culture-specific habits of thought. This conclusion is insupportable, Davidson argues, both in principle and as a matter of empirical fact. For we can and do very often make a tolerable job of interpreting unfamiliar forms of utterance, whether in cases like that of the anthropologist faced with a puzzling new piece of ethnographic data, or — nearer home — as native speakers required to construe some strange or puzzling metaphor. We do so by a mixture of inspired guesswork and basic assumptions about the truth, intelligibility and semantic structure of human language in general. Understanding simply couldn't get off the ground unless there existed this general willingness to assume, first, that other people make sense of experience in ways not radically unlike our own, and second, that the attitude of holding-true — of attaching a particular significance to sentences that get things right — is as important for them as it is for us.

These beliefs are not optional, Davidson thinks, or merely a product of our own ethnocentric values and assumptions. Rather, they are the necessary *precondition* for any hope we may have of getting to understand other people's language and behaviour. That is to say: unless we operate what Davidson calls this basic 'principle of charity' — the principle that holds it more likely than not that their ascriptions of truth-value to statements will correspond pretty much to our own — we will have no way of comparing the various possible accounts of what their words or actions signify, and thus of deciding which come closest to fulfilling the requirements of rational accountability. The hypothetical test case here is that of the anthropologist confronted with a language and culture whose conventions are maximally remote from his or her own. A native informant might point to some object and utter a word, apparently by way of straightforward ostensive definition. But according to some philosophers — among them W.V. Quine — this situation is nowhere near as simple as it seems, since the native informant might be offering all kinds of information as regards the object concerned.[3] It could be a matter of the object's desirability, of its threatening character, its tribal-totemic role, some bit of it or aspect of its past history, the unlikelihood of coming across it *here*, or any number of alternative hypotheses. From this Quine moves to his general thesis: that we cannot translate between cultures, language-games or different 'forms of life' without at some point coming up against the problem of deciding just which interpretive gambit will best make sense of the informant's words or behaviour. This problem cannot be resolved, he argues, by appealing to supposedly invariant features of language, like the gesture of naming an object by simply pointing straight at it. For ostensive definition is itself a language-game, one that only makes sense — as Wittgenstein remarked — in the context of a cultural form of life which might always turn out to be peculiar to us, or to speakers trained in our particular set of naturalized responses and expectations.[4]

Thus Quine denies the very possibility of 'radical translation', if by this is meant a kind of rock-bottom assurance that people can indeed communicate effectively across cultures by first getting down to the basics and then building up a more complex set of definitional equivalents. Any putative 'translation manual' compiled on these principles would still have to face the disturbing possibility that the native informants were in fact trying to communicate something quite different, and that therefore its entire system of semantic links, collocations and associative networks was based on a total misunderstanding of everything that had passed between the communicating parties. For Quine, therefore, 'radical translation' is a strictly impossible undertaking. And this predicament extends far beyond the somewhat exotic instance of an anthropologist working from scratch within a totally alien culture. Similar problems can arise, he argues, with any attempt to assign meanings to statements in our own language, especially where these involve some unfamiliar or problematic terms of description, but even where there seems to be no obstacle in the way of straightforward comprehension. For it is always the case that those terms just *might* have been used in a sense either markedly or subtly at odds with our normal ways of understanding.

One such deeply entrenched idea concerns the categorical distinction between analytic statements (those whose truth is self-evident by virtue of their logical form) and synthetic propositions whose truth is a matter of empirical warrant, and must therefore be subject to revision if some piece of counter-evidence should at length turn up. In one form or another, this distinction has been maintained by most philosophers from Aristotle to Kant and contemporary logicians. But for Quine it is nothing more than a contingent fact about the way we presently divide up our discourse into different orders of truth-claim.[5] The analytic/synthetic distinction is one of those deeply entrenched ideas which to us have the appearance of holding good for all possible worlds of experience and knowledge. But in fact, Quine argues, it only strikes us this way because it happens to occupy a central place in the fabric of connected ideas and beliefs that make up our existing context of discourse. Thus we tend to suppose that empirical (or synthetic) propositions are those at the furthest remove from a priori self-evident truth, statements whose validity depends entirely on their matching up with facts of observation, and which therefore exist on the outermost edge of that same network or articulated web of beliefs. But to Quine this whole picture seems radically misconceived. There is, he asserts, no reason to suppose that what we *now take as* indubitable truths must appear so to those with a different world-view, or even to ourselves if there suddenly occurred a radical shift of discursive values and priorities. Such a shift could just as well begin with some upset at the 'periphery' of knowledge, some discovery that started out by unsettling our empirical beliefs and then, so to speak, worked inward to disturb the hitherto unshakable structure of assumptions identified with a priori logic and truth. In short, such distinctions had better be regarded as holding good only for all present and practical purposes, and not as possessing any ultimate validity.

Davidson I comes out strongly against what he sees as the disabling relativist assumptions bound up with Quine's way of posing these questions. He does so by denying that truth must always be a product of codes, conventions and language-games that determine what shall normally count as true in any given cultural context. On the contrary, Davidson argues: we can make no sense of such assertions unless we acknowledge some basic level of understanding that allows us to recognize these local instances of cultural difference. Hence his objection to the so-called 'Sapir–Whorf hypothesis', namely, the idea that since experience is always mediated by language — since language provides the very concepts and categories by which we interpret experience — therefore it is impossible to translate from one language (or cultural context) to another without inescapably imposing our own habits of thought and perception. But such arguments fail, according to Davidson, as soon as they claim to offer some account of the cultural differences involved.[6] Thus 'Whorf, wanting to demonstrate that Hopi incorporates a metaphysics so alien to ours that Hopi and English cannot, as he puts it, "be callibrated", uses English to convey the contents of sample Hopi sentences' (*Inquiries*, p. 184). Davidson's argument here amounts to a form of transcendental-deductive riposte, showing that Whorf — and others of the same persuasion — cannot for a moment accept the consequences of their own relativist position. Where they fall into error, he suggests, is in thinking that every language must impose some ultimate 'conceptual scheme', some network of signifying codes and conventions peculiar to itself, such that any standards of validity and truth will be internal to that one language and hence beyond the grasp of speakers or translators belonging to a different language group. But this is to get the whole matter upside down, Davidson argues. The very idea of a 'conceptual scheme' must logically depend on our possessing the means to interpret and compare what evidence we have, deciding where the salient differences occur on the basis of at least some measure of reciprocal grasp. Such agreement 'must take the form of a widespread sharing of sentences held to be true by speakers of "the same language", or agreement in the large mediated by a theory of truth contrived by an interpreter for speakers of another language' (*Inquiries*, p. 197). For otherwise — and this is Davidson's central point — it simply wouldn't make sense to talk about alternative conceptual schemes, since we would have no way of knowing or describing just where and how they differed from our own.

This is one of the ways in which Davidson arrives at his anti-relativist conclusion. Another is more technical and has to do with a form of canonical notation for truth-functional semantics developed by the logician Alfred Tarski. On this account, as Davidson describes it, a satisfactory theory of truth for a language L must entail, for every sentence s of L, a theorem of the form 's is true if and only if p' where 's' is replaced by a description of s and 'p' by s itself if L is English, and by a translation of s into English if L is not English. [*Inquiries*, p. 194]

This way of stating the matter amounts, as Davidson admits, to a form of elaborate tautology, and is in any case not much use when dealing with the complexities of natural language. What his argument comes down to in practical terms is the point that we couldn't make a start in understanding *any* kind of language without the two basic assumptions, (1) that some statements must indeed be veridical, and (2) that its speakers must at least have a grasp of the conditions that have to be satisfied in order for this or that statement to count as true. Thus 'the methodological problem of interpretation is to see how, given the sentences a man accepts as true under given conditions, to work out what his beliefs are and what his words mean' (*Inquiries*, p. 162). From this point one can go on to interpret those other, problematical instances where it may be that some deep-seated difference of assumptions is getting in the way of an adequate grasp. But there is no reason (so Davidson argues) to follow those thinkers, like Whorf and Quine, who would persuade us that such instances are paradigmatic, or that all translation must involve such ultimate problems. For it is precisely on account of their exceptional nature — our knowledge that they are *not*, in fact, typical cases — that these problems can be recognized as such and referred to other, more perspicuous contexts where meaning is not in doubt. What enables us to do just that is the general conviction that language makes sense, that truth-conditions hold across the boundaries of cultural difference and therefore that translation is not the impossible enterprise that sceptics would have it.

Thus 'we compensate for the paucity of evidence concerning the meaning of individual sentences not by trying to produce evidence for the meanings of words but by considering the evidence of a theory of the language to which the sentence belongs' (*Inquiries*, p. 225). The main task of this holistic approach is to make explicit the various presuppositions that speakers of a language must bring to bear in producing and interpreting statements held to be true. The same applies to those forms of utterance where truth is not directly in question, where meaning comes about through fictive, metaphorical or other such devices which cannot be accounted for in truth-conditional terms. For here also the condition of intelligibility is that we recognize such cases for what they are and then make sense of them by looking to the context in which they occur. This would be impossible, Davidson argues, if convention went all the way down; if meaning were entirely a product of the cultural codes or signifying structures that determine the limits of intelligible sense. 'Philosophers who make convention a necessary element in language have the matter backward. The truth is rather that language is a condition for having conventions' (*Inquiries*, p. 280). And furthermore, the condition for having language at all — or for knowing what to make of it in any given context — is that we grasp what is involved in the paradigm case of sentences that do possess the character of truthful statements.

If Davidson is right — 'Davidson I', the philosopher whose arguments I have so far attempted to summarize — then clearly this poses a considerable challenge to current post-structuralist theory. For it is a basic premise of all such thinking that language is indeed conventional through and through; that meaning consists in the 'arbitrary' link between signifier and signified, a link sustained only by the system of culture-specific relations and distinctions that makes up any given language. On this view, questions of truth and reference simply don't arise, at least within the terms of a general linguistics or semiotic theory whose aim is to account for the structural economy of language as a self-contained signifying system, and *not* to explain how this or that sentence achieves the condition of truthful utterance. Thus Saussure takes it as axiomatic that the sign is a localized point of intersection between two distinct planes: on the one hand the system of *phonological* contrasts that enables us to register meaningful differences of sound, on the other the network of *semantic* relations that comprise all our operative concepts and categories.[7] For Saussure, as for Whorf, this entails the further point that we cannot raise questions of reference or truth except in relation to some signifying practice (or 'conceptual scheme') which alone makes sense of such questions. It is this way of thinking that induces us, in Davidson's view, to invert the real order of priorities, to treat convention as the basis of all language, or the source of what counts as valid or true within any given language. But the problem disappears, he would argue, as soon as we switch these priorities around and see that the appeal to conventions in fact explains nothing: that the very idea of a conceptual scheme is logically dependent on our prior grasp of the truth-conditions that must presumably operate across all languages. For unless we accept this fact — namely, that 'whether we like it or not, if we want to understand others, we must count them right on most matters' (*Inquiries*, p. 197) — we shall simply have no grounds for comparison when it comes to assessing the finer points of cultural difference.

So the following might be Davidson I's critique of post-structuralism, consonant with what he has to say about Whorf and the logical shortcomings of relativist doctrine. Post-structuralism goes wrong when it takes Saussure's notion of the arbitrary sign — a notion adopted strictly for the purposes of structural-linguistic description — and extrapolates from it a wholesale theory of language, meaning and interpretation. More specifically, it errs by ignoring the fact that sentences, not individual words or signs, are the units of intelligible meaning, and that any attempt to assign meaning to sentences must involve the appeal to some form of truth-conditional logic before we can begin to grasp how they function in larger contexts of discourse. From this basic error post-structuralism goes on to assert (like Foucault) that 'truth' is nothing more than a localized effect of power/knowledge, of the will-to-truth that gives certain hegemonic discourses the power to impose their perspective on other, more marginal languages.[8] Thus from Foucault's avowedly Nietzschian standpoint, truth is nothing more than a species of persistent rhetorical illusion, a pretence that we can get outside this arena of competing discursive strategies to some detached high ground of critical reason whence to adjudicate the issue between them. Then again there are those, like Roland Barthes, who celebrate the advent of a new kind of writing, a practice that breaks altogether with mimetic constraints or the myth of authorial presence, and which thus opens itself up to a utopian play of plural signification.[9] This writing would constitute an implicit critique of those repressive ideologies — like the discourse of high classic realism — which have hitherto worked to enforce what amounts to a restricted economy of language, meaning and representation.

Davidson's counter-argument to all such claims can be stated briefly enough. What they fail to remark is the elementary fact that language — even fictional language — can only make sense on condition that *some* sentences be taken to refer successfully, or to possess the basic attributes of validity and truth. Otherwise our response when confronted with one of Barthes's hypothetical limit-texts would be something like that of the Whorfian ethno-linguist exposed to a radically alien form of life and convinced that, since meaning is entirely a matter of cultural convention, therefore no means could possibly exist for translating observation-sentences from one language to another. And the same would apply to Foucault's idea that truth is nothing more than a reflex product of discursive power-relationships, a value attached to certain forms of utterance that currently enjoy that status. For if this were indeed the case — if we possessed absolutely no means of distinguishing truthful from false, fictitious or merely indeterminate statements — then the relativist would be in the untenable position of asserting it as a generalized truth about language that language could assert no truths. What Davidson says about Whorf would then apply equally to Foucault, with the difference that Whorf's hypothesis at least captures something of the genuine puzzlement that must sometimes result from the encounter of radically alien cultural life–forms. Even so, Davidson writes, 'there does not seem to be much hope for a test that a conceptual scheme is radically different from our own if that test depends on the assumption that we can divorce the notion of truth from that of translation' (*Inquiries*, p. 195). And for Foucault, this puzzlement would have to extend to every single act of interpretation, even where the language or the text in question belonged squarely within our own cultural heritage. For it is, Davidson argues, an unavoidable consequence of relativist thinking — or of any such appeal to linguistic conventions as a bottom-line of accountability — that we are left with no good reason to suppose that understanding can *ever* take place on a footing of reciprocal intelligibility. Hence the need for an alternative paradigm, one based on the reasonable premise that 'from the moment someone unknown to us opens his mouth, we know an enormous amount about the sort of theory that will work for him — or we know we know no such theory' (*Inquiries*, p. 278). In the latter case the fact of our perceiving the problem will itself provide a starting-point for the process of reinterpretation.

So it might seem that Davidson's arguments come out clean against the kind of radical conventionalism that unites thinkers like Whorf, Saussure, Foucault and Barthes. But this is to assume that Davidson I is demonstrably right on all the basics; that any workable theory of interpretation will have to start out from the conditions that hold in the case of truthful utterances; and that therefore the only right reading of Davidson's work is one that applies exactly this set of assumptions to his own texts. But there is, as I have mentioned, another way of construing those texts that has proved more adaptable to the purposes of post-structuralism, and more attractive to commentators — notably Richard Rorty — who would wish to have done with all such talk of truth, epistemology and right reading. This is not the place for a detailed exposition of Rorty's neo-pragmatist outlook. Very briefly, he argues that philosophy went wrong when it took (with Descartes and Kant) a turn toward epistemological questions as its area of chief concern.[10] Truth became a matter of accurate *representation*, of achieving a proper correspondence between ideas, propositions or a priori concepts on the one hand, and experience, perception or sensuous intuitions on the other. Henceforth the various schools would divide not so much on the question of whether such knowledge was available, but on how best to attain it. Thus rationalists started out from transcendental assumptions about the nature, the constitutive powers and limits of human reason in general, while empiricists largely rejected such claims and sought a grounding for knowledge in the supposed self-evidence of straightforward sensory perception. Kant sought to reconcile these two conflicting creeds by demonstrating first, in the transcendental mode, that we could only make sense of experience in so far as its forms were given a priori through concepts of pure understanding, and second that these forms must necessarily match up with our sensuous intuitions, since otherwise there was nothing to prevent reason from becoming lost in metaphysical abstractions of its own giddy devising. Hence Kant's claim to have effected nothing less than a 'Copernican revolution' in the history of thought. It would now be the task of a truly critical philosophy to examine its own truth-claims and establish more precisely the powers and the limits of human cognitive enquiry.

But on Rorty's view this was just one more attempt to solve problems which only existed because philosophers had dreamed them up in the first place. It is here that Davidson enters the picture as one of those modern 'post-analytical' thinkers who can help us out of this conceptual fix by showing how it rests on mistaken notions about language, meaning and truth. For the main source of all such delusions, according to Rorty, is the idea that thought and language depend on 'conceptual schemes', or systems of representation, whereby reality is somehow construed in accordance with our sense-making concepts and categories. For Kant, these had the character of strictly a priori truths, intrinsic to the nature of human thought and perception, and therefore invariant across all languages, thought-systems or cultures. To others (like Quine) this claim has seemed implausible, since different languages may impose different ways of conceiving the distinction between analytic or a priori concepts on the one hand, and contingent or empirical facts on the other. At most there may be sentences which the observer can label 'stimulus-analytic', i.e. sentences in our own and some other language which are uttered in the same context, and with apparently similar objects in view, and which therefore it is reasonably safe to pair off in any basic translation manual. But this only gives grounds for a kind of *ad hoc* inductive guesswork, and would certainly not justify any larger claims of a generalized a priori character. For such claims could be warranted only if we had some means of knowing for sure that we had grasped the operative truth-conditions for at least some sentences of the language in question. This cannot be the case if, as Quine argues, our very notions of truth, meaning and analyticity are bound up with the language we speak and the structure of beliefs embedded in that language. Thus Quine serves Rorty as a prime example of the way that philosophy has at last given up on the quest for knowledge, as opposed to presently valid or workable belief.

Davidson I offers various reasons for rejecting this kind of argument. They involve (as we have seen) his denial that anything useful is achieved by appealing to 'conceptual schemes', and his assertion that some form of truth-conditional theory is simply indispensable to coherent thinking about issues in the province of language and translation. However, Rorty sees no great problems in assimilating Davidson to his own neo-pragmatist view of what's best for philosophy in its current, 'post-analytic' situation. He does so by pointing to those elements in Davidson's theory which appear to weaken the idea of 'truth' to a point where — as Rorty would argue — it serves no real argumentative purpose and might just as well be dispensed with. In *Philosophy and the Mirror of Nature* (1980) Rorty suggests that Davidson's work 'can best be seen as carrying through Quine's dissolution of the distinction between questions of value and questions of fact — his attack on the linguistic interpretation of Kant's distinction between the receptivity of sense and the a priori concepts given by spontaneity'.[11] That is to say, Davidson has helped along the process of belated self-deconstruction by which philosophy has come round to the view that those distinctions are simply redundant, that they are the product of a certain (now obsolete) line of metaphysical talk which contributed nothing to our knowledge of the world except a whole series of insoluble 'problems' which will surely disappear as soon as we find some alternative, preferable idiom.

Quine's essay 'Two Dogmas of Empiricism' is Rorty's chief model for this way of shedding unwanted epistemological baggage. He finds Davidson a useful ally in the same campaign, or at least that side of Davidson's thinking which apparently lends itself to the purpose. For the upshot of rejecting all talk of 'conceptual schemes' is surely (as Rorty would have it) that we must give up thinking of *truth* as some ultimate correspondence between knowledge on the one hand and objects of knowledge on the other. This only made sense so long as the main problems of philosophy presented themselves in epistemological terms, that is to say, through metaphors of the mind as a 'mirror of nature', or of concepts as more or less accurately picturing the world through a kind of internal representation. Once this picture loses its hold, we can simply dispense with such misleading notions and accept that truth is nothing more than an honorific title, a name attached to those ideas and beliefs that count as true for all current practical purposes. Any theory that claimed to do more — whether in Kantian terms, by matching up concepts with sensuous intuitions through some form of transcendental deduction, or by analysing language into its logical or truth-conditional components — would then appear simply unworkable or beside the point. Such ideas went along with the notion of philosophy as a quest for epistemological grounds, an enterprise whose ultimate purpose was give us better, more cogent reasons for believing what commonsense had always in any case led us to believe. But it has now turned out, after so much misdirected effort, that belief (so to speak) goes all the way down; that there is no difference between holding-true on the basis of shared values and assumptions and *knowing* what is true on grounds of purported rational self-evidence. '"Truth" in the sense of "truth taken apart from any theory" and "world" taken as "what determines such truth" are notions that were (like the terms "subject" and "object", "given" and "consciousness") made for each other. Neither can survive apart from the other.'[12] These terms are all involved — so Rorty argues — in a play of specular representations which has held philosophy captive at least since Descartes and Kant, and which continues to exert a seductive and mystifying power over many thinkers in the modern analytical tradition.

So truth-claims are fallacious in so far as they take this strong Kantian form, starting out from the idea of a 'conceptual scheme' and then trying to *prove* that this particular scheme is the one that demonstrably gets things right. And they are merely redundant in so far as they appear (as with most modern versions) in a weaker form, translating Kant's epistemological arguments into a linguistic register, and claiming that the project can best be carried through by examining the truth-conditional structure of language or the difference between analytic and synthetic propositions. For this way of thinking is equally vulnerable to Quine's argument: that we can make sense of such distinctions only in terms that derive in the end from our own, culture-specific concepts and categories. We might as well admit, Rorty urges, that truth is indeed as the pragmatist would have it: 'what's good in the way of belief'. Any desire to think otherwise — any residual craving for grounds, first principles, clear and distinct ideas, concepts of pure understanding or whatever — is nothing more than the old metaphysical yearning for a knowledge ideally exempt from the vagaries of mere consensus belief. It can best be cured, Rorty thinks, by remarking first how this project has collapsed under the pressure of argument from 'post-analytical' thinkers like Quine, and second (by a less technical route) that we just can't be in a position to know anything other or anything more than those things we actually believe. For there is no difference between believing this or that to be the case, and claiming to *know* — on whatever grounds — that our belief corresponds to the truth of the matter. Belief just *is* the condition of thinking that one has good warrant or adequate grounds for believing whatever one does. Saying 'I believe x' is exactly the same as saying 'I hold it to be true that x is the case', or 'I know for a fact that x'. Nothing is added to the belief-statement except perhaps a measure of rhetorical emphasis or subjective commitment. This is indeed, as Rorty would argue, the end-point of all epistemological or truth-based theories: that they answer to our need for something more to believe in than consensus, 'warranted assertability', or simply 'what's good in the way of belief'. But the mere fact of our having this need — this desire to distinguish opinion from knowledge, *doxa* from *episteme*, that which we (perhaps wrongly) hold true from that which we genuinely know to be the case — gives no grounds at all for thinking such distinctions valid in epistemological terms. On the contrary, Rorty asserts: it just goes to show, once again, that what counts as true for us and like-minded individuals will always be decided in the last instance by appeal to some consensus of shared values and beliefs.[13]

Thus Rorty offers an approving summary of William James's view that '"true" resembles "good" or "rational" in being a normative notion, a compliment paid to sentences that seem to be paying their way and that fit in with other sentences which are doing so'.[14] It has no work to perform — certainly no conceptual or epistemological work — apart from this purely honorific function. And he thinks that Davidson can be read as providing further good arguments for the same pragmatist position. On Rorty's account, what is valuable in Davidson is the doing away with 'conceptual schemes' and with all those other kinds of surplus metaphysical baggage that philosophers produce in the effort to justify such talk. What is less helpful from this point of view is Davidson's insistence on adopting a truth-conditional theory of meaning as a hedge against the threat of linguistic or cultural relativism. In fact there is no great problem here, Rorty thinks, since we can always point to those passages where Davidson concedes that such truth-conditions must be taken as holding between all the sentences that count as true in any given language, and thus (in the end) as being culture-specific in pretty much the way that pragmatists would have them. This is where Davidson II parts company with the far stronger truth-claims apparently advanced by Davidson I. For if the argument comes down to this weak version of the thesis — that meaning is fixed by truth-conditions, but that these must in turn be relativized to the whole set of sentences believed true by speakers in a certain cultural community — then it might seem that nothing much is gained by continuing to talk in these terms.

Truth thus becomes a piece of redundant technical equipment, an obsolete notion brought in just to save appearances, or to give some semblance of epistemological rigour to a theory that would work perfectly well without it. Thus, according to Rorty,

> [t]he point of constructing a 'truth theory of English' is not to enable philosophical problems to be put in a formal mode of speech, nor to explain the relationship between words and the world, but simply to lay out perspicuously the relation between parts of a social practice (the use of certain sentences) and other parts (the use of other sentences).[15]

On this account there is nothing more to Davidson's talk of truth than a sense that there *ought* to be some way of hooking up sentences with the real-world objects or states of affairs that enable us to pick out truthful from other kinds of utterance. But there is no need to carry on thinking in this way if one chooses instead to follow out the holistic implications of Davidson's theory, his point that we can assign truth-conditions to sentences only on the basis of a generalized grasp of the relations holding between all sentences of the language concerned. From here it is no great step to the pragmatist conclusion that truth comes down to what is warranted as such by our current beliefs, language-games, cultural forms of life or whatever. One can then treat Davidson in much the same fashion that Rorty recommends with Hegel and others; that is, by discounting what they say about reason, truth, ontology or other such delusive metaphysical absolutes, and picking out those passages that happen to fall square with the general pragmatist view.[16] In Davidson's case this amounts to a claim that we can lop off the truth-conditional apparatus, along with its realist premises, and then simply keep what's left: a coherence-theory in which 'truth' functions as an intra-linguistic (and to this extent a more or less redundant) term.

In a recent essay Davidson sets out to clarify his differences with Rorty. He agrees that (in Rorty's words) 'nothing counts as justification unless by reference to what we already accept', and that therefore, in this ultimate sense, 'there is no way to get outside our beliefs and our language so as to find some test other than coherence'. But he differs in thinking that there is still a real question as to how, given all this, 'we nevertheless can have knowledge of, and talk about, an objective public world which is not of our making'.[17] Rorty considers this a world well lost, since it was never (in his view) anything more than a construction out of various philosophical pseudo-problems, notably those post-Cartesian metaphors of mind as the 'mirror of nature', and knowledge as an accurate matching-up of inward with outward representations. If Davidson I had only taken the point of the arguments advanced by Davidson II, then he would have seen that coherence — or the way that our beliefs hang together at any given stage of the ongoing cultural conversation — is all that is required to put an end to such otiose metaphysical talk. But Davidson clearly rejects this reading of his own work, and does so moreover on grounds of rational self-evidence which — according to Rorty — just can't be had, since all truth-claims in the end come down to the question of whether or not they happen to fit with our current pattern of values and beliefs. If Rorty is right about Davidson then Davidson must himself be wrong about at least one part (and it would seem a major part) of his own philosophical enterprise. That is to say, Davidson II has provided the necessary arguments for regarding 'truth' as a dispensable term, for accepting a coherence-theory (a holistic account of meaning and context) as the best available alternative, and thus for denying Davidson I any privileged voice as to how we should interpret his work.

Rorty meanwhile manages to occupy a position where no counter-argument could possibly prove him wrong. For whatever may be Davidson's · intentions, his truth-claims, reasonings, ontological commitments or whatever, the pragmatist can always set them aside as so much redundant conceptual baggage, incapable of resolving the issue one way or the other. So it is simply beside the point for Davidson to argue — in what amounts to a kind of transcendental deduction — that we couldn't make sense of language at all unless we took it for granted that most sentences (in our own or another tongue) were either true or at any rate intelligible in terms of some truth-conditional schema. For Rorty, this just goes to show once again that 'true' is synonymous with 'good in the way of belief', that it is the label we normally apply to what works for present argumentative purposes (in Davidson's case, the purpose of 'proving' pragmatism in some sense wrong), and that nothing more is to be had in the way of ultimate justification. It is therefore no embarrassment to Rorty's position that this means discounting a great deal of what Davidson I has to say on the topic. For the pragmatist needn't claim to get anything right, or to interpret Davidson in a manner that he (Davidson) would acknowledge as capturing the essential points of his argument. There is no ultimate truth of the case, whether as regards our knowledge of objects and events in the world, our ways of construing utterances about them, or our reading of texts (like Davidson's essays) that take some particular stand on such matters. It is enough that any reading should fulfil the main conditions of (1) playing its role in an ongoing cultural 'conversation', (2) hanging together in an interesting way with other contributions to the same broad enterprise, and (3) making sense — acceptable sense — on whatever terms are provided by the present-day consensual rules of the game. And it so happens, as Rorty reads the signs, that pragmatism is currently the best option for fitting everything together in a large, historically satisfying picture.

This viewpoint is expressed most concisely in a passage from *Consequences of Pragmatism* where Rorty sketches in some background detail for the current neo-pragmatist turn.

> The history [of recent analytic philosophy] has been marked by a gradual "pragmaticization" of the original tenets of logical positivism . . . I think that analytic philosophy culminates in Quine, the later Wittgenstein, Sellars, and Davidson — which is to say that it transcends and cancels

itself. These thinkers successfully, and rightly, blur the positivist distinctions between the semantic and the pragmatic, the analytic and the synthetic, the linguistic and the empirical, theory and observation . . . Davidson's holism and coherentism shows how language looks once we get rid of the central presupposition of Philosophy: that true sentences divide into an upper and a lower division — the sentences which correspond to something and those which are 'true' only by courtesy or convention.[18]

There is no point sticking with 'technical' programs in philosophy — whether Kantian, logical-positivist, truth-conditional or whatever — which haven't yet come up with the goods and (for reasons attributable to Davidson II) are unlikely to do so. In this case there would be no compelling reason for the commentator to get Davidson 'right', or give due weight to his arguments about meaning and truth. Rather, the aim would be to make sense of Davidson's writings from a post-philosophical, post-analytic or generally 'postmodern' viewpoint. It wouldn't matter — or at least wouldn't count as a decisive objection — that much of what Davidson writes goes clean against the pragmatist drift of Rorty's understanding. Any arguments brought up by Davidson I in defence of a stronger truth-conditional theory — one that held out for the logical primacy of sentences that do 'correspond' or refer to factual states of affairs — would of course fail to carry conviction with anyone persuaded by Rorty's account of how philosophy has developed in recent times. They would fail not because they didn't give reasons (logically adequate reasons) for conceiving of language in this way, but because the conversation has now moved on and left such reasonings pretty much devoid of interest, appeal or consensus–viability.

Davidson's response to Rorty (cited above) makes it clear that he doesn't think his work gives warrant for settling the question on pragmatist terms. While certainly espousing no form of metaphysical realism, he still wants to argue that there *is* a genuine difference — and not just a choice of alternative vocabularies — between Rorty's and his own way of posing the issue. Rorty has confused matters, according to Davidson, by assuming that any talk of 'truth' must involve some version of the scheme/content dualism, the idea that sentences are made true by their matching up with real-world objects or events through some kind of inward mirroring process. Certainly this is just the sort of notion that Davidson wants to do away with by discouraging talk of 'conceptual schemes' and other such phantom entities. But there is no reason to suppose that this error infects all strong versions of the truth-conditional claim, or indeed all forms of correspondence-theory. For it is facts, situations or states of affairs that determine the relevant truth-conditions, and not — as Rorty's metaphor suggests — objects, realia or discrete events. Thus (in Davidson's words) '*that* experience takes a certain course, that our skin is warm or punctured, that the universe is finite . . . makes sentences and theories true' (*Inquiries*, p. 194). The plausibility of Rorty's deconstructive move comes from his lumping all realist philosophies into the same metaphysical basket, treating them as mere technical variations on a common (deluded) theme. However, this involves a determinate misreading of Davidson, one that assumes him not to have pursued the logic of his own best insights. What Davidson is saying is not that sentences are true because they have a meaning that somehow corresponds (through a covert appeal to the old metaphor) with the way things are in reality. In fact Davidson has no use for such ill-defined appeals to 'meaning', regarding them as just another place-filler for talk of 'conceptual schemes'. The relation between paradigm sentences and factual states of affairs is one that avoids such question-begging terms by taking truth (not meaning, convention or other intermediary concepts) as its logical point of departure.

So Rorty is getting the matter backwards when he suggests that Davidson (Davidson I) has failed to follow out the consequences of his own pragmatist position. What makes a sentence true is not that its 'meaning' corresponds to some pre-given, ultimate reality whose nature in this case could never be determined outside the language (or conceptual scheme) in question. Rather, it is the fact that we always start out — as Davidson says — in the position of knowing a great deal about the kinds of evidence, justification, reasonable inference and so forth that will work for any conceivable language, no matter how remote from our own. Hence his objection to those, like Whorf, who are over-impressed by the sheer variety of languages and cultures on display, and who thus fall into the relativist trap of assuming that translation must be in some sense a radically impossible enterprise. Their mistake is to suppose that these localized problems of linguistic and cultural grasp cannot in principle be sorted out by reference to the much wider areas of agreement that must exist between all communities of language use. This agreement, says Davidson, 'may take the form of a widespread sharing of sentences held true by speakers of "the same language"', or it may be a matter of 'agreement in the large mediated by a theory of truth contrived by an interpreter for speakers of another language' (*Inquiries*, p. 192). This latter would count against the kind of ethno-linguistic relativism espoused by thinkers like Whorf, or those obstacles to the project of 'radical translation' that are often taken to follow from Quine's brand of ontological scepticism. The first line of argument — having to do with problems of grasp between speakers of 'the same language' — would serve as a rejoinder to the pragmatists, post-structuralists, Kuhnian philosophers of science and others who raise the idea of conceptual schemes (alternatively, 'paradigms' or 'discourses') into a doctrine that denies the commensurability of different orders of knowledge. In each case Davidson asserts just the opposite: that we do, when required, manage to get a grip on languages or discourses outside our immediate cultural domain, and that our starting-point for any such attempt will be the truth-conditions, rational constraints, procedures of logical inference and so forth which we *must* take as holding for the language in question if it is to make sense at all for us or for anyone else. In short, translation is a feasible project — whatever the distance of cultural horizons — because there exists this large central core of necessary presuppositions.

This is why the pragmatist version of Davidson cannot (or should not) claim to be a right reading, one that respects either the logic or the intended force of his argument. For it is a reading which chooses to pass clean over a crucial point in Davidson's argument: namely, that any workable account of language, meaning and interpretation will have to be grounded in something more than a coherence or consensus model of truth. This is not to say that Davidson is committed to one or other of the classical alternatives, whether a naïve correspondence-theory or a version of foundationalist epistemology which would leave him open to all the well-worn objections rehearsed by (among others) Quine, Rorty and Davidson himself.[19] Rather, it is to claim that these alternatives don't exhaust the field, and that there is a way of addressing the issue that can satisfy the twin conditions of (1) taking truth as something more than 'truth relative to this or that language, culture or system of beliefs', while (2) not going along with ideas of correspondence or privileged epistemic access that would beg the whole question from a relativist viewpoint. This position has been argued by thinkers like Jürgen Habermas and Karl-Otto Apel, theorists who take their bearings partly from the Frankfurt tradition of post-Kantian critical thought, and partly from developments in Anglo-American philosophy of mind and language.[20] For the rest of this chapter I shall be looking at one essay in particular, Apel's 'The Problem of Philosophical Foundations in Light of a Transcendental Pragmatics of Language'.[21] I shall argue that this offers not only some useful points of comparison with Davidson's thinking, bu: a means of defending his central propositions against the generalized pragmatist drift that Rorty finds everywhere in current 'post-analytical' philosophy.

Apel starts out by distinguishing different kinds of foundationalist truth-claim. 'From the point of view of transcendental pragmatics, the logical process by which sentences are deduced from sentences — indeed, all "axiomatics" — can only be considered as an objectifiable means within the context of the argumentative grounding of statements through epistemic evidence' (Apel, p. 271). That is to say, there is no question of simply rejecting the pragmatist argument, adopting a straightforward neo-Kantian approach and asserting that truth can be arrived at through critical reflection on the a priori powers and limits of human cognitive grasp. One could maintain this position only by ignoring the problems that arise as soon as one considers the extent to which truth-claims are in fact argued out, refined and developed through an ongoing dialogue whose rules are set by some existing community of shared interests and assumptions. In this sense at least the anti-foundationalist will always have knock-down arguments in plenty against anyone who seeks to put philosophy back on an epistemological footing, or to rehabilitate truth-as-correspondence in any of its classical forms. But we can take the full force of these objections — so Apel argues — without giving up on the idea of truth as something more than 'what's good in the way of belief'. For there is still the choice between Rorty's kind of pragmatism — one that in the end has no use for truth, reducing it to the way that beliefs hang together in some given cultural context — and Apel's 'transcendental pragmatics', a theory which seeks to conserve truth not just as an honorific term but as simply indispensable to any form of reasoned philosophical or scientific thought.

This is why Apel denies that we can separate the 'argumentative grounding of statements' from the question of 'epistemic evidence'. Certainly it is the case, he acknowledges, that agreement within some existing consensus is the precondition for a statement's possessing any warrantable claim to truth. But equally such claims must also be subject to agreed-upon procedures of verification, procedures that involve (among other things) the effort to match up hypotheses with experimental data, or the selection between rival theories in light of continuing research. This principle extends beyond the specialized domain of scientific method to the practices of everyday language use and inter-subjective understanding. For here also we must start from the knowledge that statements can be more or less truthful, informative or relevant to the matter in hand; that there will (at least in the majority of cases) be better reasons for accepting or rejecting such claims than the mere appeal to consensus belief; and that ultimately what counts as a good reason is the fact that some statements do correspond to the way things are in reality. So we are *not* confronted with an ultimate choice between, on the one hand, some version of metaphysical realism (or foundationalist epistemology) which ignores the role of discursive constraints in the social production of truth, and on the other a wholesale pragmatist creed which rejects all talk of truth as so much obsolete conceptual baggage. Rather, it is a question of seeing how these viewpoints cannot (or need not) get into conflict; how the 'argumentative grounding' of statements is always bound up with the presupposition that such statements can be checked against the facts in some not merely circular, trivial or self-confirming way.

We shouldn't be misled into thinking that Apel's choice of the term 'transcendental pragmatics' signifies a broad measure of agreement with Rorty's pragmatist position. On the contrary: what Apel sets out to defend is a strong truth-conditional theory of interpretive reason whose grounds are 'transcendental' in a sense much akin to the Kantian use of this term. Thus he argues (1) that sentences can indeed be assessed in terms of their ultimate truth-value, (2) that this process of assessment is carried on by a community of rational enquirers, and (3) that what qualifies a proposition as true is not just the present state of consensus belief within that community but also their readiness to make trial of it against evidence that may overthrow the consensus. To this way of thinking, Apel writes,

> it makes no sense to speak of 'appeal to epistemic evidence' without presupposing linguistic discourse as a context for interpretation and logical coherence. Likewise, it makes no sense to speak of substantial argumentative discourse without presupposing certain epistemic evidence, which the particular participants of discourse apply as their

criteria of truth in the argumentative procedure of building a discourse.
[Apel, p. 26]

In support of this contention Apel cites the example of modern
theoretical physics, where successive 'crises' have been brought about
by a perceived mismatch between the different orders of evidential
reasoning. On the one hand experiments may fail to confirm some
particularly powerful or elegant hypothesis. In this case the upshot
may be either that the theory is eventually abandoned as problematic
evidence keeps coming in, or that it is borne out in the long run
when science develops the technical means (maybe a microscope with
higher powers of resolution) to validate what had been, up to then,
an attractive but epistemically ungrounded hypothesis. On the other
hand, there may exist situations where a certain hypothesis continues
to appear both counter-intuitive and devoid of experimental warrant,
but where its sheer argumentative cogency and rigour compels
widespread assent. Such was at one time the case, Apel argues, with
those alternative geometries or space–time dimensions presupposed
by the General Theory of Relativity.

From this it might seem that the Rortyan pragmatist must have the
last word; that 'truth' is indeed what counts as such within a given
community of knowledge, and therefore cannot be defined in terms
of correspondence or epistemic access. Apel rejects this conclusion,
arguing instead that the business of sustaining an apparently counter-
evidential hypothesis must always be justified *at some point* by the
appeal to an available method of verification. Thus the testing of such
theories 'is carried out by means of measuring instruments which for
their part, in both their function and their manufacture, presuppose
evidence in the sense of the perception of ideal space, which is
paradigmatic in the "protophysical" language-game of Euclidean
geometry' (Apel, p. 270). That is to say, any hypothesis will have to
make sense not only in terms of its role within some specialized
discourse of speculative knowledge, but also in the context of those
checks and procedures that count elsewhere as providing well-
founded scientific evidence. 'This example', says Apel, 'elucidates the
a priori necessary connection between argumentation related to
discourse and (sufficient justification by means of) appeal to epistemic
evidence' (p. 270). His point also holds for those less specialised uses
of language where truth is not a matter of stringent verification but
of knowing, in a general way, that some kinds of utterance have a
genuine claim to be more accurate, more reliable or closer to the facts
than others.

There are two main points that Apel seeks to establish by taking this
example from modern theoretical physics. One is the insufficiency of
any Cartesian or Husserlian appeal to intuitive self-evidence, apodictic
certainty, a priori concepts of pure understanding or the like. For
such arguments cannot account for the fact that their truth-claims are
validated only within a certain discourse of knowledge, a discourse
whose terms must at least make sense and carry some degree of

logical conviction with users of the same language.[22] 'Like Descartes, Husserl could not even bring to his own consciousness the indubitability of his ego-consciousness, in a form both intelligible and valid for him, unless he could formulate this insight as an argument in the framework of a transcendental language-game of an ideal communication community' (Apel, p. 280). It is impossible to set aside the arguments of those (like Wittgenstein in his remarks on the 'private language' fallacy) who point to the radical incoherence of foundationalist thinking, at least in so far as such thinking is tied to notions of privileged epistemic access.[23] The analogy from physics supports this case by offering evidence that there are forms of knowledge that presently lack any kind of epistemic self-evidence, but for which it suffices that their claims hold good within a given, albeit highly specialized community of language-use. This is why it was possible for proponents of relativity theory 'to question the intersubjective validity of classical physics on the basis of a reinterpretation of experience through explanatorily more powerful theories', even though the older model still accorded not only with commonsense perception but with 'certain a priori evident connections between representations, as subjective conditions of the possibility of primary experience (for instance, conceptual connections in the sense of Kant's "forms of intuition" and "schematized categories")' (Apel, p. 269). There can always develop situations like this where the constraints of a language, discourse or set of intra-theoretical assumptions count for more than the appeal to any kind of epistemic self-evidence. But — and this is Apel's second main point — science would scarcely exist as such if the truth-claims arrived at through this process of purely argumentative enquiry were not ultimately subject to procedures of empirical verification. The same applies to 'ordinary', non-scientific discourse in so far as interpretation depends on our grasping the structures of logical inference, the truth-conditions and semantic implications that we just couldn't grasp were it not for the fact that language *paradigmatically* refers to objects of real-world experience. In short, the very notion of argumentative validity — of 'truth' as the product of general agreement within some currently existing paradigm — can only make sense on the prior assumption that statements may successfully refer to the world and thus lay claim to a stronger (epistemic) order of truth.

Where the pragmatists go wrong, from this point of view, is in assuming that the two kinds of theory cannot possibly be reconciled. That is, they equate all epistemic truth-claims with the sort of rock-bottom foundationalist argument that denies to language (or to discourse in its knowledge-constitutive aspect) any role in the social production of truth. Since clearly this position must be untenable — since we cannot conceive of any knowledge that could ever be arrived at outside some context of validating argument — they conclude that truth is *purely and simply* a product of consensual discourse. But, according to Apel, this line of argument leaves them open to a form of transcendental *tu quoque*: namely, that the pragmatist reduction of truth to what's good in the way of belief can offer no means of distinguishing valid from invalid forms of consensus knowledge. For if, as Rorty argues, the purported 'foundations' of rational discourse come down to nothing more than some particular language-game or choice of 'final vocabulary', then there is no possibility of criticizing false claims-to-truth on the basis of better, more cogent or adequate arguments. That such arguments will never be foundational in the absolute, Kantian sense — that they will always seek validation according to a set of currently prevailing discursive rules and constraints — is therefore no reason for espousing the wholesale pragmatist position and rejecting all talk of truth. 'From the point of view of a transcendental pragmatics of language, the fact that evidential consciousness achieves intersubjective validity only as publicly acknowledged language-game paradigms shows that giving reasons in arguments necessarily leads back to appeals to epistemic evidence' (Apel, p. 271). If this were not the case then the activity of giving reasons could be nothing more than a species of circular argument that would always confirm its own inbuilt logic of assumptions. What therefore distinguishes Apel's 'transcendental pragmatics' from the anti-transcendental version propounded by Rorty is precisely his insistence that rational debate cannot be conducted in the absence of epistemic truth-claims.

At this stage Rorty would doubtless respond by arguing first that any such claims must involve some appeal to foundationalist criteria — thus running into all the familiar problems — and second, that Apel has already undermined these delusive foundations by conceding that 'truth' can only be arrived at through the process of intersubjective debate. So one might just as well (indeed must, for consistency's sake) abandon all forms of transcendental argument and accept the pragmatist point without further ado. However, it is precisely this way of posing the issue that Apel seeks to avoid by way of his appeal to the 'transcendental pragmatics' of discourse involved in every kind of rational, truth-seeking enquiry. The pragmatist fallacy rests on the argument that since all reasoning is conducted in the context of particular languages, paradigms or communities of discourse, therefore reasons can only hold good in so far as they cohere with certain culture-specific values and assumptions. In the end this involves a covert appeal to conventions or 'conceptual schemes', despite Rorty's agreement with Davidson that such talk just obscures the issue. For if truth is indeed defined (for all practical purposes) by the way that statements fit in with some prevailing consensus, then it is hard to envisage just how such a fit could come about unless on the basis of a matching-up between shared structures of meaning or belief. One could argue further that Rorty gets into this awkward position by the same route that leads him to misconstrue Davidson: namely, his refusal to countenance any stronger form of truth-claim than the pragmatist reduction of all such issues to the level of consensus belief.

This is why Apel rejects the wholesale pragmatist argument and proposes instead a 'transcendental pragmatics' that would not lead on to such circular reasoning.

By virtue of the propositional acts (the identifying acts of reference and predication) upon which the formation of judgments depends, epistemic evidence is interwoven from the outset with language use and the capacities of knowing subjects . . . Justification, as giving reasons for the validity of knowledge, must always rest on the possible evidential consciousness of the particular knowing subjects (as autonomous representatives of the transcendental knowing subject as such) and on the a priori intersubjective rules of an argumentative discourse in the context of which the epistemic evidence, as subjective proof or objective validity, has to be brought to the level of intersubjective validity. [Apel, pp. 261–2]

This is a Kantian form of argument in so far as it locates the possibility of truth in the achievement of a state of rational (enlightened) consensus, a knowledge brought about by critical reflection on its own claims to validity. It is distinguished from Rorty's pragmatist position partly on account of the role played within it by the knowing, self-critical subject; partly by the link that it maintains between knowledge and questions of epistemic evidence; and partly by the fact that it holds out for an informed or rational consensus — for truth at the end of enquiry — and thus maintains the necessity of criticizing false ideas and beliefs, no matter how widely accepted these may be in some given cultural context. It is Kantian also in the sense that it argues from the 'conditions of possibility' for human understanding in general, that is to say from the fact that we would be in no position to argue, criticize, give reasons or engage in purposeful debate unless we acknowledged the truth of its premisses. But it doesn't involve the kind of foundationalist truth-claim that would render it vulnerable to those arguments so deftly rehearsed by Rorty in his deconstructive reading of the mainstream tradition. Such grounds are unavailable, as Apel makes clear, since 'the Kantian claim of the definitive completeness of the "system of pure reason" can no longer be maintained; our task is rather that of progressively opening up new transcendental horizons, which grow wider with the expansion of the human knowledge that we are questioning as to its conditions of possibility' (Apel, p. 273).

Davidson can best be read in light of these qualified but none the less powerful Kantian arguments. That is to say, we should accept his holistic approach (the idea of truth-conditions as holding between all sentences of a given language) along with the stronger theory in which truth figures as a matter of epistemic warrant. The alternative (pragmatist or post-structuralist) reading is one that must finally reject such claims and regard truth as wholly relative to the language, discourse or cultural paradigm in question. On this account (as argued by S. Pradhan in a recent article on Davidson and Derrida) one can indeed embrace the holistic implications while discounting any version of the strong truth-conditional or epistemic theory.[24] Thus Davidson may be taken to agree with Derrida on the following points: (1) that the appeal to linguistic 'conventions' in fact explains nothing, since signs, sentences and speech-acts can always be 'grafted' into novel or unlikely contexts where they continue to function despite the absence of normative constraints; (2) that such appeals would in any case involve a kind of infinite regress, since a rule would be required to determine just how, when and where the relevant condition came into force, and this rule would be dependent in turn upon some third-order level of linguistic convention; and (3) that we should therefore dispense with such question-begging talk and make do with what Pradhan calls a 'minimalist semantics', one that allows speech-acts to function across the widest possible range of contexts without always asking how their 'meaning' allows them so to function. This is why Davidson and Derrida both have an interest in anomalous cases, speech-acts that would count (on conventionalist terms) as deviant, non-standard or somehow 'parasitical' in relation to other, authentic or normative uses of the same verbal formula.[25]

Such is Derrida's response to John Searle, pointing out that *all* speech-acts are iterable, i.e. capable of being cited, parodied, taken 'out of context' etc., so that Searle runs up against insuperable problems in attempting to distinguish genuine from non-genuine varieties. Davidson is arguing to similar effect when he denies that 'deviant' uses of language (e.g. metaphor or malapropism) have to be referred back to our grasp of the proper, literal meaning before we can begin to make sense of them.[26] For there is nothing that could serve as an adequate 'scheme', or set of agreed-upon interpretive conventions, for effecting this shift from the level of deviant to non-deviant usage. Quite simply, 'the same declarative sentence may have the same meaning when used to make an assertion, to tell a joke, to annoy a bore, to complete a rhyme, or to ask a question' (*Inquiries*, p. 269). This is so not because (as Searle would argue) the normal case provides guidance enough for interpreting deviant instances, but because no semantic conditions determine the possible range of meaning that attaches to any given speech-act in context. Hence the need for a 'minimalist semantics', one that can account for this capacity of signs to function across a vast (potentially infinite) range of contexts without falling back on redundant talk of conventions, conceptual schemes and so forth. In Pradhan's words:

> If a sentence can be put to any use, and if its meaning does not restrict its use in any way and it retains the same meaning in the context of those multiple uses; or if a sign can always be removed from its context and grafted into another context and its identity as a sign does not hamper its functioning as that sign in those new contexts; then we had better posit only the minimum required semantically to constitute that sentence or that sign as that unit of language.[27]

From this it follows — according to Pradhan — that truth on the Davidsonian model must somehow be relativized to the entire language or set of logico-semantic relations which determines what shall count as a proper understanding of each particular utterance. 'Even though a theorem which states the truth conditions of a sentence explicitly refers only to that sentence and no other linguistic element, nevertheless to understand what is stated in stating the truth conditions of a sentence we must bring in its relation to other linguistic elements.'[28] Thus Davidson can be seen as concurring with Derrida in the argument that meaning cannot be fixed by any appeal to convention, to normative ideas of context or to theories of the sign (or individual speech-act) as possessing a semantic identity that would make it possible to distinguish proper from improper uses. In which case truth more or less drops out of the picture, except in the largely redundant guise of 'truth relative to some particular language as a whole'.

This argument amounts to yet another version of that same linguistic-conventionalist idea that Davidson is so anxious to avoid. Pradhan, like Rorty, chooses to stress certain elements in Davidson's thinking — those that can be used to make the link between his broadly holistic approach to language and post-structuralist notions of the arbitrary sign — while ignoring his insistence that any such theory must also take account of epistemic constraints upon the class of sentences held true. Thus, in Davidson's words, '[a] sentence or theory fits our sensory promptings, successfully faces the tribunal of experience, predicts future events, or copes with the pattern of our surface irritations, provided it is borne out by the evidence' (*Inquiries*, p. 193). And this despite the fact that any such theory or sentence will always be construed, and its truth-claims assessed, in some broader context that may extend from the idiom of a specialized sub-group, research programme, 'interpretive community' or whatever to the whole linguistic and cultural tradition within which that idiom arose. Davidson's chief point is that these two requirements don't necessarily conflict; truth can be *both* a matter of epistemic warrant *and* a matter of the way propositions hang together with others in the same language.

Thus it is wrong to suppose that there must be some ultimate choice between, on the one hand, foundationalist theories that isolate truth from the context of discursive or linguistic justification, and on the other the wholesale pragmatist view that truth is simply what counts as such according to our present, culture-specific aims and purposes. On this point Davidson would surely concur with the line of 'transcendental-pragmatic' argument advanced by thinkers like Habermas and Apel. That is to say, he accepts that truth-claims must indeed be subject to a process of validation in and through language, a process whereby they come to be accepted by members of the relevant community. But it is also prerequisite to any workable theory of truth and interpretation that an appeal should be open from language — or the realm of intra-discursive concepts and meanings — to the conditions under which statements are tested against various kinds of epistemic evidence. Otherwise, as Davidson argues, we could never make a start in that process of assigning determinable truth-conditions which is always presupposed in attempts to clarify the meaning of any given utterance. 'Of course truth of sentences remains relative to language, but that is as objective as can be. In giving up the dualism of scheme and world, we do not give up the world, but re-establish unmediated touch with the familiar objects whose antics make our sentences and opinions true or false' (*Inquiries*, p. 198).

There is no doubt that Davidson's writings — or selected passages from them — can be so construed as to offer support for the pragmatist/post-structuralist standpoint in matters of language, truth and representation. Furthermore, this approach has the dubious advantage of placing itself effectively beyond criticism by denying that there can be, when all is said and done, any right reading or demonstrable truth of the Davidsonian text. But in so doing it has to ignore not only some crucial aspects of his argument but also — more importantly — the entire logical structure of assumptions upon which that argument rests.

References

1. See especially Ernest Le Pore (ed.), *Truth and Interpretation: essays on the philosophy of Donald Davidson*, Oxford, Basil Blackwell, (1986).
2. Ludwig Wittgenstein, *Philosophical Investigations*, G.E.M. Anscombe (trans.), Oxford, Basil Blackwell, (1953), pp. 2–10 and *passim*.
3. See W.V. Quine, *From a Logical Point of View*, Cambridge, Mass., Harvard University Press, (1953).
4. Wittgenstein, *Philosophical Investigations* (op. cit.), p. 89 ff.
5. Quine, 'Two Dogmas of Empiricism', in *From a Logical Point of View* (op. cit.), pp. 20–46.
6. Donald Davidson, 'On the Very Idea of a Conceptual Scheme', in *Inquiries into Truth and Interpretation*, London, Oxford University Press, (1984), pp. 183–98. Hereafter cited in the text as *Inquiries*.
7. Ferdinand de Saussure, *Course in General Linguistics*, Wade Baskin (trans.), London, Fontana, (1974).
8. See for instance Michel Foucault, *Language, Counter-Memory, Practice*, Donald F. Bouchard and Sherry Simon (trans.), Oxford, Basil Blackwell, (1977) and *Power/Knowledge: selected interviews and other writings*, Brighton, Harvester, (1980).
9. See particularly Roland Barthes, *S/Z*, Richard Miller (trans.), London, Jonathan Cape (1975) and the essays collected in *Image–Music–Text*, Stephen Heath (trans.), London, Fontana, (1977).
10. Richard Rorty, *Philosophy and the Mirror of Nature*, Princeton, NJ, Princeton University Press, (1980).
11. Ibid., p. 261.
12. Rorty, *Consequences of Pragmatism*, Minneapolis, University of Minnesota Press, (1982), p. 15.
13. This line of argument has been taken up by neo-pragmatist literary critics who seek to demonstrate that 'theory' is a pointless, misguided or redundant activity. See especially Stanley Fish, *Is There a Text in this Class?*, Cambridge, Mass., Harvard University Press, 1980); Steven Knapp and Walter Benn Michaels, 'Against Theory', *Critical Inquiry*, Vol. VIII, (1982), pp. 723–42; Knapp and Michaels, 'Against Theory 2: hermeneutics and deconstruction', *Critical Inquiry*, Vol. XIV (1987), pp. 49–68. In this second article they cite Davidson's work in support of their case against theories that rest on the idea of meaning as a product of conventions or conceptual schemes. However, their version of Davidson is similar to Rorty's (and yet more extreme) in its acceptance of a thoroughgoing pragmatist approach to questions of meaning and interpretation. For Knapp and Michaels, meaning is synonymous with authorial intention, but only because it doesn't make sense to raise 'theoretical' issues of validity, truth, etc.

14. Rorty, *Consequences of Pragmatism* (op. cit.), p. xxv.
15. Rorty, *Philosophy and the Mirror of Nature* (op. cit.), pp. 261–2.
16. See especially Rorty, 'The World Well Lost' and 'Dewey's Metaphysics', in *Consequences of Pragmatism* (op. cit.), pp. 3–18 and 72–89.
17. Davidson, 'A Coherence Theory of Truth and Knowledge', in Le Pore (ed.), *Truth and Interpretation* (op. cit.), pp. 3–18, 72–89.
18. Rorty, *Consequences of Pragmatism* (op. cit.), p. xviii.
19. Rorty rehearses these arguments succinctly in his 'Introduction' to *Consequences of Pragmatism*, pp. ix–xlvii.
20. See for instance Jürgen Habermas, *Knowledge and Human Interests*, Jeremy Shapiro (trans.), London, Heinemann, (1972); Habermas, *Communication and the Evolution of Society*, Thomas McCarthy (trans.), London, Heinemann, (1979); Karl-Otto Apel, *Towards a Transformation of Philosophy*, London, Routledge and Kegan Paul, (1980).
21. Apel, 'The Problem of Philosophical Foundations in Light of a Transcendental Pragmatics of Language', in Kenneth Baynes, James Bohman and Thomas McCarthy (eds), *Philosophy: end or transformation?*, Cambridge, Mass., MIT Press, (1987), pp. 250–90. Hereafter cited in the text as Apel.
22. Jacques Derrida pursues a similar line of argument in his early work on Husserl. See Derrida, *Edmund Husserl's 'Origin of Geometry'*, John P. Leavey (trans.), Stony Brook, Nicolas Hays, (1978).
23. On this topic see for instance Saul Kripke, *Wittgenstein on Rules and Private Language*, Oxford, Basil Blackwell, (1982).
24. S. Pradhan, 'Minimalist Semantics: Davidson and Derrida on meaning, use, and convention', *Diacritics*, Vol. XVI (Spring, 1986), pp. 66–77.
25. See Derrida, 'Signature Event Context', *Glyph*, Vol. I, Baltimore, Johns Hopkins University Press, (1977), pp. 172–97; also John R. Searle, 'Reiterating the Differences', *Glyph*, Vol. I, pp. 198–208; and Derrida's response to Searle, 'Limited Inc abc', *Glyph*, Vol. II (1977), pp. 162–254.
26. See Davidson, 'What Metaphors Mean', in *Inquiries* (op. cit.), pp. 245–64 and 'A Nice Derangement of Epitaphs', in Richard E. Grandy (ed.), *Grounds Of Rationality*, Oxford, Basil Blackwell, (1986), pp. 157–74.
27. Pradhan, 'Minimalist Semantics' (op. cit.), p. 75.
28. Ibid., p. 74.

3 Pope among the formalists: textual politics and 'The Rape of the Lock'

Except in its most obvious physical aspect — the shape of words on the page — it is hard to attach any clear meaning to the idea of poetic 'form'. This concept may indeed be a species of enabling fiction, having more to do with the interpretative rage for order than with anything objectively 'there' in the text. Or it may be the product — in Paul de Man's words — of a close 'dialectical interplay' between poem and reading, such that the poem takes on a precarious unity of form in answer to the critic's subtle teasing-out of unifying themes and figures.[1] Criticism would then be caught up in a process of aesthetic mystification whereby its own desire for unity and closure was ceaselessly confirmed in the act of reading. To interpret is always to aim at an encompassing grasp of the text which would charge every detail with relevant meaning and so demonstrate the presence of genuine 'organic' form. Yet clearly it is the reading, as much as the poem, whose integrity is at stake in this quest for a validating wholeness of vision. Interpretation must always be able to show that its methods are sufficiently subtle, complex and responsive to bring out the deep-lying sources of coherence vested in the literary text. Any reading that fails in this objective — that leaves certain details unaccounted for, or confesses to finding the text incoherent — is thereby shown up as inadequate.

This assumption runs largely unchallenged from Coleridge to the American New Criticism. It is taken for granted that poetry possesses a richness and complexity of verbal resource that mark it off clearly from 'ordinary' language, and that criticism is best, most usefully employed in drawing attention to this difference. Poetry becomes an autonomous mode of discourse, belonging to a separate linguistic domain where commonplace logic no longer holds good and truth is bodied forth through metaphor, paradox and other such privileged rhetorical figures. Interpreters may bring great subtlety to bear in their reading of literary texts. They may even, like Coleridge, carry speculation to the point where it becomes very hard to draw any firm juridical line between poetry, criticism and theory. There were even those among the New Critics, like Allen Tate, who sometimes suspended the orthodox bans to the extent of wondering what criticism might become if freed from its strictly subservient role *vis-à-vis* the literary text.[2] But these were entertained as heretical notions to be set firmly aside when it came to the business of serious practical criticism. T.S. Eliot's pitying reference to 'the sad ghost of Coleridge, beckoning from the shades' was sufficient reminder of the ills and delusions to which criticism was prone once it abandoned its proper subordinate role.[3]

For the orthodox New Critics this amounted to a virtual policing operation, a matter of beating the strict ontological bounds that separate poetry from other kinds of language, including the language of criticism. A whole apparatus of doctrinal checks and sanctions was erected to maintain this division of realms. Critics might theorize as much as they pleased, but only on the understanding that their theories belonged to a second-order discourse which reflected on the powers and the limits of criticism itself, rather than seeking to make sense of poetry by imposing an alien logic of explanatory concepts. Thus Cleanth Brooks declared flatly that 'the principles of criticism define the area relevant to criticism; they do not constitute a method for carrying it out'.[4] Poetry has its own special claims to truth, quite distinct from those of rational explication on the one hand or generalized interpretative theory on the other. To confuse these realms — so the New Critics argued — was to lose sight of whatever gave value to poetry as a language transcending commonplace habits of thought and perception. It is this danger that John Crowe Ransom has in mind when he remarks that any adequate 'logic of poetic figure' would effectively constitute 'a logic of logical aberrations, applicable to the conventions of poetic language'.[5] This is because poetry — unlike criticism or critical theory — has nothing to do with the standard requirements of logical consistency or truth. Only by respecting its inwrought structures of rhetorical implication ('paradox', 'irony' and other such figures) can criticism hope to preserve poetic truth against the various 'heresies' that constantly threaten its autonomous mode of existence.

Chief among these heresies was the idea that poetry could be paraphrased, or made to yield up its meaning in a language of perspicuous plain-prose sense devoid of 'poetic' figuration. Thus the New Critics admired William Empson for his extraordinary close-reading skills, but sounded a warning note when it came to Empson's habit of providing all manner of paraphrastic hints and suggestions by way of making the poem more accessible. Empson's readings, as Ransom put it, might just as well apply to 'a piece of infinitely qualified prose'.[6] For the New Critics it was a high point of principle that poetry existed in a separate dimension of rhetorical complexity which no prose paraphrase — however subtly qualified — could hope to reach. The same applied to those other rampant 'heresies' which sought to interpret poetry in terms of such 'extraneous' contexts of knowledge as history, biography or cultural politics. Of course the New Critics never quite lived up to their own high principles here. Reading, say, Brooks on Marvell's 'Horatian Ode', one is aware of the way that historical facts and biographical background are smuggled in, so to speak, under cover of mere close attention to 'the words on the page'.[7] Like Eliot before him, Brooks wants to argue that the special quality of Marvell's poem — its poise, sophistication, perfected balance of attitudes — comes of its detachment from the pressures of politics and historical circumstance. The 'Ode' thus becomes a test-case for criticism, or more specifically for the kind of criticism that values such qualities of civilized wit and finds little use for mere documentary 'background'. Yet it is clear that Brooks starts out with a good working knowledge of Marvell's highly ambivalent career during and after the Civil War period. His apparently easy switch of loyalties from Cromwell to the restored monarchy is implicit in everything that Brooks has to say about Marvell's sophisticated handling of civic and martial themes. What Brooks's essay achieves on its own account — and programmatically, as part of the wider New Critical enterprise — is the same aesthetic distancing from history and politics that it finds so strikingly embodied in Marvell's poem.

But this achievement is not without its own specific weight of ideological prejudice. Behind Brooks's reading — nowhere spelled out but informing every last detail — is that potent mythology of English cultural decline which T.S. Eliot raised into a virtual dogma of modern literary opinion. Marvell stands in as the last representative of a civilized tradition whose values were threatened, even as he wrote, by the turmoils of the English Civil War. At about this time, in Eliot's famous phrase, there occurred a 'dissociation of sensibility', a lapse from political and cultural grace whose effects we have yet to understand, let alone overcome.[8] The Civil War marked the transition from a stable, divinely sanctioned order of society to one in which religious and political discord would henceforth work their mischief. Along with these social upheavals went a seismic shift in what might be called — though Eliot would scarcely have used such a phrase — the relations of literary production. For Shakespeare, Donne and their contemporaries, 'thought' and 'emotion' had existed in a happily unselfconscious harmony, with the intellect existing (as Eliot wrote of Donne) 'at the tips of the senses'. But then began that long sad period of secular decline when poetry could only alternate between extremes of 'dissociated' thought and emotion, the Augustans on the one hand (to adopt Eliot's drastically simplified picture) and the Romantics — or their latter-day Georgian descendants — on the other. It is not hard to see how Marvell fits in with this wholesale historical myth. Living through the period of civil strife, and living on (what is more) to become a satirist and a party-political poet in the new age, Marvell yet managed to produce a handful of lyrics and obscurely 'topical' poems whose complexity lifts them above mere history or circumstantial record. He thus becomes the touchstone for a critical method which elevates the virtues of 'paradox' and 'irony' into a measure of poetry's power to transcend the mundane realities of history and politics.

This background narrative, worked up from the myth of Eliot's devising, is deeply inscribed within New Critical practice. More specifically, it goes along with that rhetoric of detachment or aesthetic autonomy which works to keep such interests safely at bay. Eliot's 'tradition' is effectively what substitutes for history when the latter is reduced to a potent myth of secular decline and fall. It is a timeless dimension of aesthetic transcendence where the great creative minds of European culture converse without hindrance of mere historical or socio-cultural difference. 'Tradition' thus becomes a kind of imaginary museum, a space where the 'monuments' of past achievement compose themselves into an ideal order, determined by a sense of deep-laid cultural continuity and not by mere accidents of historical time and place. All these factors converge in the reading of Marvell proposed by Eliot and refined by Brooks. Leaving out the politics — or treating it as incidental background, fit matter only for the poet's play of non-committal attitude — the 'Ode' can then serve as a perfect example of how poetry transcends such unworthy concerns.

Post-structuralism takes issue with the 'old' New Critics on each of these closely connected points of principle. It rejects the idea that poetry is a special kind of language, radically different from those other discourses (of history, criticism, literary theory) which must therefore learn to respect its sovereign autonomy. De Man's essay on the New Criticism shows how this doctrine self-deconstructs as soon as one focuses attention on its characteristic language and strategies of argument. The discrepancy between precept and practice becomes most apparent when the New Critics draw upon metaphors and images of natural process to support the idea of 'organic' form. In de Man's words:

> Instead of revealing a continuity affiliated with the coherence of the natural world, [this] takes us into a discontinuous world of reflective irony and ambiguity. Almost in spite of itself, it pushes the interpretative process so far that the analogy between the organic world and the language of poetry finally explodes. This unitarian criticism finally becomes a criticism of ambiguity, an ironic reflection on the absence of the unity it had postulated.[9]

The upshot of de Man's essay is to show that the New Critics were unable to maintain any strict demarcation between the language of poetry and those other kinds of language that belong (so they thought) to a separate discursive realm. This leads to a further implication: that criticsm itself is often drawn into complex and duplicitous strategies of reading which deserve the same close attention that interpreters normally pay to 'literary' texts. It is precisely by failing to discover any firm ontological ground for their distinction between poetry and criticism that these interpreters point beyond their own express doctrines to a deconstructive reading of poetry and criticism alike. According to de Man, it is often in their moments of singular 'blindness' — blindness, that is, to the rhetorical complexity of literary texts — that critics may provide the maximum 'insight' for readers alert to such symptoms.

This suggests that we should read criticism in a way quite distinct from received ideas of its proper utility and purpose. It is not (as the New Critics would have it) a discourse standing apart from the literary text, supplying certain insights and even, on occasion, certain guidelines of 'method' but in no sense aspiring to occupy the same rhetorical domain. For post-structuralists, on the contrary, poetry and criticism exist in a close (if often strained and contradictory) relationship, such that no dogmatic conviction on the critic's side can hold them forcibly apart. This is because texts of all kinds — poetry, criticism, philosophy, historical narrative — can be shown to exploit the same rhetorical techniques and to place similar problems in the way of any straightforward (veridical or referential) reading. It is no longer a case, as it was for the New Critics, of resisting the claims of a positivist literary scholarship bent upon reducing the text to so many background facts or evidential sources. Such claims rested on the presupposition that *other* forms of discourse gave access to a truth beyond the equivocal, self-occupied character of 'literary' language. Thus the old quarrel between 'scholars' and 'critics' was not so much a genuine difference of principle as a matter of seeking alternative solutions to the same root dilemma. For all that they resisted its intrusive claims, the New Critics effectively yielded to scholarship the right to adjudicate in questions of straightforward factual self-evidence. Their only defence in face of such attack was to tighten up the sanctions surrounding that imaginary entity, the 'literary' text.

Post-structuralism goes various ways around to subvert this rigid demarcation of textual bounds. In de Man it takes the form of a deconstructive reading that presses the logic of New Critical theory to the point where it has to confront its own aberrant rhetorical drift. Elsewhere the point is made by taking texts from supposedly different discursive realms and reading them alongside each other to draw out their co-implicated rhetorics and strategies of argument. Thus for instance some of the best recent criticism of Wordsworth has more or less explicitly read him in the light of concepts and analogies drawn from Hegel's *Phenomenology of Mind*.[10] The point of such readings is not to claim 'philosophical' authority for what would otherwise be just another piece of workaday literary criticism. Philosophy is not conceived as an ultimate truth-telling discourse whose superior logical grasp enables it to illuminate the poem's more perplexed or obscurely metaphorical passages. Rather it is a question of allowing both texts to enter into a process of mutual interrogative exchange where commonplace distinctions between 'poetry' and 'philosophy' become increasingly hard to maintain. For the 'old' New Critics there was just one concept from Hegel — that of the 'concrete universal' — that served to underwrite their claims for the absolute autonomy of poetic form.[11] Removed from the context of Hegelian dialectic — of everything pertaining to history and change — it figured as a purely metaphysical support for the idea of poetry as a self-contained language indifferent to everything outside its own domain. What T.S. Eliot derived from Hegel (*via* his philosophic mentor F.H. Bradley) was the same kind of de-historicized idealist doctrine which enabled him to formulate 'tradition' as a timeless communing of minds, and poetry as a matter of unconsciously discovering some 'objective' verbal form for one's otherwise inchoate emotions.[12] As with Bradley, so with Eliot, this led to a species of transcendental solipsism. 'Tradition' becomes a kind of echo-chamber for the mind disenchanted with history and withdrawn into its own private vision of a purely synchronic cultural order.

It is a very different Hegel who figures so importantly in current post-structuralist criticism. In place of the 'concrete universal' — that ideal pretext for severing the connection between poetry, history, philosophy and other kinds of discourse — Hegel now provides the means to imbricate those languages one with another and thus to reopen an intertextual dialogue. One result of this process is that criticism can now be read with an eye to those rhetorical strategies and blind-spots which give it a symptomatic interest on its own account. In the remainder of this chapter I shall be looking at one fairly typical modern compilation — a *Casebook* on Pope's 'The Rape of the Lock', edited by John Dixon Hunt[13] — and attempting to draw out some of these problematic issues. I have chosen the *Casebook* for two main reasons. First, it is a kind of implicit New Critical manifesto, reprinting several essays (by Brooks among others) which are clearly meant as exemplary readings of their kind. Furthermore they are presented as in some sense resolving those 'problems' with the poem encountered by earlier, less sophisticated critics. Thus, the *Casebook* has a narrative line of its own, a tale of confusions and partial insights eventually redeemed by a criticism capable of rising above such limited views. Second, anthologies like this are often prescribed as 'background' reading for students, whose use of them — as a handy source of ideas but certainly not as *texts* for close reading — falls in exactly with New Critical precept. Therefore my argument is intended to have pedagogical as well as 'purely' theoretical implications. What those students had much better do, instead of mining the *Casebook* for authoritative 'insights', is read the critics with a mind alert to their interpretative strategies and moments of symptomatic blindness.

There is more than one reason for selecting 'The Rape of the Lock' as a suitable case for this kind of intertextual reading. It is a 'problem' poem not only in the sense that it has generated volumes of commentary, but also in the way that it has set these critics at odds with each other and even — at times — with their own principled commitments. As with Marvell, there is a marked tendency to insulate the poem from its social and political context, thus making it the more amenable to modern techniques of close-reading. This goes along with the desire to turn back the clock of history and treat Pope (again like Marvell) as a poet in whom there survived — intermittently at least — something of the old 'metaphysical' virtues. Leavis's essay 'The Line of Wit' is a classic example of this strategy at work.[14] It sets out to identify those elements in Pope's verse that relate him to Donne and the early-seventeenth century, qualities that almost disappeared from later English poetry — so the argument runs — partly through

Milton's malign influence and partly through the pressures of socio-
political change engendered by the Civil War. That Milton was pre-
eminently the poet of Civil War politics — an out-and-out partisan
and not, like Marvell, an artful balancer of options — gives this story
an added plausibility. In Pope's case, as even the New Critics can
hardly deny, poetry and politics are so far intertwined as to make it
very hard to read him without some knowledge of the relevant
'background'. Nevertheless there are certain techniques, most of them
represented in this *Casebook*, for minimizing the historical damage and
restoring Pope to something very like the 'metaphysical' state of
innocence and grace.

What comes across most strikingly in Brooks's reading is his effort
to contain the poem's sexual politics by treating it — in standard New
Critical style — as an allegory of aesthetic transcendence. More
precisely, it is Pope's special virtue to supply such a perfectly assured
ironic gloss to his narrative war-of-the-sexes that the episode becomes
a fine demonstration of New Critical theory in practice. Thus according to Brooks, the whole purpose of Pope's supernatural machinery
(the 'iridescent little myth of the sylphs') is to symbolize the working
of those social conventions that 'govern the conduct of maidens'. The
poem represents a good-humoured and tolerant attempt to 'do
justice', as Brooks puts it, to 'the intricacies of the feminine mind' (p.
141). Like the modern critic, Pope is well provided with sophisticated
means of taking pleasure in the episode without permitting more
serious thoughts to intrude. 'For in spite of Pope's amusement at the
irrationality of that mind, Pope acknowledges its beauty and its
powers.' Powers to seduce, to beguile and entertain, but always
within the strict limits laid down by a male sense of realism, balance
and proportion. For there are — as both Pope and Brooks do well to
remind us — certain elementary natural facts behind the shadow-play
of Pope's delightful 'machinery' and Belinda's equally delightful
courtship rituals. The poet and the critic are neither of them seriously
deceived by the elaborate conventions which Belinda — to her cost —
takes for real. Pope 'has absolutely no illusions about what the game
is'. Like Brooks, he is in possession of a balanced outlook which
knows precisely where to draw the line between convention and
reality, civilized pretence and natural fact. That he can hold these
opposites so perfectly in balance is a tribute not only to Pope's
artistry but also to his male-commonsense firmness of judgement. He
is certainly 'not to be shocked', Brooks writes, 'by any naturalistic
interpretation of the elaborate and courtly conventions under which
Belinda fulfils her natural function of finding a mate' (p. 144).

Beyond the surface detail of Brooks's reading is a scene of recognition where the critic discovers exactly those admirable qualities in the
poem that characterize his own interpretative stance. Of course one
could hardly expect otherwise, given that the critic was drawn or
impelled to interpret the poem in the first place. But there is more
going on when it comes to Brooks's reflections on Belinda and the
nature of female sexuality. His reading produces a series of implicit
equations that associate poetry (or poetic convention) with 'the

intricacies of the feminine mind', and criticism — or Brooks's kind of formalist criticism — with the masculine power to comprehend and sensibly judge those intricacies. If 'Pope's interpretation of Belinda's divinity does not need to flinch from bawdy implications', it is because both Pope and his like-minded critic have the fine breadth of judgement to take these opposed attitudes on board with perfect equanimity. Women (like poems) have a special licence to indulge their 'intricate' subtleties of feeling far beyond the limits properly observed by the discourse of male reason. Thus Belinda can display all the giddy symptoms of 'feminine' temperament — from coquettry to an absurdly exaggerated horror at her own (merely symbolic) 'rape' — and yet remain an object of male delectation. For it is a mark of Pope's maturity of judgement (and no less a virtue in Brooks's reading) that these female vagaries are not condemned but transformed into fit material for a wise and witty poem. Thus Pope 'definitely expects Belinda to be chaste; but, as a good humanist, he evidently regards virginity as essentially a negative virtue, and its possession, a temporary state' (p. 147). Belinda's histrionics are a passing show, the product of an overwrought virginal mind whose hypocrisies her male admirers (poet and critic) can afford to treat with humorous indulgence. 'She'll soon get over it' is the worldly-wise moral that Brooks finds implicit in Pope's supreme equanimity of tone.

All this chivalry turns out to have sharp limits when it comes to the more disturbing implications of Belinda's 'rape'. Brooks follows Pope in his will not to flinch from a manly recognition of the literalized meaning that persistently lurks within the metaphor. Thus he quotes Belinda's 'anguished' exclamation:

Oh hadst thou, cruel! been content to seize
Hairs less in sight, or any hairs but these!

and remarks that it 'carries on, unconsciously, the sexual suggestion' present throughout the poem (p. 146). But in this case the message is clear enough: that Belinda is more concerned with superficial appearances than with any real threat to her maidenly virtue. In Brooks's words, 'something of the bathos carries over to the sexual parallel: it is hinted, perhaps, that for the belle the real rape might lose some of its terrors if it could be concealed'. So there is, it seems, another and less attractive side to the terms on which criticism tolerates Belinda's character. Either the rape is just an elaborate game, in which case her reactions are absurdly overwrought (and perhaps, Brooks suggests, an extension of Belinda's seductive powers by other, more devious means). Or, if there is a hint of some real as opposed to merely metaphorical rape, then Belinda's concern for social appearances does begin to look like vanity or worse. Thus the upshot of all Pope's fine generosity — his attempt, as Brooks describes it, to 'do justice to the intricacies of the feminine mind' — is to place Belinda in a classic double-bind or no-win situation.

Brooks sees nothing of this, convinced as he is that 'Pope's tact is perfect', a matter of delicately making allowance for the whims and caprices of female temperament. What he chiefly admires is the poet's ability to fend off premature judgements by maintaining an attitude of finely-poised ironic reflection. 'The detachment, the amused patronage, the note of aloof and impartial judgement — all demand that the incident be viewed with a large measure of aesthetic distance' (p. 152). Even here Brooks's language betrays the slide into a tone of condescending male amusement at Belinda's expense. Behind this rhetorical shift lies the familiar New Critical evaluative stance which rates poems according to their level of 'detached' ironic self-containment. The very notion of poetic 'form' is equated by Brooks with this power to keep a multitude of feelings and responses in play while refusing to judge between them. 'It is, finally, the delicate balance and reconciliation of a host of partial interpretations and attitudes' (p. 152). Yet it is hard to square such statements with the cruder forms of irony and the patronizing tone that enter Brooks's language when he lines up with Pope on the side of male 'realism'. Then most often it is a matter of insinuating home truths which the 'feminine mind', for all its intricate turns, cannot properly grasp. Such superior knowledge on the male's part is not without its moments of unguarded brutality.

> Pope knows that the rape has in it more of compliment than of insult, though he naturally hardly expects Belinda to interpret it thus. He does not question her indignation, but he does suggest that it is, perhaps, a more complex response than Belinda realizes. (p. 152)

'Naturally' Belinda can hardly appreciate that ultimate achievement of civilized wit that discovers such rich possibilities for irony in treating the rape as more 'compliment' than 'insult'. That pleasure is reserved for those unflinching spirits whose largeness of view equips them to write, or to fully appreciate, such poetry as this.

In the course of Brooks's reading one can make out another covert drift of analogical thinking, this time one that associates the finely wrought balance of poetic 'form' with the elusive, precarious nature of female 'virtue'. Brooks makes a point of denying that 'form' has anything to do with mechanical conventions or rigid ideas of how poetry ought to be structured. Rather it is a question of tonal balance, of that infinitely subtle and qualified irony through which Pope achieves his best effects. The New Critics were collectively ill at ease when it came to defining precisely what they meant by 'form' in poetry. The various rhetorical tropes that they raised into touchstones of poetic value ('paradox', 'irony', etc) were all too easily taken for dogma and reified as structures objectively 'there' in the poem. Consequently the New Critics often had to insist, like Brooks, that these tropes were devices of no special value in themselves, but only in so far as they served to communicate a complex and rewarding variety of sense. The effect of such qualifications was to set up a kind of infinite regress, with 'form' defined only in tentative, provisional terms and always subject to further complicating hints of ambivalence or irony.

In some of Brooks's essays — like the piece on Donne's 'Canoniza-tion' in *The Well Wrought Urn*[15] — the poem has a tight enough rhetorical structure for its 'form' to be presented as more or less synonymous with its play of tone and attitude. Thus Brooks can turn the poem into a perfect New Critical allegory of reading, with the urn as symbol of poetry's power to contain and memorialize the extremes of human experience. Elsewhere, as when writing about Marvell or Pope, it is more difficult for Brooks to effect this transition from the level of meaning and attitude to the level of totalizing 'form'. His response, as we have seen, is to invoke a series of detached or 'plac-ing' ironies on the poet's part in order to forestall any premature reduction to a crudely moralizing import. The effect of this manoeuvr-ing is to set them both up — poet and critic — as arbiters of a rich and complex experience beyond the mere conventions of literary style. And it is woman (Belinda) who figures in Brooks's reading as a creature so far taken in by those conventions as to exemplify the same liabilities and limits as the notion of poetic 'form'. What this notion must include, according to Brooks, is 'much more than the precise regard for a set of rules and conventions mechanically applied' (p. 152). As Pope sees beyond the female self-regard that attaches such importance to appearances, so Brooks envisages a larger, inclusive realm of poetic meaning that puts the mere mechanics of 'form' firmly in its place. 'Belinda's is plainly a charm-ing, artificial world; but Pope is not afraid to let in a glimpse of the real world which lies all about it' (p. 152). Unlike the well wrought urn of Donne's devising, Belinda is a frail vessel whose womanly flaws the critic obligingly rotates to view.

Other commentators on 'The Rape of the Lock' are far less subtle than Brooks in announcing this commonplace prejudice. Aubrey Williams hunts out all manner of sources for the emblem of woman as 'the weaker vessel', from the New Testament to Shakespeare, Herrick, Gay, Keats and Freud.[16] And he sets up a similar suggestive parallel between Belinda's weakness and the complex fascination which she, like the poem, exerts upon the male reader. Thus: 'although Pope's view of her is laced with irony, Belinda's beauteous virginity is somehow rendered more precious, and our regard for it somehow more tender, by recognition of how easily it can be marred or shattered' (p. 227). When Williams takes issue with Brooks, it is on account of Brooks's failure to heed these omens of catastrophe and his consequent tendency to make the poem turn on matters of 'taste' rather than moral questions. What they signify to Williams is a deeper-running current of serious suggestion: that Belinda does indeed suffer some kind of 'fall', that her perfection is rudely shattered and that (in Williams's deft phrasing) 'she does lose her "chastity", in so far as chastity can be understood, however teas-ingly, as a condition of the spirit' (p. 228). There are several kinds of 'teasing' suggested here, all from a male point of view. There is Belinda's artful use of her own virgin sexuality, deployed (however 'unconsciously') as a means to heighten her seductive charms. There is the teasing implicit in the male critic's down-to-earth reminder that chastity 'as a spiritual condition' is really beside the point, though good for some neatly turned displays of poetic conceit. Along with these suggestions goes a hint of how the poem — itself a frail vessel of seductive contriving — puts itself constantly at risk (like Belinda) from the wrong kind of male attention. There seems, Williams writes, 'as much danger in taking the poem too lightly as there is in taking it too seriously: the poem seems able to tease us into thought as well as out of it' (p. 228). The two kinds of teasing, sexual and aesthetic, both have to do with form, convention and the risks attendant on mistaking artifice for real-life behaviour.

Williams's glancing allusion to Keats suggests how issues of aesthetic form here become closely intertwined with sexual and erotic implications. If the poem teases criticism into and out of thought, then it shares this power with Belinda's artful yet dangerous use of her feminine charms. The aesthetic ideal implicit in formalist criticism — that of the poem as a pure, self-enclosed product of verbal artifice — exacts the same tribute of mixed feelings as Belinda's dissimulating conduct. Thus Williams's language oscillates between a 'tender regard' for her 'beauteous virginity' and talk of the 'narcissistic self-love' that drives her to make such a show of it. In the same way, Williams reproaches Brooks for yielding too readily to the poem's aesthetic blandishments — to matters of form, taste, convention — and thus ignoring its moral import. If Brooks had only attended more closely to the implications of Belinda's 'fall' (along with the associated metaphors of woman as the 'weaker vessel') he would surely have resisted this temptation. The beguiling influence of aesthetic form is as powerful yet also as fragile as anything mustered by Belinda's arts. In the last analysis Williams, like Brooks, wants an end to this teasing play and an honest acknowledgement (on the poet's, if not on Belinda's part) that the sexual situation is for real. Thus: 'Pope further intensifies the issues (and the element of free choice) by his hints, delicate though they be, that Belinda actually acquiesces, however faintly, in the "rape" (p. 228). Thus poet and critic are agreed in demanding that the girl leave off her artificial pretences and face up — at whatever 'unconscious' level — to some plain home truths about the female mind.

There are two main topics or centres of attention in this running debate among the modern commentators. One is the question of Belinda's 'character', shading off easily (as we have seen) into generalized pronouncements about female nature. The other has to do with interpretative method and the balance of priorities between such matters as form, attitude and tone. That these topics are linked in devious ways — that the 'problem' of Belinda is oddly tied up with the 'problem' of aesthetic form — I have suggested through my reading of Brooks and Williams. A familiar pattern begins to emerge as the critics take issue over various details of Pope's elusive text. On the one hand they conceive themselves as speaking up for truth against the falsehoods or the partial insights of other, less sophisticated readings. Thus the *Casebook* has several essays of a broadly New Critical persuasion that compete in their attempts to do full justice to Pope's satiric range and subtlety of tone. On the other hand these critics adopt a certain stance in regard to Belinda (or 'woman' in general), the effect of whose presence in the poem is both to disconcert and to redouble their truth-seeking efforts. Woman takes on those aesthetic attributes — of ambivalence, paradox, dissimulating irony — which the New Critics expressly prized yet obscurely mistrusted in poetry. So Belinda becomes, in effect, a surrogate victim of the tensions and strains which these critics are unable to resolve in their own methodology. Her 'world' is represented as a self-enclosed domain of mere 'good form' and polite convention. Meanwhile the interpreters can confidently join with Pope in discovèring the limits of that female world and gently but firmly reminding Belinda of the sexual realities outside.

One might recall those passages in Derrida's *Spurs* where he shows how the image of woman has figured obsessively as lure and provocation in the discourse of male reason. Woman provokes by her 'unmasterable' distance, her standing-off from the masculine protocols of reason, dignity and truth. With Nietzsche especially, this issues in a kind of mixed fascination and loathing, a fix upon woman as the virtual embodiment of everything that philosophy — 'serious' philosophy — needs to abjure. Thus Nietzsche in his overtly misogynist vein excoriates woman for her fickleness, her concern with appearances and scandalous disregard for truth. Yet Nietzsche is himself in the process of challenging (or deconstructing) those very claims-to-truth that have ruled the discourse of philosophic reason from Socrates to Hegel and beyond. Thus there develops, in Nietzsche's writing, a perverse association of themes by which 'woman' comes to stand — however obliquely — for those liberating energies that might yet break with the weight of received ideas.

> Woman . . . is twice model, at once lauded and condemned. Since she is a model for truth she is able to display the gift of her seductive power, which rules over dogmatism, and disorients and routs those credulous men, the philosophers. And because she does not believe in the truth (still, she does find that uninteresting truth in her interest) woman remains a model, only this time a good model. But because she is a good model, she is in fact a bad model. She plays at dissimulation, at ornamentation, deceit, artifice, at an artist's philosophy. Hers is an affirmative power. And if she continues to be condemned, it is only from the man's point of view where she repudiates that affirmative power and, in her specular reflection of that foolish dogmatism that she has provoked, belies her belief in truth.[17]

Other names for this 'dissimulating non-truth of truth' are (as Derrida suggests) 'style' and 'writing', since philosophy has traditionally repressed the knowledge of its own rhetorical character in pursuit of an idealized self-presence of truth immune to such trivial distractions. So 'woman' becomes, by the strangest of involuntary reversals, the emblem of everything that beckons beyond the delusive regime of metaphysical truth.

The drastic ambivalence of Nietzsche's writing on the 'woman question' is reproduced — albeit more tactfully — in critical discussion of
Pope's Belinda. Here also there is a strain of manly disapproval which
occasionally rises to shuddering contempt at the artifice of female life.
Dr Johnson strikes this tone in a passage from his 'Life' of Pope
which the *Casebook* includes among its 'Extracts from Earlier Critics'.
'The whole detail of a female life is here brought before us, invested
with so much art of decoration that, . . . we feel all the appetite of
curiosity for that from which we have a thousand times turned
fastidiously away' (p. 69). It is the word 'fastidious' that heightens
the sense of outraged masculine values, suggesting as it does that
Johnson's reaction has about it something of the exaggerated 'female'
sensitivity to matters of form and appearance. As with Nietzsche, the
topic is one that gets under the critic's elaborate defences and then
proceeds to work a subtle confusion of established gender-role ideas.
Thus Johnson goes on, in yet more absurdly hyperbolical style, to
justify his own animadversions by remarking the effect of female
behaviour on the conduct of society at large. 'The freaks, and
humours, and spleen, and vanity of women, as they embroil families
in discord, and fill houses with disquiet, do more to obstruct the
happiness of life in a year than the ambition of the clergy in many
centuries' (p. 69). Of course one wouldn't find any modern critic
prepared to let prejudice ride in such an overtly moralizing style. Yet
the upshot of all their sophisticated reading techniques is still to
devise new and more elaborate ways of putting Belinda down.

In fact those 'earlier critics' were often more aware of the politics
— sexual and dynastic — bound up with the problems of interpreting
Pope's allegorical design. Thus Hazlitt cites a passage from
Shakespeare, remarking on its elemental grandeur, and then observes
how 'there is none of this rough work in Pope . . . His Muse was on
a peace establishment, and grew somewhat effeminate by long ease
and indulgence' (p. 92). Hazlitt is writing from the standpoint of a
later, more pressured situation when events in France and the
backlash in Britain had forcibly involved poetry with politics and put
an end to the idea of poets living undisturbed 'on a peace establishment'. There is a certain contempt in Hazlitt's description, carried (as
usual) by the habit of thought which associates poetic artifice with all
things womanish or 'effeminate'. However, there is also a clear
understanding that Pope's peculiar kind of formal perfection has
political and ideological overtones beyond this immediate impression.
'The balance between the concealed irony and the assumed gravity is
as nicely trimmed as the balance of power in Europe' (pp. 93–4). If
there is something effete about Pope's way of writing, it is none the
less a style whose formal attributes and implicit values can always be
enlisted on the side of conservative reaction. To celebrate Pope, as the
modern critics do, for his qualities of 'balance' and perfect ironic
detachment is to fall in with that mystified image of a bygone
civilized order which Hazlitt was quick to perceive in the conservative
ideologues of his day.

One can see this process very plainly at work in Martin Price's essay 'The Problem of Scale: the game of art'. Price goes through most of the usual moves to establish the poem as a well-nigh miraculous achievement of verbal art and Belinda as the vessel whose graces and flaws enable the poet to bring this miracle about. The sylphs and gnomes of Pope's supernatural 'machinery' are, says Price, 'in their diminutive operation, like those small but constant self-regarding gestures we may associate with a lady conscious of her charms' (p. 238). Yet these very frailties of female nature are so worked upon by Pope's transformative art that they become an emblem of everything that raises humanity above mere animal instinct. Like many of the commentators, Price invokes the time-honoured trope by which poetry is seen as an agent of redemption, a means of lending ideal permanence to the passing show of mortal beauty. Thus: 'the elevated lock is, in a sense, the poem, shining upon beaux and sparks, but upon all others who will see it, too'. So the lock stands in synecdochically, not only for Belinda (who is thereby redeemed from all the ills that female flesh is heir to), but also for the poem, by whose magical powers this whole transformation is successfully carried through. But if woman is thus saved from her natural state, it is only on condition that she play the proper role as defined by prevalent male ideas of 'feminine' artifice and charm. She then becomes the acme of perfection for a backward-looking vision of order which locates the social virtues in a bygone age and discovers mere chaos and anarchy in everything since.

It is hardly surprising when Price caps his argument by quoting Edmund Burke on the sad decline from older standards of moral and aesthetic taste.

> It is gone, that sensibility of principle, that chastity of honour, which felt a stain like a wound, which inspired courage while it mitigated ferocity, which ennobled whatever it touched, and under which vice lost half its evil, by losing all its grossness [quoted by Price, *Casebook*, p. 242]

This passage lends itself ideally to the purpose of a criticism bent upon refining away all the traces of history or sexual politics inscribed within Pope's text. Any crudely literal understanding of the 'rape' is discountenanced by Burke's harking back to a time when such 'grossness' was rendered unthinkable — sublimated out of view — by a more refined state of moral sensibility. In Hazlitt this notion of a past golden age went along with a sense, a keenly historical sense, of the politics implied by any such form of retrospective idealization. Burke's example was evidence enough that the transposition of aesthetic values into the sphere of history and politics was a move now co-opted by the forces of reaction, whatever its earlier, more radical claims. There is something of the same differentiating irony when Byron speaks of 'the ineffable distance in point of sense, harmony, effect . . . between the little Queen Anne's man, and us of the Lower Empire' (p. 101). What Hazlitt and Byron implicitly resist is the kind of ahistorical mythologizing impulse that annuls such distance in the name of some ideal aesthetic or social order. However, when Price quotes the passage from Burke, it is assumed to carry a timeless authority and weight of self-evidence beyond all mere fluctuations of political climate. Like the poem itself, Burke's words are translated to a realm of precarious yet somehow enduring truth where they hold out against the ravages of secular decline. In the Cave of Spleen episode we are offered, according to Price, 'one of the strongest pictures of disorder in the age . . . a sense of the strength of the forces that social decorum controls and of the savage distortion of feeling that it prevents' (p. 240). Thus the tonings of Burke's counter-revolutionary rhetoric are carried over perfectly intact into Price's reading of Pope.

There is one modern essay in the *Casebook* that does raise questions about the politics of interpretation and the New Critical tendency to render such questions invisible by placing poetry beyond reach of historical discourse and critique. The author is Murray Krieger, himself a noted defender of the 'old' New Criticism, but also a theorist aware of its failings from the viewpoint of other, more politically sensitive modes of reading. Krieger's title, 'The "Frail China Jar" and the Rude Hand of Chaos', suggests that his essay will follow the by now familiar pattern, constructing a mythology of aesthetic form against the 'chaos' of modern (political) reality. And indeed, up to a point, this is the line his argument adopts. Thus it happens — as so often in New Critical debate — that Krieger takes issue with a fellow-interpreter (Cleanth Brooks once again), suggesting that there is more to be said, or more subtle and adequate ways of saying it. Even Brooks, according to Krieger, has 'not quite pursued his approach to this poem to a unified conclusion'. He has rested content with 'merely complicating the dimensions of the poem . . . and so leaving it, exposed but not regrouped, in all its multiplicity' (p. 203). It is thus left for Krieger to press Brooks's scattered insights to their proper (formalist) conclusion and thereby demonstrate both the unifying power of Pope's imagination and the full critical grasp of a method that can adequately celebrate that power.

In Krieger's closing statement, after an intertextual reading with *The Dunciad* and parts of the *Essay on Man*, this method achieves its own apotheosis. The passage is worth quoting at length since it brings out very clearly the aims and ontological commitments of New Critical method.

> Powerless against chaos — that disintegrating force of historical reality whose 'uncreating word' extinguished 'Art after Art' — the frail universe could win immortality with the very evanescent quality that doomed it: for 'quick, poetic eyes' it glows, gem-like, a sphere beyond the reach of the 'universal Darkness' that buried all. [p. 219]

On the face of it this stands as the perfect summation of all those rhetorical strategies and ploys that the New Critics raised to such a high point of principle. Allusions to the *Dunciad* are skilfully interwoven with an argument that sets off the timeless values of art against the 'chaos', the 'disintegrating force' of historical process.

This attitude is confirmed elsewhere in Krieger's essay when he states simply that 'the permanence of art must be preferred to the dynamic causality of history'.

As usual, it is Belinda, and Belinda's virginity, that serves as a focus for this contrast between natural and artificial orders of being. Krieger is more precise, more rhetorically exacting than most interpreters when he isolates the two chief tropes — metonymy and zeugma — through which the transformation is achieved. Metonymy (taking the lock to stand for Belinda's body) is what enables the allegory to work its effect while keeping its distance from any crudely literal sense. Zeugma, the yoking of two distinct idioms to a single verb ('Or stain her honour, or her new brocade') is the single most effective of Pope's rhetorical tricks, in so far as it creates an ironic clash between seemingly disparate orders of value. Thus Krieger can argue that the poem finally brings about a 'miraculous conversion', such that 'the "frail china jar" becomes more precious than virginity — in effect comes to be not merely a symbol for virginity, but even an artificial substitute for it in this world of artifice' (p. 212). To the extent that it deploys a more 'technical' idiom to refine upon this commonplace trope, Krieger's essay rejoins the New Critical tradition whose values and priorities it scarcely disturbs.

Yet, on a closer reading, there are signs in Krieger's text that the different analytical terms go along with a tendency to problematize those truths about poetic language that the New Critics took as a matter of working faith. For one thing, Krieger holds out against the somewhat homespun New Critical rhetoric which assimilates metonymy to metaphor, and thus ignores any problems in the way of its own transcendentally unifying vision. Krieger's essay was published in 1961, long before the advent of deconstruction or of Paul de Man's powerful demystifying texts on the rhetoric of metaphor and symbol. Nevertheless there are moments when Krieger very strikingly anticipates de Man's astringent critique of the truth-claims vested in these privileged figures of thought. The more orthodox New Critics were apt to build a vision of universal harmony and truth on the basis of details (like Belinda's lock) which they took, in a vaguely encompassing sense, as metaphors of the human condition. Krieger is himself intermittently willing to go along with such claims, but elsewhere he insists (like de Man) that it is wrong to be taken in by this rhetorical ploy; that metonymy and metaphor need to be distinguished; and that most 'metaphors' come down in the end to aggregates of metonymic detail. Thus with Pope it is a question of resisting inflated metaphorical accounts by viewing the poem as 'a mockery of the self-conscious seriousness displayed by trivial characters over a trivial occurrence'. In that case we will see them 'indulging the logical fallacy of metonymy: they have mistaken the lock of hair, actually incapable of being violated, for the lady's body — vulnerable, but unassaulted by the baron' (p. 203). There is more to this passage than a simple insistence on getting one's terminology right and not confusing two distinct figures of speech. What Krieger is effectively deconstructing — against the main drift of his essay —

is the strong vested interest in totalizing tropes (like metaphor and symbol) which underwrites the claims of New Critical method.

The comparison with de Man will seem less far-fetched if one takes account of a symptomatic footnote to Krieger's essay. The note concedes that he has been using the key-term 'zeugma' in two distinct senses, only one of them answering to its proper usage as defined by rhetorical theory. A genuine case of zeugma is one where the double meaning hangs on a single verb, thus involving a *grammatical* as well as a rhetorical dimension to the well-wrought pun. This condition is satisfied by classic examples of the kind: 'Here thou, great Anna! whom three realms obey, Dost sometimes counsel take — and sometimes tea'. Of Krieger's instances, only one (he thinks) conforms to the strict pattern: 'Or stain her honour, or her new brocade'. The others are cases where the rhetorical effect is much the same although the grammar doesn't properly conform to type. These figures Krieger describes as 'mere antitheses of four distinct parts, with each object controlled by its own verb' (p. 219). Thus in the lines 'Whether the nymph shall break Diana's law, Or some frail China jar receive a flaw' there is no instance of zeugma, strictly defined, but there is the strong sense that disparate scales of value are being neatly played off through a shrewd turn of style. This enables Krieger to claim that, 'in a rhetorical if not in a grammatical sense', these tropes all exploit the same kind of verbal resource. Only in rare cases do we find what Krieger calls 'the short-circuited perfection of the grammatical device'. The others are 'effective, but less complete, and thus less brilliant examples yielding the same rhetorical effect'.

In several late essays de Man drew attention to the link between rhetorical and ideological forms of mystification. In particular he pointed to the ways in which philosophers and literary critics had effectively collapsed the vital distinction between logic, grammar and rhetoric.[18] This threefold division — the basis of the classical *trivium* — was pushed out of sight (so de Man argues) by the rise of an aesthetic ideology which privileged metaphor and symbol as the highest, most expressive forms of language. What this attitude entailed, on the negative side, was a marked disregard for metonomy, allegory and other such merely 'mechanical' tropes. These figures held out against the Symbolist drive to sink ontological differences and treat language as a visionary discourse of pure, unmediated truth. They insisted on the arbitrary nature of the sign, the irreducible gap between signifier and signified, and the fact that meaning was constructed in language by a process that constantly deferred or undermined the hypostatic union dreamt of in Symbolist aesthetics. Thus the 'valorization of Symbol' always occurs at the expense of allegory and coincides historically with 'the growth of an aesthetics that refuses to distinguish between experience and the representation of this experience'.[19] What metonymy and allegory have in common is their power to deconstruct this mystification of language by ceaselessly revealing the rhetorical sleights of hand upon which its claims are ultimately based. In 'the world of the Symbol', de Man writes, 'it would be possible for the image to coincide with the substance', since sign and reality are 'part and whole of the same set of categories'. With allegory, on the other hand, meaning can only consist 'in the repetition of a previous sign with which it can never coincide, since it is of the essence of this previous sign to be pure anteriority'.[20] Metonymy exerts a similar force of deconstructive leverage since it focuses attention on the artifice involved — the element of random or piecemeal selectivity — in any act of figural substitution. Where metaphor implies a totalizing grasp, a perfect reciprocity between 'vehicle' and 'tenor', metonymy puts up an active resistance to this strong rhetorical drift.

Hence de Man's repeated demonstration of the ways in which under-privileged tropes (like metonymy and allegory) work to undo the high Romantic claims of symbol and metaphor. Hence also his suggestion that criticism return to that division of discourse (logic, grammar, rhetoric) laid down by the classical *trivium*. For it is precisely in the tension *between* these disciplines or levels of analysis that de Man locates the most important area for deconstructive critique. It is here, he argues, that mystified rhetorical strategies get a hold upon language by systematically eliding the conflicts of sense which would otherwise threaten their self-assured grasp. This comes out most clearly in the problems that develop as one reads a text with an eye to those repetitive (or 'quasi-automatic') patterns of meaning that resist a purely metaphorical account. By calling attention to this resistance — showing, as de Man very often does, how metaphor typically self-deconstructs into chains of metonymic detail — theory can effectively hold out against the powers of linguistic mystification. From this it follows, according to de Man, that 'more than any other mode of enquiry . . . the linguistics of literariness is a powerful and indispensable tool in the unmasking of ideological aberrations, as well as a determining factor in accounting for their occurrence'.[21] On the one hand literary language gives endless opportunities to those who would erect a wholesale system of mystified values on the basis of a favoured few rhetorical tropes. Such is the New Critical way of elevating figures like 'paradox' and 'irony' to the status of touchstones for the absolute measurement of poetic worth. However, there is also — as de Man would argue — an opposite, demystifying use for the 'linguistics of literariness', one that can recognize those strategies for what they are precisely by virtue of its own close involvement with textual and rhetorical critique. Thus de Man writes contemptuously of critics who attack deconstruction on the grounds of its supposed 'apolitical' character.

> Those who reproach literary theory for being oblivious to social and historical (that is to say ideological) reality are merely stating their fear at having their own ideological mystifications exposed by the tool they are trying to discredit. They are, in short, very poor readers of Marx's *German Ideology*.[22]

If deconstruction makes a virtue of attending closely to the rhetoric of literary (and critical) texts, this is not — as some Marxist critics would have it — a last-ditch retreat from the pressures of political commit-ment. For it is often at this level of textual analysis that thought can best unmask those effects of ideological blindness and duplicity to which language is always prey.

This brief excursion into de Man's later essays may help to define the exact point at which Krieger parts company with the orthodox New Critical reading of 'The Rape of the Lock'. His insistence on distinguishing metonymy from metaphor is a move beyond the mystified ontology of poetic language that treats all the kinds and varieties of trope as aspiring to a single, metaphorical condition. It is true that Krieger takes only a cautious and limited step in this direc-tion. Thus his footnote no sooner explains the distinction than it seems to withdraw, for all practical purposes, onto safer New Critical ground. ('My point is, however, that in a rhetorical if not a gram-matical sense, there is a similar yoking of two disparate worlds in all these instances.') His reading is indeed, to a very large extent, organized around those selfsame rhetorical strategies that operate in Brooks and other such adepts of formalist method. In this sense Krieger's essay differs from itself as much as it differs from orthodox New Critical practice. This difference is by no means confined to a somewhat more exacting deployment of rhetorical terms. Ultimately it leads to a questioning of all those aesthetic assumptions which the New Critics raised into a safeguard against the pressures of historical awareness.

Not that Krieger deconstructs the formalist position with anything like de Man's tenacity or will to expose its blind-spots of argument. He remains a New Critic by rooted persuasion, arguing that poetry has the power to express lasting truths through a language that transcends the limiting conditions of plain prose statement. More recently Krieger has defended such claims against the threat of a deconstructionist theory that would seem to annul every kind of ontological privilege and reduce poetry to an undifferentiating rhetoric of tropes. In his book *Poetic Presence and Illusion* (1980) Krieger suggests that Renaissance poets like Sidney and Spenser were shrewdly beforehand with these modern debates.[23] On the one hand they were trained up in a long tradition of rhetorical theory which laid great stress on the elaborate conventions and the artificial character of poetic language. On the other, they devised a whole range of redemptive tropes by which to thematize the permanence of verbal art-forms, their power to resist the encroachments of time and the vicissitudes of cultural change. Hence those metaphors in the courtly love tradition that represent the poem as conferring on the beloved an immortality beyond reach of her natural charms and graces. Such tropes are an emblem, so Krieger would argue, of poetry's power to hold out against the various disintegrating forces that afflict other kinds of language. Among these forces must be counted the drift toward a generalized intertextuality whose effect is to undermine belief in the 'presence' (or capacity for autonomous self-preservation) traditionally ascribed to poetry.

These themes are all present in Krieger's reading of 'The Rape of the Lock'. They amount, as I have said, to a highly refined and sophisticated set of variations on the standard New Critical technique that treats the poem as a self-sustaining allegory of aesthetic transcendence. Thus Pope can finally afford to acknowledge the hard truths of Belinda's mortal condition, but 'only because he is granting a resurrection to the metonymic lock which has been appropriately hailed by the "Beau monde" that it symbolizes' (p. 218). The rhetorical drift here — from 'metonymy' to 'symbol' — shows very clearly what de Man has in mind when he writes of the prematurely 'totalizing' drive that motivates all rhetorics based upon symbol and metaphor. In this case it allows Krieger's essay to rise to an impressive peroration where the poem is inscribed 'midst the stars' (with Belinda's name), and 'the illusory universe . . . like the "Beau monde" constructed as a work of art . . . testifies to the persistence, the indomitable humanity of its creator's classic vision' (pp. 218–9). It would be hard to find a more consummate example of formalist poetics in the service of a transcendental aesthetic creed.

Against this one can set the various indications that Krieger had already found problems with the 'old' New Criticism, not least with its tendency to lift poems into a realm of idealized meaning and value immune to the assaults of time. One such indication is the fact that his essay brings in 'The Dunciad', not merely as a source of local contrasts and comparisons, but by way of a genuinely intertextual reading that threatens the whole aesthetic ideology built upon 'The Rape of the Lock'. In the end Krieger sees a victory for art against the 'uncreating word' of anarchic reality, the 'disintegrating force' that history applies to the products of human imagination. But it is a victory achieved through such a complex and tortuous process of argument that Krieger appears to be constantly setting up obstacles to his own wished-for interpretative vision. Of all texts (or intertexts), the 'Dunciad' goes furthest to undermine that sense of metaphysical grace that Krieger glimpses, precariously figured, in 'The Rape of the Lock'. The point is made again, from a different angle, when he takes Epistle I of the 'Essay On Man' as an instance of Pope's rather shallow and simplistic benevolist creed, his belief that all was for the best if one could only make out the hidden purpose of things. Krieger regards this as a piece of slightly desperate nostalgia, a backdated myth quite out of touch with the realities of Pope's time and place. It offers 'a kind of *ersatz* and decapitated replica of the unified, catholic, psychologically and aesthetically soothing thirteenth-century universe' (p. 212). Krieger is firm enough in rejecting this myth and the species of naïve wish-fulfilment that goes along with it. Yet there are, as we have seen, still signs in Krieger's essay of that other powerful myth of historical decline and aesthetic transcendence which Eliot and the New Critics after him took as an article of faith. This puts considerable strain on his argument when it comes to distinguishing the good from the bad (or the merely escapist) uses of myth. Once again, the interpreter is on trial along with the poem, his reading subject to the same kinds of complicating doubt and tension.

For it is only through the highest refinements of formalist method that 'The Rape of the Lock' can be made to appear an object of such transcendent aesthetic worth that it stands apart from the naïvely idealized strain of Pope's lesser productions. Otherwise the poem and Krieger's reading must seem to fall into the same habit of substituting myth for the complex realities of human experience.

Krieger's intentions are plain enough. He wants to point up the peculiar excellence of 'The Rape of the Lock' by contrasting it first with Pope's pious platitudes in the 'Essay on Man', and then with the vision of universal chaos vouchsafed in the 'Dunciad'. This allows him to take the most completely 'artificial' of Pope's creations and argue that in truth it represents a supremely balanced response to those fallacious opposite extremes. His rejecting the archaic mythology of the 'Essay on Man' is a credibilizing gesture which insists that Krieger's essay — like the better poem — is strong enough to withstand a good deal of demythologizing treatment. 'Once Pope feels secure that he has established Belinda's world as one we can cherish . . . he dares introduce materials from other and realer worlds more openly as if to prove the power of his delicate creation' (p. 209). The same can be said of Krieger's essay, balanced on a knife-edge of critical tact between the claims of an ideal aesthetic order and those of a tough-minded demythologizing stance. Hence the uneasy co-existence within that essay of orthodox New Critical tropes with tentative moves into a larger domain of aesthetic and historical speculation. The signs of this incipient passage 'beyond formalism' are there to be read in Krieger's attentiveness to intertextual meaning, his insistence (up to a point) on the metaphor/metonymy distinction, and his refusal to countenance wholesale mythologies of Western cultural decline.

This commentary will seem rather off-the-point if one accepts what Krieger has to say in his opening paragraph. Here he maintains that New Criticism is not, as popular prejudice would have it, a species of 'ivory-tower' formalism that ignores history on principle. His essay is intended partly as a practical demonstration that the close-reading of literary texts 'can illuminate even so un-new-critical an area as the history of ideas' (p. 201). But at this point Krieger feels obliged to enter a series of methodological caveats. It may be, he writes, that this exercise will turn into 'a kind of mythology of idealized generalizations', a myth which allows certain 'ideological commonplaces' to bear more weight than the 'careful historian' would permit. To this extent, as Krieger seems willing to acknowledge, the interests of history are still subdued to those of a harmonized aesthetic understanding. If this results in his essay 'doing violence' to those other kinds of commonplace that govern the historian's enterprise, then Krieger remains unrepentant. For 'surely', he argues, 'this is one of the chief functions of poetry, this violation of the commonplace' (p. 201). His language here can hardly fail to call up echoes of that other 'violation' whose literal or figurative sense the poem and its critics so skilfully hold in balance. Oddly enough, in this particular passage, it is the myth-making artifice of poetry that inflicts such 'violence' on historical understanding, and not — as one might suppose — the other way around. There are similar ironies and double-edged comparisons everywhere in Krieger's essay. Thus: 'the rape of the lock is more to be avoided in honor's world than are the more sordid, but less openly proclaimed, assaults in classical legend and in London back-alleys' (p. 204). Once again Pope's achievement is precariously balanced between opposite extremes: brute fact and fiction, sordid reality and myths of Arcadian innocence. What Krieger visibly strives to maintain is an attitude transcending these hateful antinomies. But equally visible in the rhetoric of his essay are the twists and argumentative detours that result from a formalist aesthetic pushed up against its limits of self-authenticating method.

One result of what he calls 'this somewhat reckless allegorical excursion' is that Krieger brings poetry more closely into contact with philosophy and the history of ideas. The contact is fleeting and offered in the spirit of a merely suggestive analogy. Nevertheless it prefigures, in a tentative way, that erosion of the old ontological bounds that ensued upon the break with New Critical precept and practice. In this passage Krieger is reflecting on the extreme fragility and artificial nature of that civilized world whose ideal embodiment is the rhyming couplet of Pope.

> As the Humes and the Kants convincingly reveal in shattering the false, dogmatic security of this world, the price of the construct is a metaphysical flimsiness — a naivete, the reverse side of its symmetrical delicacy — that made it easy prey to the rigors of critical philosophy and the ravages of social-economic revolution. [p. 213]

Here again there is an element of mythical projection, a running-together of 'critical philosophy' (conceived in no very precise terms) with the process of cultural attrition through social change. Certainly it is a passage that bears all the marks of that gloomy prognosis which was T.S. Eliot's legacy to modern criticism. Yet in Krieger's version there is a countervailing stress on the 'flimsiness', the lack of historical foundations for any mythology that sets up a golden age of past achievement against which to measure the symptoms of latter-day decline. Kant is drawn in, not merely as a typecast 'rationalist' destroyer of communal wisdom, but also — more pointedly — as one who called such myths to account by exposing their dependence on the ideal constructions of human intellectual and imaginative vision. Thus the passage — like so much in Krieger's essay — seems to allegorize its own predicament, caught between a powerful literary myth of origins and a will to deconstruct that myth by moving outside its privileged aesthetic ground.

Krieger is among the subtlest and most resourceful of those theorists who have continued to work within the broad confines of New Critical method. Others, like Geoffrey Hartman, have seized upon the hermeneutic freedoms offered by alternative sources in (mainly Continental) theory.[24] In Hartman's case the move beyond formalism has led to his dispensing with all those customary terms of distinction that marked off 'literature' from 'criticism' on the one hand, and criticism from philosophy (or 'theory') on the other. His writing thus breaks altogether with that principled division of realms which the New Critics sought to maintain. Yet in reading their texts, as I have tried to show here, one is constantly aware of those other discourses crowding in upon the narrow preserves of aesthetic autonomy and truth. What Krieger writes of the 'Essay On Man' could just as well apply to his own beleaguered position as a rearguard defender of New Critical values. In Pope's reassertion of a bygone 'cosmic solidarity' one detects, according to Krieger, 'the insecurity that was aware of its vulnerability and of the surrounding hordes of modernism already closing in' (p. 213). Such criticism verges on a conscious recognition of its own deep involvement with the vision of order so precariously achieved by Pope. At this point it becomes quite impossible to draw a line between commentary 'on' the poem and commentary as a kind of reflexive critique that both displays and interrogates its own founding assumptions.

Of course Pope guessed what the critics would soon be at, and determined to play them off the field by supplying an absurd pseudonymous gloss. 'A Key to the *Lock*' by Esdras Barnivelt appeared soon after the poem and affected to warn the innocent reader against being taken in by its subtle contrivances. 'This unhappy division of our Nation into Parties' is the cause, Pope suggests, of all the covert political meanings that are presently passed off upon an unsuspecting public by poets of deeply mischievous intent. Hence the need for an answering subtlety of method on the interpreter's part.

> In all things which are intricate, as Allegories in their own Nature are,
> . . . it is not to be expected that we should find the Clue at first sight;
> but when once we have laid hold on that, we shall trace this our Author
> through all the Labyrinths, Doublings and Turnings of this intricate
> Composition. [p. 35]

Indeed the poem has not lacked for ingenious commentators ready to pursue those labyrinthine doublings and turnings. But Pope's prediction is wide of the mark — in the long term at least — when he attributes this seeking-out of occult meanings to the spirit of rampant party-political prejudice. Far from reading politics into the poem, criticism has developed the most elaborate techniques for keeping such questions either safely out of sight or firmly subordinate to its own aesthetic concerns. 'Unhappy divisions' of any kind — sexual or political — give way to the desire for a harmonizing myth that transcends all forms of disruptive or complicating difference. It is at those moments when this project encounters resistance that the critics are beguiled into allegories of reading more intricate than anything dreamed of by Pope's pseudonymous scribe.

References

1. See Paul de Man, 'Form and Intent in the American New Criticism', in *Blindness and Insight: essays in the rhetoric of contemporary criticism*, London, Methuen, (1983), pp. 20–50.
2. See especially Allen Tate, *The Forlorn Demon*, Chicago, University of Chicago Press, (1953).
3. T.S. Eliot, *The Use of Poetry and the Use of Criticism*, London, Faber (1933), p. 63.
4. Cleanth Brooks, 'My Credo' (contribution to 'The Formalist Critics: a symposium'), *Kenyon Review*, Vol. XVIII (1951), pp. 72–81; p. 78.
5. John Crowe Ransom, in *Critical Responses to Kenneth Burke*, William Ruekert (ed.) Minneapolis, University of Minnesota Press, (1969), p. 156.
6. Ransom, 'Mr Empson's Muddles', *The Southern Review*, Vol IV (1938/9), pp. 322–39; p. 330.
7. See Cleanth Brooks, *The Well Wrought Urn*, New York, Harcourt, Brace, (1947).
8. T.S. Eliot, 'The Metaphysical Poets', in *Selected Essays*, London, Faber, (1964), pp. 288–99.
9. de Man, *Blindness and Insight* (op. cit.), p. 28.
10. See the two essays on Wordsworth reprinted in Paul de Man, *The Rhetoric of Romanticism*, New York, Columbia University Press, (1984). Also Geoffrey Hartman, *Wordsworth's Poetry, 1787–1814*, New Haven, Yale University Press, (1964), and David Simpson, *Wordsworth And The Figurings Of The Real*, London, Macmillan, (1982).
11. See especially W.K. Wimsatt, *The Verbal Icon*, Lexington, University of Kentucky Press, (1954).
12. See T.S. Eliot, *Knowledge and Experience in the Philosophy of F.H. Bradley*, London, Faber, (1964).
13. John Dixon Hunt (ed.), *'The Rape of the Lock': A Casebook*, London, Macmillan, (1968).
14. See F.R. Leavis, 'The Line of Wit', in *Revaluation*, Harmondsworth, Penguin, (1967), pp. 10–41.
15. Cleanth Brooks, *The Well Wrought Urn* (op. cit.), pp. 10–20.
16. Aubrey Williams, 'The "Fall" of China', in Hunt (ed.), *A Casebook* (op. cit.), pp. 220–36. All further references to essays in the *Casebook* given by page number in the text.
17. Jacques Derrida, *Spurs: Nietzsche's Styles*, Barbara Harlow (trans.), Chicago, University of Chicago Press, (1979), pp. 67–9.
18. See especially Paul de Man, 'The Resistance to Theory', *Yale French Studies*, No. 63 (1982), pp. 3–20. Also, for a more summary statement, 'The Return to Philology', *Times Literary Supplement*, No. 4158 (10 December 1982), pp. 1355–6. These essays are reprinted de Man, *The Resistance to Theory*, Minneapolis, University of Minnesota Press, (1986).
19. De Man, 'The Rhetoric of Temporality', in *Blindness and Insight* (op. cit.), pp. 187–228; p. 188.
20. Ibid., p. 207.
21. De Man, 'The Resistance To Theory' (op. cit.), p. 11.
22. Ibid.
23. Murray Krieger, *Poetic Presence and Illusion*, Baltimore and London, Johns Hopkins University Press, (1979).
24. See for instance Geoffrey Hartman, *Beyond Formalism*, New Haven, Yale University Press, (1979); *'The Fate of Reading' and other essays*, Chicago,

University of Chicago Press, (1975); *Criticism in the Wilderness: the study of literature today*, New Haven, Yale University Press, (1980); and *Saving the Text: Literature/Derrida/Philosophy*, Baltimore and London, Johns Hopkins University Press, (1981).

4 Post-structuralist Shakespeare: text and ideology

For Shakespeare criticism, as for current post-structuralist theory, a good deal hinges on the crucial ambiguity of Derrida's cryptic statement: 'there is no "outside" to the text' ('il n'y a pas d'hors-texte').[1] On the one hand this can be taken to signify a literary formalism pushed to the extreme, a last-ditch retreat from 'reality' into the solipsistic pleasures of textual freeplay. Such is the reading widely convassed by those who reject post-structuralist theory in the name of a commonsense or humanist tradition founded on the doctrines of mimetic realism. But Derrida's statement is capable of a different reading, one which answers more precisely to the context and logic of its appearance in *Of Grammatology*. This would bring out the reverse implication of a radically 'textualist' argument. If reality is structured through and through by the meanings we conventionally assign to it, then the act of suspending ('deconstructing') those conventions has a pertinence and force beyond the usual bounds of textual (or 'literary') interpretation. Maintaining those bounds is the business of a commonsense philosophy which stakes its authority on a stable relation between world and text, the real and the written, object and representation. This mimetic economy is firmly established by Plato and becomes, in effect, the grounding rationale of Western philosophic tradition.[2] It is questioned only at moments of stress when the *texts* of that tradition appear to threaten its otherwise self-regulating norms.

This point deserves emphasis in view of certain current polemical attacks on post-structuralist and deconstructive theory. Such ideas, it is argued, amount to a merely delusive and self-indulgent 'radicalism', a fetishistic cult of the text which can only end by severing all connection between literature (or criticism) and practical reality. These arguments are employed both by Marxists[3] and by critics who conceive themselves as speaking up for plain commonsense truth against all the varieties of bother-headed theory, Marxist versions included. What these opponents have to ignore — in line with the traditional prejudice which unites them — is that such arguments are challenged at root by the extended, non-reductive sense of 'textuality' that Derrida brings into play. There are powerful institutional forces at work in the assumption that texts are mimetic or second-order constructs, referring back always — by whatever kind of mediating process — to a first-order realm of empirical reality. To deconstruct that assumption, in all its manifold forms, is to turn back the logic of commonsense discourse at precisely the point where it thinks to challenge the activity of deconstruction. The 'question of the text' is not to be so lightly dismissed by a tradition which, of internal necessity, has failed to think through its effects and implications.

In his latest writings Derrida has laid increasing stress on this power of deconstruction to breach and subvert the instituted orders of discourse. Text 'overruns all the limits assigned to it', refusing the conventional protocols of genre, method or answerable style. It embraces, in Derrida's words, 'everything that was to be set up in opposition to writing (speech, life, the world, the real, history . . .)'.[4] And this not by way of reducing such activities to an undifferentiated signifying flux, but by challenging the systems of discursive propriety which hold them each within clearly marked bounds. Hence Derrida's reiterated stress on the wider (pedagogical and ultimately political) effects of deconstruction. What 'the institution' cannot tolerate, he writes,

is for anyone to tamper with language, meaning both the *national* language and, paradoxically, an ideal of translatability that neutralizes this national language. Nationalism and universalism . . . It can bear more readily the most apparently revolutionary ideological sorts of 'content', if only that content does not touch the borders of language and of all the juridico-political contracts that it guarantees.[5]

Among such institutions, I shall argue, is that of literary criticism at large, and more specifically the history of Shakespeare studies as inscribed within the national culture. The question of the text and its 'juridical' limits is nowhere posed with more insistent (and problematic) force.

The link between Shakespeare and ideas of 'the national language' is one which hardly needs documenting here. From Dr Johnson to F.R. Leavis, critics have looked to Shakespeare for linguistic intimations of an 'Englishness' identified with true native vigour and unforced, spontaneous creativity. Johnson, of course, ran into all kinds of difficulty when he tried to square this ideal with the practical business of editing Shakespeare. 'Nationalism and universalism' — to recall Derrida's formulation — turn out to have sharply paradoxical consequences for Johnson's project. On the one hand Shakespeare has to be accommodated to the eighteenth-century idea of a proper, self-regulating discourse which would finally create a rational correspondence between words and things, language and reality. From this point of view Johnson can only deprecate the tiresome 'quibbles' and redundant wordplay which so flagrantly transgress the stylistic norm.[6] On the other hand, allowances have to be made for the luxuriant native wildness of Shakespeare's genius, its refusal to brook the 'rules' laid down by more decorous traditions like that of

French neo-classicism. This clash of priorities in turn creates all the manifest twists and contradictions of Johnson's argument in the *Preface* to his edition. Patriotic self-interest, the idea of a 'national language' and of Shakespeare as its chief exemplar, comes up against a powerful universalist creed which effectively consigns such interests to the status of provincial special pleading.

What is at stake here is the question of the text as posed by two conflicting ideologies, each with a prepossessing claim upon eighteenth-century 'taste' and reason. Propriety of style is a matter of observing the economy of reference which ideally should relate words and things in a one-to-one system of disambiguated usage. Such was the famous Royal Society programme for placing English on a rational, scientific basis by severely curbing its dependence on metaphor and other dangerous liabilities of natural language. In this respect Johnson stands squarely within the Lockian tradition of positivist thinking about language, logic and epistemology.[7] Shakespeare's unfortunate proclivities of style — his 'quibbles', 'clinches', 'idle conceits' and so forth — represent a constant threat to the civilized consensus which works to maintain this proper economy. But tugging against Johnson's rationalist creed is an equal and opposite determination to hold Shakespeare up as the naturalized voice of a peculiarly English character and style. And where is this genius to be located if not in the very excesses of temperament and language that Johnson is so often constrained to criticize?

The following passage from the *Preface* brings out the deep-lying rationalist assumptions in Johnson's dealing with Shakespearian style.

> Not that always where the language is intricate the thought is subtle, or the image always great where the line is bulky; the equality of words to things is very often neglected, and trivial sentiments and vulgar ideas disappoint the attention, to which they are recommended by sonorous epithets and swelling figures [Johnson, pp. 67–8]

What Johnson expressly objects to here is the disturbing non-coincidence of 'language' and 'thought', and the corresponding failure to observe a due proportion (or 'equality') between words and things. Such delinquencies of style present a twofold danger to the stable currency of meaning. They threaten both the *expressive* relationship which holds between word and idea, and the *representational* function which consists in an adequate matching-up of language and the world. Disorders of reference — brought about by figural excess — are simultaneously felt as disorders of identity, breaking or suspending the privileged tie between words and expressive intent. This amounts to an implicit morality of style, an assumption that language should properly say what it means and mean what it says. Unbridled figuration — where words, in Wittgenstein's phrase, threaten to 'go on holiday' — leaves the interpreter uncomfortably bereft of such assurance. Shakespeare's equivocal style refuses, as it were, to take responsibility for the 'sonorous epithets' and 'swelling figures' that compose its own discourse.[8]

This ethical charge is rarely far from the surface in Johnson's denunciatory strain. A quibble to Shakespeare, most famously,

> is what luminous vapours are to the traveller; he follows it at all adventures, it is sure to lead him out of his way . . . It has some malignant power over his mind, and its fascinations are irresistible . . . A quibble was to him the fatal *Cleopatra* for which he lost the world, and was content to lose it. [Johnson, p. 68]

The question of style here takes on a whole strange dimension of associated myth and metaphor. Ironically, the passage might be seen to exemplify the very linguistic vices that Johnson treats with such contempt. He is most in danger of yielding to the power of seductive multiplied metaphor precisely when criticizing Shakespeare for the selfsame fault. One recalls, in this connection, Derrida's copious examples of how figurative language invades the discourse of philosophy even where attempts are made — as by Locke — to expunge its insidious effects.[9] To adapt Bacon's saying: 'drive metaphor out with a pitchfork, yet she will return'. A perverse compulsion seems to operate here, turning language back against its own self-regulating ordinance.

In Johnson, this phenomenon is all the more disturbing for the sexual overtones — of yielding, seduction, abandoned self-mastery — which mark its emergence. The metaphor of wordplay as a 'fatal Cleopatra' is just one of many suggestions, in the *Preface* and elsewhere, that work to associate feminine wiles with the mischiefs created by unbridled linguistic figuration. The straightforward virtues of a 'manly' style — vigorous, commonsensical, unembellished, plain-dealing — are opposed to the weaknesses attendant upon metaphor and other such womanish devices. Rationality demands that the seductive ornaments of language be kept within bounds by a firm sense of masculine propriety and discipline. Otherwise, as Johnson repeatedly complains, good sense is all too often overwhelmed by the blandishments of figural language. Such distractions are evidently not to be borne by a critic and editor so intent upon distinguishing the virtues from the vices in Shakespeare's plays.

'It is impossible to dissociate the questions of art, style and truth from the question of the woman'.[10] Thus Derrida, in a reading of Nietzschian metaphor which seeks to deconstruct, or turn back against itself, the 'phallocentric' discourse of male mastery and power. Derrida traces a strange concatenation of themes beyond the explicit message of Nietzsche's virulent anti-feminism. Woman is the very antithesis of philosophic truth, she whose 'seductive distance' and 'dissimulating ways' are traps set on purpose to lure the philosopher out of his appointed path. Truth-seeking discourse is deflected from its aim by an 'abyssal divergence' which 'engulfs and distorts all vestige of essentiality, of identity, of property'. If woman is 'but one name for that untruth of truth', then the other names are 'style', 'metaphor' and 'writing' — temptations which likewise beckon to philosophy from the distance of an unmasterable charm and provocation. The question 'what is woman?' founders on the rock of this dissimulating non-identity. 'One can no longer seek her, no more than one could search for woman's feminity or female sexuality. And she is certainly not to be found in any of the familiar modes of concept or knowledge.'[11]

So much, one might say, for the standing provocation which instigated Nietzsche's well-known rabid anti-feminism. Yet within those same texts, as Derrida reads them, there also emerges the outline of a counter-interpretation, one which would affirm the undoing of truth by the stratagems of 'feminine' style. Thus Derrida quotes a passage from 'The History of an Error' where Nietzsche, tracing the symptoms of intellectual decadence, seizes on the point at which 'it becomes female' (*'sie wird Weib'*). Yet it is precisely the case that Nietzsche's own writings exploit those very symptoms of decline as a tactical resource against the truth-claims of philosophy from Socrates to Hegel. By his practice of a 'literary', aphoristic style, Nietzsche sets out to undermine all the system-building constructs of traditional thought. What he writes about the intellect's 'becoming-female' could just as well be applied, point for point, to Nietzsche's own 'dissimulating' strategies. As Derrida writes:

> The question of the woman suspends the decidable opposition of true and non-true . . . The hermeneutic project which postulates a true sense of the text is disqualified under this regime. Reading is freed from the horizon of the meaning or truth of Being, . . . whereupon the question of style is immediately unloosed as a question of writing.[12]

This is sufficient, Derrida argues, to deconstruct Heidegger's reading of Nietzsche, a reading which claims to speak the truth of his text while perforce ignoring the co-implicated questions of 'woman' and 'style'.

This might seem all very remote from Dr Johnson and the major issues of eighteenth-century Shakespeare scholarship. Yet there is, after all, a similar paradoxical strain about Johnson's contemptuous yet fascinated dealing with Shakespeare's seductive wordplay. That his own critical language, like Nietzsche's, shows signs of the same infectious malaise would suggest that the analogy is not so far-fetched. What we read in the *Preface* are the twists and blind-spots of an argument pressed beyond the limits of consistent sense by its own contradictory commitments. Johnson, as I have argued, is caught between two opposing ideologies, each with its attendant structure of linguistic and critical presupposition. The major topics of the *Preface* all relate, more or less directly, to this underlying clash of codes. Was Shakespeare a wild, untutored genius or one who transcended (and effectively transformed) the dictates of conventional propriety? Can his plays survive the test of rational judgement, or must reason itself come to terms with the signal fact of his achievement? And above all, the matter of Shakespearian *style*: can such excesses be justified despite their offence against reason, dignity and truth?

Johnson returns contradictory answers to each of these questions. As regards Shakespeare's language, his talk of 'luminous vapours' and 'malignant powers' may be set alongside the confident claim that

> he who has mazed his imagination in following the phantoms which
> other writers raise up before him, may here be cured of his delirious
> ecstasies by reading human sentiments in human language . . . [Johnson,
> p. 61]

Such manifest inconsistencies are commonly put down to Johnson's
last-minute haste in composing the *Preface*, or, more charitably, his
judicious habit of weighing up alternative viewpoints. What is
overlooked by such generalized accounts is the way that Johnson's
text both stages and evades a more specific conflict of ideological
motives. The signs of that tension are there to be read in the aberrant
figural turns which conventional eighteenth-century wisdom would
confine to the margins of sense.

'Marginal' is precisely the term Johnson uses by way of modestly
playing down the significance of textual commentary *vis-à-vis* the text.
'I have confined my imagination to the margin', he writes, unlike,
presumably, those overweening editors who allow their emendations
to disfigure the text, instead of decently recording them in footnotes.
The *Preface* winds up on a curious note of ironic diffidence mixed with
defensive self-esteem. Textual criticism is a thankless labour, its
efforts at best a humble contribution and at worst a monument to
misguided scholarly ingenuity. And yet, Johnson writes, it is an art
which, properly performed, 'demands more than humanity
possesses', so that 'he who exercises it with most praise has very
frequent need of indulgence' (Johnson, p. 84). The licence which
Johnson elsewhere extends to Shakespeare is in this case applied to
his own present labours. On the one hand the editor–critic is cast as
a harmless drudge whose activities are strictly subservient and
marginal to the text he would faithfully transmit. On the other,
textual scholarship becomes a kind of surrogate creative act, requiring
a well-nigh superhuman measure of moral and imaginative strength.
'Let us now be told no more of the dull duty of an editor.'

And yet, as the *Preface* repeatedly insists, Johnson counts himself a
foe to 'conjecture', or to textual emendations which cross the line
between self-effacing scholarship and creative licence. Such
speculative ventures on the critic's part are a hazard which
commonsense wisely avoids. It is, Johnson warns,

> an unhappy state, in which danger is hid under pleasure. The
> allurements of emendation are scarcely resistible. 'Conjecture has all the
> joy and all the pride of invention, and he that has once started a happy
> change is too much delighted to consider what objections may rise
> against it. [Johnson, p. 96]

Figures of allurement, seduction, dangerous pleasure: the passage can
hardly fail to recall Johnson's strictures on the 'fatal Cleopatra' of
Shakespearian wordplay. For the critic to indulge in speculative fancy
is a weakness complicit with the dramatist's worst excesses. It

offends, that is to say, against the principled economy of logic and sense which insists on a proper correspondence between signifier and signified, language and intent. In his redaction of previous editorial efforts, Johnson recollects how he encountered 'in every page Wit struggling with its own sophistry, and Learning confused by the multiplicity of its views' (Johnson, p. 95). Confusion worse confounded is the only result of allowing conjecture to practise its arts upon such powerfully seductive and bewildering material.

Yet of course it is that very confusion in the sources — textual corruption as well as the aggravating wordplay — which called forth the editors' unhappy labours in the first place. Criticism may be deluded if it thinks that mere ingenuity (wit) can point the way back to plain good sense. But with Shakespeare, as Johnson has often perforce to admit, the sense may lie so far beyond the common bounds of 'propriety' and 'truth' as to render such distinctions untenable. Sober scholarship is no better placed than speculative fancy when it tries to bring order to such resistant material. Editorial surmise becomes lost in the labyrinths of figural undecidability. How can one distinguish, on scholarly grounds, between the malign genius of Shakespearian wordplay and the multiplied errors and confusions attendant on the process of textual transmission? Johnson's desire for stability and the permanence of truth demands that he cling to some vestigial faith in the authority of origins, in the text as providing suffi-cient guidance as to its own most authentic form. Commonsense might then at least hope to unravel the worst of those super-induced perplexities created by the muddle-headed copyists and critics. Yet even this chastened ambition seems wildly optimistic in the face of such intractable problems. That the commentator should so often turn out to be mistaken 'cannot be wonderful, either to himself or others, if it be considered that in his art there is no system, no principal and axiomatical truth that regulates subordinate positions' (Johnson, pp. 95–6).

This throws a whole series of paradoxes into Johnson's professed editorial creed. How can speculation be 'confined to the margin' where texts are perceived as standing in need of such elaborate restorative treatment? How can criticism aim at any kind of settled or consensual reading where the vagaries of textual transmission are compounded by the lawlessness of Shakespeare's equivocating style? Commentary becomes, in Johnson's words, a self-acknowledged 'art', rather than a matter of regulative 'system' or 'axiomatical truth'. It is bound to transgress the prescriptive line between creation and criticism, text and context, meaning and the margins of meaning.[13] This in turn bears directly on those areas of sensitive concern that Derrida associates with language in its 'juridical' or legislative aspect. Commonsense requires that the peculiar licence extended to a poet like Shakespeare should at least be prevented from working its mischief on the efforts of rational prose commentary. Yet this trans-action is not achieved on such amicable terms as might be suggested by a simple parcelling-out of different linguistic domains. 'Where any passage appeared inextricably perplexed', Johnson writes, 'I have endeavoured to discover how it may be recalled to sense with least violence' (Johnson, p. 93). Thus the restoration of tolerable 'sense' may involve a certain violence, a willed imposition of commonsense juridical norms. If reason is in danger of being contaminated by Shakespeare's sophistical language, the opposite is also the case: that Shakespeare may be literally disfigured by the rational sense-making efforts of the scholar.

I have pressed rather hard on these problematic aspects of Johnson's text because they point symptomatically to larger questions about the practice and tradition of Shakespearian criticism. These may be summarized as follows. First, there is the matter of textual scholarship, its relation to 'the text' on the one hand and problems of interpretation on the other. That these distinctions may be blurred, as in Johnson, is an index of their artificial character, their obedience to certain specific laws of discursive economy. Any notion of the sacrosanct literary text — whether as an object of scholarly or of critical attention — is rendered problematic by the instance of Shakespeare. Then again, there is the question of how Shakespeare's significance, as a textual phenomenon, is processed and constructed within the constraints of a dominant ideology. These constraints may be far from monolithic or logically consistent. They may indeed give rise to obvious internal contradictions, as with Johnson's facing about between an abstract universalism and a nationalist ideology of language. As a result, his role is constantly shifting: from self-effacing editor to speculative critic and then, beyond that, to those weighty moralizing passages which effectively re-write Shakespeare on their own preferred terms of imaginative 'truth'.

It is here that we find the central and continuing paradox of Shakespeare criticism, from Johnson's day to the present. Outside theological tradition, no body of writings has been subjected to more in the way of interpretative comment and textual scholarship. Yet the upshot of this activity — visible already in Johnson's edition — is to cast increasing doubt on the power of criticism to distinguish between the two. No doubt this is partly a matter of contingent historical circumstance. Criticism, as Johnson so often complains, rushes in with manifold fictions of its own to redress the delinquent carelessness of Shakespeare and his copyists. But there is also a more general lesson to be drawn, one which returns us to the question of the text as raised in post-structuralist theory. Shakespeare is an extreme but representative case of the way in which commentary works to erase all the firm, juridical limits surrounding that imaginary entity, the literary text. Even textual scholarship, with its self-denying ordinances, finds itself repeatedly crossing over from a strictly ancillary to a kind of rival-imaginative role.

It may be the case, as Raymond Williams has argued, that this distinction between 'literature' and other kinds of writing was not yet an issue for Johnson and his contemporaries.[14] It was only in terms of the nineteenth-century 'culture and society' debate that such ideas took on a definite and complex ideological character. 'Literature' — like 'culture' itself — came to connote a whole alternative order of human aspirations and values, an imaginative creed set firmly against the grim utilitarian outlook of 'society' at large. Dr Johnson, as Williams remarks, gets along with a generalized notion of literary activity which includes many kinds of writing — poetry, history, criticism — and has no need, as yet, for such charged ideological distinctions. However, the absence of 'literature' as a key-term in Johnson's lexicon doesn't at all signify a lack of concern with those issues which were later to emerge in more sharply contested form. With Johnson we witness the beginnings of that powerful ideology within English criticism which sets up 'literature' as a paradigm of imaginative health, and Shakespeare in turn as the test-case and touchstone of literary values at large. And this despite the fact that Johnson, of course, judges Shakespeare by his own 'eighteenth-century' standards, and often finds him wanting. What is more significant, as I have argued, is the encounter thus staged between an as yet ill-defined ideology of literature and an answering (but deeply confused) critical practice.

'Nationalism and universalism' — Derrida's terms are still very pertinent here. Since Johnson, critics have ceased by and large (with a few exceptions, like Tolstoy and Shaw) to lament Shakespeare's 'barbarous' language and corresponding lack of stern moral fibre. The problem is no longer posed in such overtly ideological terms. But they have still had to acknowledge, in various ways, what is felt as the exorbitant character of Shakespearian English, its resistance to rational or commonsense accounting. On the one hand the plays are held up, by critics from Coleridge to Leavis, as the central and definitive achievement of literary language at full creative stretch. Of literary *English*, that is, although there is often a larger (and vaguer) claim in the background: that Shakespearian English embodies an ideal of cooperative thought and sensibility transcending all rootedness in time and place. By such means has criticism managed to reconcile the otherwise contradictory demands of 'nationalism' and 'universalism'. Yet there remains, on the other hand, a persistent problem in accommodating Shakespeare's language to any kind of moral or prescriptive norm. The rhetorical excess which so troubled Johnson continues to vex a critic like Leavis, though the anxiety issues in a typically displaced and indirect form. To watch this displacement at work is to see how criticism repeatedly falls into traps and contradictions of its own ideological creating.[15]

Leavis's essay on *Othello* is a typically combative and charged piece of writing.[16] It sets out not only to interpret the play but to treat it as a primer for criticism, a test-case of what responsive reading ought to be when measured against the vital complexity of Shakespeare's language. It also carries on a running polemic against A.C. Bradley and his idea of 'character' as the primary, psychological reality of Shakespearian drama.[17] More specifically, Leavis pours scorn on Bradley's portrayal of Iago as a villain of near-superhuman resourceful cunning, and of Othello as his nobly suffering idealized counterpart. Leavis's arguments are sufficiently well known and require no detailed summary here. Sufficient to say that he views Othello as laid open to Iago's insinuating wiles by a fatal combination of weaknesses in his own temperament. The Bradleian account is a falsification of the play resulting from the naïve assumption that Othello's opinion of himself is also the opinion that we, as audience or readers, are supposed to entertain. In fact, Leavis argues, the contrary signs are unmistakably there in Othello's strain of grandiloquent rhetoric, his indulgence in manic alternating moods of heroic projection and plangent self-pity. Othello falls victim to flaws in his own make-up which are merely obscured by viewing him 'like Bradley' as the noble dupe of a devillishly complex and interesting Iago.

'Like Bradley' has a pointed ambiguity here. Bradley's account of *Othello* is branded by Leavis as 'naïve', 'sentimental' and 'idealizing' — as sharing, in short, precisely that complex of temperamental flaws that Leavis detects in Othello himself. This is in keeping with the logic of Leavis's argument, and gives rise to some neatly turned jokes at Bradley's expense. Thus 'Iago's knowledge of Othello's character amounts pretty much to Bradley's knowledge of it (except, of course, that Iago cannot realise Othello's nobility quite to the full) . . .' (Leavis, p. 137). Or again, with more heavy-handed irony: 'to equate Bradley's knowledge of Othello with Othello's own was perhaps unfair to Othello' (p. 138). Every detail of the Bradleian account can be held up to ridicule as yet another instance of patent simple-mindedness and sentimentality. The difference of views between Bradley and Leavis becomes oddly intertwined with the drama played out between Othello and Iago. Leavis conceives himself as speaking up for a tough-minded realist assessment of the play inherently at odds with Bradley's 'idealizing' approach. One desirable result, as Leavis sees it, is to undermine the romantic fascination with Iago as a character of baffling complexity and sinister appeal. Leavis's counter-idealist reading is at any rate 'a fit reply to the view of Othello as necessary material and provocation for a display of Iago's fiendish intellectual superiority' (p. 138).

Leavis can therefore claim support for his reading in the fact that this is, after all, Othello's and not Iago's tragedy. Bradley's account has the absurd result of reducing the play to 'Iago's character in action'. Nor is he alone in this, since the Bradleian reading — as Leavis ruefully observes — has been current, even prevalent at least since Coleridge. It thus remains for Leavis, writing in the face of this 'sustained and sanctioned perversity', to cut through the layers of sentimental falsehood and restore the play to its rightful interpretation.

> The plain fact that has to be asserted . . . is that in Shakespeare's tragedy of *Othello* Othello is the chief personage — the chief personage in such a sense that the tragedy may fairly be said to be Othello's character in action (p. 139).

Yet there is clearly a sense in which the logic of Leavis's argument tends to undercut this confidently orthodox assertion. His attitude of prosecuting zeal towards Bradley cannot help but carry over into his treatment of Othello, just as — conversely — Othello's romanticized self-image finds an echo and analogue (according to Leavis) in Bradley's reading. There is, furthermore, a touch of Iago's corrosive or deflationary cynicism in the way that Leavis sets out to confront those twin representatives of virtuous self-ignorance, Othello and Bradley. The latter, 'his knowledge of Othello coinciding virtually with Othello's', sees nothing but doomed nobility and pathos. By a further twist of the same interpretative logic one can see how Leavis plays a Iago-like role in destroying the illusion of Othello's nobly suffering innocence. If Bradley's blinkered idealism is, as Leavis says, 'invincible', so also is Leavis's ruthlessly debunking approach.

It is not uncommon for critics to become thus involved in curious patterns of compulsive repetition which take rise from their resolutely partial understanding of a literary text. Criticism belongs to what Freud called the work of 'secondary revision', a process aimed at achieving some consistency of 'fit' between manifest and latent sense, but also producing all manner of disguise, repression and 'uncanny' repetition of themes. This compulsion is most in evidence where critics deal with an overtly ambiguous narrative like Henry James's *The Turn of the Screw*. The text seems to support two opposite interpretations, the 'psychological' and 'supernatural', and to offer no consistent means of deciding between them. Recent deconstructionist readings have shown how critics mostly espouse one side or the other, and are thus forced to suppress or unconsciously distort any textual evidence which controverts their reading.[18] If the story turns — as the 'naturalists' would have it — on neurotic delusions suffered by James's governess–narrator, then her symptoms are oddly reproduced in the gaps and obsessional lapses of argument displayed by the critics. Such 'Freudian' readings are likewise crudely reductive in their wholesale, unmediated use of psychoanalytic terminology and method. On the other hand, the 'supernatural' version of James's tale requires that the interpreter pass over some striking indications of neurosis and paranoid delusion on the part of the governess. In both cases there is an inbuilt bias of approach which unconsciously produces its own tell-tale symptoms of thematic displacement and reworking.

Post-structuralism is perhaps best characterized by its willingness to acknowledge this predicament, rather than set itself up as a 'meta-language' ideally exempt from the puzzles and perplexities of literary texts. The structuralist enterprise aimed at precisely this ideal: that criticism should aspire to a 'science' of the text which would finally uncover its invariant 'grammars' of structure and style. This approach laid down a firm disciplinary line between literature and the systematic discourse of knowledge which sought to comprehend it. Such ambitions soon gave way as critics like Roland Barthes came to recognize the inadequacy of formalistic methods and the way in which textual signification exceeds all merely heuristic limits. Barthes's *S/Z* (1970) marked a turning-point in this passage from structuralist to post-structuralist thinking.[19] At the same time Jacques

Derrida was developing his powerful deconstructive critique of traditional epistemic categories, including that conservative notion of 'structure' which he found implicit in Saussure, Lévi-Strauss and others.[20] Textuality was recognized as breaking all the bounds of a conceptual regime which had striven to hold it in check, betokening a correspondent shift in the relations between literature, criticism and textual theory. As the latter relinquished its claim to sovereign knowledge, so it took on something of the complex, contradictory character normally attributed to 'literary' language.

Shoshana Felman reveals the extraordinary lengths to which this process can be carried in her reading of various critics on *The Turn of the Screw*. 'The invitation to undertake a reading of the text is perforce an invitation to *repeat* the text, to enter into its labyrinth of mirrors, from which it is henceforth impossible to escape (Felman 1977, p. 190). Interpretation can only repeat, in compulsive fashion, the acts of misreading exemplified by various, more or less deluded characters *within the tale*. Any attempt to provide an omniscient critical reading is always foredoomed to this chronic partiality of viewpoint. As Felman puts it:

> In seeking to 'explain' and *master* literature, in refusing, that is, to become a *dupe* of literature . . . the psychoanalytic reading, ironically enough, turns out to be a reading which *represses the unconscious*, which represses, paradoxically, the unconscious which it purports to be 'explaining'.[21]

This applies as much to self-styled 'theoretical' criticism as to essays of a more traditional interpretative cast. Such distinctions break down against the 'uncanny' transference which carries across from the narrative to its various symptomatic partial readings. The tale is contagious in the sense that it creates a frustrated desire for coherence, one which can never be satisfied except by certain self-defeating acts of textual repression.

Leavis's essay on *Othello* bears all the marks of this obscure compulsion at work. It is to Iago that Leavis attributes a 'deflating, unbeglamouring, brutally realistic mode of speech' (Leavis, 1952, p. 144). Yet the same description could equally be applied to Leavis's essay, working as it does to 'deflate' and 'unbeglamour' the nobility of character mistakenly imputed to Othello. At times this curious transference of roles comes close to the surface in Leavis's prose.

> Iago's power, in fact, in the temptation-scene is that he represents something that is in Othello . . . the essential traitor is within the gates. For if Shakespeare's Othello too is simple-minded, he is nevertheless more complex than Bradley's. Bradley's Othello is, rather, Othello's; it being an essential datum regarding the Shakespearian Othello that he has an ideal conception of himself. [Leavis, pp. 140–41]

What makes Othello more rewardingly 'complex' than Bradley can show is the fact that his character (as Leavis reads it) partakes somewhat of Iago's destructive nature. By the same odd logic it is Leavis's account of *Othello* which raises the play to a level of dramatic complexity undreamt of in Bradley's naïve philosophy. The undoing of simple-minded virtue takes place not so much 'in' the play — since Othello is already thus tainted — but in the contest of readings between a tough-minded Leavis and a feebly romanticizing Bradley. As with James's tale, so here: interpretation is drawn into a scene of displaced re-enactment where critics have no choice but to occupy positions already taken up by characters within the play.

This lends an added resonance to Leavis's metaphor of the 'traitor within the gates'. A certain logic of host-and-parasite is insistently at work in Leavis's essay. It operates by a series of thematic reversals, substituting 'maturity' for 'innocence' ('Bradley, that is, in his comically innocent way'), 'realism' for 'idealism' and — ultimately — 'Leavis' for 'Bradley'. In each case the second (dominant) term has a Iago-like ambivalence, exposing simple-minded virtue to the trials of an undeceiving, rock-bottom worldly knowledge. Leavis attacks the sentimental reading which prefers to see the play 'through Othello's eyes rather than Shakespeare's'. His own account is designed to correct this romantic bias by focusing attention on those qualities of Othello's language — in particular, his rhetoric of nobly suffering pathos — which supposedly should lead us to a proper 'Shakespearian' reading. In fact it is quite obvious that Leavis is simply substituting one interpretation for another, his own drastically 'deflating' account for Bradley's idealizing version. The claim that his approach enables us to see Othello 'through Shakespeare's eyes' is merely an enabling fiction, though one that few critics seem prepared to forego. What we are really offered, despite this legitimizing ploy, is a compound of *Leavis's* familiar views on the nature of 'maturity' and 'intelligence' as manifest in English verse. Othello's great flaw, like Bradley's after him, consists very largely in a failure to grasp the Leavisite criteria of poetic health and strength.

Leavis makes the point plainly enough in objecting to Bradley's description of Othello as 'the greatest poet' among Shakespeare's tragic heroes. For Leavis, this provides just one more example of Bradley's inveterate romanticism, his habit of seeing Othello through Othello's own self-deluding eyes.

> If the impression made by Othello's own utterance is often poetical as well as poetic, that is Shakespeare's way, not of representing him as a poet, but of conveying the romantic glamour that, for Othello himself and others, invests Othello and what he stands for. [Leavis, p. 143]

Those 'others' include Bradley but not of course Leavis, or indeed Iago, who makes some very effective points of his own about Othello's 'romantic glamour'. All the same it is hard to see that Leavis's case rests on anything more than his predisposed view of what constitutes 'the Shakespearian use of language'. That view rests in turn, as I have argued, on a complex of deeply ideological assumptions about language, thought and sensibility. Poetry is conceived as expressing the truth of a complex and properly self-critical response to the varieties of lived experience. 'Intelligence', 'maturity' and 'life' are the fixed coordinates around which Leavis constructs his highly selective 'tradition' of English poetry. It is a view of literary history which locates its main high-point in the early seventeenth century (Shakespeare and Donne), and which judges later poets — especially the Romantics — against that mythical ideal of a 'unified sensibility' belonging to a long-lost 'organic' culture. If Milton and Shelley, among others, are tried by this standard and found sadly wanting, so also is Shakespeare's Othello.

Leavis set out his main criteria in a number of early *Scrutiny* pieces.[22] Among other critical touchstones (like 'thought' and 'judgement'), he offered close readings of several short poems intended to emphasize the difference between 'emotion' and 'sentimentality'. The hallmark of sentimental poetry, Leavis argued, was its surrender to a mood of plangent, self-regarding pathos unchecked by any sense of 'mature' critical restraint. Such is the standard that Leavis applies to Othello's characteristic strain. It involves, Leavis writes, 'an attitude towards the emotion expressed — an attitude of a kind we are familiar with in the analysis of sentimentality' (Leavis, p. 143), which of course presupposes that Othello's rhetoric is placed, or shown up for what it is, by the implicit contrast with Shakespeare's most vital ('creative-exploratory') style. Leavis would have it that this contrast is self-evident, at least to any reader 'not protected [like Bradley] by a very obstinate preconception'. Romantic misconceptions should be easy to rebut 'because there, to point to, is the text, plain and unequivocal'. This would make it odd, to say the least, that critics have differed so widely over the play's interpretation, and that Leavis should feel summoned to redeem such a history of multiplied error and delusion. But this is to ignore the more likely explanation: that Leavis has invented his own *Othello* in pursuit of an imaginary coherence required by certain pressing ideological imperatives.

These motives are evident in the curious shifts of argumentation which Leavis adopts in the course of his essay. The central appeal is to a normative idea of human 'character' and 'experience', closely related to the virtues of 'mature', self-critical intelligence which Leavis finds at work in all great poetry. Shakespeare's genius has to consist in this consummate union of truth-to-experience and language raised to its highest creative power. Othello, says Leavis, 'is (as we have all been) cruelly and tragically wronged', so that 'the invitation to identify oneself with him is indeed hardly resistible' (Leavis, p. 153). There is irony here at Bradley's expense, but also a measure of acceptance, necessary if Othello is to retain any remnant of genuine 'tragic' dignity. For it is the nature of Shakespeare's genius, as Leavis goes on to argue, that it 'carries with it a large facility in imposing conviction locally'. Othello's self-deceiving rhetoric must be taken to possess at least a certain moving force if the play is to achieve its effect. 'He is (as we have all been) cruelly and tragically wronged' — the essay founders on this quite undecidable mixture of Iago-like irony and generalized 'human' pathos. Such are the conflicts engendered by a reading which stakes its authority on presupposed absolute values of language, morality and truth. At the close, Leavis writes, 'he is still the same Othello in whose essential make-up the tragedy lay'. It is on this notion of 'essential' human nature, both as norm and as measure of 'tragic' deviation, that Leavis's essay splinters into so many diverse and conflicting claims.

From Johnson to Leavis there occurs a marked shift in the ideological values sustaining the project of Shakespearian criticism. For Johnson the prime imperative is to stabilize the text by application of commonsense criteria, and to reach a corresponding measure of agreement on issues of interpretative truth. Underlying this approach is a generalized assurance that language, though forced against its natural grain by Shakespeare's deplorable excesses, can yet be restored to something like a rational, perspicuous order of sense. Johnson's praise for the universality of Shakespearian drama ('his story requires Romans or kings, but he thinks only on men') goes along with his faith — however sorely tried — in the joint account-ability of language, reason and truth. With Leavis, this appeal to commonsense universals has given way to a more embattled ideology, one which pits the truth of individual experience against all forms of abstract generalization. There is, so Leavis argues, a close and exemplary relation between Shakespeare's 'creative-exploratory' language and the process of anguished discovery through which his protagonists attain to authentic self-knowledge. This becomes the measure of Othello's characterizing weakness, his rhetorical evasion of the truths borne home by his own tragic predicament.

Johnson stands near the beginning, Leavis near the end of a certain dominant cultural formation in the history of Shakespeare studies. It is an effort of ideological containment, an attempt to harness the unruly energies of the text to a stable order of significance. With Johnson this takes the form of a conservative textual-editorial policy allied to an overt moralizing bent which very often issues in flat contradictions of precept and practice. With Leavis, it produces a reading of Othello ruptured by striking inconsistencies of statement, logic and intent. Beneath them runs the reassuring persuasion that dramatic 'character' has its own coherence, and that language must properly be always in the service of authentic human experience. What Leavis so forcefully rejects in Bradley — the idea of 'character' as a simple, real-life analogue — takes a different but related shape in his own appeal to the characterizing force of Shakespearian language. Thus Othello in Act V is 'still the same Othello', while Iago represents 'a not uncommon kind of grudging, cynical malice' (p. 154). In the end Leavis can only reduplicate Bradley's cardinal error in a form of displaced but none the less naïve and reductive moraliz-ing judgement.

Post-structuralism affords an understanding of the ideological compulsions at work in this persistent allegory of errors. It provides, most importantly, an argued theoretical perspective on that effort to recuperate Shakespeare's text in the name of autonomous subjectivity and universal human experience. From Johnson to Leavis, a tradition has grown up in which the plays are subjected to a powerful normative bias, an imposition of meanings and values as conceived by the dominant ideology. It is in the will to secure this stability — to repose, as Johnson hoped, on 'the permanence of truth' — that criticism runs into all those strange divagations of sense which mark the history of Shakespeare studies. Textual scholarship and interpretation are likewise afflicted by this chronic uncertainty of aim. As Johnson labours against multiplied errors and delusions, so Leavis rebuts the 'potent and mischievous' influence of Bradleian criticism, only to write another chapter in the case-book of endlessly dissenting views. Shakespeare's meaning can no more be reduced to the currency of liberal-humanist faith than his text to the wished-for condition of pristine, uncorrupt authority. All we have are the readings which inevitably tell the various partial and complicated stories of their own devising.

References

1. Jacques Derrida, *Of Grammatology*, Gayatri Chakravorty Spivak (trans.), Baltimore, Johns Hopkins University Press, (1976), p. 73.
2. See Derrida, 'Plato's Pharmacy', in *Dissemination*, Barbara Johnson (trans.), London, Athlone Press, (1981), pp. 61–171.
3. See for instance Terry Eagleton, *Walter Benjamin, or towards a revolutionary criticism*, London, New Left Books, (1981).
4. Derrida, 'Living On: border-lines', in *Deconstruction and Criticism*, Harold Bloom *et al.* (eds), London, Routledge and Kegan Paul, (1979), pp. 75–176.
5. Ibid., pp. 94–5.
6. Samuel Johnson, 'Preface to the Plays of William Shakespeare', in *Dr Johnson on Shakespeare*, W.K. Wimsatt (ed.), Harmondsworth, Penguin, (1969), pp. 57–98. Hereafter cited in the text as Johnson.
7. On this topic see especially Paul de Man, 'The Epistemology of Metaphor', *Critical Inquiry*, Vol. V (1978), pp. 13–30.
8. On this prevalent mistrust of rhetoric and the effects of unbridled metaphor or trope, see Derek Attridge, *Peculiar Language: literary language from the Renaissance to Joyce*, London, Routledge, (1988).
9. See for instance Derrida, 'White Mythology: metaphor in the text of philosophy', in *Margins of Philosophy*, Alan Bass (trans.), Chicago, University of Chicago Press, (1982), pp. 207–71.
10. Derrida, *Spurs: Nietzsche's Styles*, Barbara Harlow (trans.) Chicago, University of Chicago Press, (1979), p. 71.
11. Ibid., p. 71.
12. Ibid., p. 107.
13. For a text that positively celebrates confusions like this, see Geoffrey Hartman, 'Crossing Over: literary commentary as literature', *Comparative Literature*, Vol. XXVIII (1976), pp. 257–76.
14. See Raymond Williams, *Keywords*, London, Fontana, (1976) and *Marxism and Literature*, London, Oxford University Press, (1977).
15. Attridge (op. cit.) gives a detailed historical account of how this tension developed betwen normative and 'peculiar' (deviationist) ideas of literary language.
16. F.R. Leavis, 'Diabolic Intellect and the Noble Hero: or the sentimentalist's

Othello', in *The Common Pursuit*, London, Chatto and Windus, (1952), pp. 136–59. Hereafter cited in the text as Leavis.

17. A.C. Bradley, *Shakespearean Tragedy*, London, Macmillan, (1904), reprinted (1961). See also Katherine Cooke, *A.C. Bradley and his Influence on Twentieth Century Shakespearean Criticism*, Oxford, Clarendon Press, (1972) and Terence Hawkes, *That Shakespeherian Rag: essays on a critical process*, London, Methuen, (1986).

18. For two such readings in the diagnostic mode, see Christine Brooke-Rose, '"The Turn of the Screw" and its Critics: an essay in non-methodology', in *A Rhetoric of the Unreal*, Cambridge, Cambridge University Press, (1981) and Shoshana Felman, 'Turning the Screw of Interpretation', in *Literature and Psychoanalysis: the question of reading — otherwise*, Yale French Studies, Nos 55/56 (1977), pp. 94–207. My chapter on Pope in this volume (pp. 84–108) finds some comparable blind-spots and moments of revealing *parti pris* in critics of 'The Rape of the Lock'.

19. Roland Barthes, *S/Z*, Richard Miller (trans.), London, Jonathan Cape, (1975).

20. See especially Derrida, 'Force and Signification', 'Genesis and Structure', and 'Structure, Sign and Play', in *Writing and Difference*, Alan Bass (trans.), London, Routledge and Kegan Paul, (1978), pp. 3–30; 154–68 and 278–93.

21. Felman, op. cit., p. 193.

22. See Leavis, 'Thought and Emotional Quality' and 'Reality and Sincerity', reprinted in *The Living Principle*, London, Chatto & Windus, (1975).

5 Law, deconstruction and the resistance to theory

There are several fairly obvious points of contact between literary criticism and legal studies. Lawyers, after all, spend much of their time interpreting texts, whether for the purpose of establishing case-law precedents, determining the scope of statute provisions or debating issues (like that of judicial reform) which cannot be settled by appeal to first principles or the evident facts of the case. In jurisprudence, as in literary studies, such debates tend to polarize between those who believe in the authority of origins, intentions or historical warrant, and those who argue for a more liberal approach to questions of legal precedent, regarding law as a text open to reinterpretation in the light of changing social and political realities. For every position adopted by the partisans of this or that literary theory one can find a corresponding argument developed in the context of legal interpretation. Thus some take the view that a poem or an article of law has just one right interpretation; that to discover its meaning must always be a matter of respecting the author's or the framer's intention; and that any attempt to divorce these notions (as by relativizing language or law to present-day interests and values) must therefore undermine the whole interpretative enterprise.[1] At the opposite extreme there are those who deny that we can ever have knowledge of an author's intentions, or indeed — supposing such evidence were available — that it could count decisively for or against any particular reading. Such arguments may appeal to 'unconscious' levels of meaning in the text, to the fact that some crucial word or phrase might have taken on a new significance, or (more generally) to the way in which our readings are always to some extent shaped by present-day habits of cultural response. In which case, these theorists argue, we had better give up the deluded quest for intentions or authorial meaning, and concentrate instead on making the best possible sense of the text in hand according to the range of interpretative options currently available.[2]

These debates grow more sharp-edged at times like the present when consensus values have come under strain, when governments are perceived to be manipulating law in their own ideological interests, and when any appeal to judicial neutrality can easily appear just a species of pious fraud. Such is the current situation in legal studies, where theorists are raising the kinds of question that have hitherto been largely confined to the province of literary criticism. A brief glance at the law journals is enough to show that disciplinary boundaries are beginning to break down and that legal discourse no longer possesses anything like the sovereign autonomy that it has always claimed. The very move to treat law as somehow on a par with literary criticism and interpretation is itself a clear sign of this widespread mood of unrest. It is present not only among dissident fractions — those like the Critical Legal Studies group who would question every tenet of received juridical wisdom — but along among other, mainstream-liberal thinkers who wish to preserve the authority of law while seeking new ways to ground that authority in various models of textual or narrative understanding. That such issues are raised more often in the context of American than of British jurisprudence is not surprising given the differences between the two legal systems. In America judges have much greater powers to revise, reinterpret or even overturn acts of state legislature by appealing to principles supposedly enshrined in the Constitution, principles which are often so vaguely worded as leave room for all kinds of funda-mental disagreement. Thus debate tends to focus on controversial issues in the area of human rights, on the appointment of Supreme Court judges with markedly political ends in view, and on the way that policy decisions are arrived at under cover of a speciously objec-tivist rhetoric. In British law, conversely, there is no last appeal to articles of a written constitution, and hence less room for such basic conflicts as to how some particular clause or provision should best be construed. Judgments are based for the most part on case-law precedent, or on statutes that are thought to be largely self-explanatory or well enough provided with supplementary rules to guide their application in this or that context. Of course there is plenty of localized controversy over judgments which do appear 'political' in some way, or instances where the statute or precedent in question has to be stretched unduly to accommodate the case in hand. But these instances rarely give rise to the kind of widespread dispute, or the conflicts of theoretical position, that characterize the discourse of American law.

This helps to explain why American legal theorists have lately shown such an interest in topics like post-structuralism, deconstruc-tion and narrative poetics. The idea of law as an autonomous discipline has come to seem not only an instance of narrow profes-sionalism but a means of heading off crucial questions as to the motives, ideology and social effects of past and present legislation. By opening up their discipline to recent developments in the area of literary theory these thinkers hope to put such questions very firmly back on the agenda and thus to strip away the self-validating aura of legitimacy that has hitherto worked against the aims of radical legal reform. At least this is the case with the Critical Legal Studies group, who enlist deconstruction (or their own selective reading of it) as a weapon against every last precept and principle of established judicial thought. In particular, they seek to expose the antinomies of classical liberal reason, the idea of the individual citizen before the law as a self-acting, autonomous subject pursuing his or her chosen ends in a community of likewise autonomous individuals constrained only by rules arrived at on the basis of their freely willed assent. This picture, whether in its Kantian or updated Rawlsian form, they regard as merely a fraudulent disguise for the operations of a capitalist market system which in fact compels the subject's acquiescence by presenting these as the only terms on which to make sense of social reality. Thus law can be seen as a mystifying discourse which secures its own authority and power by equating the way things contingently are — the inequalities, coercions and effects of social injustice — with a 'commonsense' perception of the way things must be according to the tenets of liberal thought. Deconstruction can then be called upon to reveal the contradictions that emerge when such thinking is pushed up against its limits in various problematic instances. The same applies to those other antinomies — of fact/value, 'original meaning' versus current application, the letter of the law as opposed to its (presumably more enlightened) spirit — which plague the discourse of judicial reason. In each case, so these theorists argue, the liberal consensus can be shown to self-deconstruct and thus lay bare the legitimizing ruses which have hitherto concealed its political and self-interested character.[3]

Foucault and Derrida provide the main points of theoretical departure for this radical revisionist exercise. From Foucault comes the notion that power and knowledge are always inseparably linked; that what counts as truth or justice at any given time is a reflex of the various social, political and disciplinary interests that between them dominate the field of discursive representation.[4] Thus law can be seen as the discourse which, more than any other, translates the effects of self-legitimizing power into a 'knowledge' — a set of rules, conventions, ethical and professional codes — immune to questioning by virtue of its sheer coercive force. Their use of Derrida is (as I shall argue) more questionable, though it does have a certain *prima facie* plausibility. After all, deconstruction is chiefly concerned with the logic of value-laden binary distinctions, contrasting terms (like the fact/value or the private/public law paradigm) which can always be shown, on closer reading, to exist in a state of reciprocal dependence which renders their difference 'undecidable' in any given case, and which thus works to destabilize the system of received categorical ideas.[5] One can see why Derrida's example has provided them with rhetorical strategies in plenty for deconstructing the values and assumptions of liberal jurisprudence. Most usually, however, these strategies come down in practice to a habit of repeatedly 'trashing' instances of legal precept and practice by exposing the contradictions, the logical non-sequiturs or clashes of overt and covert principle that surface everywhere in the rhetoric of legal authority. Thus they have often been labelled 'nihilists' by opponents who regard their position (not without reason) as a species of last-ditch Nietzschian irrationalism incapable of putting up alternative arguments for a better, more consistent or socially responsive practice of applied jurisprudence.[6] It is the same misunderstanding of literary deconstruction — on the part of exponents and detractors alike — which has led to its dismissal as an attitude of 'anything goes', a kind of self-licenced hermeneutic free-for-all with not the least regard for standards of argumentative rigour and truth.

But Critical Legal Studies is only one version (albeit the most extreme) of this appeal from law to theories of language, discourse and textual understanding. Again, one finds a whole range of implied hermeneutic models (or standpoints in relation to meaning and truth) which in turn reflect differences of political and ideological view. They are united at least in rejecting any straightforward intentionalist account which regards law as basically determinate so long as it preserves a due respect for the framers' meaning. They are typically more interested in 'hard cases', i.e. those that resist adjudication according to firmly entrenched principles or clear-cut case law precedents. Where the intentionalist or proponent of 'original mean- ing' assumes that the determinate instance must always be taken as the norm — in other words, that hard cases can only be resolved by appeal to some established, clarifying instance — these thinkers suppose just the opposite, regarding all law as in some degree subject to effects of undecidability, differences between the model and the case in hand which complicate the process of arriving at a fair and just estimate. Here again, deconstruction offers parallel arguments for the idea that every reading of a text will always be to some extent a misreading, a version that selects certain details, meanings or struc- tural features at the expense of other details which could just as well have figured in the critic's account. The only kind of 'reading' that could escape this predicament is one that simply transcribes the text verbatim and hence would not count (except maybe in one of Borges' fables) as belonging to the realm of interpretation at all. Thus for many legal theorists the distinction between clear-cut and 'hard' cases is one that fails to stand up, not only in the field of common-law judgment (where obviously the fit between past and present instances is subject to various complicating factors), but also in that of statute law, where even the most explicit or carefully worded provisions may still give rise to far-reaching disagreements as regards their meaning and range of application.

Such arguments mostly stop well short of the out-and-out sceptical position espoused by the Critical Legal Studies group. But they acknowledge that law is in some sense at least a radically inter- pretative enterprise; that any general rules for the conduct of legal discourse will necessarily partake of this textual or hermeneutic dimension; and that therefore something is to be gained by exploring analogies with current ideas in the domain of literary theory. Some of these analogies have a fairly traditional cast, aiming to defend the principled character of legal interpretation against its more radical or 'nihilist' detractors. Thus Ronald Dworkin proposes that we think of law as a kind of 'chain-novel', a story whose episodes are added along the way by a series of guest-contributors (judges, legal theorists, constructive critics of the system), and whose coherence is preserved by their willingness to treat it as an ongoing communal narrative and not just a pretext for imposing some solution that answers to short-term aims and interests.[7] Thus a valid contribution will be one that both acknowledges the claims of established precedent and accepts that those claims will often need to be revised, modified or reinterpreted in light of changing social conditions. Dworkin's main point in developing the analogy with fiction is that lawyers and students of jurisprudence, like the chain-novelist, cannot simply opt out of the story so far and decide to give it an ingenious twist unrelated to previous episodes. Their obligation is threefold: (1) to ensure that the narrative hangs together as a record of intelligible arguments, decisions and consequences; (2) that each new contribution should also be a principled and good-faith response to present social needs; and (3) that the concern of everyone involved in this enterprise should be with what Dworkin calls 'law as integrity', or the effort to present legal practice in the best intellectual and moral light. By working on these assumptions, he argues, we can avoid both the kind of dogmatic literalism which cleaves to old values through a blind respect for tradition and precedent, and the opposite danger of a radical approach which destroys all sense of law as a continuing dialogue between past and present. Thus Dworkin's use of the 'law-as-literature' paradigm is one that rejects its more extreme implications but treats it as broadly analogous to the process of enlightened communal debate enshrined in the principles of liberal justice.

Then there are those of a pragmatist persuasion, like Stanley Fish, who see little point in appealing to 'principles', since judgments in law — as in literary criticism — always come down to a matter of consensus belief, and cannot be provided with anything more in the way of legitimizing grounds. Fish first developed this line of argument in response to the various claims and counter-claims advanced by literary theorists.[8] Theirs was a strictly impossible enterprise in so far as they sought to give reasons, theoretical reasons, in support of this or that interpretative creed. On the one hand there were critics, like E.D. Hirsch, who adopted a strong hermeneutic stance, who equated meaning with authorial intention, and argued that criticism could scarcely make a start unless it respected this primary rule of recognition.[9] Texts might accrue different kinds of 'significance' with the passage of time and the changing conditions of cultural climate or reader response. But their *meaning* remained unaffected, according to Hirsch, since it was fixed for all time by the author's intention, by the logical necessity that what the text means should correspond to what the author originally meant it to mean. Hirsch goes a long way around in defending this position, making use of arguments from speech-act theory, Husserlian phenomenology and other philosophical sources. But he is mistaken, Fish thinks, in wanting to bring up all this heavy theoretical machinery. For if meaning and intention are synonymous terms — if language only makes sense in so far as we take it to realize a speaker's or author's intentions — then there is really nothing more to be said on the topic, and certainly no need for theories which purport to explain the relation between meaning and intent. Such theories only serve to complicate the otherwise self-evident fact that what a text means just is what the author must have intended it to mean.[10]

Fish is equally dismissive of theories that reject this intentionalist viewpoint, those which argue (whether on New Critical, Marxist, Freudian or deconstructionist grounds) that reading neither can nor should be constrained by notions of what the author originally meant. In its moderate form this argument holds simply that the 'words on the page' are all the evidence we have, that even if there were some well-attested record of authorial intention for this or that work we should still have no way of knowing for sure that the intention had been realized, or that the work hadn't come to mean something other or more than the author acknowledged.[11] For the Freudian, such swerves from original intent are evidence of 'unconscious' motives and desires, while the Marxist interprets them as symptoms of ideological conflict and strain, signs that a text has come up against the limits imposed by its own, inevitably partial and distorting world-view. Deconstruction pursues this negative hermeneutic to the point where meaning becomes strictly 'undecidable', where logic is undone by the ruses of figural language, and texts can be shown to subvert any reading that construes them on straightforward intentionalist terms. Such at least is the vulgarized account of deconstruction put about by those who wish to represent it as a species of feckless intellectual nihilism. In fact, as will emerge from any attentive reading of Derrida or de Man, deconstruction is far from denying the claims of logic or authorial intention, since those claims are built into the very structure of all linguistic understanding. What is at issue is the idea that meaning can be wholly accounted for in intentionalist terms, or that logic as the paradigm of rational discourse cannot be subject to effects of rhetorical displacement or undecidability. Deconstructive readings regularly focus on passages where these distinctions begin to break down, where meaning exceeds the grasp of any simplified intentionalist account, or where rhetoric turns out to place obstacles in the path of a clear-cut logical argument. This can only be achieved through a scrupulous attention to those details of the text — including its professions of intent, its truth-claims, structures of logical implication and so forth — which must provide the starting-point for any competent reading. This is why critics are wide of the mark when they charge deconstruction with showing no regard for the elementary protocols of logic or the claims of authorial intention. The point is not to reject such claims out of hand but to show how they are inscribed within a larger system, an economy of meaning and representation which cannot be fully accounted for on terms like these.[12]

Fish would be totally unimpressed by such arguments. For him, deconstruction is just one more example — albeit a particularly bad case — of what goes wrong when meaning is treated as a problem in need of theoretical solution. Hirsch fails to stick with his own best insight by first urging that meaning and intention are synonymous terms, and then going on to offer arguments, methods or procedural grounds for establishing the relevance of authorial intention as if there were some possibility that the two might not coincide, or that critics might be tempted to read quite against what they take to be the author's intent. Deconstruction starts out from the opposite, sceptical premiss, i.e. that textual meaning is always indeterminate, that intentions cannot govern the rhetorical production of sense and that therefore the activity of reading raises questions undreamt of in Hirsch's philosophy. According to Fish this is to ignore the simple point that imputing intentions just *is* what we do when we interpret language, spoken or written. Any positive theorist who thinks, like Hirsch, that principles are needed to support this case — since without them intentions might just get forgotten — is effectively embracing the very same fallacy he or she sets out to refute. The negative theorists (Derrida and de Man) are even more confused since they raise that fallacy into a wholesale programme for dispensing with intentions and construing texts as if meaning were a figment of rhetorical codes devoid of all communicative purport.[13]

In fact, Fish argues, we can only understand what these critics are saying in so far as their proposals make sense according to shared assumptions about meaning, context and authorial intent. In general terms those assumptions are a matter of the language, the tradition or cultural 'form of life' within which all speakers necessarily operate. More specifically, they have to do with a certain 'interpretive community', in this case the community of teachers, critics and scholars who habitually read and interpret such texts.[14] Deconstruction may adopt a stance on such matters which generates widespread resistance and appears to place it way beyond the realm of commonly acceptable belief. But it can only be mistaken if it thinks thereby to shake the foundations of critical discourse, or to shift the whole debate onto a radically different ground. For deconstruction, like any other form of argument, must always presuppose a large measure of shared understanding as to the sense of words, the conventions that determine what shall count as a relevant or useful piece of work, and beyond that the framework of accepted beliefs that provide the very sense of belonging to a given intellectual tradition. In this case the community in question is composed of all the colleagues, fellow-critics, members of university appointment panels, publishers' readers, book-reviewers and so forth who together must have the last say in deciding which texts make the academic grade and which are consigned to the limbo of incompetence, mere eccentricity or 'unprofessional' conduct. It is at this level — through the tacit community of judgments that define the self-image of a culture, profession or intellectual form of life — that texts assume what significance they have and establish their claim to be taken seriously. So professionalism, for Fish, is neither a vice nor a virtue but a simple, inescapable fact of intellectual life. Appealing against it, or pretending to criticize consensual values from some alternative ground of theory or principle, is therefore an utterly hopeless endeavour, one which must fail either because it doesn't make sense to members of the relevant community or because (more probably) it *does* make sense — at least to the extent of generating meaningful dialogue — and therefore belongs squarely within the tradition it thinks to deconstruct.

This argument is carried across from Fish's writings on literary criticism to his articles on law and jurisprudence.[15] Thus he thinks that no purpose can ultimately be served by appealing to 'principles' in Dworkin's manner. Such appeals may bring comfort to enlightened liberals who think that something more is required than a mere invocation of consensus beliefs; that these beliefs may be distorted or swung to accommodate the interests of political parties or pressure-groups; and that law without principles must therefore be deficient in the virtues of integrity and justice. But this is to get the matter backwards, Fish argues, since no talk of principles can make the least difference to what we believe and put into practice as judges, lawyers, legal theorists or others within the relevant community. Dworkin goes wrong not so much in espousing his liberal beliefs — which may have great merit in social, political and ethical terms — but rather in thinking that belief is not enough, and that principles are needed in order to provide some ultimate justification.[16] In fact this talk is just another form of handy psychological back-up, a means of strengthening his own convictions and at the same time convincing others by appearing to have grounds, moral or argumentative grounds, for the values he wants to promote. Thus Fish takes the standard pragmatist line that truth can amount to nothing more than 'warranted assertability', or simply 'what's good in the way of belief'. Truth-claims of whatever kind — whether in law, criticism, ethics, science or any other discipline — have to be construed in accordance with the standards of meaning, relevance and value established by the interpretive community concerned. Having 'theories' or 'principles' may help by getting one a hearing within that community, by carrying an added rhetorical weight or just creating the illusion that one's beliefs are well founded, justified or ultimately true. But in the end belief, so to speak, goes all the way down; to believe in some principle just *is* to accept it as true, whatever the additional assurance to be had by offering reasons and grounds.

Thus the appeal to first principles is much like the desire among hermeneutic theorists like Hirsch to give arguments for thinking that meaning is intentional, or that texts can be rightly understood only in so far as one is able to establish what the author meant. There is simply no point in trying to connect up meaning and intention if it is just a plain fact about language that we can't make sense of it except on intentionalist terms. Equally, the appeal to principles in law — principles of integrity, social justice, human rights, free speech, equal opportunities or whatever — might just as well be couched in the language of straightforward belief and conviction as in the language of Kantian or Rawlsian liberal theory. For these arguments convince to the extent that they embody some persuasive or desirable belief, and not by virtue of their abstract reasoning as to the nature of social obligation, the character of ethical judgment in general or the grounds for believing in this or that programme of enlightened judicial reform. To suppose otherwise is to think that one could step outside the ongoing dialogue and occupy some alternative ground (like Rawls's 'original position') from which to adjudicate such questions on a basis of disinterested rational enquiry.[17] This position would still need to account for itself on terms that made sense according to commonly received values and beliefs. We therefore come back to the same pragmatist argument that Fish deploys against every version of the appeal to 'theory' or legitimizing principles. That is to say, there is no point in adopting this line of talk unless to give some extra persuasive force to beliefs which are already in place and will therefore be unaltered in consequence.

The case is somewhat different with negative theorists, those like the Critical Legal Studies group who wish to 'deconstruct' even the most liberal ideas of justice, reason and truth. For here we find the opposite delusion, Fish argues: the idea that one can get outside some existing consensus not in order to provide better reasons for accepting this or that item of belief, but to bring the whole edifice tumbling down by exposing its lack of solid foundations or ultimate justifying grounds. These theorists set out to 'delegitimize' law by showing how its various principles get into conflict, how rulings which seem clear-cut or unambiguous are in fact 'undecidable' in some given case and how any attempt to frame laws which allow for such difficult cases will inevitably take such an abstract or generalized form as to offer no real guidance when it comes to their practical application. From which the delegitimizers conclude that law is not only incoherent but based on a species of massive and systematic fraud, a means of imposing politically motivated judgments while claiming the authority of principle, precedent or other such authorizing gambits.

Thus a theorist may invoke Derrida's debate with John Searle in order to deconstruct the assumptions that operate in contract-law, i.e. the idea that an utterer's intentions can be read off more or less unproblematically from the document in question, and that where this proves impossible one can always appeal to the relevant context (the conditions under which the agreement was entered into) by way of clearing up any residual doubts.[18] These assumptions can be shown to produce some fairly sizable paradoxes as soon as one asks (like Derrida) what criteria we possess for distinguishing genuine, 'serious' speech-acts from those that are merely cited, rehearsed or performed in jest; and again, by what normative or *de jure* standards we can possibly set limits to the range of contexts in which a speech-act might count as appropriate or legally binding.[19] Or the theorist might seize on certain normative distinctions like that between case law and statute law, the former involving some measure of adaptive reinterpretation from case to case, while the latter is thought to possess determinate meaning and scope, and therefore to stand in no need of such local adjustment. But this distinction breaks down, so the sceptic would argue, for the same reason that emerges in the course of Derrida's or de Man's reading of philosophic texts. That is to say, such readings arrive at a point where it is no longer possible to distinguish the 'constative' and 'performative' aspects of language, the level at which a text (apparently) states what it means and the level at which that meaning turns out to depend on rhetorical or figural devices, tropes which cannot be accounted for in terms of straightforward referential or logical sense. On these grounds the theorists contend that law is indeterminate through and through; that its discourse is everywhere plagued by such disabling aporias; and that therefore no talk of principles, integrity or other such quasi-legitimizing ruses can save it from the rigours of a thoroughgoing deconstructive critique.

It is not hard to see how this argument plays straight into the hands of an equally thoroughgoing pragmatist like Fish. For he can point out once again that the sceptic is caught in a classic double-bind or no-win predicament. Unless the critical theorist mounts his or her case in a language acceptable to others in the legal community, they will fail to convince anyone (or anyone qualified to judge) that their opinion counts, that their articles merit publication or that what they have to say makes sense in the context of ongoing legal debate. There is thus no question of their theory providing, as they are often apt to suggest, some alternative ground from which to criticize every form of current juridical wisdom. They are trapped in a yet more disabling paradox when they reject all theories, past and present, that attempt to legitimize the discourse of law by appealing to principles, reasons or foundationalist truth-claims. Such appeals, they argue, can only serve the purpose of diverting attention from real-world (social and political) conflicts of interest, conflicts which had better be openly discussed than covered up by high-sounding abstract talk. To this extent the Critical Legal Theorists are themselves adopting a pragmatist stance. What they fail to see — as Fish shrewdly remarks — is that this argument leaves no room for their own kind of *soi-disant* radical theory.

> I call this error 'anti foundationalist theory-hope', the hope that because we now know that our foundations are interpretive rather than natural (given by God or nature), we will regard them with suspicion and shake ourselves loose from their influence. But any such hope rests on the possibility of surveying our interpretive foundations from a vantage-point that was not itself interpretive; and the *im*possibility of doing that is the first tenet of anti-foundationalist thought. It follows then that anti-foundationalist thought cannot have the consequences that many hope that it will have, which is to say no more than that anti-foundationalism cannot itself (without contradiction) be made into a foundation.[20]

In short, these thinkers are substituting one delusion for another, arguing that theory has no use whatsoever in propping up the truth-claims of liberal justice, while believing that their own kind of negative theory can shift the whole ground of consensual debate. Where their case falls down (according to Fish) is in its failure to follow right through to the otherwise inevitable pragmatist conclusion.

That is to say, all theory-talk is just another way of debating particular beliefs, and no theory will ever do more than advance or contest those beliefs on the terms available within some existing community of values and interests.

Fish's arguments do have considerable force when applied to the kinds of wholesale scepticism espoused by certain deconstructionists and exponents of Critical Legal Studies. For it is clearly the case that these thinkers are in some sense undermining the ground they want to stand on, or putting forward theories which cannot stand up according to their own professed principles. They are open to the standard *tu quoque* argument which Socrates deployed against Protagoras, and which philosophers have since then used (with minor variations) against the more extreme forms of relativist doctrine. That is, they are committed to the idea that all truths are a species of rhetorical imposture — mere fictions adopted for this or that suasive purpose — but at the same time they take this argument for a truth about the ultimate limits of human knowledge or cognitive grasp. The deconstructionist invites this riposte when he or she states it as a matter of fact that (for instance) the truth-claims of philosophy will always be undone by rhetorical tropes beyond its power to comprehend or control; that speech-acts are always, inescapably caught up in a generalized 'iterability' which renders their meaning undecidable in any given context; or that language is everywhere suspended between constative and performative orders of sense whose effect is to destabilize each proposition at the moment of utterance. One can indeed find such claims advanced at various points in the writings of Derrida and de Man. But there they are 'earned', so to speak, through a considerable labour of textual exegesis, a process of argument that could scarcely be further from the free-for-all attitude of hermeneutic licence that often gets mistaken for 'deconstruction' by friends and enemies alike.

Thus de Man may reach the point (as he does in an essay on Rousseau's *Social Contract*) of questioning whether laws can ever be framed so as to meet the requirements of justice, consistency and relevance in changing social and historical contexts.[21] Legal discourse can function effectively only in so far as its statements possess (or are taken to possess) an authority that transcends such accidents of time and place. If laws are to command general allegiance and not appear simply an instrument of power in the hands of some dominant social group, then their language has to claim a general validity beyond the demands of this or that specific case-in-hand. This need finds expression in the 'grammar' of law, in the system of generalized statements, clauses and abstract provisions which give the appearance of applying in a purely objective, machine-like way without the least admixture of circumstantial interest or motive. 'Just as no law can ever be written unless one suspends any consideration of applicability to a particular entity including, of course, oneself, grammatical logic can function only if its referential consequences are disregarded' (*AR*, p. 269). Otherwise it will be evident that laws are framed with some particular social end in view, that their provisions are by no means arrived at through a process of disinterested judgment, and that citizens' rights and obligations are imposed not (as Rousseau would have it) by the general will working through its selfless elected representatives but by those with the power to enforce their notion of a just and well-ordered society. What enables law to maintain its authority against such challenge is the way that speech-acts of a basically prescriptive or coercive character are passed off · as statements of principle enounced from no particular, self-interested subject position. So it comes about (according to de Man) that the generalized 'grammar' of legal discourse secures assent by concealing precisely those enactments of a soverign juridical will that bring it into being in the first place.

This process of concealment comes up against its limits whenever the law has to be applied to some particular case. 'It cannot', de Man says, 'be left hanging in the air, in the abstraction of its generality. Only by thus referring it back to particular praxis can the *justice* of the law be tested, exactly as the *justesse* of any statement can only be tested by referential verifiability, or by deviation from this verification' (*AR*, p. 269). What is at issue here is the question how far law can provide for its own proper application by establishing rules, criteria or principles that could offer guidance in specific cases. On the one hand such rules would need to operate at a high level of generality corresponding to the ethical truth-claims vested in the notion of absolute justice. On the other they would have to come to terms with the fact that no such abstract decision–procedure could possibly encompass the various instances, facts or case-histories which might be taken as falling under the law in question. Thus the principles of justice will always be couched in a language of the utmost generality which nevertheless allows for numerous conflicting interpretations, disagreements of the kind that typically preoccupy American theorists of constitutional law. At the opposite extreme — where judgment is based very largely on case-law precedent, with no explicit appeal to such principles — any decision will always be context-specific and a matter of comparing the 'facts of the case' with some other such legally documented set of facts. This is why, in de Man's reading, a work like the *Social Contract* both states and conceals the necessary conditions of its own rhetorical working. As a legislative text it must seek to ensure an obedience to its own dictates which can only be achieved through the instituting power of language in its radically performative aspect. In order to legitimize this power — to represent it as serving the interests of universal reason as well as those of a generalized public good — the *Contract* must adopt a dissimulating rhetoric that covers its own performative tracks. It is here, de Man writes, 'in the description of a political society, [that] the "definition" of a text as a contradictory interference of the grammatical with the figural field emerges in its most systematic form' (*AR*, p. 270).

Now there is much in these pages from *Allegories of Reading* that would offer theoretical support for the Critical Legal Studies position.

De Man puts forward some powerful arguments for treating law as a textual phenomenon, a field of rhetorical forces and tensions that can best be understood through the kind of close-reading more often brought to bear upon literary works. Such a reading will raise considerable problems for those other, more familiar forms of argument which set out to demonstrate that law is a consistent, self-validating enterprise; that its seeming contradictions or antinomies can always be resolved by application of higher-order principles; or that 'hard cases' should best be treated as marginal, deviant instances, capable of clear adjudication simply by referring them back to clear-cut precedents.[22] Each of these arguments breaks down at the point where decision–procedures no longer serve, where rules give way to interpretation and where rhetoric (rather than 'grammar' or logic) turns out to be the last ground of appeal. But where the Critical Legal Theorists adopt this stance as a kind of a priori programmatic creed — thus laying themselves open to Fish's shrewdly aimed objections — de Man arrives at it only in the course of a densely argued chapter on one particular text. This is not to say that de Man's observations would apply only to the *Social Contract*, or only to texts with a similar range of thematic and rhetorical concerns. In fact it is one of his strongest claims that the antinomies revealed in this reading of Rousseau could be found in *any* legislative text that attempted — as all such writings must attempt — to reconcile the various conflicting requirements of a discourse on politics, justice and truth. What makes the *Contract* an exemplary case is the undeceiving rigour of Rousseau's language, its extreme rhetorical complexity and the way that it provides (as de Man would claim) all the materials for its own deconstructive reading. Any lessons to be drawn from it must respect this condition and not move off at the first opportunity into statements of a generalized negative import.

De Man's central point in this essay is that law gives a force of real-world practical consequence to linguistic and rhetorical devices for which we may lack any adequate conceptual model. What Rousseau explicitly sets out to offer is a theory, a 'constitutional machine' which would in turn provide the blueprint or working model for future acts of legislation. If this could be achieved, then 'the text of the law and the law of the text would fully coincide and generate both the *Social Contract*, as a master text, and a set of contractual rules on which the constitution of any state could be founded' (*AR*, p. 271). Such an ideal is unattainable for reasons that begin to emerge as de Man works his way through passages of the *Contract* that register the presence of two quite distinct and incompatible orders of meaning. 'It turns out . . . that the "law of the text" is too devious to allow for such a simple relationship between model and example, and the theory of politics inevitably turns into the history, the allegory of its inability to achieve the status of a science.' (Ibid.) Again, this conclusion finds a parallel in the claim often advanced by adherents to the Critical Legal Studies' position: namely, that attempts to place law on a footing of integrity, consistency, principle or justice are in fact merely a species of *post-hoc* rationalization, adopted to conceal its actual foundations in prejudice, class-interest and the will to power. But this argument is presented — with rare exceptions — at a level of blanket generality which achieves nothing like the force, the analytical rigour and cogency of de Man's essay on Rousseau.

There are two main reasons for this difference. One is de Man's habit of sticking close to the text and allowing discrepant details to register at the point where they create the maximum resistance to our settled presumptions about meaning, truth and interpretive method. The second is his absolute refusal to erect 'deconstruction' into a kind of alternative orthodoxy, a self-assured method or technique of reading which takes it more or less for granted that those presumptions are ill-founded and incoherent. 'The legal machine, it turns out, never works exactly as it was programmed to do. It always produces a little more or a little less than the original, theoretical input' (*AR*, p. 271). This would apply equally to deconstructive readings which avoid the difficult business of textual exegesis for sake of moving straight on to large pronouncements about language and meaning in general. De Man makes this point most forcefully in his late essay 'The Resistance to Theory'.[23] Such resistance is not confined, he argues, to those traditionalist scholars and critics who reject deconstruction as a 'nihilist' attack on all the values that have hitherto sustained the enterprise of humanistic studies. It is also to be felt within theory itself, at the point where deconstruction is tempted to advance generalised claims that would then substitute for the activity of close-reading. For it is de Man's main contention, here and elsewhere, that rhetoric (or language in its figural aspect) will always put obstacles in the path of any reading that seeks to reduce it to some preconceived method, model or structural grammar. As with the *Social Contract*, so here: the 'machine' turns out to work well enough, but with results that may be a lot more complicated than anything allowed for by 'the original, theoretical input'.

It is not just a matter of external pressures, of the widespread institutional 'resistance to theory' that would simply ignore these questions or treat them as marginal to the critic's proper concerns. What interests de Man far more is the resistance specific to theory itself, or to the kind of reflective and meticulous close-reading that is caught, so to speak, between the permanent temptation of theory and the constant risk that its project will run aground on details that problematize all its working assumptions. This is why de Man proposes a return to the model of the classical *trivium*, the discipline which combined the study of logic, grammar and rhetoric as a basis for all humanistic enquiry. In its orthodox form this discipline required that logic be treated as the main component, since it bore directly on matters of reason and truth. Grammar was seen as essentially an adjunct to logic, a study of the ways in which language reproduced the elements of logical structure and form. In so far as rhetoric retained a place in this system it could only be as a strictly ancillary discipline, one that studied language in its persuasive (as opposed to its rational or truth-selling) aspect, and which mostly confined its efforts to compiling an exhaustive taxonomy of figural devices. The model was thus firmly hierarchical in its mode of application, giving logic pride of place, setting grammar in the service of logic, and assimilating rhetoric to a generalized 'grammar' of tropes which would finally ensure its logical accountability.

De Man's main purpose in reviving the *trivium* is not to confirm this classical sense of priorities but to show just how easily its terms can be reversed or displaced when subjected to the rigours of textual close-reading. For it then becomes apparent that rhetoric, so far from obeying the dictates of grammar and logic, in fact has autonomous signifying properties which cannot be reduced to any such orderly, self-contained system. De Man offers various examples of this persistent desire to maintain the sovereignty of logic over rhetoric by way of an all-embracing taxonomic grammar that would keep figural language firmly in its place. The tradition begins with Descartes and the Port-Royal grammarians who took it for granted that 'the grammatical and the logical functions of language are co-extensive', and that grammar should therefore be treated as 'an isotope of logic' (*RT*, p. 14). Among present-day theorists de Man cites the instance of A.J. Greimas's structural semantics, a generalized theory whose claims extend to the various languages or discourses (including that of law) which supposedly exhibit striking regularities of codified structure and form.[24] For Greimas, 'grammar stands in the service of logic which, in turn, allows for the passage to a knowledge of the world' (*RT*, p. 14). This latter comes about through the idea that logic articulates the basic structures of thought and perception, achieving at best a direct correspondence between concepts, propositions and real-world states of affairs. Hence what de Man perceives as the link between rationalist epistemology and a certain phenomenalist account of language and reference which takes it for granted that words should match up with the objects of immediate sensuous cognition. It is thus by bringing together logic, language and phenomenal self-evidence that philosophy can claim to be a truly foundational discipline, without any need to account for language in its other, less orderly rhetorical forms.

One version of this belief — nowadays out of fashion but still, de Man argues, capable of exerting a covert influence on theories of language and perception — is the Cratylist idea that sound and meaning are somehow intimately related, that the sensuous properties of words have a close kinship with their semantic nature. The field where such notions have retained their greatest currency is that of aesthetics and literary theory. 'To the extent that Cratylism assumes a convergence of the phenomenal aspects of language, as sound, with its signifying function as referent, it is an aesthetically oriented conception; one could, in fact, consider aesthetic theory . . . as the complete unfolding of the model of which the Cratylian conception of language is a version' (*RT*, p. 9). For if there is one article of faith that unites the most divergent schools of critical thought — from the Romantics, through T.S. Eliot to the American New Critics, the Russian Formalists and exponents of reception-theory — it is the idea that there exists a uniquely 'poetic' use of language, one that is able to surmount all those bad antinomies (subject and object, thought and feeling, concepts and sensuous intuitions) which have hitherto plagued the discourse of abstract reason. Aesthetic understanding is the mode in which these distinctions fall away, at least momentarily, giving access to a realm of ideally unified sensibility. There is no room here to pursue the various arguments by which de Man brings out the impossible nature of this enterprise, or more specifically the kinds of textual resistance that rise up against it in the major works of Romantic critical thought.[25] Sufficient to say that he regards it as the source of a mystified theory of language and perception, one that begins with an angled misreading of certain crucial passages in Kant, and which then continues to exercise its power whenever the categories of aesthetic understanding encroach on the domain of history, politics and ideological critique. What results from such confusions is a tendency to naturalize language and thought by assimilating rhetoric, which might otherwise obstruct this process, to the orders of logic or grammar on the one hand and phenomenal cognition on the other.

This is why de Man rejects the commonplace account that would treat post-Kantian aesthetic theory — from Schiller, Wordsworth and Coleridge to their various present-day heirs — as standing in firm opposition to the tenets of rationalist philosophy and the modern scientific world-view. On the contrary, he argues: there is a basic solidarity between the move that connects logic, via grammar with the world of scientific *realia*, and the move that attributes to poetry (or to other forms of aesthetic experience) the power of manifesting sensations directly in a language of heightened phenomenal vividness and force.

> This is a clear instance of the interconnection between a science of the phenomenal world and a science of language conceived as definitional logic, the pre-condition for a correct axiomatic-deductive, synthetic reasoning . . . In such a system, the place of aesthetics is preordained and by no means alien, provided the priority of logic, in the model of the *trivium*, is not being questioned. [*RT*, p. 13]

The model, that is to say, holds good just so long as rhetoric is confined to its proper, subordinate role; for in this case it must remain strictly unthinkable that language should in any way disrupt or controvert the assured correspondence between logic and the forms of phenomenal cognition. But different possibilities begin to emerge when rhetoric is analysed more closely as a dimension of language that may not, after all, lend itself to treatment in logical or grammatical terms. It then becomes clear that figural language has a life of its own, a tendency to generate meetings or trains of implication which exceed all the powers of logical grasp. This is the point, de Man writes, at which rhetoric intervenes 'as a decisive but unsettling element which, in a variety of modes and aspects, disrupts the inner balance of the model and, consequently, its outward extension to the nonverbal world as well' (*RT*, p. 14). For what emerges most strikingly from the reading of literary texts is the sheer *impossibility* of pinning language down to a clear-cut 'grammar' or taxonomy of tropes and devices.

Such, according to de Man, is the chief lesson to be learned from those methodical theorists like Greimas whose efforts are always 'strategically directed toward the replacement of rhetorical figures by grammatical codes' (*RT*, p. 15). Their work has considerable value, but mainly on account of its revealing gaps and inconsistencies, those problems which it cannot afford to recognize, given the nature of its own prior commitments. In short, 'the grammatical decoding of a text leaves a residue of indetermination that has to be, but cannot be, resolved by grammatical means' (Ibid.). This 'residue' can be accounted for only in rhetorical terms, as the effect of figural tropes and displacements that exceed any clear-cut logic of meaning or style. Thus it turns out, in de Man's most succinct formulation, that

> this undoing of theory, this disturbance of the stable cognitive field that extends from grammar to logic to a general science of man and of the phenomenal world, can in its turn be made into a theoretical project of rhetorical analysis that will reveal the inadequacy of grammatical models of non-reading (*RT*, p. 17).

Such theories (like Greimasian structural semantics) are models of 'non-reading' in the sense that they tend to substitute methodological aims and ambitions for the detailed activity of textual exegesis. To this extent they are heirs of the classical *trivium*, effectively maintaining the priority of logic and grammar, and seeking to reduce figural language to the compass of a systematic theory.

Hence de Man's claim that the close-reading of texts — especially of texts that foreground their own rhetorical dimension — can often produce more in the way of demystifying insight than any appeal to generalized theories of language, ideology or representation. For such theories will be out to confirm their own governing set of assumptions, and will therefore tend to treat the text in hand as just another useful illustrative instance. There is a strong temptation to abandon the inherently risky, unpredictable ground of close-reading, and to take refuge in large theoretical claims that override any possible resistance from the text. 'Mere reading, it turns out, prior to any theory, is able to transform critical discourse in a manner that would appear deeply subversive to those who think of the teaching of literature as a substitute for the teaching of theology, ethics, psychology, or intellectual history.'[26] This is why rhetoric figures in de Man's criticism as the name for that disruptive element in language that resists all forms of premature method, ideology or aesthetic mystification. For it is at this level, — in the field of rhetorical displacements, drives and substitutions which cannot be accounted for in systematic terms — that a text will most often work to obstruct our settled habits of response. 'Tropes, unlike grammar, belong primordially to language. They are text-producing functions that are not necessarily patterned on a non-verbal entity, whereas grammar is by definition capable of extra-linguistic generalization' (*RT*, p. 15). So it is that 'mere reading' can generate resistance to theories that would otherwise fail to register those disruptive forces within language.

What de Man has to say about literary language would apply equally to the discourse of legal theory and interpretation. Here also, criticism can best get a hold by attending to the strains and contradictions that emerge when theorists attempt to clarify law in accordance with precept or principle. His essay on the *Social Contract* has an obvious relevance to problems in the field of statute law, where supposedly there is little room for variant readings, and where language is taken to possess a determinate (constative) force which precisely delimits its meaning and scope of application. Yet, as many commentators have recognized, this can be only a notional ideal, a species of enabling legal fiction that soon breaks down when confronted with the vagaries of real-world judicial practice. Thus the distinction between clear-cut and 'hard' cases is at most a matter of degree, since no legal utterance can make full provision in advance for the range of possible events, contexts and circumstances that it may be required to cover. Indeed, legal history is itself the product of this openness to variant readings, this failure of the text to specify precisely what would count, from case to case, as an adequate interpretation. 'Considered performatively, the speech act of the contractual text never refers to a situation that exists in the present, but signals toward a hypothetical future . . . laws are promissory notes in which the present of the promise is always a past with regard to its realisation.' (*AR*, p. 273). There will always be this problem with any attempt to derive the authority of law from some primary 'rule of recognition', some grounding act or primordial context of agreement from which all subsequent rules and obligations are taken to follow.

De Man makes the point in rhetorical terms by invoking the figure of *metalepsis*, the trope that reverses cause and effect through a shuttling exchange of priorities. Thus Rousseau describes how a people might be brought to 'appreciate the sound maxims of politics' if 'the social spirit that [these] institutions are to produce should preside over their elaboration' (*AR*, p. 274). That is to say, laws are justified through a kind of metaleptic reversal, one that starts out from the desirable effects they are thought to have produced in some subsequent state of society, and then proceeds to legitimize those same future benefits by decreeing that the framers, as good-willed citizens, must have made provision for this and no other arrangement. 'Men should be, prior to the laws, what they are to become through them.' In this sentence Rousseau states the crucial paradox of all such appeals to original intent or framer's meaning. It is a paradox with far-reaching implications, especially — as we have seen — in the context of American constitutional law, where differences of view on fundamental issues are often debated as if these came down to a clash of rival interpretative theories. Thus conservatives may claim to base their reading of the relevant clause on a decent respect for what the framers had in mind, while radicals deny that we can possibly have such knowledge or, if we could, that the interests of justice are best served by appealing to anachronistic values and beliefs. Meanwhile there are those — mostly liberals like Dworkin — who adopt a midway position, one that upholds the 'integrity' of law as a matter of respecting tradition and precedent while also striving, on principled grounds, to make the best possible sense of its less determinate provisions in light of changing social and political needs. In each case the parties to this dispute will take up a particular stance with regard to questions of hermeneutic method and theory. Conservatives maintain that the radical–revisionist position reduces the law to a free-for-all of naked political interests, an unprincipled relativism devoid of authority and truth. The radicals respond by pointing to clauses like the Equal Rights Amendment, where clearly the framers had no idea that their provisions might one day be extended to oppressed minorities like the slave population. The liberals attempt to get over this problem by broadening the concept of original intentions, by conceding that there may indeed be reason to revise our idea of what the framers had in mind, but arguing that we can in fact respect the spirit of their laws by construing them to mean what a good-willed judge would presently incline to make of them.

Thus it is clear that the kind of 'metaleptic' reversal which de Man points out in the *Social Contract* also has its place in current debates about legal interpretation and judicial review. The framers are credited (on the liberal view) with having made allowance for subsequent enactments which might not have figured as part of their original intention, but which can now be seen as working to legitimize both their and our own visions of a just, equitable social order. Cause and effect are thus reversed: the text which should, on more traditionalist assumptions, mean simply and precisely what it says, and so stand proof against later misreadings, in fact turns out to be justified only in so far as its provisions make tolerable sense according to the wisdom of present-day exegetes. Conservatives may appear to avoid this problem altogether by insisting on the absolute primacy of the framer's meaning, and therefore condemning the revisionist enterprise as a species of unprincipled relativism. But their case runs up against the obvious objection that we simply cannot take the framers to have meant what we now understand by concepts like Equal Rights; that any serious attempt to respect their 'intentions' on the issue of slavery would turn back the history of enlightened reform to a stage beyond any (including the most conservative) ideas of social justice. There is always a sense in which past enactments have authority and force only to the extent that they answer present needs. Thus the legal text, as de Man describes it, exists in a permanent state of suspension between 'constative' and 'performative' modes, on the one hand appearing to stipulate precisely the terms on which it must be understood, while on the other looking to a future history of 'authorized' readings, revisions and extensions which it cannot determine in advance, but which none the less provide its only possible source of retroactive authority. Such is the form of 'metaleptic' substitution — the habit of justifying laws by treating them, however covertly, as past effects of present causes — which de Man finds at work in Rousseau's discourse and in every attempt to construe legal history on self-legitimizing terms.

He makes the point succinctly in a passage that also takes us back to the arguments and terms for analysis proposed in 'The Resistance to Theory'. There, we recall, it was rhetoric (or language in its tropological aspect) that threatened to disturb the 'stable cognitive field' which would otherwise extend straightforwardly from logic, through grammar to the realm of phenomenal cognition. In the case of the *Social Contract*, he writes,

> [t]he discrepancy within the contractual model . . . will necessarily manifest itself phenomenologically, since it is defined, in part, as the passage, however unreliable, from 'pure' theory to an empirical phenomenon. The noncoincidence of the theoretical statement with its phenomenal manifestation implies that the mode of existence of the contract is temporal, or that time is the phenomenal category produced by the discrepancy. [*AR*, p. 273]

Laws have application or practical warrant only to the extent that their language is taken to possess referential force, to 'fit the facts' of some particular case in hand. But they also lay claim to a universality, a respect for the standards of absolute justice that transcends each and every such localized instance. De Man's seemingly extravagant assertion, that 'textual allegories on this level of complexity generate history' (*AR*, p. 277), may appear less paradoxical in light of what actually goes on in the context of day-to-day judicial debate. Thus statutes and case-law precedents alike are treated as embodying some ultimate claim to justice which none the less requires a constant effort of contextual reinterpretation, an effort that takes account of those material factors and circumstances that cannot be subsumed under the abstract ideal. This in turn gives rise to the history of variant legal creeds and philosophies, the debate between conservatives, liberals and radicals, all of whom adopt some particular view of how the balance can best be struck. What de Man suggests is that the rhetoric of law, the tensions that develop in its language between 'constative' and 'performative' modes, may be at the root of these differences and affect them in ways not fully understood by exponents of this or that principled viewpoint.

Now there might, on the face of it, seem little to choose between de Man's deconstructionist reading of the *Social contract* and the arguments put forward by the Critical Legal Studies group. They also make a practice of exposing contradictions and antinomies, pointing to areas where law is indeterminate, and claiming that judgements are arrived at not on the basis of impartial reasoning, or in pursuit of justice and truth, but always under pressure of competing political interests. Furthermore, they would appear to follow his example by treating legal discourse in rhetorical terms, as a language that works to persuade, win over or (most often) simply to coerce subjects into accepting the current institutional status quo. Any attempt to derive a code of practice from first principles, rules or natural justice is regarded by these 'delegitimizing' critics as a ruse in the service of authority and power. Their main target is the doctrine of legal 'formalism', classically defined (in the words of Roberto Unger) as 'belief in the availability of a deductive or quasi-deductive method capable of giving determinate solutions to particular problems of legal choice'.[27] This belief found its most articulate expression in the work of Hans Kelsen, the neo-Kantian theorist who sought to ground jurisprudence in a self-sufficient system of a priori concepts, ground-rules and normative terms, and hence to save it from the looming threat of cultural and ethical relativism.[28] This strong version of the formalist case has since been subjected to widespread criticism and nowadays has few adherents. Yet the doctrine survives, according to Unger, in current attempts to distinguish between questions that belong strictly within the province of legal debate, and issues that open into wider contexts of socio-political argument. Formalism in this sense can be defined more generally as 'a commitment to, and a belief in the possibility of, a method of legal justification that contrasts with open-ended disputes about the basic terms of social life, disputes that people call ideological, philosophical, or visionary'.[29] It is the aim of the Critical Legal Studies movement to demolish the grounds of any such distinction, to show that legal reasoning is always bound up with particular interests, values, priorities or visions of the social good. This can best be achieved (so the argument continues) by treating the discourse of law as a species of applied rhetoric, all the more so when its strategy includes an appeal to abstract talk of principles, theories or legitimizing grounds.

However this approach, as I have suggested, differs from de Man's in one crucial respect: it is advanced at a level of highly generalized argument that seldom takes account of particular problems in the reading of this or that legal text. This is why a pragmatist like Fish can so easily demonstrate the basic incoherence of the Critical Legal Studies programme, the fact that on their own grounds of argument these theorists could not possibly give any reason for criticizing law as currently practised, or as perceived by those whose job it is to interpret and justify legal discourse. In order to mount such a case, as Fish understands it, they would have to occupy a position outside the prevailing consensus, a standpoint that would yield some radically different 'theoretical' view of the practices concerned. And this position is not available if what they say is right and all theories may be reduced to one or another form of rhetorical persuasion. Fish is in fact quite happy with this line of talk since it bears out his own pragmatist belief in the ultimate uselessness of theory. Let me quote once more from Fish's recent essay to recall the main points at issue.

> In what follows I will contend (1) that in whatever form it appears the argument for theory fails, (2) that theory is not and could not be used . . . to generate and/or guide practice, (3) that when 'theory' is in fact used it is in the way that Unger so dislikes, in order retrospectively to justify a decision reached on other grounds, (4) that theory is essentially

a rhetorical and political phenomenon whose effects are purely contingent, and (5) that these truths are the occasion neither of cynicism nor of despair.[30]

The Critical Legal Studies people would accept items 3 and 4 as holding good of mainstream (conservative or liberal) attempts to prop up the authority of law. They might also acknowledge the force of items 1 and 2, though not without certain misgivings, since such a thoroughgoing scepticism with regard to the relevance of theory would seem to have awkward consequences for their own strong revisionist enterprise. And item 5 they would surely see as evidence of Fish's basically conservative standpoint, his willingness to sink all differences of view — including disagreements about theory — by appealing to the values and normative assumptions of an existing consensus. But according to Fish they don't have this option of picking out some items and rejecting others to suit their argumentative needs. If the case against theory is valid at all then it applies to every form of theoretical endeavour, including such attempts to discredit other kinds of theory while smuggling one's own back in, so to speak, by a side entrance.

Fish calls this 'the characteristically left error of assuming that an insight into the source of our assumptions . . . will render them less compelling'.[31] On the contrary, he argues: such knowledge cannot possibly effect any change in our thoughts, beliefs, values or actions since it only serves to show that we have no choice but to work on those same assumptions. Theory is thus 'without consequence' in the sense that it leaves us exactly where we started, as members of a certain 'interpretative community' whose values we inevitably take on board, even (or especially) when we try to theorize their character. Of course one could turn this argument back upon Fish and claim that he himself has a theory of interpretative communities by which he seeks to explain significant features of our social, cultural and professional lives. But such a move would misfire, he points out, since the whole point of adopting this pragmatist line is to deny that it can finally make any difference whether or not one happens to accept it. In short,

> [theory] is entirely irrelevant to the practice it purports to critique and reform. It can neither guide that practice nor disturb it. Indeed, the insight that interpretative constructs underlie our perceptions and deductions cannot do anything at all. It cannot act as a direction to seek something other than interpretative constructs, because there is no such other thing to be found; and it cannot act as a caution against the influence of interpretive constructions now in place because that influence will already be at work contaminating any effort to guard against it.[32]

Theory is perfectly acceptable to Fish so long as it entertains no delusions of grandeur, no ambition to exist on a separate plane from the beliefs, discourses and practices which make up an ongoing cultural consensus. What he rejects in the Critical Legal Studies' programme is a stronger notion of theory, one that implies (for all their arguments to the contrary) that there must be some alternative vantage-point from which to carry out such criticism.

Their position is indeed vulnerable to this line of *tu quoque* response because it deals with the antinomies of law only in very general terms, and not at the level of textual engagement that one finds in a critic like de Man. They also tend to equate rhetoric with language in its purely suasive or performative aspect, an emphasis that leads them to ignore those problematic tensions between logic, grammar and rhetoric that de Man sets out to analyse. This is where Fish locates the main weakness in their argument: the self-exempting clause whereby every other form of legal reasoning comes down to mere rhetorical imposture, while Critical Legal Studies can somehow escape this predicament and expose the whole business as a species of elaborate fraud. But his objections would entirely miss the mark if applied to de Man's very different account of what constitutes a rhetorical reading. The point is best made in an essay on Nietzsche where de Man tracks the emergence of two distinct meanings that attach to the term 'rhetoric'.[33] One — the more familiar in everyday parlance — has to do with language in its purely suasive aspect, its power to achieve certain effects through the use of well-judged verbal techniques. It is in this sense of the word that 'rhetoric' has acquired a shady reputation, one that goes back to Plato's case against the sophists and still carries much the same weight of high-toned moral disapproval. But the term also applies to that study of linguistic tropes and devices which can have precisely the opposite effect of exposing, and thus counteracting this insidious persuasive power. 'Nietzsche's final insight', as de Man writes,

> may well concern rhetoric itself, the discovery that what is called 'rhetoric' is precisely the gap that becomes apparent in the pedagogical and philosophical history of the term. Considered as persuasion, rhetoric is performative but when considered as a system of tropes, it deconstructs its own performance. [*AR*, p. 131]

It is the second of these aspects, the source of Nietzsche's most powerful demystifying insights, that escapes any treatment of rhetoric confined to remarking its persuasive or coercive force. This may help to explain why the Critical Legal Studies project can muster so little resistance in the face of wholesale pragmatist arguments like those adopted by Fish. For it is impossible, on these terms, to conceive of any discourse that would break with the meanings, values and assumptions of some existing cultural consensus. The only use for 'theory' would then be to confirm that there is no getting outside this closed circle, and that all attempts to criticize its workings must perforce end up on the same pragmatist ground.

De Man addresses this point in some paragraphs from 'The Resistance to Theory' where he writes about Fish and the seductions of a certain, over-simplified philosophy of rhetoric. What drops out of sight when language is treated on purely performative terms is that conflict between rhetoric-as-persuasion and rhetoric as the undoing of its own suasive powers that de Man finds everywhere at work in Nietzsche's texts. The pragmatist approach is necessarily blind to such conflicts, since it regards language as performative through and through, and thus discounts the very possibility of tensions arising between logic, grammar and rhetoric. This is why de Man persists in working with a model based on the classical *trivium*, even though he finds problems with that model which considerably complicate its normative uses. In short:

> to empty rhetoric of its epistemological impact is possible only because its tropological, figural functions are being bypassed. It is as if . . . rhetoric could be isolated from the generality that grammar and logic have in common and considered as a mere correlative of an illocutionary power . . . Speech-act oriented techniques of reading read only to the extent that they prepare the ground for the rhetorical reading they avoid. [*RT*, pp. 18–9]

Such theories avoid the difficulties of reading in so far as they equate rhetoric with a generalized suasive or performative dimension that would simply exclude a priori any evidence of complicating factors in the text. It is by means of this pre-emptive device that Fish can refute the claims of Critical Legal Studies, at least in so far as those claims rest on a simplified law-as-rhetoric paradigm.

It would be wrong to suggest that such criticisms apply in every case where post-structuralist theory has been imported into the context of legal debate. One exception is a recent book by Peter Goodrich that takes full account of these developments but argues its way to a different and more promising conclusion.[34] Goodrich begins, in familiar style, by attacking the presumptions of legal formalism as exemplified in Kelsen's neo-Kantian treatise *The Pure Theory of Law*. He points out some interesting parallels between Kelsen's project and that of Saussurian structural linguistics. Both were conceived out of the desire to re-establish their disciplines on a normative, 'scientific' basis, and thus turn back the relativist or historicizing trend of late nineteenth-century thought. In Kelsen's case this involved a strict (and in practice, Goodrich argues, a strictly unworkable) distinction between truths of law and matters of social or circumstantial fact. Only thus, according to Kelsen, can law be 'delimited against nature', or 'the science of law as a science of norms . . . delimited against all other sciences that are directed toward causal cognition or actual happenings'. This formalist position derives on the one hand from Kant's various arguments for distinguishing analytic from synthetic orders of truth-claim. On the other it serves to insulate law from any messy involvement with political or ideological questions, since these could only compromise its normative status as a source of timeless, self-validating rules and concepts. Thus Kelsen goes so far as to assert that 'even an anarchist, if he were a professor of law, could describe positive law as a system of valid norms, without having to approve of this law'.[35]

Goodrich concurs with the proponents of Critical Legal Studies in regarding this project as inherently misguided, as a pseudo-solution to problems that arise not within law as a self-contained system of axiomatic truths, but through its application in various contexts where political interests are always in play. But he goes a lot further than those theorists usually do in deconstructing the normative arguments of Kelsen's text, bringing out the tensions that consistently emerge between its principles of 'pure theory' (couched in seemingly neutral or constative terms) and its way of enforcing such principles through recourse to a suasive, and authoritarian, rhetoric. Indeed, the main object of Goodrich's book is to argue for a closer liaison between legal studies and those disciplines (including literary theory) that might help to loosen the hold of formalist doctrine. They can do so, he argues, by showing how law is always a contested domain, a site of struggle where various languages, discourses or rhetorical strategies in the end count for more than any abstract appeal to reason, justice or truth. But this doesn't mean that all forms of legal argument should henceforth be treated on the levelling terms of a rhetoric that would offer no grounds for distinguishing valid from invalid judgments. Such claims merely reflect a narrowed and impoverished concept of rhetoric, one that (in de Man's phrase) can be 'emptied of its epistemological impact . . . only because its tropological, figural functions are being bypassed'.

In fact Goodrich has a chapter that traces this decline through its various historical stages, finding it already prefigured in Aristotle's distinction between logic (or the domain of necessary truths) and rhetoric (or the art of gaining assent through deployment of well-chosen topics and analogies). Where his account differs from de Man's is in treating the devaluation of the term as a process internal to rhetoric itself, or the discipline that traditionally bore that name, rather than relating it to the other components of the classical *trivium*.[36] Thus the marginalized status of rhetorical study is connected with the tendency, 'from Quintilian onwards, to reduce the discipline from a domain of three equal divisions — argument, composition and style — to the greatly restricted, monistic and largely formal study of style (*elocutio*) alone' (Goodrich, p. 103). This had the effect of severing rhetoric from any serious concern with argumentative validity and truth. 'It was thus to become, in the post-classical era, an incremental, didactic and largely empty form of study, focused almost obsessively on the word and its multifarious role in the figures of speech' (Goodrich, p. 103). This would seem to go against de Man's contention that the 'rhetoric of tropes', or study of language in its self-complicating figural aspect, is the point at which criticism attains its highest power of demystifying rigour and insight. But as Goodrich goes on to develop his argument it becomes clear that he, like de Man, wishes to conserve this critical power against the widespread tendency to devalue rhetoric by equating it straightforwardly with persuasive language.

Thus his reading of various legal theorists — in particular Kelsen and Hart — doesn't merely dismiss their arguments as so many forms of rhetorical imposture, but seeks to elucidate specific points of conflict between generalized statement and performative effect. This stance is maintained in Goodrich's treatment of particular case-histories, notably *Bromley London Borough Council v. Greater London Council*, where Bromley challenged the GLC over its policy of raising a supplementary rate to subsidize reductions in public transport fares. Goodrich offers a detailed account of the proceedings, especially the way that certain crucial terms ('economic', 'reasonable', 'public accountability', 'fiduciary obligation' and so forth) became the focus of an ideological debate carried on by way of largely covert rhetorical devices. His aim is to expose this hidden agenda, and to show that when the case went forward to the Court of Appeal and the House of Lords (where GLC policy was ruled unconstitutional) its outcome was decided just as much on policy grounds, and not — as the judges' pronouncements would suggest — through a process of neutral deliberative argument. Thus Goodrich draws attention to a whole range of judicial gambits whose effect is to represent the GLC case as motivated solely by (misguided) political aims, while the adversary interest amounts to nothing more than a straightforward compliance with the dictates of law and rational accountability.

This attitude is spelled out most clearly in the judges' opinion that the GLC, having promised the cheaper fares policy as part of its election manifesto, was nevertheless under no obligation to implement that plan on coming to power. 'The duty owed to the electorate emerges as in this case promissory and indirect, while the duty owed to ratepayers is direct and proprietary and would, on this occasion, appear to override the electorate's policy preferences' (Goodrich, p. 196). In short, it is assumed (in formalist fashion) that law should properly exclude all concern with ideological issues and operate on a strictly normative, value-free and 'reasonable' basis of judgment. But, as Goodrich points out, this principle is distinctly selective in its mode of application, since it works to discredit the GLC's quite overt appeal to social and policy matters, while aligning its own, professedly neutral stance with the rival set of interests represented by Bromley Borough Council and its disgruntled ratepayers.

> The *sovereignty* of legal discourse is not only expressed tacitly in the axiomatic character of much of the argument and its manipulation of evaluative epithets, but also explicitly in the assertion of the independence of the legal issues from the political debates . . . The language of the text, however, would appear to indicate the precise opposite. The reasonableness of the G.L.C.'s substantive decision is a constant object of ethically imbricated comments, their duty to the electorate is legally circumscribed, and the meaning of the term 'economic' is considered in relation to transport policies that range from the arbitrary and socialistic to the business-like and fair. [Goodrich, p. 199]

This passage makes it clear that Goodrich is far from wanting to collapse the distinction between judgments arrived at through a process of open, rational debate and judgments that appear to adopt this standpoint while in fact finding room for all manner of covert rhetorical ploys. His approach certainly entails a vigilant mistrust of legal theories that claim to separate formal from substantive issues, or rights and obligations as defined within law from those that admit disagreement with regard to socially desirable objectives. Such theories merely serve, as in this case, to bolster a myth of judicial neutrality and ensure that certain kinds of political argument are treated as pretextual impositions, failing to meet the normative standards supposedly required under law. But this is not to claim that all such debates come down to a contest of rhetorical strategies where notions of validity or rational warrant are simply beside the point. As Goodrich writes, 'it is only by critically analysing the details of the language and discursive processes inherent within the legal text that the preconstructions, preferred meanings, rhetorical and ideological dimensions generally of legal discourse can be rationally challenged within the legal institution itself' (Goodrich, p. 204). For this challenge to be effective it has to take account of those tensions that develop between rhetoric in its suasive and its critical or self-deconstructing aspect.

It will then be seen that Fish's line of argument only appears to possess such a knock-down force because it treats rhetoric entirely at the level of straightforward performative effect. That is to say, it ignores the possibility that a close reading of legal texts may uncover inconsistencies, gaps and contradictions that go completely against some received, canonical understanding. This is why any project like Critical Legal Studies needs to theorize its position but also to leave room for a certain 'resistance to theory', a resistance that is produced in the reading of texts that may problematize all its favoured working assumptions. One last passage from de Man will help to make the point more effectively. It proposes what amounts to an 'ethics of reading', an attentiveness to discrepant details of the text that will treat them (in almost Kantian terms) as deserving of respect on their own account, rather than enlisting them as a means toward the end of some preconceived interpretation.

> Understanding is not a version of one single and universal Truth that would exist as an essence, a hypostasis. The truth of a text is a much more literal and empirical event. What makes a reading more or less true is simply the predictability, the necessity of its occurrence, regardless of the reader's or of the author's wishes . . . It depends, in other words, on the rigour of the reading as argument. Reading is an argument . . . because it has to go against the grain of what one would want to happen in the name of what has to happen.[37]

It is only by remaining alert to these signs of textual resistance that theory can break with the closed circle of interpretive foreknowledge or consensus beliefs which, according to Fish, must always set limits to any such revisionist project. Otherwise the pragmatists will inevitably have the last word, a message that translates into political terms as the powerlessness of theory, or criticism in general, to effect any change in the currently prevailing discourse of authority and power. Deconstruction undoubtedly holds useful lessons for critical legal theorists in search of a strategy for contesting this defeatist doctrine. But they are not, as I have argued, lessons of a kind that can simply be taken as read, or applied in such a fashion as to generate theories detached from the reading of particular texts.

References

1. For a recent defence of this strong intentionalist standpoint see P.D. Juhl, *Interpretation: an essay in the philosophy of literary criticism*, Princeton, NJ, Princeton University Press, (1980).
2. This position is argued most forcefully in Roland Barthes, *S/Z*, Richard Miller (trans.), London, Jonathan Cape, (1975) and 'The Death of the Author', in *Image–Music–Text*, Stephen Heath (trans.), London, Fontana, (1977).
3. See for instance J.M. Balkin, 'Deconstructive Practice and Legal Theory', *Yale Law Journal*, Vol. 96 (1987); Clare Dalton, 'An Essay in the Deconstruction of Contract Doctrines', *Yale Law Journal*, Vol. 94 (1985); Gerald Frug, 'The Ideology of Bureaucracy in American Law', *Harvard Law Review*, Vol. 97 (1984); Alan Hunt, 'The Theory of Critical Legal Studies', *Oxford Journal of Legal Studies*, Vol. 6 (1986); Allan C. Hutchinson, 'From Cultural Construction to Historical Deconstruction', *Yale Law Journal*, Vol. 94 (1984); David Kairys (ed.), *The Politics of Law: a progressive critique*, New York, Pantheon Books, (1982); Mark Kelman, 'Interpretive Construction in the Substantive Criminal Law', *Stanford Law Review*, Vol. 33 (1981) and 'Trashing', *Stanford Law Review*, Vol. 36 (1984); Duncan Kennedy, 'The Structure of Blackstone's *Commentaries*', *Buffalo Law Review*, Vol. 28 (1979); Patrick Monaghan and Allan C. Hutchinson, 'Law, Politics and the Critical Legal Scholars', *Stanford Law Review*, Vol. 36 (1984); Christopher Norris, 'Suspended Sentences: textual theory and the law', in *The Contest of Faculties*, London, Methuen, (1985); Joseph William Singer, 'The Player and the Cards: nihilism and legal theory', *Yale Law Journal*, Vol. 94, (1984); David Trubek, 'Complexity and Contradiction in the Legal Order', *Law and Society Review*, Vol. II (1977) and 'Where the Action Is: critical legal studies and empiricism', *Stanford Law Review*, Vol. 36 (1984); Mark Tushnet, 'Critical Legal Studies and Constitutional Law: an essay in deconstruction', *Stanford Law Review*, Vol. 36 (1984); Roberto M. Unger, *The Critical Legal Studies Movement* (Cambridge, Mass., Harvard University Press, (1986). For further references, see Duncan Kennedy and Karl E. Klare, 'A Bibliography of Critical Legal Studies', *Yale Law Journal*, Vol. 94 (1984).
4. See especially Michel Foucault, *Discipline and Punish: the birth of the prison*, New York, Pantheon, (1977); *Power/Knowledge: selected interviews and other writings*, Brighton, Harvester Press, (1980); *The Foucault Reader*, Paul Rabinow (ed.), New York, Pantheon, (1985).
5. See Jacques Derrida, *Of Grammatology*, G.C. Spivak (trans.), Baltimore, Johns Hopkins University Press, (1976); *Positions*, Alan Bass (trans.), London, Athlone Press, (1981); *Margins Of Philosophy*, Alan Bass (trans.), Brighton, Harvester Press, (1982). Of particular relevance in this context are Derrida's essays 'The Law of Genre', *Glyph*, Vol. 7, (1980) and 'Devant la loi', in A. Phillips Griffiths (ed.), *Philosophy and Literature*, Cambridge, Cambridge University Press, (1984).
6. See for instance Stephen L. Carter, 'Constitutional Adjudication and the

Indeterminate Text: a preliminary defence of an imperfect muddle', *Yale Law Journal*, Vol. 94 (1984); John Stick, 'Can Nihilism Be Pragmatic?', *Harvard Law Review*, Vol. 100 (1986).

7. Ronald Dworkin, 'Law As Interpretation', *Critical Inquiry*, Vol. 9 (1982). This argument is developed at greater length in Dworkin, *Law's Empire*, London, Fontana, (1986).

8. See Stanley Fish, *Is There a Text in this Class? The authority of interpretive communities*, Cambridge, Mass., Harvard University Press, (1980). The issue is debated from various points of view in W.J.T. Mitchell (ed.), *Against Theory: literary theory and the new pragmatism*, Chicago, University of Chicago Press, (1985).

9. E.D. Hirsch, *Validity in Interpretation*, New Haven, Yale University Press, (1967).

10. See Fish, 'Consequences', *Critical Inquiry*, Vol. II (1985).

11. For a classic statement of this position, see W.K. Wimsatt and Monroe C. Beardsley, 'The Intentional Fallacy', in Wimsatt, *The Verbal Icon*, Lexington, University of Kentucky Press, (1954).

12. The point is made with particular emphasis in Derrida, 'Plato's Pharmacy' and 'The Double Session', in *Dissemination*, Barbara Johnson (trans.), London, Athlone Press, (1981).

13. See Fish, 'Consequences', (op. cit.).

14. Fish, *Is There a Text in this Class?* (op. cit.).

15. See Fish, 'Working on the Chain Gang: interpretation in the law and in literary criticism', *Critical Inquiry*, Vol. 9 (1982); 'Fish v. Fiss', *Stanford Law Review*, Vol. 36 (1984); 'Dennis Martinez and the Uses of Theory', *Yale Law Journal*, Vol. 96 (1987).

16. For Dworkin's response, see 'My Reply to Stanley Fish (and Walter Benn Michaels): please don't talk about objectivity any more', in W.J.T. Mitchell (ed.), *The Politics of Theory*, Chicago, University of Chicago Press, (1983).

17. John Rawls, *A Theory of Justice*, London, Oxford University Press, (1972).

18. See for instance Balkin, 'Deconstructive Practice and Legal Theory' (op. cit.), pp. 767–77.

19. See Jacques Derrida, 'Signature Event Context', *Glyph*, Vol. 1 (1977); John R. Searle, 'Reiterating the Differences', *Glyph*, Vol. 1 (1977); Derrida, 'Limited inc. abc', *Glyph*, Vol. 2 (1977).

20. Fish, 'Dennis Martinez and the Uses Theory' (op. cit.), p. 1,796.

21. Paul de Man, 'Promises (*Social Contract*)', in *Allegories of Reading: figural language in Rousseau, Nietzsche, Rilke, and Proust*, New Haven, Yale University Press, (1979). Hereafter cited in the text as *AR*.

22. For a sceptical treatment of this doctrine, see W.T. Murphy, 'Old Maxims Never Die: the "plain meaning rule" and statutory interpretation in the "modern" federal courts', *Columbia Law Review*, Vol. 75 (1975).

23. Paul de Man, 'The Resistance to Theory', in *The Resistance to Theory* Minneapolis, University of Minnesota Press, (1986). Hereafter cited in the text as *RT*.

24. See A.J. Greimas, *Structural Semantics*, Daniele McDowell, Ronald Schleifer and Alan Velie (trans.) Lincoln, University of Nebraska Press, (1983); 'Analyse sémiotique d'un discours juridique', in *Sémiotique et les Sciences Sociales*, Paris, Seuill, (1976). For a broadly similar approach, see Bernard Jackson, *Semiotics and Legal Theory*, London, Routledge and Kegan Paul, (1985).

25. See especially Paul de Man, *Blindness and Insight: essays in the rhetoric of contemporary criticism*, London, Methuen, (1983) and *The Rhetoric of*

Romanticism, New York, Columbia University Press, (1984).

26. De Man, 'The Return to Philology', in *The Resistance to Theory* (op. cit.), pp. 21–6.
27. Unger, *The Critical Legal Studies Movement* (op. cit), p. 1.
28. Hans Kelsen, *The Pure Theory of Law*, Berkeley, University of California Press, (1967).
29. Unger, *The Critical Legal Studies Movement* (op. cit.), p. 1.
30. Fish, 'Dennis Martinez and the Uses of Theory' (op. cit.), p. 1,781.
31. Ibid., p. 1,796.
32. Ibid., p. 1,797.
33. De Man, 'Rhetoric of Persuasion (Nietzsche)', in *Allegories of Reading* (op. cit.), pp. 119–31. Hereafter cited in the text as *AR*.
34. Peter Goodrich, *Legal Discourse: studies in linguistics, rhetoric and legal analysis*, London, Macmillan, (1987). Hereafter cited in the text as Goodrich.
35. Kelsen, *The Pure Theory of Law* (op. cit.), p. 218. Cited by Goodrich, p. 39.
36. On this topic see especially Walter Ong, *Ramus, Method and the Decay of Dialogue*, Cambridge, Mass., Harvard University Press, (1958).
37. De Man, 'Foreword' to Carol Jacobs, *The dissimulating Harmony*, Baltimore, Johns Hopkins University Press, (1979), pp. vii–xiii.

6 De Man unfair to Kierkegaard? an allegory of (non)-reading

This will be a reading of two very different texts, one a short story by Donald Barthelme, the other a late (and so far unpublished) essay by Paul de Man. The story is entitled 'Kierkegaard Unfair to Schlegel' and concerns — among other things — the uses of irony, the ethics of interpretation, and the bearing of these questions on history, politics and the art of just getting along from day to day.[1] In so far as 'postmodernism' means anything at all, this is a paradigmatic piece of postmodernist fiction. That is to say, it offers a series of loosely associated memories, quotations, fragmentary dialogues, comic *non-sequiturs* and suchlike, to the point where all illusions of verisimilitude finally break down and one is left (or so it seems) with a mere assort-ment of textual bits and pieces. The story is 'about' Kierkegaard, about Kierkegaard's reading of Friedrich Schlegel and also about the narrator (unnamed) who has problems of his own in trying to decide whether Kierkegaard was unfair to Schlegel. Meanwhile there is the essay by de Man, entitled 'The Concept of Irony', which makes it sound very much like a reading of Kierkegaard, but in fact more concerned with Schlegel, Fichte and other philosophers in the post-Kantian idealist tradition.[2] De Man starts out by saluting Kierkegaard for having written, quite simply, 'the best book on irony that's available' (*CI*, p. 1).[3] He concludes, after a long and very complex process of argument, by noting that all of Schlegel's interpreters, Kierkegaard included, have 'had to invoke history as a means of defense against irony' (*CI*, p. 43). On the way to this conclusion Kierkegaard figures for the most part as an off-stage presence, a voice that is silenced while Schlegel (and de Man) pursue their own lines of thought.

One might venture a modified version of Barthelme's query: is de Man fair to Kierkegaard in framing his essay with a title ('The Concept of Irony') which so pointedly creates the false expectation that this will be a study of irony from something like a Kierke-gaardian standpoint? Or again — to put the question in more general terms — why has Kierkegaard so seldom been read or written about by deconstructionist literary critics who must surely realize that his work prefigures their own in many crucial respects? The answer, I think, is there to be read in both Barthelme's story and de Man's essay. It has to do with Schlegel and the topic of Romantic irony; with Kierkegaard's insistence on subjugating the aesthetic to the ethical and, ultimately, the religious realms of value; and with that whole seductive notion of self-reflexivity (or *mise-en-abyme*) that marks the discourse of 'literary' deconstruction, even where it strives for the highest degree of analytical cogency and rigour. In Kierkegaard, Romantic irony is the name for that most dangerous of secular illusions, the idea of an unconditional freedom achieved by disowning all responsibility for the meaning or truth of one's words. For the ironist, as for Nietzsche, existence is justified as a purely aesthetic phenomenon, an endless opportunity for self-delighting play with the roles, masks or adoptive personae that offer themselves from one situation to the next. Barthelme's narrator makes the point concisely enough:

> An irony directed against the whole of existence produces, according to Kierkegaard, estrangement and poetry. The ironist, serially successful in disposing of various objects of his irony, becomes drunk with freedom . . . Irony becomes an infinite absolute negativity. Quote irony no longer directs itself against this or that particular phenomenon, against a particular thing unquote. Quote the whole of existence has become alien to the ironic subject unquote. For Kierkegaard the actuality of irony is poetry. [Barthelme, pp. 164–5]

But the narrator, unlike Kierkegaard, sees this as no reason for rejecting romantic irony, or for treating it as merely a stage on the path to some higher (ethical or religious) form of understanding. Kierkegaard is 'unfair to Schlegel' in so far as he misreads the ironist's case, equating subjective freedom with an attitude of downright amoralism or 'anything goes'. Furthermore, Kierkegaard ignores the difference between fictional and philosophic discourse, since the text in question is Schlegel's novel *Lucinde*, which Kierkegaard nevertheless proceeds to interpret as if it were advancing ethical truth-claims.[4] On balance then the narrator inclines toward Schlegel's side of the argument, as might be expected in a work of postmodern fiction where meanings, values and narative viewpoints are no sooner established than thrown into doubt. Indeed there is an obvious elective affinity between postmodernism and Romantic irony, in that both make a point of systematically subverting all those commonplace or normative ideas.

Still it is worth pursuing the story a bit further since Barthelme is not content to stage this encounter between Kierkegaard and Schlegel as a straightforward parable where fiction wins out over the claims of sober, literal-minded philosophic truth. His narrator goes on:

> I find it hard to persuade myself that the relation of Schlegel's novel to reality is what Kierkegaard says it is. I have reasons for this (I believe, for example, that Kierkegaard fastens upon Schlegel's novel in its prescriptive aspect — in which it presents itself as a text telling us how to live — and neglects other aspects, its objecthood for one) but my

reasons are not so interesting. What is interesting is my making the statement that I think Kierkegaard is unfair to Schlegel . . . because that is not
what I think at all. Because of course Kierkegaard was fair to Schlegel.
In making a statement to the contrary I might have several purposes —
simply being provocative, for example. But mostly I am trying to
annihilate Kierkegaard in order to deal with his disapproval. [Barthelme,
pp. 165–6]

So there is more to this narrator than might be supposed if one
took him to be simply defending Schlegel against Kierkegaard, or
promoting the claims of romantic irony at the expense of ethical
commitment. As in many of Barthelme's stories, the appearance of a
throwaway postmodern style goes along with a sense that all this talk
must be covering up some deeper disturbance, some problem that can
only be overcome by constantly shifting narrative perspectives and
keeping it at a safe distance of aesthetic style and technique. In this
case the story is framed as a question-and-answer routine between
the narrator and an unnamed respondent, perhaps a psychoanalyst (if
we choose to read it that way), or maybe some other, less accommodating voice of his own conscience. The narrator's problem is that
he needs to take refuge in irony, wants to make out the best possible
case for Schlegel, but knows that in the end it just won't do except
as a form of escapist reverie.

Along the way we hear quite a bit about his sexual fantasies, his
marital and domestic problems, and his sense that there is not much
point getting involved in political events — anti-nuclear marches and
so forth — since these, like everything else, come down to a form of
ineffectual self-display which can only be handled ironically.

Q. Do you think your irony could be helpful in changing the government?
A. I think the government is very often in an ironic relation to itself. And
that's helpful. For example, we're spending a great deal of money for
this army we have, a very large army, beautifully equipped . . . Now the
whole point of an army is — what's the word? — deterrence. And the
nut of deterrence is credibility. So what does the government do? It goes
and sells off its surplus uniforms . . . And immediately you get this vast
clown army in the streets parodying the real army . . . And of course the
clown army constitutes a very serious attack on all the ideas that support
the real army including the basic notion of having an army at all.
[Barthelme, p. 162]

Perhaps there is a case to be made for irony on something like
Bakhtinian grounds: as a kind of 'carnivalized' subversive laughter
that undermines the discourse of authority and state-sponsored
values.[5] But ultimately this argument is made to look inadquate,
shown up as a species of aesthetic self-indulgence on a level with the
narrator's failed attempts to cope with his problems through the
solvent of an all-embracing, all-forgiving irony. In short, the story
comes round to a position where it is Kierkegaard, not Schlegel, who
seems to have the last word; where existence cannot be redeemed or
justified as an aesthetic phenomenon, and instead bears witness

(as 'Q' puts it) to 'the unavoidable tendency of everything particular to emphasize its own particularity' (Barthelme, p. 167).

The last we hear of this dialogue is an anecdote from the life of Louis Pasteur, seeking money to continue his researches from the wife of a wealthy department-store owner. When Pasteur, much embarrassed, looks at the cheque it has been made out in the sum of one million francs. Upon which (as Q narrates the episode) 'they both burst into tears'. And then the closing sentence: 'A. (bitterly): Yes, that makes up for everything, that you know that story'. I think we are to take it that the ironist is pretty much played off the field at this point. The effect is to disconcert the *hypocrite lecteur* whose sympathies have so far been enlisted on the side of the gamy postmodernist narrator. One is left in the kind of awkward situation that Kierkegaard contrives for his unregenerate readers: that of the aesthete (or romantic ironist) lured by the subtlest of narrative devices into accepting a position which then turns out to be untenable from any good-faith, consistent or humanly responsible standpoint. Barthelme brings the message home through a series of interpolated hints and reflections which show up the narrator's failure to grasp his own compromised position. Thus 'Q. (aside). He has given away his gaiety, and now has nothing'. Far from establishing how Kierkegaard is 'unfair' to Schlegel, it would seem that the story at last comes round to a full vindication of Kierkegaard's claim that romantic irony is a perilous thing, that it stands in the way of authentic self-knowledge and leads (in Wallace Stevens's phrase) to an endlessly seductive, irresponsible play with the 'intricate evasions of as-if'.

Of course it is still possible — here as with Kierkegaard — to read against the grain and refuse to give in to such forms of high-handed ethical coercion. That is, one could treat *all* of Kierkegaard's texts (including the ethical, religious or 'edifying' discourses) as belonging to the order of aesthetic production, as written (and who is to prove otherwise?) from some pseudonymous, ironic, or noncommital standpoint, and therefore as open to a postmodern reading indifferent to questions of ultimate truth. There is nothing that can actually prevent such a reading, as I have argued elsewhere in an essay that goes about as far as possible toward deconstructing Kierkegaard's arguments, his value-system and narrative strategies.[6] In fact Kierkegaard himself baits the trap by organizing his entire life's work around a series of supposedly stable and controlled oppositions — aesthetic/ethical, ethical/religious, fictive/authentic, pseudonymous/first-hand, ironic/serious and so forth — which are only held in place by his (and the reader's) willingness to take them on faith. The deconstructionist will have no trouble in showing that these binaries are finally 'undecidable', that they rest on nothing more than the arbitrary privilege accorded to one term in each pair, and that therefore the whole project of Kierkegaard's writing — its attempt to lead the reader through and beyond the seductions of irony or aesthetic understanding — comes up against the obstacle of our simply not knowing how to take this or that particular pronouncement in context. Kierkegaard will then be seen to provide all the materials, inducements and rhetorical strategies for a deconstructive reading of his own texts. This would apply not only to those works (like the first volume of *Either/Or*) that belong to his so-called 'aesthetic' production and which more or less explicitly ask to be read as ironic, pseudonymous, or expressing a viewpoint at several removes from Kierkegaard's own.[7] In the end there is no telling, so the argument would run, just where to draw the line between these strategies of aesthetic indirection and that other, authentic or 'edifying' portion of Kierkegaard's discourse which supposedly renounces such literary tricks and brings us face to face with ultimate issues of ethical and religious truth.

Of course one could appeal to his own account in *The Point of View for my Work as an Author* where Kierkegaard claims to do just that, to redeem or justify his output in retrospect, by pointing out the various strategic devices that marked his 'aesthetic' production, and treating those texts as a mere prelude to the work of religious edification.[8] But this opens up a whole series of further questions, since there is no absolute or binding obligation to accept *The Point of View* at its own valuation, as a species of privileged discourse that would somehow transcend the doubts and obliquities of his other, less 'authentic' productions. This is why Kierkegaard worries such a lot about irony, as Barthelme's narrator observes. 'If what the ironist says is not his meaning, or is the opposite of his meaning, he is free both in relation to others and in relation to himself. He is not bound by what he has said. Irony is a means of depriving the object of its reality in order that the subject may feel free' (Barthelme, p. 164). It is against this false and illusory freedom, as displayed so seductively by romantic ironists like Schlegel, that Kierkegaard directs the main force of his arguments. But irony is not so easily laid to rest, especially when Kierkegaard has himself provided such a range of sophisticated ruses, alibis and narrative pretexts for *not* taking him at his word. In Barthelme's tale, as I have argued, the question is thrown back into the ironist's court through a series of telling rejoinders that leave him nonplussed and introduce a different voice into the narrative, one that implicitly speaks up for Kierkegaard as against Schlegel, and which thus brings about a gradual shift from aesthetic to ethical ground. Nevertheless the temptation remains to read this as a paradigm 'postmodernist' text, a fable whose multiplied perspectives, meta-narrative games and throwaway style undercut any earnest desire, on the reader's part, to detect some edifying purpose at work.

I have put quite a weight of exegetical pressure on Barthelme's little tale, partly because it will bear such treatment readily enough, but also on account of its relevance to issues in current critical thought. For here it seems to me that Kierkegaard has figured as a strong but troubling precursor, one whose influence is often to be felt but whose texts have received far less than their share of attentive close reading. Deconstruction has evolved very much in the wake of German idealist aesthetics, in particular that phase of post-Kantian thinking that led philosophers and poet-critics like Schlegel, Novalis, Solger and Kierkegaard to treat irony as a topic of central importance. De Man makes the point by noting how different is the attitude to irony displayed by a cagey modern critic like Wayne Booth. For him, what is most important is to get some conceptual grip on the topic, to recognize the signs of ironic intent and thus not be caught in the embarrassing position of a literal-minded fall-guy, straight man or dupe. This accords with Booth's marked preference for 'stable' or 'definite' irony, for the well-behaved sort that has the virtue, once recognized, of offering a hold for interpretation and not running wild in the dangerous sphere of 'absolute infinite negativity'.

Thus Booth has a revealing footnote, cited by de Man, where he briefly entertains this latter notion but then declares it off bounds for the purpose of an adequate critical approach. 'Pursued to the limit', he writes,

> an ironic temper can dissolve everything, in an infinite chain of solvents. It is not irony but the desire to understand irony that brings such a chain to a stop. And that is why a rhetoric of irony is required if we are not to be caught, as many men of our time have claimed to be caught, in an infinite regress of negations. And it is why I devote the following chapters to 'learning where to stop'.[9]

To de Man, on the contrary, this statement signals a distinct anxiety on Booth's part, a desire to bypass or to sublimate those other, less reputable kinds of irony that might just get out of hand. For if Schlegel and Kierkegaard are agreed on one point, it is the fact that irony is not indeed a 'concept', and that any attempt to describe its workings in a more or less controlled or systematic fashion will at last run up against insuperable problems. In this situation it can always turn out that the roles get reversed and the irony rebounds on those canny rhetoricians, like Booth, who think it possible to conceptualize the workings of irony.

Thus de Man notes that one of Schlegel's most rewarding texts on the topic is entitled 'Uber die Unverständlichkeit' ('On the Impossibility of Understanding'), a title that declares the paradoxical nature of his project from the very outset.[10] Irony defeats the best efforts of conceptual understanding because it cannot be treated as just one trope among others, a device whose effects could be safely reduced to the compass of a generalized theory or method. 'If indeed irony is tied to the impossibility of understanding, then Wayne Booth's project of understanding irony is doomed from the start because, if irony is *of* understanding, no understanding of irony will ever be able to control irony and to stop it, as he proposes to do' (*CI*, p. 8). Some critics (and here he cites Northrop Frye) have attempted to avoid this undesirable conclusion by arguing that irony is a trope in the root (etymological) sense of the word; that it represents a swerve or a turning-away from the plain-prose, literal meaning.[11] If so, de Man thinks, then it is a veritable 'trope of tropes', a figure that somehow has to include all those other, more easily specified devices (metaphor, metonymy, synecdoche etc.) whose workings it can always complicate to the point of an ultimate undecidability. In short, a critic like Booth might have found it more difficult to accommodate irony to his own tidy scheme of things 'if he had been more cognizant of the German tradition which has dealt with this problem, rather than centering his argument as he does on the practice of eighteenth-century English fiction' (*CI*, p. 8).

Commentators are divided on the issue of just how closely deconstruction relates to these developments in German idealist aesthetics, especially their stress on the ironic (or 'self-reflexive') character of literary texts.[12] There is a clear enough link in the work of critics like Geoffrey Hartman and J. Hillis Miller, those who started out from an interest in romantic poetry or nineteenth-century fiction, and whose earlier writings (up to the mid-1970s) were much influenced by phenomenological theory and the so-called 'criticism of consciousness' school.[13] In their case one can see how the 'turn' came about; how an engagement with themes of self-consciousness, irony and the subject–object dialectic gave way to a 'deconstructionist' rhetoric of the specular, reflexive, or endlessly self-questioning text. This amounted to a shift of privileged vocabulary, one that led directly from a finely nuanced language of the self and its modes of experience to a somewhat more austere but related concern with the problematic nature of textual representation. Thus Hartman and Miller continue in the line of speculative thinking established by precursors like Schlegel, despite what appears their sudden conversion — under Derrida's influence — to a criticism purged of existential or subjective residues. They are still in some sense 'critics of consciousness', though now less inclined to treat the self as an originating source, a locus of authentic experience and more apt to see it as a construct of the various tropes, displacements or rhetorical devices that characterize literary language.[14] The emphasis has changed, but the readings they produce are by no means incompatible with a broadly phenomenological approach.

With de Man, as always, matters are more complicated, since his work was marked from the beginning by a much greater sense of self-denying rigour, a refusal to suppose — like the early Hartman or Hillis Miller — that criticism could or should achieve the kind of inward, sympathetic grasp that annulled the very distance between text and commentary. For him, such beliefs were mere wishful thinking, a product of the delusive 'hermeneutic circle' that seemed to establish a condition of ideal reciprocity, while in fact merely reflecting the critic's own interests, values and ruling assumptions. Hence that pattern of co-implicated 'blindness' and 'insight' that de Man finds at work in just about every school of current interpretative thought, from the American New Critics to Blanchot, Poulet, the early Lukacs and even Jacques Derrida's otherwise exemplary reading of Rousseau.[15] In each case he points out the moments of necessary failure — the rhetorical blindspots, swerves from intent, conflicts between precept and practice — that ensue when criticism seeks to achieve a full understanding of the text. This argument is conducted, or so it might seem, in a language of the utmost impersonal rigour, one that holds out against the kind of subjective pathos, the fallacy of unmediated presence or inwardness, that de Man diagnoses in critics like Poulet and the phenomenological school.

All the same it is quite clear that his approach in *Blindness and Insight* owes much to the tradition of romantic irony and its stress on the divided, non-self-identical, infinitely reflexive quality of literary language. Where these critics regularly fall into self-imposed error is in thinking that commentary can ever reduplicate — or summon to mind through an act of sympathetic recreation — the state of consciousness enjoyed by an author in the moment of creative inspiration. This error comes about through their failure to acknowledge the ontological distance, the gap that opens up not only between text and commentary but within the very act of critical understanding conceived in authentically temporal terms. This is why 'irony' and 'allegory' figure as more or less synonymous key-words in de Man's middle-period writings. Irony signifies the power of an 'infinite absolute negativity', a refusal to hypostatize notions of the self, of meaning, origins or interpretative truth as an end-point to the otherwise vertiginous process of textual *mise-en-abyme*. Thus critics go wrong — and here he singles out Jean Starobinski — when they treat irony as 'a preliminary movement toward a recovered unity, as a reconciliation of the self with the world by means of art'.[16] And he then cites a passage from Peter Szondi's essay on Schlegel where this same misreading occurs, where irony is treated as destructive and negative only in so far as it rejects the possibility of some ultimate reconciliation between real and ideal. 'Every word in this admirable passage is right from the point of view of the mystified self, but wrong from the point of view of the ironist . . . Friedrich Schlegel is altogether clear about this. The dialectic of self-destruction and self-invention which for him . . . characterizes the ironic mind is an endless process that leads to no synthesis' (RT, p. 220).

The same applies to allegory — that other privileged term in de Man's critical lexicon — in so far as it names the authentic predicament of a language caught up in structures of temporal difference, unable to achieve the kind of pure, unmediated presence claimed by the proponents of a high-romantic Symbolist creed.

> Whereas the symbol postulates the possibility of an identity or identification, allegory designates primarily a distance in relation to its own origin and, renouncing the nostalgia and the desire to coincide, it establishes its language in the void of this temporal difference. In so doing, it prevents the self from an illusory identification with the non-self, which is now fully, though painfully, recognised as a non-self. [RT, p. 207]

These passages make it clear that de Man's demystifying rhetoric — his refusal to invest in the pathos of subjective identification — still draws much of its critical force from the tradition of romantic irony and its stress on the divided, self-reflexive character of all 'authentic' understanding. In subsequent texts like *Allegories of Reading* he will exploit a whole range of analytic terms (metaphor/metonymy, performative/constative, rhetoric/gramar and so forth) which appear to renounce this residual pathos, but which still derive much of their persuasive power from the knowledge that consciousness can never 'coincide' with its object, that language occupies the 'void' of a temporal difference which always prevents or frustrates the desire for a sympathetic meeting of minds.[17] In short, deconstruction remains very much an heir to the discourse of romantic irony, despite its efforts (in de Man's case at least) to transform that discourse into a rigorous epistemology of tropes that would renounce the 'nostalgia and the desire to coincide'.

Some commentators — Rodolphe Gasché among them — take this as evidence that 'literary' deconstruction is a mistaken or aberrant enterprise, one that has based itself on a highly selective and philosophically inadequate reading of Derrida's texts.[18] For Gasché, deconstruction is concerned only marginally with those themes that so preoccupy the literary critics: the idea of poetic or fictional language as an endless textual *mise-en-abyme*, a self-reflexive medium where subject and object dissolve in the specular regressions of an 'infinite absolute negativity'. This distortion has come about (he argues) because literary critics want to use deconstruction for their own interpretative purposes, especially in the field of romantic poetry, where such readings have indeed produced some powerful and illuminating criticism. All the same they have failed to register what Gasché takes as the properly philosophical import of Derrida's work: namely, its involvement with that line of post-Kantian critique that runs via Fichte and Schelling to Hegel, and which has to do with ultimate problems in the nature of mind, language, and representation. Thus Derrida's deconstructive key-terms ('supplement', 'differance', 'writing', 'parergon' and so forth) are described by Gasché as 'quasi-transcendentals', words that cannot be reduced to concepts or grounding intuitions but which none the less constitute the very possibility of thought and discourse in general. 'Focusing on an analysis of those heterogeneous instances that are the "true" conditions of possibility of reflection and speculation without being susceptible to accommodation by the intended totality, Derrida's philosophy reinscribes, in the strict meaning of this word, reflection and speculation into what exceeds it: the play of the infrastructures'.[19] It is the error of 'literary' deconstruction to ignore this infrastructural dimension of Derrida's thought and to concentrate instead on that thematics of reflexivity which lends itself more readily to the purpose of interpreting romantic and modern texts.

Gasché's book which I discuss at greater length in Chapter 9 is entitled *The Tain of the Mirror*, a reference to the lacklustre backing of tinfoil (French *étain*) which itself reflects nothing, but in the absence of which no mirroring effects could occur. Hence his argument by analogy that 'reflection and reflexivity . . . are precisely what will not fit in Derrida's work — not because he would wish to refute or reject them in favor of a dream of immediacy, but because his work questions reflection's unthought, and thus the limits of its possibility'.[20]

The literary avatars of deconstruction have mistaken its true (philosophical) pertinence in the interests of adapting it to a style of reading that allows full scope to their own, more limited but self-promoting concerns. I think this argument is convincing as applied to critics like Hartman and Hillis Miller, those for whom deconstruction is a means of continuing the tradition of high romantic argument under a different but closely related rhetorical guise. But it doesn't work so well with de Man, and this for reasons I have already hinted at. De Man never wholly breaks with that tradition, even where his language appears to repudiate any hint of subjective pathos. But he presses much further in the direction that Gasché himself indicates, toward the kind of ascetic or rigorous epistemology of tropes that would get 'behind' the play of specular reflexivity to the 'conditions of impossibility' (Gasché's phrase) that both enable such reflection and render it finally 'undecidable' in terms of any adequate philosophical grounding.

We can shortly return to his essay 'The Concept of Irony' and see just how de Man establishes this distance from a thematics of the self-reflexive text, or of irony conceived in subjective or existential terms. I want to suggest also that this move entails a curiously partial treatment of Kierkegaard, an approach to the ethics of reading that manages to bypass, ignore or short-circuit Kierkegaard's prolonged meditations on the topic. What occurs in de Man's essay — as in much of his later writing — is a wholesale reduction of ethical questions to the level of a generalized tropology, a field of rhetorical drives, substitutions and displacements which are taken to define the limiting conditions of this or any discourse. Romantic irony becomes, in one of de Man's most cryptic formulations, the 'permanent parabasis of the allegory of tropes' (*CI*, p. 33). This leads to an avoidance of ethical reflection in any but the most oblique and attenuated sense, an ethics — in so far as that term still applies — that would leave no room for autonomy, self-determination, moral choice, human agency or other such 'subjectivist' notions. I shall argue, in short, that de Man's essay avoids any serious engagement with Kierkegaard because it seeks to pass directly from the topic of romantic irony to a reformulation of this topic in purely fictive, tropological or linguistic terms. But this can only be achieved in so far as ethics becomes just the name for a certain, albeit highly sophisticated practice of reading, one that obeys the deconstructionist imperative to take nothing on trust and attend always to the letter of the text.

Hillis Miller has developed this line of argument in a recent book much influenced by de Man's late essays. There is, Miller writes, 'a necessarily ethical moment in [the] act of reading as such, a moment neither cognitive, nor political, nor social, nor interpersonal, but properly and independently ethical'.[21] This moment occurs when reading comes up against stubborn, resistant, or problematic details in the text, details one is tempted to ignore or reinterpret in the interests of maintaining coherence and sense. It is the mark of an 'ethical' reading, in Miller's understanding of the term, that it should hold out against such easy satisfactions and allow the text to dictate its own terms of understanding, no matter how far these disrupt or complicate our normative habits of response. His book goes on to offer examples of this readerly imperative at work, starting out with Kant (where the stark antinomies of moral law can only find expression in fictive, allegorical or figural terms), and then taking passages from George Eliot, Trollope and Henry James where these novelists reflect on the problem of doing justice to characters, works and events of their own contriving. In each case Miller sets out to show how 'the moral law gives rise by an intrinsic necessity to storytelling, even if that storytelling in one way or another puts in question or subverts the moral law'. (*ER*, p. 2) This interest in the narrative dimension of ethical thinking is one that Miller shares with other current philosophers, among them Bernard Williams and Alasdair MacIntyre.[22] In their case however it serves to envisage a way beyond the conflicts and aporias produced by any system, like Kant's, that sets up a realm of moral absolutes or categorical imperatives divorced from the self-understanding of situated human agents. For Miller, on the contrary, the 'ethics of reading' is a constant reminder of the totally inscrutable, paradoxical or aporetic character of ethical discourse, a lesson that he finds most powerfully stated in Kafka's *The Trial*. From Kafka to Kant is no great distance on Miller's reading, since in Kantian ethics likewise 'it is never possible to be sure that duty is not a fiction in the bad sense of an ungrounded act of self-sustaining language, that is, precisely a vain delusion and chimerical concept, a kind of ghost generated by a sad linguistic necessity' (*ER*, p. 24).

These formulations are clearly much indebted to de Man and his way of recasting ethical issues in a rhetorical, linguistic or tropological register. They show just how far Miller has travelled since his writings of the 1960s, when he could still treat the encounter between critic and text as in some sense a meeting of minds, an attempt to evoke the author's imaginative presence through a species of inward, sympathetic communing. There is no reason to suppose that it was crucially or chiefly his reading of de Man that made this appear henceforth an impossible dream. But in *The Ethics Of Reading* that influence is something like a law for Miller, an overriding instance of the quasi-Kantian imperative that separates the commonplace, naïve pleasures of reading from the duty of subjecting those pleasures to a sternly self-denying ordinance, a critique of the errors that once made them possible. For de Man, he writes,

> ethical obligations, demands, and judgments work in the same way as the court system in *The Trial* works . . . , that is, as one perpetually unverifiable referential dimension of an irresistible law, in de Man's case, a law of language . . . The failure to read or the impossibility of reading is a universal necessity, one moment of which is that potentially aberrant form of language called ethical judgment or prescription. [*ER*, p. 51]

Deconstruction is thus very far from seeking (like Williams or MacIntyre) to restore ethics to a realm of humanly intelligible motives, values and life-forms, a narrative dimension where such issues could

be treated in terms of individual and communal good, and not held
up to some abstract, inscrutable instance of moral law. On the
contrary, it sharpens the Kantian antinomies by presenting them as
so many by-products of a basically linguistic predicament, a perpetual
'interference' (as de Man would have it) between the constative and
performative aspects of language, or the 'grammar' and the 'rhetoric'
of tropes.

Hence the whole series of flatly paradoxical injunctions that run
through Miller's text, asserting both the ultimate 'freedom' of reading
(as an activity bound, in Kantian terms, to accept responsibility for its
own interpretative conduct) and also the absolute, unconditional
necessity that reading should respond to what is there in the text.
Some of Miller's most striking examples are taken from Henry
James's *The Art of the Novel*, where the author revisits his own earlier
productions and muses, with a kind of quizzical detachment, on the
problems of now doing justice to them from a retrospective standpoint. 'What indeed', asks James, 'could be more delightful than to
enjoy a sense of the absolute in such easy conditions? The deviations
and differences might of course not have broken out at all, but from
the moment they began so naturally to multiply they became, as I
say, my very terms of cognition.'[23] These 'deviations and
differences' are those that obtrude between James's desire to make
sense of his novels according to his present recollection of their
themes, style, narrative techniques and so forth, and his discovery —
coming back to them now after so many years — that very often they
don't correspond in the least to what he thinks (or perhaps once
thought) he was trying to do. Thus James's scrupulous practice of
self-criticism becomes a model of the 'ethics of reading' in general,
the duty to suspend our preconceived notions of what a text ought
to mean, and to cultivate instead a sharpened awareness of those
anomalous, disruptive or heterogeneous details that refuse the
consolations of the 'hermeneutic circle'. In Miller's words:

> What is oddest of all about James's testimony to his experience of re-
> reading is the relative value accorded to the two different versions of it.
> One might expect that the positive experience of perfect concordance
> would be the better of the two, since such a fit would positively ratify
> the previous text . . . But no, the experience of discrepancy is the
> exemplary and productive form of reading. [*ER*, p. 117]

And this on the grounds — as de Man would insist — that reading
is properly an 'argument' with the text, a process that cannot be
assimilated to any model of harmonious, inward, or intuitive
understanding, but which none the less stakes its 'ethical' claim on
the will to respect as fully as possible the very 'terms of cognition'
(in James's phrase) that the text proposes. Yet there is no guarantee,
far from it, that those terms will correspond to anything in the nature
of a straightforward ethical expression of intent on the author's part.
For, according to de Man, 'understanding is an epistemological event
prior to being an ethical or aesthetic value'.[24] 'Epistemology' is here
conceived as the product of an all-encompassing rhetoric of tropes, a

'logic' of figural turns and displacements that marks the very limit of intelligible discourse. It is hard to imagine an ethics of reading more completely at odds with traditional ideas of what criticism and scholarship are all about.

We can now return to that essay of de Man on Kierkegaard, having taken a long excursion which I hope the reader will forgive (but not forget). As I have said, it is not really so much an essay 'on' Kierkegaard as a text that invokes his authority in passing ('the best book on irony that's available'), while in fact pursuing the topos of romantic irony in a quite un-Kierkegaardian direction. What de Man sets out to achieve, like Hillis Miller in *The Ethics of Reading*, is the assimilation of ethics to narrative poetics and, beyond that, to a generalized rhetoric of tropes that will deconstruct (or render intensely problematic) any notion of the subject as an autonomous, self-acting, responsible moral agent. The avoidance of Kierkegaard in de Man's essay is more than a casual oversight. It is a symptom of his marked and persistent refusal to envisage any form of ethical discourse that would appeal to some wider, inter-personal or social realm of values.

One might recall, in this connection, Miller's strong desire to establish the credentials of an ethics of reading that would always take priority over politics, history or other such rival claimants. Where these latter kinds of interest are most often 'vague and speculative', a focus on the ethics of reading at least has the virtue, as Miller sees it, of dealing with 'the real situation of a man or woman reading a book, teaching a class, writing a critical essay' (*ER*, p. 4). Yet of course this begs the question of just what constitutes a 'real' situation, since the Marxist or the feminist could easily object that Miller's whole approach is a strategy for evading criticism of the class- or gender-based stereotypes that inform every act of reading. 'No doubt that "situation" spreads out to involve institutional, historical, economic, or political "contexts", but it begins with and returns to the man or woman face to face with the words on the page' (Ibid.). The very structure of this sentence makes it clear that Miller is conceding very little, or offering with one hand what he then promptly takes back with the other. For him, as for de Man, the ethics of reading is an absolute and sovereign imperative, one that 'begins with and returns to . . . the words on the page'. The gist of this sentence is not, I think, seriously distorted by my having left out Miller's reference to 'the man or woman face to face' with those words. For if politics and history are marginalized in the ethical 'moment' of reading, or remain only as 'vague and speculative' contexts, then the same goes for any notion of the situated reader as more than a rhetorical subject-position, a product of the various textual operations that Miller sets out to describe.

De Man's essay on Kierkegaard is a set-piece demonstration of this deconstructive process at work. Its stages of argument may be summarized briefly as follows. Romantic irony (of the kind that Schlegel advocates and Kierkegaard treats with principled mistrust) is envisaged in basically subjective terms, as a specular or self-reflexive movement of thought that cannot be held in check by any method or regulative system of concepts. It is a notion, as we have seen, that provokes real anxiety in critics like Booth, those who are quite happy to write about irony so long as it doesn't overshoot the mark and leave them bereft of adequate signposts. (Leavis on Swift would have offered another example very much to de Man's purpose here.)[25] But to treat it like this — as a matter of 'distance within a self, duplications of a self, specular structures within which the self looks at itself from a certain distance' (*CI*, p. 13) — still leaves the option of recuperating irony in terms of an inward, dialectical progress through stages of increasingly complex self-knowledge. This is where de Man finds fault with those interpreters (like Starobinski and Szondi) who hold out the promise of some ultimate resting-point or moment of 'reconciliation' achieved by the subject in its quest for heightened self-knowledge through the stages of ironic reflection. It is, he writes, a 'common (and morally admirable) mistake', one that answers to a genuine need — a constitutively human desire — for belief in the self as a knowing, will-ing and autonomous agent of meaning and choice. To this extent the partisans of romantic irony are making a 'morally admirable' mistake when they treat it as the 'prefiguration of a future recovery', or 'the reconciliation of the self with the world by means of art' (*RT*, p. 219). They are none the less deluded, de Man argues, in so far as they locate this saving possibility in language itself, or in the power of language to encompass or articulate that self-reflexive movement of thought whereby such reconciliation is thought to occur.

It is evident from what Schlegel has to say on the topic that this process cannot be held in check by any act of self-stabilizing knowledge or control on the ironist's part. 'Contrary to Szondi's assertion, irony is not temporary (*vorläufig*) but repetitive, the recur-rence of a self-escalating act of consciousness' (*RT*, p. 220). Up to this point de Man's interpretation of romantic irony corresponds fairly closely to Kierkegaard's treatment, including his attitude to artist–philosophers like Schlegel, those whose outlook would prevent any serious engagement with ultimate (ethical or religious) questions. Thus they both see nothing but error and delusion in Hegel's idea that the 'unhappy consciousness' can somehow transcend its own predicament, or arrive at a stage where all conflicts and divisions would at last be resolved in the moment of achieved self-knowledge. They are likewise agreed in detecting a form of existential bad faith in that desire to exploit the freedoms of romantic irony while drawing back from its further, more unsettling implications. Thus the exercise 'may start as a casual bit of play with a stray loose end of the fabric, but before long the entire texture of the self is unravelled and comes apart' (*RT*, p. 215). The words are de Man's, from a passage discuss-ing Baudelaire's essay on the French art of caricature, but they could easily be attributed to Kierkegaard. That is to say, they have the tone of a moral injunction, a warning to the aesthete (or the adept of romantic irony) that this may become a dangerous game, one that can 'unravel' our most basic ideas of human dignity and truth.

Where the difference comes in is at the point of ethical reckoning, the point where Kierkegaard renounces irony, or treats it as merely a transitional phase, a stage on the path to that higher, religious wisdom that would have no need for such heuristic devices. Irony is the hallmark of Kierkegaard's pseudonymous productions, those that go various oblique ways around to point up the limits of 'aesthetic' understanding and thus conduct the reader through and beyond that falsely limiting perspective.[26] The result — as in Volume One of *Either/Or* — is to encourage a degree of subjective involvement with the fictional protagonist, his erotic life-style and detached, irresponsible attitude to experience, while at the same time persuading us to view that experience from a different, more critical standpoint. However the irony doesn't stop there, since it applies also to the ethical perspective, the claims of Hegelian *Sittlichkeit*, or civic, institutional morality, advanced by Judge William in Volume Two. Thus the reader is led on to perceive the limitations of that philosophy also, and to enter on the path of religious education that is Kierkegaard's ultimate purpose. Here again we are deluded, or find ourselves reading in bad faith, if we think to have fathomed that purpose as soon as the religious shows up on the horizon of discourse. For Kierkegaard has reserved yet another distinction, that between 'Religiousness A' and 'Religiousness B', the former still caught (or so we are given to understand) within a form of 'immanent' or non-dialectical relation to authentic self-knowledge.[27]

There is no room here for a detailed exposition of the arguments by which Kierkegaard establishes this difference. Very briefly, 'Religiousness A' is an attitude that has progressed so far as to acknowledge the gulf between reason and faith, the secular and the sacred, temporal existence and eternal values. But it does so in the belief that these antinomies might yet be transcended through a movement of thought that 'annihilates' the individual subject and allows him or her to partake of the infinite by adopting (so to speak) a God's eye view. This constitutes an advance over the ethical standpoint in so far as it locates the source of all authentic values in a realm quite separate from the codes and conventions of this or that socio-political order. But it still fails to register what Kierkegaard perceives as the *absolute* disjunction between temporal and eternal values, a distance that cannot be overcome by any power of reflective thought. 'Religiousness A' has this much in common with Hegelian dialectic: it seeks to find a way through and beyond the antinomies of self-conscious spirit, but to do so by collapsing ontological distinctions and reducing the eternal and the infinite to concepts of speculative reason. It therefore remains, in Kierkegaard's terms, a form of 'immanent' thinking, one that would reconcile the disjunct realms of secular and religious value by treating them from the standpoint of a higher wisdom conceived, as it were, *sub specie aeternitatis*.

This is not the case with 'Religiousness B', the position that Kierkegaard adopts in his serious or 'edifying' texts, and which therefore, according to the *The Point of View*, offers the only authentic perspective from which to interpret all his other writings. For now there is no question of consciousness attaining a knowledge of the eternal or the infinite that would bring them within the compass of a purely immanent, speculative reason. Nor is it possible any longer to envisage some form of reconciliation between secular and religious orders of value, or existence in the here-and-now of worldly morality and obedience to the dictates of divine will. 'Religiousness B' is the stage arrived at when the subject acknowledges his or her absolute lack of understanding in the face of such demands; when reason comes up against its limits and no guidance is offered by custom, morality, civic virtue or even the doctrines of received religion. It is the predicament that Kierkegaard presents most starkly in *Fear and Trembling*, his investigative treatment of the parable of Abraham and Isaac.[28] What this episode involves, as he reads it, is not — as in Hegel's account of tragedy — a clash between two great opposing social or ethical codes, such that the protagonist is forced to opt for one and stand condemned by the other. On the contrary, it shows Abraham obeying a divine command that must appear utterly abhorrent according to any conceivable system of human interests or values. So it is with the believer who has attained to 'religiousness B', a faith that goes beyond all rational warrant, that renounces the dictates of social obligation, of ethical conscience and even, at the limit, of religious duty as commonly conceived. For in this harshly paradoxical vision of divine purpose there is no common measure, no point of intersection between the finite and the infinite, that would allow the individual to apply such standards in making some ultimate choice of life.

This seems to me frankly an appalling message and one that could justify any kind of barbarous behavior in the name of religious conviction. My point here is not to defend the upshot of Kierkegaard's tortuous arguments but to show just how different is de Man's way of renouncing the specific temptation presented by a certain understanding of romantic irony. For Kierkegaard, as we have seen, this temptation consists in treating life as an aesthetic phenomenon, a pretext for those intricate evasions of the self that can multiply perspectives beyond all ethical accounting. Yet irony can also be the first step toward confronting this attitude with its own radical insufficiency, and thus beginning the long journey that ends with true religiousness. For de Man, by contrast, what has to be renounced is the notion of irony as a self-reflexive medium, an inward or subjective odyssey of the spirit undertaken in the hope of achieving some higher wisdom. 'It is in this way, to the extent that I have written about the subject, that I have dealt with it myself, so that what I have to say now is in the nature of an auto-critique, since I want to put in question this possibility' (*CI*, p. 14). He will now avoid any hint of that subjective pathos, that residual legacy of Hegel's 'unhappy consciousness' that clings to the treatment of romantic irony in his own previous writings. But with de Man, this leads in nothing like the same direction as Kierkegaard's path of deepening inwardness and authentic self-knowledge. What replaces the reflexive or specular reading of romantic irony is a throughgoing textualist 'rhetoric of tropes', a project that seeks to undo such illusory ideas by explaining them as figments of a purely *linguistic* process, one that will always have accounted in advance for the movements of self-conscious thought.

Thus when de Man, like Miller, comes to argue for a so-called 'ethics of reading', he does so in terms that could scarcely be further removed from Kierkegaard's account of the ethical stage. It becomes, in short, a deconstructionist variant on the Kantian categorical imperative: to read or interpret always in such a way that the upshot of one's choices will be inscribed in a rhetorically undecidable (or aporetic) scene of instruction. According to de Man, it is only through a species of self-mystifying 'blindness' — a refusal to acknowledge the fictive or tropological aspect of all understanding — that the self can narrate such exemplary tales for its own subsequent edification. A work like *The Point of View* would then be able to claim no special authority, no warrant for distinguishing the 'aesthetic' works from those other portions of Kierkegaard's authorship (itself included) which ask to be read in a different, more 'serious' or self-authenticating mode. Such distinctions would be wholly undermined by de Man's argument — as pursued, for instance, in his reading of Rousseau's *Confessions* — that autobiographical or truth-telling narratives are always caught up in a fictive situation beyond their power to determine or control. Thus 'the more there is to expose, the more there is to be ashamed of; the more resistance to exposure, the more satisfying the scene, and, especially, the more satisfying and eloquent the belated revelation, in the later narrative, of the inability to reveal'.[29]

It is not hard to see how the strategies deployed in this reading of Rousseau might apply to the entire life's work that Kierkegaard describes in *The Point of View*. Such an account would begin by suspending the difference between 'aesthetic', 'ethical' and 'religious' productions; go on to analyse the complex patterns of fictive or rhetorical self-justification involved in Kierkegaard's 'edifying' works; and end by asserting the 'undecidability' of any text that purports to speak the truth of an author's intentions from some retrospective viewpoint of superior inwardness or self-understanding. De Man does precisely this in his chapter on Rousseau, and it is an approach which, as I have argued elsewhere, does much to complicate and problematize the nature of Kierkegaard's confessional project. In particular it throws a very different light on his account of the break with his fiancée Regine Olsen, a break that Kierkegaard wants us to interpret as an act of willed renunciation, carried out in the service of a higher (religious) duty which already demanded the setting aside of all secular, domestic or erotic attachments.[30] Everything would ultimately find its place in this providential narrative, not only Kierkegaard's 'aesthetic' productions but also those episodes in his life that partook of a likewise duplicitous, roundabout or seemingly unprincipled character. To de Man's way of thinking, on the contrary, there is no reason why we should ascribe this truth-telling status to *The Point of View* or any other of Kierkegaard's first-person 'edifying' discourses. They must all be seen as equally entangled in a process of self-generating narrative excuses and justifications which far outruns any straightforward, honest version of events.

What de Man has to say about Rousseau's treatment of Marion (the servant girl whom he falsely accused of stealing a ribbon, and whose life was apparently ruined in consequence) could just as well apply to Kierkegaard's tortuous account of his reasons for breaking with Regine. One need only transpose the names and relevant details to see how closely such a reading would fit. Thus:

> What Rousseau [Kierkegaard] *really* wanted is neither the ribbon nor Marion [neither marriage nor Regine], but the public scene of exposure which he actually gets . . . This desire is truly shameful, for it suggests that Marion was destroyed [or Regine abandoned], not for the sake of [his] saving face . . . but merely in order to provide him with a stage on which to parade his disgrace, or, what amounts to the same thing, to furnish him with a good ending for Book II of his *Confessions* [or suitable material for *The Point of View* and its kindred works]. [AR, p. 285]

This account, for all its seeming perversity, would follow quite logically from de Man's deconstructionist premises. These derive in turn from his reduction of the self to a product of those purely rhetorical drives, substitutions and displacements that constitute the field of subjective knowledge and desire. This is why the late essay on Kierkegaard offers such a useful point of entry into de Man's thinking. For it is here that we find his most explicit rejection, not only of romantic irony in its self-reflexive or specular form, but of any attempt, like Kierkegaard's, to move beyond it in the direction of a deeper, more authentic understanding. The essay makes it clear that de Man regards this as simply one more strategy of evasion, adopted in order to safeguard the self against a knowledge that would otherwise subvert its claims to freewill or ethical accountability.

When de Man here signals the shift of emphasis in his own work he is referring to those essays in *Blindness and Insight*, especially 'The Rhetoric of Temporality', where irony figures (along with metonymy and allegory) as a means of deconstructing the privileged truth-claims vested in the ideas of symbol and metaphor. What the former pair have in common is a power of resisting the drive toward premature totalization, the desire for a language that would actually achieve the consummate union of subject and object, mind and nature, time and eternity envisaged by the poets and their mainstream interpreters. To acquiesce in such claims is a kind of hermeneutic bad faith, a failure to perceive what language inevitably reveals in its moments of un-self-deluding insight. Metonymy, for instance, achieves this effect by stressing the contingent, material or context-bound aspects of linguistic production, those elements of meaning that cannot be subsumed within a high-romantic ethos of metaphor and symbol. (De Man's pages on Proust in *Allegories of Reading* offer perhaps the most striking example of what happens when this process gets under way.) Irony exhibits this demystifying power raised to its highest degree, since here there is no question of halting the process, arresting it (as critics like Booth would wish) at a point where meaning might yet coincide with the wishes, intentions or conscious design of a self-possessed authorial subject.

This is why irony figures as the 'tropes of tropes', the name of that disruptive drift within language that opens up a movement beyond reach of critical recuperation. Thus 'ironic language', in de Man's words,

> splits the subject into an empirical self that exists in a state of inauthenticity and a self that exists only in the form of a language that asserts the knowledge of this inauthenticity. This does not, however, make it into an authentic language, for to know inauthenticity is not the same as to be authentic. [*RT*, p. 214]

Already, as this passage makes clear, de Man thinks of consciousness as caught up within an all-encompassing system of tropes, one that entirely governs its field of operation and permits of no appeal to some higher, more privileged form of understanding. But he makes the point, here as elsewhere in *Blindness and Insight*, in a language that still carries overtones of loss, self-division and the sorrow that inheres in this state of unhappy consciousness. That is to say, de Man's rhetoric somewhat undermines his argument that 'authentic' self-knowledge is forever beyond reach, so that criticism had better accept this fact and not treat it as further cause for an existential brooding on finitude, mortality or the limits of language and thought. At this point there remains at least the hint of a nostalgic backward glance to that imaginary realm where meaning and consciousness had not yet come apart, and where the 'empirical self' — now condemned to exist in bad faith — might once have found utterance in a language adequate to its own expressive purposes. Although de Man very forcefully rejects this idea, his language contrives to suggest it none the less through its recourse to a Kierkegaardian idiom of 'authentic' versus 'inauthentic' states of awareness. These terms cannot entirely avoid the implication that genuine self-knowledge is indeed possible, even if, as de Man argues, the end-point of such knowledge is to bring home the fact of its existing only as a wishful illusion brought about by effects of language.

In 'The Concept of Irony' de Man turns aside from Kierkegaard to Fichte, in whose work he finds an exemplary attempt to account for the self and its modes of experience in purely linguistic or tropological terms. The commonplace version of Fichte's role in post-Kantian philosophy would go roughly as follows. Kant's great claim was to have offered a solution to the problem of epistemological scepticism by showing (as against radical empiricists like Hume or radical idealists like Berkeley) that there could, indeed must, be some ultimate correspondence between sensuous intuitions on the one hand and a priori concepts of pure understanding on the other. Philosophers had run into a blind alley by asking the wrong sorts of question, by thinking that since all knowledge of the world was mediated by our own perceptions, concepts and categories, therefore we could never hope to have more than a subjective or prison-house view of external reality. Kant's 'Copernican revolution' in the history of thought was to turn the telescope around, so to speak, and ask what exactly were the powers and limits of human cognitive grasp. Philosophy would then have its work cut out in establishing those facts of intersubjective experience (time, space, causality etc.) that were given in the form of synthetic a priori knowledge, and were therefore beyond all reasonable doubt for us as human knowers. Ontological questions, or the old anxiety as to what actually existed 'out there', could be treated as a world well lost in comparison to this new-found role for philosophy as an enterprise grounded in the nature of human understanding and the communal pursuit of truth. Indeed, Kant argued, such anxieties could only be misplaced, since it didn't make sense for us as rational subjects to doubt the evidence of our sensuous cognitions and the concepts under which they must be brought in order to constitute an intelligible world of experience. 'Concepts without intuitions are empty; intuitions without concepts are blind.' Thus Kant thought to bring about a shift of perspective that would render any radical scepticism henceforth unthinkable.

Subsequent thinkers, chief among them Fichte, Schelling and Hegel, professed themselves wholly unconvinced by this Kantian solution. For there was, as they remarked, a very sizable gap between Kant's rigorous 'transcendental deduction' of the concepts and categories presupposed in all forms of synthetic a priori knowledge, and his insistence — as a matter of commonsense necessity — that these must possess some ultimate truth-to-reality as given in the form of sensuous intuitions.[31] Hegel would eventually develop this critique into a full-scale phenomenology of mind or spirit, a dialectical account of how consciousness had passed through various, increasingly complex forms of mediated thought and perception, beginning at the level of primitive sense-certainty and ending with the advent of an Absolute Reason that subsumed and transcended this entire pre-history. Before him, Fichte and Schelling had grasped the two opposite horns of the Kantian dilemma, with Fichte adopting an extreme subjectivist viewpoint while Schelling expounded a quasi-objective 'dialectics of nature'. It thus remained for Hegel to synthesize these twin extremes into a philosophy that claimed to reconcile such bad antinomies by grasping their emergence, so to speak, from inside — through an effort of narrative reconstruction — and then coming out on the high plateau of Absolute Reason. Such is at least the commonplace or text-book account of German idealist thinking in the wake of Kant's critical philosophy.

De Man thinks this a mistaken reading, especially as regards Fichte and his supposedly 'subjectivist' re-processing of issues in the Kantian philosophy of mind.[32] 'Fichte is not essentially to be thought of as the philosopher of the self, if we think of the self (as we necessarily have to) in terms of a dialectic of subject and object, a polarity of self and other' (*CI*, p. 18). Our need to think in these terms is deeply bound up with our desire to conserve some privileged position for the knowing, willing, self-acting subject of Western humanist discourse. It is not — as de Man readily admits — just one position among others, a viewpoint that we might be brought to abandon by reflecting more closely on the self's involvement with structures of linguistic predication. Still there is also a need — even, as de Man would have it, a kind of ethical imperative — to subject such ideas to the undeceiving rigour of a full-scale tropological analysis. This is what Fichte most strikingly performs in his treatment of the self and its modes of experience as subject-positions that exist solely by virtue of their place within a pre-given structure of linguistic possibility. Thus:

> the self is for Fichte the beginning of a logical development, the develop-ment of a logic, and as such has nothing to do with the experiential or the phenomenological self in any form, or at least not originally, not first of all. It is the ability of language to posit, the ability of language to *setzen*, in German. It is the catachresis, the ability of language catachretically to name anything, by false usage, but to name and thus to posit anything language is willing to posit. [*CI*, p. 19]

This passage will strike a familiar note for anyone acquainted with other late texts by de Man. It is the idea of language as possessing a certain impersonal, machine-like quality, a power to generate meaning-effects that appear wholly devoid of intentional significance (whether 'conscious' or 'unconscious'), and that seemingly function in a realm quite apart from human agency or will. Elsewhere — as in his essays on Shelley and Walter Benjamin — this issues in a series of bleak pronouncements with regard to the utterly contingent character of language and its resistance to the humanizing pathos sought out by interpreters in the mainstream romantic tradition.[33] What emerges most clearly in 'The Concept of Irony' is the fact that this involves a strategic avoidance of Kierkegaard, or a reading that goes a long way around to contest, subvert or indeed misconstrue the significance of Kierkegaard's work.

For there are aspects of de Man's essay that will cause some surprise to readers of Kierkegaard who take that work at anything like its professed level of argument. One such passage is the curious remark that 'Hegel and Kierkegaard, in a sense, were concerned with dialectical patterns of history, and, somewhat symmetrically to the way it can be absorbed in a dialectic of the self, irony gets interpreted and absorbed within a dialectical pattern of history, a dialectics of history' (*CI*, p. 14). Now of course this reading goes clean against what Kierkegaard advances as his own chief objection to Hegel, namely the tendency of Hegelian dialectic to erect a great edifice of concepts and theory which leaves no room for the individual subject as a thinking, willing and situated agent who must ultimately bear full responsibility for his or her choices of existence. Why should de Man ignore this difference — fundamental as it is to all of Kierkegaard's writings — and instead try to level him with Hegel as a thinker in the German idealist line of all-embracing speculative thought? (One might note, in this connection, his curious slip in 'The

Rhetoric of Temporality' (p. 209) where de Man lists Kierkegaard along with Schlegel, Solger and E.T.A. Hoffman as notable exponents of romantic irony in the *German* philosophical tradition.) I think the main reason is de Man's determination to allow for only two possible paths of development in the wake of Kantian philosophy. One leads through Schlegel (or a certain prevalent misreading of Schlegel) to the modern idea of romantic irony as a self-reflexive or specular play with the boundless possibilities of meaning and knowledge. The other is that line of more rigorous demystifying insight that results from a proper (deconstructive or rhetorical) reading of figures like Schlegel and Fichte. De Man himself, as we have seen, moves across from the one to the other of these two ways of reading: from 'The Rhetoric of Temporality' where irony is still treated as to some extent an inward, even tragic disjunction between meaning and intent, to a text like 'The Concept of Irony' where he makes every effort to conceal or to sublimate the signs of this residual pathos. What he cannot entertain is the alternative presented by a thinker like Kierkegaard, one for whom the limits of romantic irony point toward a wholly different understanding of the self in its relation to ultimate issues of ethical and religious choice.

Hence, I would suggest, the curious avoidance of any close engagement with Kierkegaard's thought in an essay that ostensibly promises just such a reading. Kierkegaard was 'unfair' to Schlegel, de Man thinks, but not in quite the way that Barthelme suggests in his story of that title. His unfairness had to do with his treating Schlegel as a proponent of romantic irony in its inward, subjective or specular guise: as a movement of multiplied reflective doubling or infinite regress within the self that would (so to speak) make a mockery of all authentic or responsible self-knowledge. In de Man's version, what Kierkegaard ignores — what he has to ignore, given his own commitments — is that other, more unsettling aspect of Schlegel's thought that reduces the self (as in Fichte's system) to a product of purely linguistic structures and tropes. 'Friedrich Schlegel's interpreters have all felt this, which is why all of them, including Kierkegaard, have had to invoke history . . . as a means of defense against this irony' (*CI*, p. 43). What de Man is alluding to here is Kierkegaard's argument, in *The Concept of Irony*, that certain thinkers are historically justified in having resort to such duplicitous strategies, while others lack this justification on account of their untimely, belated or anachronistic status. Thus:

> Socratic irony is valid because Socrates, like Saint John, heralds the arrival of Christ, and as such he came at the right moment. Whereas Friedrich Schlegel, or the German ironists his contemporaries, were not at the right moment. The only reason that they are to be discarded is because they were out of joint with the movement of history, which for Kierkegaard remains the final instance to which one has to resort in order to evaluate. So irony is secondary to a historical system. [*CI*, p. 41]

This assumes, as in the passage quoted above, that Kierkegaard is working with a broadly Hegelian concept of history, one in which thinkers are 'timely' (or otherwise) according to the progress of a world-historical spirit whose stages determine what shall count, from age to age, as valid or authentic thought. For Kierkegaard, on the contrary, there is no such appeal to a grand teleological or totalizing movement, whether of the *Zeitgeist* or the march of historical events. Authenticity resides in the self's encounter with various temptations on the path to a knowledge which is always, irreducibly specific to that self, and which cannot be subsumed within any universalist dialectics of history and spirit.

De Man might argue that Kierkegaard is deceiving himself here, and that thinking must always proceed in relation to some existent, ongoing or historically viable system of concepts and categories. But in that case it is de Man and not Kierkegaard who has imposed this requirement, and done so moreover with the object of discrediting Kierkegaard's project from a Hegelian standpoint which de Man thinks just as misguided and open to rhetorical demystification. In short, de Man's strategy is to head off any serious or sustained encounter with Kierkegaard by reading him as caught between two, equally naïve or deluded viewpoints. Either Kierkegaard is a Hegelian *malgré lui*, approving or denouncing ironists like Socrates and Schlegel on grounds of their world-historical pertinence, or he is ultimately a victim of that same romantic irony, that infinite regress of the self-reflexive subject that he thinks to have exposed in philosophers like Schlegel as a symptom of mere bad faith. For de Man, the only way beyond these alternatives is the path that he finds marked out by Fichte, the deconstruction of the self through a rigorous deployment of linguistic and tropological categories. What he simply won't recognize, and what his essay goes to great lengths to circumvent, is Kierkegaard's claim to have shown up the limits of both Hegelian dialectic *and* romantic irony by pursuing a wholly different line of thought. Such thinking would lead not the self's annihilation at the hands of rhetorical analysis but to its reconstitution at a higher, more authentic level of awareness.

There is a revealing passage in de Man's essay where he describes something closely akin to this strategy of evasion. Here, however, it is Schlegel, not Kierkegaard, whose work (as he argues) the critics have consistently ignored or misconstrued in the interests of maintaining their own interpretative mastery.

> It would hardly be hyperbolic to say (and I could defend the affirmation) that the whole discipline of *Germanistik* has developed for the single reason of doging Friedrich Schlegel, of getting around the challenge that Schlegel . . . offers to the whole notion of an academic discipline which would deal with German literature — seriously. [*CI*, pp. 10–11]

That is to say, they have interpreted Schlegel as an exemplar of romantic irony in its self-reflexive or subjectivist mode, a reading that may appear risky to critics like Booth — those who must at all costs stabilize the concept of irony — but which yet carries nothing like the same risks as a full-scale tropological treatment of the theme. Thus de

Man sees the prevalent misreading of Schlegel (and likewise of Fichte) as a symptom of the deep resistance that develops whenever a rigorous reflection on language threatens to subvert the privileged categories of self, experience and the knowing subject. But his own treatment of Kierkegaard exemplifies a similar kind of resistance, in this case a need to avoid thinking 'seriously' about Kierkegaard's arguments and truth-claims, since these represent a radical alternative to what he thinks of as the simply inescapable passage from romantic irony to a deconstructive rhetoric of tropes. To de Man it seems clear that what the mainstream *Germanisten* are avoiding when they refuse to read Schlegel, or when they read him inattentively, is the knowledge that their discipline ultimately rests on unexamined values, mystified beliefs which can muster no defence against Schlegel's kind of undeceiving rhetoric. Yet it is equally the case that de Man can only sustain this argument by excluding from the outset any possibility that Schlegel (or his own version of Schlegel) might not represent the one and only course that criticism can pursue in the wake of romantic irony. The marginalization of Kierkegaard in de Man's essay would then represent a strategic necessity, a willed exclusion that allows him to define 'authentic', rigorous or deconstructive reading as a form of categorical imperative.

De Man leaves us in no doubt that he is playing for high stakes in this attempt to demonstrate how Schlegel's interpreters (Kierkegaard included) have either treated him unfairly or missed the whole point of his writing.

> The best critics who have written on Schlegel, who have recognised his importance, have wanted to shelter him from the accusation of frivolity, which was generally made, but in the process they always have to recover the categories of the self, of history, and of dialectic, which are precisely the categories which in Schlegel are disrupted in a radical way. [*CI*, pp. 39–9]

Still it would be wrong to read this essay as merely a negative exercise, an attempt to dismantle every last notion of truth, authenticity and self-knowledge. While it certainly mounts a resistance to ethics — or to any philosophy, like Kierkegaard's, that would situate the ethical in a realm beyond reach of linguistic or narrative representation — still de Man's project claims to be ultimately an 'ethics of reading'. And in a sense, as Geoffrey Galt Harpham has argued,[34] such resistance is the very condition of ethical thinking, whether conceived in Kantian terms (as an absolute law that constrains the subject to act against his or her immediate desire), or treated as de Man and Miller would have it, as the necessity of a textual reading that 'has to go against the grain of what one would want to happen in the name of what has to happen'.[35] The discourse of ethics has always involved this idea of a split within consciousness itself, a heteronomous compulsion that resists or forbids any straightforward fulfilment of the agent's 'natural' inclinations. Thus Harpham perceives a distinct resemblance between Kant's and de Man's ethical theories. 'Both posit on the one hand a "free" subject who would, if not coerced, follow its "desires"; and on the other, some utter and external rebuke to those desires, whether in the law or in the text' (Harpham, p. 141). To this extent ethics is another name for that moment of ascesis, self-denial or resistance that constitutes the subject as a source of moral laws for its own better guidance or government.

Some philosophers, Aristotle among them, have managed to avoid this predicament by defining virtue as that form of life which permits the individual most fully to realize his or her potential gifts and attributes. This would seem to avoid the repressive hypothesis altogether, since on Aristotle's view the desire to live well, or to order one's life in accordance with the best ethical maxims, is itself a desire that subsumes and transcends all others.[36] Yet Harpham notes an 'intriguing blandness' about Aristotle's treatment of this question, a failure to address 'the difficulty, the crisis in choice, that attends the actual process of ethical decision making' (Harpham, p. 142). He goes on to argue that 'in certain respects, Aristotle's ethics is bound to the pleasure principle, and is barely an ethics at all in de Man's terms'. It is clear from this passage that Harpham takes de Man quite seriously in his claim to locate an ethical moment in the deconstructive reading of texts, a moment of resistance where the reader's desire for hermeneutic mastery or truth comes up against obstacles to its own fulfilment. For Harpham, such resistance is the characterizing mark of all ethical discourse, even where it takes the form — as with thinkers like Nietzsche or Foucault — of a wholesale attack on ethics itself as the mere dissimulation of power-interests masquerading as moral values.[37] The same applies to the Freudian (or indeed the Lacanian) re-writing of ethical categories, where desire can only be defined in relation to that which constrains, limits or represses the fulfilment of desire. Thus, according to Lacan, Kant must take credit for 'liberating ethics from the pleasure principle by driving a wedge between the subject and the moral law', thereby enabling Freud to demonstrate in turn how 'everything that Kant made transcendental lies within the subject as a condition of repression' (cited by Harpham, p. 142).

Harpham's point is that ethical 'resistance' can assume a great variety of forms, among them the resistance to ethics itself, whether in the name of a Nietzschean 'transvaluation of values' or a deconstructive will to problematize language by pointing up its inbuilt conflicts and aporias. It is in this sense, he argues, that deconstruction 'might be seen most profitably, not as a product of ethical reading, but rather as a hyperarticulated instance of ethical discourse' (Harpham, p. 140). Harpham can maintain this position despite all the seeming counter-evidence in de Man's work: his relentless undoing of normative truth-claims, his reduction of the subject to a mere effect of language, his treatment of ethics as one 'discursive mode' among others, a 'linguistic confusion' whose source is to be found in the 'structural interference of two value systems', or of language in its performative and tropological aspects. What ultimately unites de Man with moralists like Kant — or indeed with anti-moralists like

Nietzsche and Foucault, as well as strong revisionists like Freud and Lacan — is the fact that he mounts a resistance to ethics on terms that cannot in the end be other than ethical.

Thus de Man may claim, in a sentence that appears to controvert the whole drift of Harpham's argument, that ethics 'has nothing to do with the will (thwarted or free) of a subject' (*AR*, p. 164). And he adopts this stance, as we have seen, in accordance with his view that the self and its supposed attributes are in fact just the delusive side-effects of a linguistic process that brings them into being through a kind of unwilled, even mechanical necessity. Nothing could be further — or so it might seem — from Harpham's suggestion (as against Aristotle) that ethics must involve some check to the subject's immediate desires, some 'law' whose source may be internalized in the form of a Kantian moral imperative or Freudian superego, but which none the less acts to thwart or constrain the freedom of self-gratifying instinct. Yet Harpham sees this as no obstacle to his reading of de Man as a genuinely ethical thinker.

> Ethics cannot do without the subject any more than it can do without morality. Even de Man finds subjectivity an irresistible temptation, for in another passage . . . he defines reading as a chastening and purging, an 'argument' because 'it has to go against the grain of what one would want to happen in the name of what has to happen' . . . Ethical actions themselves reveal that what one 'wants' can include what one does 'not want' — the weight of necessity, compulsion, obedience to the law. [Harpham, p. 141]

And this despite everything in de Man's late texts that would appear to discountenance such a reading, in particular his treatment of romantic irony as a purely linguistic or tropological phenomenon, having nothing to do with the subjective pathos of a consciousness exposed to inward doubt and self-division. For Harpham, de Man is still an 'ethical' thinker in so far as he exemplifies the moment of ascesis, of self-denying critical rigour, that has marked the discourse of ethical philosophy from Socrates to Kant and the present.[38]

Deconstruction should therefore be seen (he argues) not as a radical break with this tradition but as striving to articulate the same questions in a textual or rhetorical mode. This applies even to those passages where de Man talks of reading as an 'impossible' activity, or of ethics as resulting from the 'structural interference of two value systems'. For his language remains very much in the grip of that 'ascetic imperative', or self-denying drive, whose exemplars range from the Christian desert fathers to those proponents of a modern 'hermeneutics of suspicion' which defines itself expressly against all forms of premature knowledge or truth-claim. If resistance is impossible in the absence of desire, then equally it is the case that desire cannot function without some resistance, some opposing force against which to measure its strength. Thus a proper genealogy of ethics, as Harpham conceives it, would proceed from the premise that 'the subject itself has a self-interfering, self-resisting, self-overcoming ethical "thickness", and that the moral law or the inhumanity of the text is no more external to the subject than are its "desires" (Harpham, p. 141). From this point of view deconstruction would stand as one more instance of the 'ascetic imperative', the law that identifies resistance to desire as the precondition of ethics, but which also defines ethics itself as the desire to resist its own more generalized or blandly accommodating precepts. As de Man puts it: 'nothing can overcome the resistance to theory since theory *is* itself this resistance'.[39] What Harpham seeks to do is transpose de Man's argument from a textualist to an ethical register, or — more precisely — establish the point that such talk of 'resistance' only makes sense as a form of ascetic imperative.

I think there is some truth in Harpham's claim, although its bearing on de Man's work remains, to say the least, highly problematic. For what can be the status of an ethics (even an 'ethics of reading') that reduces all questions of truth, responsibility and self-knowledge to a play of rhetorical codes and figurations; that rejects any appeal to human agency or will as inherently self-deluding for the same reason; and that always arrives at a stage of ultimate undecidability where the 'structural interference' of two linguistic codes is the end-point of ethical reflection? For de Man, as for Miller, it is precisely this ability to block or suspend our more habitual, commonplace habits of judgment that gives deconstruction its properly ethical force. Thus, in Harpham's words, 'ethics may suspend choice, may resist settled determinations, may remain content with articulating the issue; this is in fact the spirit in which ethical philosophers refuse to prescribe values' (Harpham, p. 144). One might compare de Man's allegories of textual 'unreadability' with the principle (widespread among contemporary philosophers) that ethics has to do with the analysis of concepts, value-terms and forms of moral argument, rather than with offering specific judgments on this or that moral issue. But Harpham himself goes on to point out the most obvious problem with any such self-denying ordinance. What it tends to overlook — or set aside in the interests of philosophic purity and rigour — is that whole dimension of human involvement that gives moral concepts their characteristic 'thickness', or their relevance to the complex situations of everyday life.

In the end it is impossible for ethics to maintain this stance of extreme analytic detachment and at the same time address itself to genuine moral problems. This applies even more to de Man's way of reading, as Harpham pointedly remarks:

> The vexation many feel about deconstruction is an obscure reflection of the fact that deconstruction is both fanatically ethical and amoral. It does not sufficiently credit the drive for interpretation which literature also stimulates, and in fact treats this drive as though it were unethical and should therefore be resisted. What we prize most in literature may be, as I suggested, its 'unreadability'. But if literature were only unreadable, it would remain at the margins of human interest, in the position which deconstruction proudly cultivates. [Harpham, p. 144]

This seems to me an admirably clear-headed statement, but one that goes further than Harpham might wish toward questioning the ethical claims of deconstruction as argued by de Man or Hillis Miller. Their work may articulate that moment of resistance or ascesis which has always, according to Harpham, characterized the discourse of ethical philosophy. But it does so precisely by excluding all reference to those thematic, historical or 'moral' concerns that provide the only possible point of contact between ethics and lived experience.

Thus the question (as de Man puts it in his essay on Proust) is 'precisely whether a literary text is *about* that which it describes, represents, or states' (*AR*, p. 57). His answer is of course a categorical negative: in so far as a text is 'about' anything, it is an allegory of those conflicts, aporias and blind-spots that mark the 'structural interference' of linguistic codes. This attitude is carried across with unrelenting rigour into de Man's various cryptic pronouncements on the 'ethics of reading'. His object is always to block any appeal to the text's thematic or experiential content by establishing the maximum possible distance between constative and performative, grammatical and rhetorical modes of understanding. Such, we may recall, is de Man's reading of the Marion episode in Rousseau's *Confessions*, where it finally appears 'that the entire construction of drives, substitutions, repressions, and representations is the aberrant, metaphorical correlative of the absolute randomness of language, prior to any figuration or meaning' (*AR*, p. 299). There is a very sizeable leap of faith from this way of posing the question to anything that would count as ethical discourse in humanly or morally intelligible terms. What de Man has achieved is an emptying-out of ethical categories to the point where they seem entirely disconnected from issues of practical choice and commitment.

This essay started out with Barthelme's question: was Kierkegaard unfair to Schlegel? It concluded (on the evidence of Barthelme's text) that the unfairness was far from one-sided; that romantic irony cannot in the end measure up to those demands placed upon language and narrative by the need for ethical self-knowledge. In de Man, the passage through and beyond romantic irony took the form of a rhetorical imperative, a will to demystify that language of authentic inwardness and truth that Kierkegaard so strenuously sought to achieve. I have suggested furthermore that the avoidance of Kierkegaard — or the very partial reading that de Man offers in the course of his reflections on romantic irony — can be seen as one signpost of the path not taken by current deconstructionist criticism. What is now put forward as an 'ethics of reading' is in fact the end-result of a singular resistance to ethics, and one that cannot readily be reclaimed, as Harpham would have it, by viewing such resistance as the precondition of ethical discourse in general. It may be argued, in the words of one recent commentator, that no matter how extreme his self-denying ordinance

de Man never actually left behind 'the wealth of lived experience' . . . For, in pointing to the necessity of renouncing it, he is in fact acknowledging the existence of temptation, and is thus already speaking about it, albeit in a negative manner. The impression of deprivation comes closer, nonetheless, to grasping the quintessence of de Man than a placid acceptance of the extreme ascesis that reigns in his work.[40]

This argument is clearly double-edged in the sense that it has to resist or discount the more unsettling implications of de Man's work in order to present them in humanly or ethically accountable terms. In short, there comes a point where one has to decide between de Man's understanding of his own project and the claims of a different, Kierkegaardian reading that would view that project as a series of increasingly elaborate rhetorical self-evasions.

No doubt it is possible, by treating Kierkegaard as de Man treats Proust or Rousseau, to reduce all his texts (the ethical and religious writings included) to so many allegories of unreadability, caught up in a self-deconstructive movement beyond their own power to command or control. What is more, this approach could claim, as de Man always does, to respect the very strictest protocols of textual close-reading, and to operate only with materials provided by the work in hand. In Kierkegaard's case it would involve the decision not to take his edifying motives on trust, but to read his entire life's-work as subject to those eminently deconstructive strategies and ruses that characterize the 'aesthetic' or pseudonymous productions. Of course such a treatment would invite the charge of sheer bad faith, of ignoring Kierkegaard's manifest intentions in pursuit of its own self-promoting puzzles and paradoxes. Then again, it might be said that Kierkegaard's intentions are by no means so obvious or open to view; that his writings, some of them at least, create such obstacles to any straightforward intentionalist account that even his 'serious', first-person statements partake of a radical undecidability. But this argument would need to be carried right through by engaging with the whole elaborate construction of narratives, meta-narratives, retrospective commentary and passages of auto-critique by which Kierkegaard seeks to educate the reader out of his or her 'aesthetic' attitude to life. That is to say, it would have to go far beyond that obsessive concern with romantic irony that Kierkegaard treats as merely one stage on the path to authentic self-knowledge. For otherwise, as I have argued, the 'ethics of reading' will encounter no resistance — no properly *ethical* resistance — in its passage from the giddying extremes of romantic irony to a thoroughgoing deconstructive rhetoric of tropes.

References

1. Donald Barthelme, 'Kierkegaard Unfair to Schlegel', in *Sixty Stories*, G.P. Putnam's Sons, New York, (1981), pp. 160–8. Hereafter cited in the text as Barthelme.
2. My thanks to Tom Keenan and Andrzej Warminski for supplying a typescript copy of this essay, transcribed from a lecture given by de Man at Ohio State University, Columbus, Ohio, on 4 April 1977, hereafter cited in the text as *CI*. There are plans for publishing at least one further

posthumous collection of de Man's later work, so this essay — or some edited version of it — may yet appear in print.

3. Soren Kierkegaard, *The Concept of Irony*, Lee M. Capel (trans.), Bloomington, Indiana University Press, (1968).

4. See Friedrich Schlegel, *'Lucinde' and the Fragments*, Peter Firchow (trans.), Minneapolis, University of Minnesota Press, (1971). De Man also cites Schlegel, *Dialogue on Poetry and Literary Aphorisms*, Ernst Behler and Roman Struc (trans.), University Park and London, Pennsylvania State University Press, (1968).

5. See especially Mikhail Bakhtin, *Rabelais and his World*, Cambridge, Mass, Harvard University Press, (1968).

6. Christopher Norris, 'Fictions of Authority: narrative and viewpoint in Kierkegaard's writing', in *The Deconstructive Turn: essays in the rhetoric of philosophy*, London, Methuen, (1983), pp. 85–106. The reader will note that I have here pursued a different line (more honestly, changed my mind) on a number of crucial issues.

7. See Kierkegaard, *Either/Or, Vols. I and II*, David F. Swenson and Lillian Marvin Swenson (trans.), New Jersey, Princeton University Press, (1971).

8. Kierkegaard, *The Point of View for my Work as an Author*, Walter Lowrie (trans.), London and New York, Oxford University Press, (1939).

9. Wayne Booth, *A Rhetoric of Irony*, Chicago, University of Chicago Press, (1974) p. 59, n. 14. Cited by de Man, *CI*, p. 7.

10. Translated as 'On Incomprehensibility' in Firchow (op. cit.), pp. 257–71.

11. The reference is to Northrop Frye, *Anatomy of Criticism*, Princeton NJ, Princeton University Press, (1957), p. 40.

12. See especially Rodolphe Gasché, *The Tain of the Mirror: Derrida and the philosophy of reflection*, Cambridge, Mass., Harvard University Press, (1986).

13. See for instance Geoffrey Hartman, *Beyond Formalism*, New Haven, Yale University Press, (1970) and J. Hillis Miller, 'The Geneva School', *Critical Quarterly*, Vol. VIII (1966), pp. 305–21.

14. This shift of emphasis can be seen most clearly in transitional works like Hartman's *'The Fate of Reading' and other essays*, Chicago, University of Chicago Press, (1975) and Miller's *Thomas Hardy: distance and desire*, Cambridge, Mass., Harvard University Press, (1970).

15. Paul de Man, *Blindness and Insight: essays in the rhetoric of contemporary criticism*, 2nd edn., revised and enlarged, Minneapolis, University of Minnesota Press, (1983).

16. de Man, 'The Rhetoric of Temporality', in *Blindness and Insight* (op. cit.), pp. 187–228; p. 219. Hereafter cited in the text as *RT*.

17. de Man, *Allegories of Reading: figural language in Rousseau, Nietzsche, Rilke, and Proust*, New Haven, Yale University Press, (1979).

18. Gasché, *The Tain of the Mirror* (op. cit.).

19. Ibid, p. 239.

20. Ibid, p. 6.

21. J. Hillis Miller, *The Ethics of Reading*, New York, Columbia University Press, (1987). Hereafter cited in the text as *ER*.

22. See for instance Bernard Williams, *Ethics and the Limits of Philosophy*, Cambridge, Mass., Harvard University Press, (1986) and Alasdair MacIntyre, *After Virtue: a study in moral theory*, London, Duckworth, (1985).

23. Henry James, *The Art of the Novel: critical prefaces*, Boston: Northeastern University Press, (1984), pp. 336–7. Cited by Miller, *ER*, p. 117.

24. de Man, 'Foreword' to Carol Jacobs, *The Dissimulating Harmony*, Baltimore, Johns Hopkins University Press, (1978), pp. vii–xiii.

25. Thus Leavis on Swift: 'The dispassionate, matter-of-fact tone induces a

feeling and a motion of assent, while the burden, at the same time, compels the feelings appropriate to rejection, and in the contrast — the tension a remarkably disturbing energy is generated . . . If Swift does for a moment appear to settle down to a formula it is only in order to betray; to induce a trust in the solid ground before opening the pitfall' (F.R. Leavis, *Revaluation*, London, Chatto and Windus, (1958), pp. 73–87. Leavis is much happier with Pope, whom he takes to represent 'an Augustanism of the most positive kind', one that appeals to eighteenth-century social and moral certitudes, and which thus provides the critic with a bedrock of assurance, even where the satire is pushed to an otherwise unnerving extreme. (Leavis, 'The Dunciad', *Revaluation*, pp. 88–96).

26. For a perceptive survey of these writings see Mark C. Taylor, *Kierkegaard's Pseudonymous Authorship*, Princeton NJ, Princeton University Press, (1975).

27. See Kierkegaard, *Concluding Unscientific Postscript*, Walter Lowrie (ed.), David F. Swenson (trans.), Princeton NJ, Princeton University Press, (1941).

28. Kierkegaard, *Fear and Trembling*, Walter Lowrie (trans.), New York, Anchor Books, (1954).

29. de Man, 'Excuses (*Confessions*)', in *Allegories of Reading* (op. cit.), pp. 278–301. Hereafter cited in the text as *AR*.

30. On this episode and its treatment in Kierkegaard's writing, see Josiah Thompson, *Kierkegaard*, New York, Alfred A. Knopf, (1973).

31. See Peter Dews, *Logics of Disintegration: post-structuralist thought and the claims of theory*, London, Verso, (1987) for a reading of Fichte, Schelling and others in the post-Kantian tradition that differs from de Man's on just about every major point.

32. De Man refers mainly to Fichte's *Grundlage der gesamten Wissenschaftslehre* (1974), translated by Peter Heath and John Lachs as *The Science of Knowledge*, Cambridge, Cambridge University Press, (1982).

33. See de Man, 'Shelley Disfigured', in *The Rhetoric of Romanticism*, New York, Columbia University Press, (1984), pp. 93–123 and 'Walter Benjamin's "The Task of the Translator"', in *The Resistance to Theory*, Minneapolis, University of Minnesota Press, (1986), pp. 73–93.

34. Geoffrey Galt Harpham, 'Language, History, and Ethics', *Raritan*, Vol. VII, No. 2 (1987), pp. 128–46.

35. de Man, 'Foreword' to Carol Jacobs, *The Dissimulating Harmony* (op. cit.), p. xi.

36. For a strongly-argued modern defence of Aristotelian ethics, see Alasdair MacIntyre, *After Virtue* (op. cit.).

37. See for instance Michel Foucault, *Language, Counter-Memory, Practice*, Donald F. Bouchard and Sherry Simon (trans.), Ithaca, Cornell University Press, (1977).

38. These ideas are developed most impressively in Harpham's recent book, *The Ascetic Imperative in Culture and Criticism*, Chicago, University of Chicago Press, (1987).

39. de Man, *The Resistance to Theory* (op. cit.), p. 19.

40. Minae Mizumura, 'Renunciation', in Peter Brooks, Shoshana Felman and J. Hillis Miller (eds), *The Lesson of Paul de Man*, Yale French Studies, No. 69, (1985), pp. 81–97.

7 Deconstruction against itself: Derrida and Nietzsche

One can best take stock of Derrida's recent work by asking what resistance it offers to the kinds of appropriative reading that Derrida has suffered at the hands of (some, not all) American deconstructionists. That is: how far does it go along with the idea of deconstruction as a species of unlimited textual 'freeplay', a break with all the rules and protocols that have so far governed the activity of interpretation? These questions are raised most explicitly through Derrida's address, in *The Ear of the Other*, to the problem of interpreting Nietzsche, in particular those aspects of Nietzsche that lent themselves to the purposes of Nazi ideology.[1] Shall we say (with Nietzsche's defenders) that his texts were subject to a gross misreading and distortion, a treatment that wrenched certain passages out of context and produced a caricature of their 'true' meaning? Or must we concede to his detractors the fact that those texts were, after all, uniquely available for just such a reading; that they did in some way rehearse or prefigure the construction placed upon them by Nazi thinkers? Derrida rejects any simplified response to these questions that would either make Nietzsche directly responsible for subsequent uses of his teaching, or — on the other hand — dismiss them as so many mere misreadings or perversions, unrelated to what Nietzsche genuinely thought. Such arguments ignore the many passages (in *Ecco Homo* especially) where Nietzsche reflects on the 'untimely' character of his writing, the absence of fit readers in his own time and the need to project his meaning forward into an always uncertain and provisional future. Clearly there was no way of knowing in advance what political programme might find a pretext in Nietzsche's meditations on history, culture and the destiny of civilization. His writings are 'speculative' in a sense unthinkable to philosophers like Hegel, those who speculate only with the purpose of reducing all past or future events to an order of self-present meaning. If Nietzsche's texts have a stake in their own future reading, it is only on this condition: that they take their chance with interpreters of a radically revisionist mind whose construals can never be definitively ruled out of court.

But this is not to say, as Derrida has too often been taken as saying, that there can henceforth be no constraints on the activity of textual interpretation. If his project were indeed reducible to this message of 'anything goes', then it would merit all the charges of irresponsibility, game-playing nihilism and so forth, brought against it by critics and philosophers of an orthodox persuasion. By taking Nietzsche as a test-case — and more specifically, Nietzsche as putative source and inspiration of Nazi ideology — Derrida is confronting these charges at their most forceful and extreme. For there is one version of Nietzsche that has proved highly acceptable to the adepts of deconstruction, including (previously) Derrida himself. This is the 'rhetorical' Nietzsche, arch-debunker of Western metaphysics, he who undermined the truth-claims of philosophy from Socrates to Hegel by insisting that all concepts came down to metaphors in the end; that 'truth' itself was merely a product of our willing bewitchment by language, or our subjection to the vast, unrecognized powers of tropological persuasion.[2] By reading selectively and concentrating on those aspects of his work apparently least compromised by subsequent events — avoiding such dangerous themes as Eternal Recurrence and the Will to Power — a case could be made for the 'new' Nietzsche as herald of this far-reaching textual revolution.

Such was the message in the closing paragraph of Derrida's 'Structure, Sign and Play', the text most often cited by Anglo-American converts to the cause.[3] Nietzsche is there invoked as the first Western thinker to have broken decisively with that age-old 'metaphysics of presence', that logocentric dream of origins and truth whose influence extends, so Derrida argues, to the work of classic structuralist masters like Claude Lévi-Strauss. The alternative is Nietzsche's antinomian vision of a writing and reading practised in the full knowledge of its freedom from all such regulative concepts and constraints. No longer turned back toward some 'transcendental signified' or moment of authentic truth — a notion that persists through all the variants of structuralist theory — language would henceforth rejoice in its openness to a potentially infinite play of figural tropes and substitutions. This explains the marked tonings of apocalypse in 'Structure, Sign and Play', a rhetoric that suggests the strange, the as-yet unthinkable prospects to be glimpsed in the reading of Nietzsche's untimely meditations. Hence also the marked appeal of this text for literary critics who were already looking for a more adventurous hermeneutic model, a release from the protocols of 'old' New Critical method and style.[4] That deconstruction in America took the path of textual 'freeplay' and became most strikingly a liberation-movement among literary theorists — albeit with important exceptions like Paul de Man — is understandable given this background of vested academic interests.

Meanwhile Derrida has taken to dividing his time between Paris and America, a fact of more than merely topographical significance. In France his main involvement since the mid-1970s has been with a group of philosophers and activist intellectuals concerned to analyse the relation between teaching and various forms of state and institutional power.[5] In America — despite his repeated avowals to the contrary — Derrida's work is still regarded for the most part as the *ne plus ultra* of a 'textualist' radicalism indifferent to all such wider political issues. He has never gone so far as to repudiate either 'American deconstruction' or those passages in his work that gave rise to this flourishing offshoot. But he has signalled his distance from it in a series of recent texts (including *The Ear of the Other*) that emphasize the need for deconstruction to engage with matters of direct political concern.

It is this context that one has to bear in mind when assessing Derrida's distinct change of tack on the topic of Nietzsche and the politics of reading. For deconstruction has likewise had to take its chance with the process of translation into a language, a culture and an academic discourse attuned to very different values and priorities. Certainly Derrida is in no strong position to determine what shall count as a proper or duly authorized use of his texts. So when Derrida reflects on Nietzsche's treatment at the hands of his latter-day exegetes — on the question how far, and in what precise sense, an author may be held accountable for readings of his work — these issues have an obvious bearing on the deconstructionist enterprise. The Nietzschean doctrine of Eternal Recurrence is one way to conceive how a teaching might at once be subject to wholly unpredictable uses and yet, in some sense, specifically lay itself open to just such a history of variant interpretations. 'By definition, it cannot let itself be heard or understood in the present; it is untimely, differant, anachronistic. Yet, since this news repeats an affirmation, since it affirms the return, the rebeginning, and a certain kind of reproduction that preserves whatever comes back, then its very logic must give rise to a magisterial institution' (*EO*, p. 20). In Nietzsche's case, this 'institution' takes the form of a future history whose shape is darkly prefigured in texts which both solicit and actively disclaim what will later be made of them. For deconstruction, one could say, the issue is caught up in a similar logic of delayed after-effects where no amount of canny prevision on Derrida's part can fend off 'unauthorized' readings. Yet he, no less than Nietzsche, has to acknowledge some peculiar stake in a movement that is associated with his name, and whose effects on present and future teaching practices he, like Nietzsche, is by no means inclined to underrate. In short, deconstruction affords no easy escape-route from the responsibilities of authorship, despite the widespread misunderstanding which would seek to indict it on precisely those grounds.

It may be, as Derrida has argued elsewhere, that effective communication is never truly guaranteed; that speech-acts function only by virtue of their 'iterability', their readiness for use in any number of possible contexts. The chance of radical misunderstanding would then seem not merely an accident that occasionally befalls language but the very condition of linguistic possibility in something like a Kantian a priori sense. But this — the point at issue in Derrida's well-known exchange with John Searle[6] — cannot (or should not) be taken at face value as a licence for endless interpretative games. While nothing guarantees the passage of 'original' meaning from one context to another — indeed, for that very reason — one still has to ask how it is that language can be open to conflicting interpretations. To fall back on a rhetoric of infinitized 'freeplay' is to ignore the plain fact that texts cannot be made to mean just anything; that conflicts arise precisely where divergent, incommensurable readings each find warrant in 'the words on the page'.

Such has been the case with Nietzsche, his writings acclaimed (or denounced) by thinkers of sharply differing persuasion, all of them able to point to passages that supposedly endorse their reading. This is no accident, Derrida argues, but an effect of the 'destinational structure', the address to an unknown future readership which has left its mark on philosophy at least since Hegel's time. Thus: 'there can always be a Hegelianism of the left and a Hegelianism of the right, a Heideggerianism of the left and a Heideggerianism of the right . . . and even, let us not overlook it, a Marxism of the right and a Marxism of the left. The one can always be the other, the double of the other' (*EO*, p. 32). It might seem the height of 'textualist' irresponsibility, this talk of political positions which flip across neatly from 'left' to 'right' acording to an errant tropology, a rhythm of rhetorical shifts, whose 'logic' outruns all such tidy prescriptions. But Derrida is now very firm in rejecting this account of what deconstruction comes down to in political terms. 'The future of the Nietzsche text is not closed. But if, within the still-open contours of an era, the only politics calling itself — proclaiming itself — Nietzschean will have been a Nazi one, then this is necessarily significant and must be questioned in all of its consequences' (*EO*, p. 31). It would certainly be wrong to identify the truth of Nietzsche's texts with the meaning discovered in them by Nazi ideologists. Such a reading would invite the obvious objection that Nietzsche has been read very differently by those with a much stronger claim to have grasped the 'syntax' of his thought, its 'subtle refinements', 'paradoxical reversals' and so forth. It will then appear that the Nazi appropriation is a travesty of what Nietzsche wrote, a 'mimetic inversion and perversion' that apparently stays close to the Nietzschean text (by selective quotation) but in fact manages to twist and exploit its rhetorical resources. In this case, Derrida insists, one must still account for the fact that such perversions are possible, and — more specifically — the fact that they have taken so extreme and virulent a form in the Nazi reading of Nietzsche. We may reject both the naïve (intentionalist) account which holds Nietzsche *ipse* responsible for his 'views', and that other, more sophisticated (hermeneutic) version which locates the truth of his work in the meaning that emerges through successive encounters between reader and text. But this leaves the question unanswered: what is it 'in' the Nietzschean text that has produced such a history of antagonistic readings? For, as Derrida writes: 'even if the intention of one of the signatories in the huge "Nietzsche Corporation" had nothing to do with it, it cannot be entirely fortuitous that the discourse bearing his name in society, in accordance with civil laws and editorial norms, has served as a legitimating reference for ideologies' (*EO*, p. 31).

Hence the insistent metaphor of hearing that runs through Derrida's text; of understanding as a matter of echoes, repercussions, sounds that register only at a certain unpredictable remove, once they have made their way through the labyrinthine channels of the ear. This topic was first broached in his Preface to *Margins of Philosophy*, where the tympanum (among other things, the membrane or diaphragm that separates the inner and outer aural cavities) figures as a topos in the deconstructive reading of Hegelian phenomenology.[7] It works to undo a whole series of classic conceptual oppositions, including the privilege that has always accrued to inwardness, self-presence, intelligible truth as opposed to the realm of mere external sensory perception. This privilege — the ground of Hegelian dialectic — is subject to a certain dislocating pressure as soon as it comes into contact with a 'logic' (that of the tympanum) which suspends the decidable difference between inward and outward, interiorized meaning and phenomenal sense. Thus the ear takes on a significance at odds with its traditional (phonocentric) role in the texts of philosophy from Plato to Hegel and Husserl. No longer can it serve as the ultimate guarantee of a meaning that always returns to source in the moment of authentic, self-present truth. What Nietzsche obliges us to think, in Derrida's reading, is the risk that goes along with entrusting one's words to the ear of the other, but also — more emphatically now — the need to reject any too quick or evasive retreat into a rhetoric of textual freeplay or 'undecidability'.

This thematics of the ear acquires more specific connotations in a passage from *Thus Spake Zarathustra* which Derrida cites as a prelude to his text. Nietzsche is here attacking the docility, the credulous and trusting attitude of contemporary 'cultured' individuals, in particular their zeal to hang upon the teacher's every word without the least sign of active, independent thought. He pictures them as victims of a chronic deformity, 'inverse cripples' in whom the over-development of a single organ has reduced them to a state of hopeless passivity. "'An ear! An ear as big as a man!" I looked still more closely — and indeed, underneath the ear, something was moving, something pitifully small and wretched and slender . . . If one used a magnifying glass one could even recognise a tiny envious face; also, that a bloated little soul was dangling from the stalk' (quoted, *EO*, p. 3). Derrida goes on to associate this repugnant passage with others from *Ecce Homo* and a little-known text on 'The Future of our Educational Institutions', dating from Nietzsche's early years as a professor of philology, and unpublished during his lifetime.[8] What emerges from this reading is a series of ambivalent but intensely political meditations on 'the ear', developing the theme of a cultural decadence brought about by the over-dependence on passive hearing. This condition, Nietzsche argues, can only be the product of our present-day liberal institutions of learning. Here one finds the cause of that hypertrophied state whereby the critical spirit is progressively weakened and its place unsurped by the faceless disciplines of a uniform liberal enlightenment. There is a need for vigorous remedies, and it is Nietzsche's all-too vigorous suggestions that take him into the rhetorical ambit of Nazi ideology. For Nietzsche, 'democratic and equalizing education, would-be academic freedom, the maximal extension of culture — all these must be replaced by constraint, discipline (*Zucht*), and a process of selection under the direction of a guide, a leader or *Führer*, even a *grosse Führer*' (Derrida's paraphrase; *EO*, p. 27). Apologists may argue that the word as yet possessed nothing of its subsequent, sinister meaning; that to take it out of context, thus allowing it 'to resonate all by itself in its Hitlerian consonance', is a crude anachronism. But this ignores the fact that any 'resonance' in Nietzsche's use of the word is not just a kind of random pre-echo, but is closely bound up with the entire network of motifs and obsessions that organize his discourse. The Nietzschean *Führer* 'is not merely a schoolmaster and master of doctrine', just as Hitler conversely 'also wanted to be taken for a spiritual and intellectual master . . . a teacher of regeneration' (*EO*, p. 28). To ignore the elective affinity here is as wrong as to hold Nietzsche directly and personally accountable for what subsequent readers have made of him.

What these early texts share with the Nazi 'perversion' of Nietzschean doctrine is that strain of contempt for degenerate values which can yet be transformed into a script, a virtual programme for the collapse of civilized culture. Again, there is the argument that Nietzsche had nothing to do with these later events in German history; that in so far as he 'predicted' them he took great pains to forestall and discountenance just such a reading. Thus (as Derrida notes) he refused to have the lectures printed, finding them in some way 'premature', unsatisfactory and declaring himself unwilling 'to publish any book that doesn't leave me with a conscience as clear as an angel's' (cited p. 25). And this veto extended to posthumous publication, since otherwise their effects (at whatever historical remove) might always be construed as 'binding on the author'. To these factors must be added the extreme rhetorical complexity of Nietzsche's stance, his play with generic conventions (those of the academic lecture-series) which he is out to mimic and thereby subvert. Thus it might seem naïve to ignore such a range of shrewdly placed obstacles and read off the symptoms of looming catastrophe in Nietzsche's apocalyptic style. On the other hand there is the risk that 'sophisticated' readings, those that take Nietzsche's rhetorical lessons to heart, may end up by evading the single most urgent question. For 'even if Nazism, far from being the regeneration called for by these lectures of 1872, were only a symptom of the accelerated decomposition of European culture and society as diagnosed, it still remains to be explained how reactive degeneration could exploit the same language, the same words, the same rallying cries as the active forces to which it stands opposed' (*EO*, p. 29). And this problem is compounded, not resolved, by the textual evidence that 'neither this phenomenon nor this specular ruse eluded Nietzsche'.

Such is the question that Derrida confronts most insistently in *The Ear of the Other*. What remains, what 'survives' of an author's name, intentions, strategies of rhetoric and style, once his writing has become the object of diverse competing interpretations? This question takes on peculiar force in the case of thinkers (like Freud) who have chanced their authority by engaging in speculative ventures which always run the risk of not being 'properly' understood. Derrida's recent essays on Freud are concerned with the complex intertextual relation between life, writing and the destiny of Freudian psychoanalysis as a movement whose fortunes its 'author' could scarcely envisage or control.[9] This is the predicament that Derrida finds so aptly figured in the famous 'fort-da' game, where the speculator (Freud) erects a new theory of libidinal drives on the chance observation of his infant grandson caught up in a curious repetitive routine.[10] The child lies in his cradle and alternately throws away his plaything, a bobbin on a string, then pulls it back with evident relief and satisfaction. The noises that he utters in the course of this game — vague approximations to the German 'fort . . . da', meaning 'gone . . . back again' — Freud interprets as a sign of his reliving the periods of intense separation–anxiety caused by the mother's absence. This anxiety is briefly assuaged by his casting out the bobbin and then triumphantly securing its return by tugging at the string. But the game could only work, Freud argues, on condition that the child underwent something like the 'original' trauma with each disappearance of the bobbin; that the feeling of renewed mastery was never quite sufficient to annul the repeated element of risk. It is on this basis that Freud rethinks the libidinal economy of meaning and desire, giving rise to his subsequent, sombre meditations on the toll of instinctual repression exacted by man's coming-to-terms with an alien social order.

So the 'fort-da' game has large implications for the future of psychoanalysis. A similar compulsion seems to operate everywhere in Freud's theorizing, in his readiness to risk a far-fetched hypothesis (like that of *Beyond the Pleasure Principle*) on a series of apparently random or 'private' observations. For indeed, as Derrida shows, there is more to this family scene than Freud's use of his grandson's behavior as a mere illustrative instance. What Derrida discerns is a running subtext of rivalries, tensions and speculative ploys on the grandfather's part, some in relation to his children and family, others having to do with the prospects of psychoanalysis as a movement, a site of future struggles and presumptive claims to power. Like his grandson with the bobbin, Freud is in the grip of a double compulsion, a game in which the stakes are both enormously high and impossible to calculate in advance. On the one hand he perpetually seeks reassurance that he is in charge of the family business; that his name still possesses the authority and power that belong to him as founder of a dynasty, a movement. On the other Freud seemingly goes out of his way to indulge in speculative flights of fancy which can only appear to compromise that authority. For what can be the 'scientific' standing of a discipline, psychoanalysis, which entertains such wild hypotheses and whose future is tied to this compulsive interest in the fortunes of a mere proper name?

These same issues arise in the context of Nietzsche and the politics of deconstruction. Here also there is the problem of knowing what to make of a text which simultaneously asserts and undermines its own powers of theoretical command. Again it is a matter of the authority attaching to a name, 'Nietzsche', whose effects (whose resonance) can always be exploited to radically different ends. Must there not be, Derrida asks (and the passage needs quoting at length),

> some powerful utterance-producing machine that programs the movements of the two opposing forces at once, and which couples, conjugates, or marries them in a single set . . . (Here, all the difficulty comes down to the determination of such a set, which can be neither simply linguistic, nor simply historico-political, economic, ideological, psycho-fantasmatic, and so on. That is, no regional agency or tribunal has the power to arrest or set limits on the set, not even that court of 'last resort' belonging to philosophy or theory, which remain subsets of this set. [*The Ear Of The Other*, p. 29]

Of course this passage raises more questions than it claims (or even hopes) to resolve. In particular, it blocks the way to any straight-forward indictment of Nietzsche, any reading that attempts (like Lukacs in *The Destruction of Reason*) to identify his thought as the source and inspiration of modern irrationalism, and thus to trace a direct line of descent from Nietzsche to the Nazi ideologues.[11] But the passage also holds that there must be certain protocols, trans-formative rules or enabling conditions that limit the freedom of inter-pretative play. It insists that we read Nietzsche against himself, or at least against that widespread (deconstructionist) account of him that fastens on the doctrine of strong misreading as a species of out-and-out hermeneutic licence.

This tells against the current neo-pragmatist move (by philosophers like Richard Rorty) that annexes deconstruction to the project of dismantling every last claim of 'enlightened' critical reason.[12] For Rorty, what is good about Derrida is his willingness to treat philosophy as just another 'kind of writing', useful in so far as it throws up interesting ideas for debate, but possessing no particular or privileged claim to truth. From this point of view, philosophers in the modern analytical tradition are simply missing the point when they try to reformulate the old (Kantian) problems in a more up-to-date linguistic idiom. The proof of this backsliding tendency, Rorty argues, is precisely their belief that those 'problems' still persist beneath and despite the shift of rhetorical terrain. What Rorty denies on pragmatist grounds is the notion that any such link could possibly obtain; that one could map out the series of *conceptual* shifts that lead, say, from Kant to Strawson's revisionist reading of Kant. Such a view must presuppose that the current neo-Kantians 'have arguments and theses which are connected to Kant's by a fairly straightforward series of "purifying" transformations, transformations which are thought to give clearer and clearer views of the persistent problems'.[13] But if philosophy is indeed just another 'kind of writing', then interpreta-tion goes all the way down, with no room left for the kind of extended, continuous debate — the working away at well-defined 'problems' — that philosophers like to think they are carrying on.

Rorty's is a thoroughly Nietzschean reading of Derrida, if the name 'Nietzsche' is taken to signify a break with all received (enlightened) ideas of argumentative consistency and truth. Deconstruction would then be the welcome upshot — welcome, that is to say, on Rorty's neo-pragmatist terms — of the Nietzschean drive to undermine that whole tradition by exposing its thoroughly rhetorical character. But this is the version of Nietzsche that is called into doubt by Derrida's more recent texts. The reason for this shift of emphasis most likely has to do with his increased political involvement, especially his collaborative work with GREPH on philosophy, education and the state. This work has entailed a complex relation to that Kantian tradition of enlightened thought which identifies critical reason, its powers and its limits, with a certain idea of philosophy's role in the modern university. To say that Derrida 'deconstructs' this idea, in the simplified sense of dismantling or rejecting its mystified claims, is to give a very partial account of what is involved. Certainly he brings out the conflicts of statement and principle that develop as Kant lays down his requirements for philosophy as a pure, 'disinterested' seeking-after-truth untouched by practical affairs of state. Such was Kant's design (in 'The Conflict of Faculties') for saving philosophy from the pressures of state interference by declaring its interests strictly theoretical and hence of no concern to the censors and apparatchiks.[14] To deconstruct this nexus of opposed valuations, of 'pure' versus 'applied' knowledge, is indeed to cast doubt on the Kantian ideal of a liberal, enlightened university system. Yet it is equally clear, as Derrida remarks more than once, that such criticism can only take effect by in some sense upholding that impossible ideal against its manifold contemporary distortions and perversions. Indeed there is no way of keeping philosophy pure — of maintaining belief in its disinterested character — at a time when, 'so long as it has the means, a military budget can invest in anything at all, in view of deferred profits: "basic" scientific theory, the humanities, literary theory and philosophy'.[15] But if the Kantian paradigm is (and always has been) a strictly impossible dream — a dream, moreover, that can often be pressed into service by the very interests it claims to oppose — nevertheless it is an indispensable means of bringing such interests to light.

Thus Derrida's aim in remarking the complicity between 'pure' and 'applied' knowledge is not to argue that the humanistic disciplines lack any critical force; that they are products, one and all, of a self-deluding enterprise congenitally blind to its own real motives. Rather, he is defending the principle of reason, the enlightenment desire for clarity and truth, in so far as that project can be 'deconstructed' to reveal what it harbours of a hidden agenda all the more powerful for its rhetoric of Kantian disinterest. As Derrida writes most explicitly: 'we cannot and we must not forego the *Aufklärung*, in other words, what imposes itself as the enigmatic desire for vigilance, for the lucid vigil, for elucidation, for critique and truth'.[16] Simply to renounce this ideal — to give it up at Nietzsche's or Rorty's bidding as an outworn fiction, a rhetorical construct, one kind of writing among others — is a move with demonstrably wide appeal to the theorists of 'postmodern' culture. It is the move that enables Lyotard to proclaim an end to all forms of enlightened critique, all those old 'meta-narratives', whether Kantian, Marxist or whatever, that pinned their faith to reason as a genuine emancipating force. One major plank in Lyotard's argument is a 'strong misreading' of Kant (to put it charitably) which ignores every protocol of reasoned exposition in order to prove the rhetorical, essentially pragmatist cast of Kantian ethical dictates.[17] Here as with Rorty such misprisions have a kind of inbuilt defence in the pragmatist belief that no logic, no standards of valid argumentation, can henceforth apply to the reading of texts. It is against this fashionable pragmatist drift that Derrida implicitly argues in *The Ear of the Other*.

These issues are focused in that early text of Nietzsche ('On the Future of our Educational Institutions') which Derrida finds so crucial to a properly political reading of his work. For it is here that Nietzsche mounts his attack on the Kantian-enlightenment idea of how a liberal institution (the modern university) answers to the principle of reason. He regards it as merely a 'ruse of the state', a species of pious fraud whereby the covert workings of political power are dressed up in a rhetoric of noble disinterest. Worst of all, Nietzsche argues, is the myth of 'academic freedom', a fiction maintained by professors (and students) who fit snugly into their allotted role as 'docile and unquestioning functionaries'. This freedom is on a par with the autonomous, self-legislating will of Kantian ethics. It is a symptom of cultural decadence, of the weak individual's failure to perceive how his or her actions and very desires are dictated from outside, though always in the form of a moral law (a 'categorical imperative') whose source is supposedly deep within one's own sovereign conscience. This delusion is writ large in the kind of unresisting liberal consensus that Nietzsche so detests in the modern university. 'Behind "academic freedom" one can discern the silhouette of a constraint which is all the more ferocious and implacable because it conceals and disguises itself in the form of *laissez-faire*. Through the said "academic freedom", it is the State that controls everything' (Derrida's paraphrase; *EO*, p. 33). The docile teacher is rewarded with the promise of a freedom to be exercised on exactly those terms that Kant laid down for the pursuit of pure (disinterested) knowledge.

In texts like 'The Principle of Reason', Derrida at times seems close to adopting this Nietzschean position *vis-à-vis* the modern university and its Kantian heritage. In particular he works to deconstruct that idea of the humanistic disciplines — philosophy, theory, criticism — as somehow surviving in a realm apart from the crude imperatives of 'applied' research.[18] Such distinctions are clearly untenable when (for instance) the US Department of Defense can enlist the aid of semioticians, rhetoricians, speech-act theorists and others by way of assessing the current stage of nuclear-strategic bluff. In this situation it becomes quite impossible to distinguish two types of 'competence': hard-headed technical expertise on the one side and 'advanced research in the humanities' on the other. Any new development in weapons technology will always go along with a shift in the posture of so-called deterrent strategy. So it comes about that decisions must be based not only on a 'rational' calculation of means and ends, but also on a sense of how the other side perceives our intentions, how they see us as perceiving theirs, how we might respond to that perception, and so on to the point where strategic reckoning exceeds all the bounds of logical predictability. 'All of them [the analysts and decision-makers] are in the position of inventing, inaugurating, improvising procedures and giving orders where no model . . . can help them at all.'[19] It is here that deconstruction has a critical edge, since to some extent it has learned how to live with the idea that logic (or the powers of rational grasp) can always be played off the field by language in its 'other', rhetorical dimension. The aporias of nuclear discourse would then present something like an ideal target for the purposes of deconstructive reading. Thus in Derrida's words: 'if there are wars and a nuclear threat, it is because "deterrence" has neither original meaning nor measure. Its "logic" is the logic of deviation and transgression, it is rhetorical-strategic escalation or it is nothing at all.'[20] But such activity would be useless, worse than useless, if it simply went along with the irrationalist drive to discredit every form of enlightened critical reason. Deconstruction would then be given over to a strain of anti-enlightenment apocalyptic thought which, in this of all contexts, is the last thing required.

So it is important to see precisely how Derrida has shifted his ground in relation to Nietzsche and the whole current line of 'postmodern', neo-pragmatist thinking which takes Nietzsche's lessons as read. Otherwise there is no effective reply to those critics of the deconstructive enterprise who regard it as a form of 'textualist' mystification, a last, desperate bid to ward off history and politics on the part of an ideologically bankrupt bourgeois-intellectual tradition.[21] Like much of his recent writing, *The Ear of the Other* finds Derrida engaging simultaneously on a number of fronts, not least that which marks the problematical encounter between deconstruction and the politics of enlightenment. It remains to be seen what effect this will have on the currency of Anglo-American debate.

References

1. Jacques Derrida, *The Ear of the Other: texts and discussions*, Christie V. McDonald, Claude Lévesque and Peggy Kamuf (trans. and eds), New York, Schocken Books, (1985). Further references given by *EO* and page-number in the text.
2. For a representative sampling, see David B. Allison (ed.), *The New Nietzsche: contemporary styles of interpretation*, New York, Dell Publishing Company, (1977).
3. Derrida, 'Structure, Sign and Play in the Discourse of the Human

Sciences', in *Writing and Difference*, Alan Bass (trans.), London, Routledge and Kegan Paul, (1978), pp. 278–93.

4. See especially Geoffrey Hartman, *Beyond Formalism*, New Haven, Yale University Press, (1970). Also Geoffrey Hartman, Harold Bloom, J. Hillis Miller *et al.*, *Deconstruction and Criticism*, New York, Seabury Press, (1980).

5. For a collective statement, see GREPH, *Qui a peur de la philosophie?*, Paris, Flammarion, (1977). Derrida gives a brief account of this recent work in 'On The University', an interview with Imre Salusinszky, *Southern Review*, Adelaide, Vol. XIX, No. 1 (1986), pp. 3–12.

6. See Derrida, 'Signature Event Context' *Glyph*, Vol. I, Baltimore, Johns Hopkins University Press, (1977), pp. 172–97; John R. Searle, 'Reiterating the Differences', *Glyph* I, pp. 198–208; and Derrida's response to Searle, 'Limited Inc abc', *Glyph* II (1977), pp. 162–254.

7. Derrida, *Margins of Philosophy*, Alan Bass (trans.), Chicago, Chicago University Press, (1982).

8. Nietzsche, 'On The Future of Our Educational Institutions', J.M. Kennedy (trans.), in *The Complete Works of Friedrich Nietzsche*, Vol. 3, Oskar Levy (ed.), New York, Russell and Russell, (1964).

9. See Derrida, 'Coming into One's Own', in *Psychoanalysis and the Question of the Text*, Geoffrey Hartman (ed.), Baltimore, Johns Hopkins University Press, (1978), pp. 114–48. Also Derrida, 'Speculating — on Freud', *The Oxford Literary Review*, No. 3 (1978), pp. 78–97.

10. Sigmund Freud, 'Beyond the Pleasure Principle', in *On Metapsychology: the theory of psychoanalysis*, Vol. XI of the Pelican Freud Library, Angela Richards (ed.), Harmondsworth, Penguin, (1984), pp. 275–337. See especially pp. 283–7.

11. Georg Lukacs, *The Destruction of Reason*, London, Merlin, (1980).

12. See Richard Rorty, 'Philosophy as a Kind of Writing', in *Consequences of Pragmatism*, Minneapolis, University of Minnesota Press, (1982), pp. 90–109. See also Rorty, 'Deconstruction and Circumvention', *Critical Inquiry*, Vol. XI (1984), pp. 1–23.

13. Rorty, *Consequences of Pragmatism* (op. cit.), pp. 92–3.

14. Immanuel Kant, *The Conflict of the Faculties*, Mary J. Gregor (trans. and ed.), New York, Abaris Books, (1979).

15. Derrida, 'The Principle of Reason: the university in the eyes of its pupils', *Diacritics*, Vol. XIX (1983), pp. 3–20.

16. Derrida, 'Of an Apocalyptic Tone Recently Adopted in Philosophy', John P. Leavey (trans.), *The Oxford Literary Review*, Vol. VI. No. 2 (1984), pp. 3–37.

17. See Jean-François Lyotard and Jean-Loup Thébaud, *Just Gaming*, Wlad Godzich (trans.), Minneapolis, University of Minnesota Press, (1986).

18. Aesthetics is of course the privileged ground for such arguments in favour of the free, 'disinterested' play of cognitive powers. For a deconstructive reading of Kant's *Critique of Judgement*, see Derrida, 'Economimesis', *Diacritics*, Vol. XI, No. 2 (1981), pp. 3–25. Similar questions are raised with regard to modern aesthetic philosophy in Christopher Norris, *The Contest of Faculties*, London, Methuen, (1985).

19. Derrida, 'No Apocalypse, Not Now (full speed ahead, seven missiles, seven missives)', *Diacritics*, Vol. XX (1984), pp. 20–31; p. 22.

20. Ibid, p. 29.

21. For two versions of this argument from very different political standpoints, see Terry Eagleton, *Walter Benjamin, or towards a revolutionary criticism*, London, New Left Books, (1981) and Gerald Graff, *Literature Against Itself*, Chicago, Chicago University Press, (1979).

8 The Politics of style and the fate of reading: on Geoffrey Hartman

'Easy pieces' they may be, compared with some of Hartman's more esoteric writings over the past two decades, but there is more going on in these reprinted essays and reviews[1] than might be guessed from the book's disarming title, or from his statement in the Preface that most of them were written 'in response to specific occasions and mostly for non-university audiences'. In fact — whatever Hartman's intention in issuing these modest disclaimers — the book is very much of a piece with those other recent texts of his where no such self-denying ordinance applied. All the same, one can see what drove Hartman to adopt this pastoral tone (taking 'pastoral', in Empson's extended sense, to describe that style of writing which affects simplicity the better to establish a complex, many-levelled relation with the reader). For one thing, Hartman admits to a growing impatience with those critics who insist — for polemical purposes — on lumping him together with the 'Yale deconstructors', and dismissing them *en bloc* as so many bother-headed abstract dialecticians. On the contrary, Hartman asserts: he has always been primarily an interpreter of texts, one whose theoretical interests have grown out of, and fed back into, the close reading of literary works. The idea has gained ground, mainly among the followers of Leavis and other 'commonsense' militants, that theory and criticism just don't mix, or only at risk of producing a discourse puffed up with its own deluded philosophical claims. It is understandable that Hartman should counter such arguments by expressly disowning the mandarin style and adopting (at least intermittently) a somewhat more down-to-earth, colloquial tone.

But this is not the whole story, as soon becomes apparent as one reads beyond the Preface and finds Hartman giving voice to some familiar themes and preoccupations. After all, it has been one of his steadiest beliefs, argued in the face of much hostility, that critics should feel themselves free to adopt what Hartman calls an 'answerable style', a language that throws off the decorous constraints enjoined by precursors like Arnold and Eliot. His own writing has ranged across several such styles, from the exuberant wordplay of *Saving the Text* to the elegiac tonings of his essays on

Wordsworth, Keats and others.[2] The point is always to insist that
there is no self-evident distinction between 'creative' and 'critical'
language; that interpretation should properly exploit the full range of
stylistic resources; and that only by doing so can criticism hope to
achieve the kind of inwardness and sympathetic grasp that counts as
an adequate response to the text. The opponents here are those self-
appointed guardians of a sacrosanct 'literary' canon who would see
criticism as a mere service-industry with no claims to creative standing on its own account. The effect of this orthodox view — the
'Arnoldian concordat' as Hartman dubs it — is to enforce a drab
monotony of style and a failure of imaginative nerve which make the
whole enterprise largely redundant. What is needed, he argues, is the
courage to recognize that no such constraints exist, save in the style
of handed-down critical decorum that has exerted such a hold on
weaker, more orthodox practitioners. The best way to break this hold
is to set about self-consciously flouting the conventions, showing —
by whatever stylistic means come to hand — that criticism is no
longer subject to a rigorous parcelling-out of domains.

One could hardly expect Hartman's 'easy pieces' to abandon this
crusade and resume the currencies of civilized critical exchange. To be
sure, there is nothing in this volume that approaches either the punning virtuosity of *Saving the Text* — Hartman's free fantasia on Derri-
dian themes — or the sheer speculative energy and drive of his best
middle-period pieces. There are even signs of a certain misgiving, as
when Hartman reflects on the cult of 'intertextuality', and wonders
whether perhaps we have gone too far toward breaking down generic
distinctions between fact and fiction, philosophy and literature,
poetry and psychoanalysis. But it would still be wrong — a perverse
misreading — to interpret these local reservations as a mere
backsliding on Hartman's part into safer, more conventional modes of
thought. What alarms him, and provokes this cautionary note, is the
sense that 'radical' new ideas can easily degenerate to the point of
becoming a new orthodoxy. In this case the danger is all the more
real for the ways in which modern mass-communications are already
working to blur the difference between facts of experience (or
documentary record) and wholesale mythologies of disinformation.
'So absurd and magnetic is this confusion that a John Hinckley and
a Jodey Foster, who have no connection, gravitate into the same field
of light' (*EP*, p. 126). In this situation, Hartman thinks, there may be
cause to mistrust the more facile versions of an 'intertextuality' which
dissolves all boundaries between real and fictive worlds. But this is
not to side with the partisans of a commonsense dogmatism whose
resistance to theory becomes the pretext for ignoring any form of
stylistic or speculative venture.

If there is a defensive edge to many of these essays, it comes of
Hartman's sense that his writings have been widely, and in some
cases wilfully, misunderstood. He finds himself attacked, by
'commonsense' critics, for stylistic self-indulgence and conceptual
overreaching; by radicals of various colour, for espousing no straightforward political creed; and by purist deconstructors (among them

admirers of de Man) for not pursuing the business of textual deconstruction with a suitably single-minded rigour. The signs of this pressured situation are there to be read in his essays, though Hartman is not given to knockabout polemics and prefers to meet the charges obliquely. For it is not, he believes, just a matter of defending his own predilections as critic, stylist and teacher. What is at stake in these debates is the 'fate of reading', or — to put it less dramatically — the future role of humanistic education in a culture increasingly dedicated to narrow concepts of means–end rationality. This is why Hartman is so anxious to reclaim the imaginative freedoms that are lost by critics who willingly accept the self-denying ethos of the modern (post-Arnoldian) consensus style. 'The stylish critics are merely shielding themselves from being argued with — say those who claim to know what argument is, despite the age-old dispute between *ratio* and *oratio*, or logic and rhetoric' (*EP*, p. 209). These opponents may argue that 'theory' is just a species of abstract mystification, devised by a bunch of self-interested mandarins with no real purpose save to keep themselves in jobs. But behind this argument Hartman detects the presence of a simplified notion of 'reading' that would finally reduce literary studies to the crudest of applied educational technologies. They assume that reading can be taught on the model of a straightforward communicative competence, such that any dwelling on problematic detail would be seen as a needless distraction. From here it is no great distance to the idea that literary studies are justified only in so far as they subserve the interests of a smoothly-running business or state machine.

Hartman looks back to I.A. Richards as one of those critics who came dangerously close to endorsing this simplified model. 'The one and only goal of all critical endeavours', Richards wrote, 'is improvement in communication.' This dream of a free, unimpeded intercourse of minds was the motive that prompted much of Richards's work, from the therapeutic nostrums of *Practical Criticism* to the later forays into Basic English and translation theory. Hartman is far from dismissing this ideal in favour of some obscurantist desire to make understanding as difficult as possible. But it does raise the awkward question of why one should attach any special value to poetry, or the teaching of literature, given that other kinds of language are much better adapted to the ends of plain communication. It is against this reductive, instrumentalist view (of reading and teaching alike) that Hartman holds out in the hope of preserving an essential role for the modern humanities. After all, what could be the use of literary studies in a culture where standards of efficiency and competence have invaded every last discipline of thought?

According to Hartman, it is precisely by contesting that model — by reading *slowly*, with a salutary sense of the problems and resistances involved — that humanists can nowadays best hang onto their vocation. As he writes (in a piece on 'Humanities, Literacy and Communication'):

Instead of speeding up thought and smoothing the tongue, a humanistic training may produce a curious stutter in both . . . In that sense the humanities are dangerous; they impede practical communication; they ask that we do not live in homogenous time; they inspire a 'self-determined indetermination' that can darken every step of thought or language. [p. 177]

It is in the space opened up by this hesitant reading, a space for reflectively coming to terms with the sense of what one has read, that Hartman locates the chief value of literary studies. This value comes of their resistance to any kind of simplified communicative model that would deny (among other things) the interpreter's freedom to cultivate an 'answerable style'. Only by *writing* (in the strong, qualitative sense of the word) can criticism forestall its own tendency to fall back on passive or routine habits of response.

One problem for Hartman is that 'theory' has a threatening as well as a benign or liberating aspect. It is welcome in so far as it frees interpretation from the grip of naïvely referential ideas about language and 'real-life' experience. This awareness of the mediating agency of words has been constant with Hartman, from his early book on Wordsworth[3] (where the approach is thematic and largely untheorized) to the recent, expressly 'deconstructionist' writings. That poets and critics are likewise caught up in this predicament — creatures of language and representation, 'living in the secondary', as Hartman puts it — is a theme to which he often returns. By claiming the privilege of an answerable style, the critic is simultaneously making the point that all language, poetry included, partakes of this 'secondary' character, no matter how strong its desire to evoke the innocence of nature and origins. Such was the burden of Hartman's book on Wordsworth, and such, in more exuberant fashion, the message conveyed by *Saving the Text*. There is no going back, he now believes, to a naturalized ontology of language and experience which would once again discover in poetry the voice of authentic, self-present truth and in criticism merely a parasitic discourse incapable of any such thing. Those who lament this state of affairs — who wish to prevent commentary from crossing the line between creative and critical endeavour — are rejecting not merely a short-lived fashion in literary theory but (as Hartman would argue) the very condition of intelligent, reflective reading. Behind such claims is the broadly Hegelian idea, that literary history is a progress through ever more complex and mediated forms of awareness. There is no possibility of simply restoring some earlier, more 'natural' state of mind, unless by breaking faith with the interpreter's historical vocation. To this extent 'theory' is inescapably a part of our modern, post-Romantic dealings with poetry and the language of mediated vision.

But there is also, in Hartman, a suspicion that theory can go too far in its drive to demystify the sources of poetic power. At times he seems to put the Hegelian machinery into reverse, suggesting that the subtleties of speculative thought may congeal into mere abstractions unless redeemed by some countervailing influence. 'Our work now', he writes, is 'less to purify the individual from immediacy and sensuousness than to sublimate fixed, determinate thoughts and so to experience the actuality of general or abstract ideas.' (*EP*, pp. 175–6).

So one finds him, in these essays, weaving a complex, often tortuous path between the claims of self-consciousness or 'theory' on the one hand, and those of a restored 'actuality' on the other. Not that Hartman is making any concessions to the commonsense view that would have poets speak their mind and critics not presume to interfere in the process. He remains more than half-way convinced that it is an 'illusion' (in poets and critics alike) that impels this quest for an authenticity prior to the ruses of textual figuration. Even so, he remarks, this drive calls out for explanation: 'it may be an illusion as vital to life as dreaming' (*EP*, p. 19). There is a similar facing-about between opposite temptations in Hartman's attempt to redeem the referential aspect of language without giving in to a commonsense creed that would leave no room for the play of interpretative thought. Several of these essays are devoted to a strategy for 'saving' at least some residual belief in a mimetic or representationalist theory of art. For otherwise, as Hartman more than once remarks, there is a danger that criticism will push too far in the breaking-down of ontological bounds. Literature would then lose every last privilege, becoming merely 'one kind of "inscription" or sign-system among others'.

Hence the summoning of Joyce (and, more pointedly, Aquinas) in the closing sentence of Hartman's essay 'Representation Now'.

> Even philosophy's insistence on clear and distinct ideas may express this 'ineluctable modality' of the perceptible that makes what we call representation the unexcludable middle between phenomenal reality and mind, between thinking in images and thinking by means of texts against them. [p. 134]

This sentence is uncharacteristic of Hartman in its juggling with heavyweight abstractions and its quite uncompromising lack of 'literary' grace. Meeting it out of context, and hazarding a guess, one would probably attribute it to Paul de Man, and indeed Hartman's essays show signs of a close and productive engagement with de Man's writing. This comes across most clearly in his efforts to articulate an aesthetic that would both acknowledge the need for theory and resist its more cramping or doctrinaire forms. De Man's late texts are especially helpful in getting to grips with Hartman's more roundabout (and sometimes rather nebulous) arguments.

De Man locates the 'resistance to theory' in the failure of aesthetic philosophy to think through the problems and antinomies bequeathed by Kant and Hegel.[4] Thought has taken refuge in a certain kind of premature phenomenalist reduction which confuses 'linguistic' and 'natural' reality, and thus short-circuits the difficult labour of reading texts with an eye to their rhetorical structure. This habit of taking the word for the deed, of implicitly accepting what poetry says when it claims to hand across sensations bodily, is the chief form of aesthetic mystification which de Man sets out to deconstruct. 'Theory' is thus opposed to traditional aesthetics in so far as the latter has typically determined to elide or repress these problems in the way of its own enterprise. And the resistance to theory, as de Man reads it, is in part a product of that same aesthetic ideology whose effects extend into the realm of cultural politics. 'By allowing the necessity of a non-phenomenal linguistics, one frees the discourse on literature from naïve oppositions between fiction and reality, which are themselves an offspring of an uncritically mimetic conception of art.'[5] In which case, as de Man goes on to argue, the work of deconstruction is also a labour of ideological critique. For it is precisely such wholesale categorical confusions — as between the fictive, the real and the natural — that underwrite all forms of ideology. Those who attack deconstruction on the grounds of its supposed apolitical character are merely (according to de Man) exposing their own philosophical blindness. They are, as he puts it, 'very poor readers of Marx's *German Ideology*'.[6]

These are some of the issues at stake in Hartman's reflections on the 'fate of reading' and the status of mimetic representation *vis-à-vis* contemporary theory. His essays all return to this complex of themes, whether explicitly (as in the passage quoted above), or obliquely, by way of musing commentaries on Blake, Wordsworth, Malraux, Freud or the films of Truffaut and Hitchcock. 'What conceptual apparatus can question, in our time, the face value of representations? Or what can undo the media illusion of direct reportage?' (*EP*, p. 125). These questions echo through the book and find no single or consistent answer. On the one hand Hartman remains highly alert to the ways in which premature naturalization, the unseemly rush from words to world, threatens to foreclose the interpretative enterprise. Also, more urgently, it props up those forms of 'media illusion' whose effect is twofold: to erase all sense of the difference between fiction and reality, and then, by various naturalizing gimmicks, to pass this confusion off as reality itself. So the first of Hartman's questions may be taken as genuinely in search of an answer. There *is*, after all, a need for some 'conceptual apparatus' that will help to undo 'the face value of representations'. But also there is an inbuilt risk with such iconoclastic theories: namely, that they can press so far toward 'undoing' the sources of mimetic illusion that reality dissolves — or is felt to dissolve — into a tissue of rhetorical codes and conventions. This unease is most apparent in Hartman's response to Roland Barthes and Parisian semiology. What he most admires in Barthes is the progress (as Hartman sees it) from an early drive to demythologize literature, along with other forms of 'bourgeois' ideology, to the subsequent, more stylish and nuanced reflections on a range of heterodox themes. What Barthes thus creates, in Hartman's words, is 'an alternative to muscular and demystifying ideologies that are highly reductive.— as reductive as philosophy when it conceives its task to be a thinking against images' (*EP*, p. 132). Hartman's own writings are best understood as a continuing attempt to achieve just that: a self-consciousness sufficient to demystify language as it were *from within*, and thus to avoid the worst excesses of iconoclastic zeal.

Hence perhaps his interest in Malraux, the subject of an earlier book (1960),[7] and of a brief but densely-argued essay reprinted in this volume. The 'Malraux mystery', as Hartman describes it, is the question why such a man — one possessed by the spirit of modernity, politics, technology and cultural change — should yet have devoted so much care to the preserving of traditional artforms. 'A man like that should have been an iconoclast, someone so disturbed by the proliferation of images that he would have to destroy them. Yet the opposite happened. He became our greatest animator of paintings, sculptures, and masks' (*EP*, p. 47). Hartman is here responding to something in Malraux that clearly connects with his own sense of the interpreter's complex predicament. The kinship lies in that ambivalence on the subject of representation which runs through this book and discovers a kind of subjective correlative in Malraux's strange case-history. Whatever its sources, Hartman writes, 'Malraux's psychology of art contains a remarkable theory of anti-mimesis, and all future aesthetics will have to deal with it' (*EP*, p. 53) — anti-mimesis' not in the full-blown, doctrinaire form that Hartman mistrusts, but rather as an openness to manifold styles and conventions whose variety defeats all the naturalizing powers of a tradition founded on ethnocentric prejudice. What is important for Hartman is the glimpse of an attitude — hardly a 'method' — that would hold together the will to conserve and the impulse to break with such 'natural' forms of perception. When he asks, at the outset, whether Malraux's 'interesting if perplexing' career can be grasped in terms of some 'central purpose', the question seems to carry more than a hint of reflexive application to Hartman himself.

But there are other, less congenial kinds of question that Hartman's critics have continued to press, especially when it comes to weighing up the politics implicit in this highly self-conscious morality of style. Michael Sprinker has stated the Marxist objections[8] in an essay that assimilates Hartman's writing to the strain of 'late bourgeois humanism' descending from nineteenth-century idealist aesthetics and diagnosed most forcefully by Herbert Marcuse. On this account, Hartman's is a complex variation on that theme of 'affirmative culture' which seeks a resolution to political conflicts in the idea of a free, harmonious play of faculties promoted by aesthetic education. This concept — developed out of Kantian premises and achieving its canonical expression in the writings of Schiller — has remained a touchstone of humanist aesthetics down to the present day. Its positive aspect (as Marcuse argues)[9] is to keep alive the genuine utopian ideal of a social order transcending the realities of injustice and class oppression. But along with this there goes a tendency to 'dematerialize' politics, to elevate culture (or aesthetic education) to the point where it loses all contact with genuine social critique. Thus Sprinker notes that Hartman, in his book on Malraux, apologized for not having more to say about the writer's political involvement, but then 'finessed the point' by arguing that Malraux was envisaging a new kind of politics, one that would 'reconstruct faith in humanism' by finding a different, more congenial role for the modern 'engaged' intellectual. By such means has criticism sought to appease its political conscience while maintaining a purebred aesthetic ideology of timeless 'disinterested' values.

Sprinker is careful to define exactly what he means in bringing these charges. 'The point is not to accuse Hartman of bad faith, but of having stumbled across a contradiction that the discourse of aesthetic humanism cannot finally resolve.'[10] But it is hard to separate these two lines of attack, or to read Sprinker's essay as anything but a detailed indictment of Hartman's whole project. And indeed there are passages in this latest book of essays where Hartman is visibly reacting to the force of such criticism by mounting a kind of oblique rearguard defence. One can hardly miss the point when he comments in passing that Barthes 'like most French intellectuals, . . . is under constant ideological pressure, and especially that of responding to Marxism and allied forms of social critique' (*EP*, p. 41). Yet there is no doubting Hartman's conviction that the 'fate of reading', or the future of the humanistic disciplines, is centrally a matter of political concern. He is no longer prepared, if indeed he ever was, to subordinate politics to aesthetics in the way that Sprinker describes. Thus Hartman quotes Schiller on the 'wound' inflicted by our modern, increasingly complex machineries of State, but then quickly adds: 'I cite this passage without any claim that what Schiller names aesthetic education could bind up this wound, or reverse the fall into division' (*EP*, p. 165).

No doubt such reservations are prompted in part by that sense of being 'pressured' to political ends that Hartman finds implicit in Barthes' late writings. But there is more to it than simply a desire to make peace (on his own 'aesthetic' terms) with a bunch of troublesome activists. What Hartman is broaching in these essays is the idea that theory — more specifically, theories of art — may be 'anti-ideological in essence' because the role of aesthetic critique is to practise a double demystification, always aware of the motives that actuate its own self-interested discourse. On the one hand Hartman certainly resists those pressures of ideological commitment that would place firm limits on the speculative exercise of mind. But on the other — as appears in that shrewdly self-distancing comment on Schiller — he is anxious to decouple critical theory from the kinds of abstract mystification carried on in the name of traditional aesthetics. For at least one cause of Hartman's 'pressured' situation is his own acute awareness of the dangers attendant on any project that nowadays seeks to 'aestheticize politics'. Sprinker's argument, though justified up to a point, fails to take stock of this countervailing impulse in Hartman's criticism.

In the end it is his notion of a politics of style that carries the main weight of Hartman's defence. Sprinker quotes a sentence from *Criticism in the Wilderness* where Hartman calls for a theory of interpretation 'that is not simply a new version of pastoral: a theory of the relation of criticism to culture and of the act of writing itself as a will to discourse with political implications'.[11] An admirable project, Sprinker comments, but not one that Hartman has in fact carried through in anything like this promising form. What Sprinker is shrewdly latching onto here is the hint that Hartman's criticism is, after all, just another 'version of pastoral', a means — in Empson's famously capacious definition — of 'putting the complex into the simple'. The politics of this would be open to the charge that has often been brought against the pastoral *genre*: that it works to naturalize a social order based on the uneven distribution of power between 'simple' (folkish) and 'complex' (or sophisticated) modes of experience. The pleasures of interpreting pastoral are those of a leisured class — renaissance courtiers or latter-day literary critics — whose fondness for the *genre* is hardly devoid of ideological interest. Empson recognizes this when he comments on the 'massive complacency' of tone and the hint of 'a cheat in the implied politics' conveyed by a poem like Gray's 'Elegy'.[12] The interpreter's claims to an 'answerable style' — the freedom to speculate in and on writing — can easily be viewed as a pastoral ploy to evade certain other, more pressing responsibilities.

What might be Hartman's line of defence against such a far-reaching ideological critique? An answer may be found, or the sketch of an answer, in the last of these essays, 'Reconnoitering Chaos: a statement on contemporary criticism'. Here Hartman makes his most determined attempt (and with a non-specialist readership in mind) to clarify the relations between art, ideology and critical writing as a hermeneutic enterprise. The essay thus stands as a summary inscription of all Hartman's work over the past two decades, from his first tentative excursions 'beyond formalism' (or beyond the hegemony of the 'old' New Critics) to his latest commentaries on Derrida and Continental theory. It also gives an outline of that sweeping historical narrative that Hartman offered as the background to his arguments in *Criticism in the Wilderness*. It is worth looking closely at this retrospective statement for any help it might offer in figuring out those elusive connections that Hartman perceives between 'writing', 'theory' and the politics of style.

The argument can be summarized roughly as follows. The resistance to theory among British and American critics comes out of an old, deep-seated mistrust of 'Continental' styles and systems of thought. It mostly takes the form of a 'commonsense' reaction against anything that threatens to exceed or disrupt the currency of normalized social exchange. This consensus was created in large part by the widespread imposition of a style — a moderate, equable, commonsense style — which henceforth became the staple of English criticism. Historically rooted in the ethos of eighteenth-century 'polite' conversation and journalism, this idiom retained its civilizing hold through a number of crises and threats from outside the established national consensus. These included, as Hartman narrates them, 'Jacobinical fears, Popery fears, the impact of French universalism and then of the French Revolution' (*EP*, p. 204). The effect was to reinforce British suspicions of any style or conceptual idiom that overstepped the natural limits laid down by a decent regard for propriety and truth. Current animosities, directed against critics like Hartman and de Man, were clearly prefigured in the British response to Hegel and others in the German tradition of hermeneutic or speculative thinking. It thus became a chief object of the commonsense tradition to talk people down — whether critics or philosophers — from the heights of 'Continental' abstraction. This could all be carried on under cover of insisting on the straightforward virtues of plainspeaking argument and good prose manners. But behind it, as Hartman argues, was a philosophic war of ideas which often came down, on the British side, to a habit of 'fee-fo-fumming against Hermann the German'. Such attitudes penetrated far beyond the confines of expressly political or philosophic discourse. 'What is Jane Austen', Hartman asks, 'but the flowering of a perpetual reflection on the humane wit of conversation compared to any other form of human display: the dance, duets, cutting a figure, theatricals, even reading (in excess)?' (*EP*, p. 204). Thus the English ideology succeeded in creating a consensus-style of civilized reason which could yet be relied upon, at moments of crisis, to call up some fairly heavyweight means of rhetorical coercion.

For the literary critic, this coercion takes the form of a widespread agreement that criticism cannot — or at any rate should not — cross the line between commentary and 'creative' writing. Hartman finds this doctrine firmly in place by the time of T.S. Eliot's 'magisterial' pronouncements on the folly of confusing these two distinct realms. More poignant is the case of Matthew Arnold, lamenting his own belated birth into an 'age of criticism' devoid (as he felt) of true creative vigour, yet unwilling to abandon the disabling prejudice that propped up this sense of cultural decline. The critic in Arnold takes the negative path of living out his own inferiority complex *vis-à-vis* the poets of a previous age whose achievements overshadow the present. He can only look forward, with patient resignation, to the advent of a new 'creative' era whose outline the critic may distantly descry but without the least hope of himself being allowed to enter the promised land. And the style of Arnold's prose, its middling formality and straitlaced decorum, goes along with this submission to a strictly ancillary or 'service' role for the critic. Such are the effects of what Hartman dubs the 'Arnoldian concordat' in subsequent literary criticism: a marked stylistic reticence joined with a belief that (in Eliot's words) there can be no such thing as 'creative criticism'.

Hartman joins battle with this modern consensus on grounds of its having effectively repressed, or rendered invisible, any signs of revolt against its cramping prescriptions. There is evidence nowadays (as indeed there always was, for those with eyes to read) that 'commentary' has well and truly crossed over into the privileged domain of 'creative' writing. Assertions to the contrary must needs ignore, among other things, the extreme self-consciousness of style and technique displayed by modern poets from Stevens to Ashbery, or the inwrought fictive commentaries devised by writers like Borges and Nabokov. Such overt mixings of the 'critical' and the 'creative' should serve as a reminder (Hartman writes) that 'the line between original text and critical commentary may always have been precarious, at least not as distinct as the conservative scholar holds it to be' (*EP*, p. 203). This 'conservatism' is not just an academic matter of traditionalist scholars jealously policing their sacred textual domain. For Hartman, what resounds in these attacks on critical theory — or on commentary that dares to 'cross over' — is a whole background chorus of repressive voices enjoining submission to the social status quo. Thus the question of interpretative style takes on a larger political aspect. Criticism cannot be ranked as absolutely inferior to 'creative' writing unless one accepts a hierarchical position that resists such threats on principle.

If we are willing to acknowledge the force of these arguments then it appears that Hartman does, after all, have an adequate response to Sprinker's challenge. His particular, highly nuanced form of 'aesthetic humanism' situates itself against a background of social and historical interests which converge on the politics of *style* (or writing) as a form of cultural critique. Certainly this is how Hartman now views his own enterprise. 'Out of this corner I too write; and what I write remains practical criticism, though I have sought to enlarge it, to insist on a new *praxis* that would not neglect theory or a reflection on the social and institutional context' (*EP*, p. 208). But a critic like Sprinker could still maintain that this amounts to no more than a shift of rhetorical tack; that Hartman has managed to historicize his project, but only in the form of an accommodating myth that yet provides a means to place 'culture' above 'politics'. And this reading might find some justification in the closing sentence of Hartman's essay, where his faith seems still, at least residually attached to a notion of aesthetic transcendence. 'This tension between intelligibility and difficulty, as between ordinary and extraordinary language, may be the only *literary* constant in any age' (*EP*, p. 218). This could easily reduce to a species of formalist mystification, an argument that resorts, in the last instance, to conceiving of literature as timelessly distinct from other, more mundane sorts of language. Hartman's texts invite such criticism, given that they virtually equate the act of writing (or the self-conscious exercise of style) with the power to resist ideologies. By this stage 'writing' has itself become a form of handy synecdoche for every kind of theory that holds out against the naturalizing ruses of a dominant (consensus) reality. Bakhtin's idea of 'polyphonic' discourse, Barthes on the pleasures of the 'writerly' text, Adorno on the rigorous 'intrasigence' of theory — all can be enlisted by Hartman on the side of a new-found hermeneutic freedom to think the possibilities of style. One might doubt, like Sprinker, that any such polymorphous bundle of ideas could really do more than 'aestheticize politics' in the old, familiar way.

At the end it may seem that Hartman's criticism is indeed one more 'version of pastoral', a means of supplying those complex satisfactions that could scarcely be yielded by other, less ambivalent forms of commitment. Empson was writing in the early 1930s, very much aware (like Hartman) of the 'pressured' situation created for artists and intellectuals at a time of stark political choices. His opening chapter in *Some Versions* — 'Proletarian Literature' — makes a point of weighing the likely objections that a communist might bring against the pastoral *genre*. Clearly there is room for all kinds of bad faith in the modern cultivation of a literary form that makes a virtue of ironic detachment and a high-class intellectual cult of 'putting the complex into the simple'. Yet finally Empson sets these misgivings aside. Pastoral may lend itself (as in Gray's 'Elegy') to the purposes of a vague yet powerful mystique based on the facts of class inequality. The interpreter of pastoral may seem to endorse this tradition by supplying his modern, sophisticated gloss. But to turn against those complex conventions in the name of some simpler, more doctrinaire politics — like the statements of orthodox Socialist Realism that Empson cites in *Some Versions* — is just another form of escape from the interpreter's difficult role. Only by acknowledging the problems they pose to any kind of hard-line political creed can such conventions be shown to exert their own pressure of self-directed irony and immanent critique. Thus Empson's later chapters, especially on *The Beggars' Opera*, demonstrate how hard it is to draw any firm, categorical line between 'pastoral' and 'counter-pastoral' uses of the basic convention. The *genre* is inherently unstable, its complexities always appearing to invite an ironic or deconstructive reading. And to keep this possibility in view is also, necessarily, to hold out against any simplified politics of art.

We can understand Hartman as making a similar point in the following passage from his essay 'Reconnoitering Chaos':

> Out of this impasse . . . a new consciousness arises. Theory, also *in* language, is not so much anti-historical as deconstructive: it lives within what it criticizes and tries to isolate certain antibodies. One of these is art, which seems to have the potential to resist ideologies while being deeply immersed in convention. [p. 213]

From the Marxist standpoint this may well seem a piece of mere tactical evasion. Certainly these essays show Hartman often engaged in rhetorical manoeuvres to outflank or circumvent the claims of political commitment. Sprinker finds many such passages in his earlier writing, and singles out one especially, from *Criticism in the Wilderness*, which appears to pinpoint the strategies involved. 'We have seen the Critic become the Commissar', Hartman writes, 'and this danger is one reason so many today prefer to see the critic subordinated in function to the creative writer, who is notoriously unconformable.'[13] This would make it very largely the fault of those party-line critics that interpretation now finds itself reduced to a secondary role without the will to deconstruct prevailing systems of authority. But Sprinker sees the drift of his rhetoric here, and spells out the underlying politics. 'Hartman knows very well that Marxist aesthetics is not synonymous with socialist realism, and he ought to know as well that Marxist politics are not synonymous with the Moscow trials and the camps.'[14] For undoubtedly there is, in Hartman's writing, a resistance to politics that often takes the form of a thinly veiled hostility toward Marxism in particular.

But perhaps this is to simplify matters in exactly the way that

Hartman regards as a threat to the liberating energies of art and the powers of aesthetic critique. The function of criticism nowadays, he writes, 'is reticence, cunning, resistance — against whatever is perceived to be fate. And, at present, propaganda or propagandistic versions of history are fate' (*EP*, p. 213). Whether or not one can accept this claim must depend at the last on whether one believes in a cultural politics that concentrates its thinking in the sphere of aesthetic ideology, and tends to disregard — or actively resist — any calls from outside that sphere. Is it really such a 'radical' gesture, as Hartman thinks, to annul the distinction between literature and commentary, or assert the latter's right to an 'answerable style' in recognition of its new-found autonomy? Responses to Hartman, especially among British critics, would indeed suggest that something more is involved than a difference in prose etiquette. What is interesting about these attacks is that they don't all come (although many of them do) from plain-prose plodders who merely resent the dexterity and brilliance of Hartman's style. Thus one finds Christopher Ricks — himself a critical stylist of impressive subtlety and resource — denouncing Hartman and Bloom for their arrogance in wanting to raise criticism onto a level with 'genuine' creative writing.[15] And this despite the fact — which he would certainly, on principle, deny — that Ricks is often more interesting to read than the poet or the passage he happens to be writing about. As with Empson, it is hard, and maybe not worth the effort, to decide now much is 'there' in the text under scrutiny, and how much a product of inter-pretation. Yet Ricks is fierce in condemning those critics (like Hart-man) who would welcome the signs of a growing *rapprochement* between creative and critical writing. A perverse compulsion seems to operate here, with interpreters refusing to acknowledge in themselves what they seek out most zealously in literary texts.

According to Hartman, this failure of nerve is one symptom of a wider (moral and political) breakdown in the present day function of criticism. The 'conservative reaction', as he terms it,

> makes of literary criticism the last refuge of Neo-Classical admonitions against mixed genres, against quitting the demarcation between criticism and art or criticism and anything else — philosophy, religion, the social sciences. [*EP*, p. 202]

Hence Hartman's tendency to raise the mixing of genres to a high point of principle, a standing rebuke to the tidy 'neo-classical' parcelling-out of disciplines and styles. Hence also the offence he gives to critics, of whatever political persuasion, who see good reason not to mix genres if the upshot is a blurring of important categorial distinctions. For Sprinker, Hartman's sin is not so much his 'mixing' of art and politics, no sin at all from a Marxist standpoint, but his promotion of a mystified aesthetic realm above the hard necessities of social critique. This objection is justified on its own terms, although Hartman (as we have seen) has strategies to counter its more reduc-tive implications. But when it comes to that other vexed question —

— of commentary 'invading' the literary text, refusing a subaltern or service role — Hartman's essays undoubtedly make their point. The best example here is 'The Interpreter's Freud', a remarkably subtle and sustained meditation on language, psychoanalysis and the power of poetry (Wordsworth's 'A slumber did my spirit seal') to draw them into strange relation. It is the poem that calls forth Hartman's commentary and — as he reads it — eludes every form of analytic grasp or description. But if criticism is thereby teased out of thought, it is impossible to say where poetry ends and commentary begins its creative work.

References

1. Geoffrey Hartman, *Easy Pieces*, New York, Columbia University Press, (1985). All further references given by *EP* and page-number in the text.
2. See Hartman, *'The Fate of Reading' and Other Essays*, Chicago, University of Chicago Press, (1975); *Saving the Text: Literature/Derrida/Philosophy*, Baltimore, Johns Hopkins University Press, (1981).
3. Hartman, *Wordsworth's Poetry, 1787–1814*, New Haven, Yale University Press, (1964).
4. See especially Paul de Man, 'Phenomenality and Materiality in Kant', in Gary Shapiro and Alan Sica (eds), *Hermeneutics: Questions and Prospects*, Amherst, University of Massachusetts Press, (1984), pp. 121–44.
5. See de Man, 'The Resistance to Theory', *Yale French Studies* No. 63 (1982), pp. 3–20.
6. de Man, 'The Resistance to Theory' (op. cit.), p. 11.
7. Hartman, *André Malraux*, London, Bowes and Bowes, (1960).
8. Michael Sprinker, 'Aesthetic Criticism: Geoffrey Hartman', in Jonathan Arac, Wlad Godzich and Wallace Martin (eds), *The Yale Critics: deconstruction in America*, Minneapolis, University of Minnesota Press, (1983), pp. 43–65.
9. See especially Herbert Marcuse, *Negations: Essays in Critical Theory*, Jeremy J. Shapiro (trans.), Boston, Beacon Press, (1968).
10. Sprinker, 'Aesthetic Criticism' (op. cit.), p. 59.
11. Hartman, *Criticism in the Wilderness: the Study of Literature Today*, New Haven, Yale University Press, (1980), p. 259. Cited by Sprinker (op. cit.), pp. 58–9.
12. William Empson, *Some Versions of Pastoral*, Harmondsworth, Penguin, (1966), p. 22.
13. Hartman, *Criticism in the Wilderness* (op. cit.), p. 162.
14. Sprinker, 'Aesthetic Criticism' (op. cit.), p. 59.
15. See Christopher Ricks, 'In Theory', *The London Review of Books*, 16 May 1981, pp. 3–6. For some other recent British responses to 'theory', see Laurence Lerner (ed.), *Reconstructing Literature*, Oxford, Blackwell, (1984); Tom Paulin, 'English Now', in *Ireland and the English Crisis*, Newcastle, Bloodaxe Books, (1984), pp. 148–54; and A.D. Nuttall, *A New Mimesis: Shakespeare and the Representation of Reality*, London, Methuen, (1984).

9 Derrida, on reflection

One would hesitate to call this bulky volume a feather in the wind, but it certainly signals something of the changed attitude to Derrida's work that has emerged among recent commentators. At last that work is beginning to receive the kind of serious philosophical attention that it has always demanded, but mostly been denied through various accidents of cultural reception-history. Deconstruction was quick to catch on among American literary critics dissatisfied with the old, workaday business of merely interpreting texts and anxious to move across into adjacent disciplines, among them that of philosophy. Their aim was not so much to make criticism more 'philosophical' as to show that the texts of philosophy could be opened up to the modes of rhetorical close-reading that critics were best equipped to provide. For some, like Geoffrey Hartman, this signalled a long overdue break with the tenets of New Critical orthodoxy, in particular the rigid boundary-lines drawn between poetry, criticism and philosophy. Henceforth the interpreter could range freely across the disciplines, exploiting all manner of stylistic resources (including those of Continental thinkers like Hegel, Nietzsche and Heidegger, all the more attractive for being sternly disowned by mainstream Anglo-American philosophers) without necessarily taking on board their more demanding or specialized arguments.[1] It thus became possible to read, say, Wordsworth alongside Hegel, Marx with Victor Hugo or Kant with Henry James, Nietzsche and Freud, in order to demonstrate the endless intertextuality of meaning and the artificial character of all attempts to separate 'literature' from other kinds of discourse.

One further benefit — proclaimed most explicitly by Hartman — was the critic's new-found freedom of style, a chance to escape from the self-denying ordinance, the decently unself-promoting decorum, handed down from Arnold, through Eliot to contemporary academic criticism.[2] No longer need critics labour under the false idea that their kind of writing was a secondary kind which had better not stray

Rodolphe Gasché, *The Tain of the Mirror: Derrida and the philosophy of reflection*, Cambridge, Mass., Harvard University Press, (1986).

onto the privileged domain of creative or poetic language. Such distinctions were held to be merely the result of an outworn habit of thinking which insisted on dividing up the disciplines along standard institutional or academic lines. If criticism could take on philosophy at its own rhetorical game then it could also make use of whatever 'poetic' tropes and devices it freely chose to exploit. Such was very largely the motivating impulse of 'literary' deconstruction in the wake of Derrida's much-publicized arrival on the North American scene. One of its effects was to alienate philosophers from what they saw, understandably, as a form of irrationalist or sophistical attack upon the principles of reason and truth. Hence the exchange between Derrida and John R. Searle on the topic of Austinian speech-act philosophy, an encounter which — as Derrida remarked — might be said never really to have taken place, since the parties were arguing at such a great distance of mutual misunderstanding.[3]

This impression was no doubt confirmed for many by the fact that Richard Rorty, most prominent of the few philosophers who engaged seriously with Derrida's work, likewise interpreted deconstruction as signalling the end of an outworn tradition. For Rorty, philosophy is indeed just a 'kind of writing', though one that has unfortunately failed to recognize this salient fact by treating itself as a privileged discourse of a priori concepts and truths. The great virtue of Derrida, as Rorty reads him, is to press home the liberating Nietzschean message that all philosophical ideas come down to metaphors in the end; that truth is the most tenacious and systematically misleading of these metaphors; and that therefore we had best give up the belief in philosophy as anything more than one, non-privileged participant voice in the ongoing cultural dialogue.[4] Literary critics may think (deludedly) that philosophers have a special kind of expertise which enables them to answer ultimate questions about the nature and limits of human understanding. On the contrary, Rorty declares: philosophy has no such superior vantage-point, and critics would do better just to take what they can in the way of handy notions and metaphors, without giving in to the old 'foundationalist' idea of epistemology as a source of ultimate truths, methods or interpretative grounds. Deconstruction is thus welcome as a propaedeutic exercise for clearing away all those bad old habits of thought. But it becomes quite pointless, Rorty argues, when it takes an epistemological turn by continuing to press the same issues of meaning, reference and truth, only to conclude that these are problematic beyond anything dreamt of by philosophers in the mainstream (post-Kantian) tradition. Then deconstruction loses its liberating force and becomes just a kind of negative metaphysics, erecting its own peculiar ontology of 'differance', 'trace' and other such privileged terms.[5]

Gasché's book is by far the most 'philosophical' account of deconstruction yet to appear. It insists that Derrida's work must be understood as a radical critique, but also a continuation, of that German idealist line of descent that runs from Kant, through Fichte and Schelling to Hegel and Husserlian phenomenology. Gasché is quite unyielding in his view that 'literary' deconstruction is a revisionist enterprise built on a fundamental misreading of Derrida's texts. This has come about, he argues, through the readiness of literary critics to pick out one or two salient 'themes' from Derrida's work, like the privilege attached to writing over speech, and then use them as a platform for advancing their own special interests. What they typically ignore is that further, more difficult stage in the deconstructive reading of a text which doesn't rest content with merely inverting a received opposition but goes on to reinscribe both its terms in another, wholly unfamiliar economy of sense. Such is the error that Rorty makes when he enlists Derrida on the side of a 'literary' discourse that would finally break with the deluded truth-claims of philosophy. 'Taking "writing" in Derrida to mean the scriptive and worldly practice of writing, a practice that would differ from its usual philosophical interpretation to the extent that the object it is about is no longer the world but texts, Rorty . . . is bound to misunderstand it as literary writing.' (Gasché, p. 274) In fact, Gasché argues, 'writing' for Derrida 'has no proper value of its own, positive or negative', and certainly not the kind of ultimate privilege that would justify literary critics (or anti-philosophers like Rorty) in their use of it as a slogan for rhetorical purposes.

The same goes for all those other terms in the deconstructionist lexicon ('differance', 'supplement', 'trace' and so forth) that Derrida appears to valorize against their more usual positive counterparts. In each case (according to Gasché) the point is not simply to invert the values of a commonplace hierarchical distinction but to push the enquiry much further back and ask what presuppositions are concealed by the structural difference in question. 'Writing' in this sense is a privileged term only in so far as, historically speaking, it has signified what Derrida calls 'the most formidable difference' from speech, self-presence and the whole logocentric scheme of conceptual priorities. It is thus the most likely candidate, Gasché argues, for the role of deconstructing those various oppositions which have worked to maintain that scheme. But this strategic pre-eminence is not to be confused with the gesture — common in some degree to all forms of 'literary' deconstruction — which would elevate writing, rhetoric or textual 'freeplay' above the claims of philosophic reason. What writing must be taken to signify in Derrida's texts is 'that synthetic structure of referral that accounts for the fact that in the play of differences between, say, speech and writing, ideality and writing, meaning and writing, philosophical discourse and writing, . . . the pole allegedly present in and of itself, which allegedly refers to itself alone, must in fact constitute itself through the element that it abases' (Gasché, p. 275). This would count against any simplified reading (like Rorty's) that took Derrida to be arguing the case against 'philosophy' in the name of a generalized writing or rhetoric that could henceforth ignore the demands of conceptual critique. Although Derrida's use of the term inevitably carries associative links with the 'vulgar', restricted or commonplace usage, nonetheless it operates (as Gasché insists) at a level of philosophic argument beyond the grasp of such straightforwardly literal readings.

Gasché has a number of points to make against what he sees as the widespread misappropriation of Derrida's texts. One is the fact that 'literature' has always been determined as in some sense the *other* of philosophy; that since Plato at least, the discourse on literary topics has taken its terms from the governing lexicon of philosophic concepts and categories. Thus literature belongs on the side of rhetoric (as opposed to reason), of metaphor (as opposed to literal or non-deviant usage) and of truth as opposed to the various kinds of fiction or imaginative licence that poets have commonly been thought to enjoy. This means that there is no getting 'outside' philosophy to some alternative ground where the concepts in question would no longer apply. A deconstructive reading must always reach the point where its notions of the 'literary' turn out to be implicated in a certain genealogy of philosophic arguments. In the case of metaphor, as Derrida remarks in his essay 'The White Mythology', it is impossible to advance a single proposition as to the nature of figural language without in the process rejoining that tradition of philosophic thinking about metaphor which has set the main terms of debate from Aristotle's day to the present.[6] The same applies to those various concepts of mimesis or poetic truth which critics have advanced by way of defence against the claims of disapproving philosophers and moralists. For again it is the case — as Gasché points out, following Derrida — that philosophy will always have occupied in advance the ground upon which these defences are mounted. 'This philosophical inauguration has not only governed the reading of literature but has determined the mode of its writing as well'. For this reason, 'if it were possible to draw one major proposition from Derrida's statements on literature, it would certainly not be that everything is literature, but on the contrary that "there is no — or hardly any, ever so little — literature"' (Gasché, p. 256).

His second line of argument follows directly from this. It has to do with the relationship between deconstruction and a certain thematics of 'reflexivity' which has more or less prevailed in literary-critical treatments of the topic. On this account, the aim of a deconstructive reading is to draw out those moments of rhetorical doubling or self-implicated paradox where the text puts its own authority into question by reflecting on the endlessly elusive character of meaning and consciousness in general. These moments produce a kind of infinite regression (more fashionably, a *mise en abyme*) which reveals the non-existence of any ultimate ground, any means of arresting the otherwise vertiginous play of specular representations. Such ideas have certainly taken hold among many of those North American literary theorists influenced by Derrida's thinking. They have been most important for critics like Hartman, interpreters of a strongly-marked speculative bent, trained up on close-reading of the major Romantic poets and anxious to find a language that would somehow respond to the subtleties, the windings of self-conscious memory and desire, encountered in the canonical texts of that tradition. Thus Hartman starts out (in his early book on Wordsworth) as a critic of broadly phenomenological persuasion, seeking to articulate the most intimate structures of mind, meaning and experience that emerge in the course of Wordsworth's growth toward mature self-knowledge.[7] Such understanding, he insists, is both elusive and subject to constant visions and revisions, since there is no 'unmediated presence' — whether of nature as Wordsworth perceives it or of Wordsworth's perceptions as they strike the reader — which could offer any ultimate guarantee that true communication had taken place. Still Hartman writes in the belief that poetry is in some sense a meeting of minds, and that criticism is best engaged in the kind of inward yet reciprocal dialogue that works toward a sense of achieved understanding.

His later 'deconstructionist' essays show Hartman increasingly coming to doubt this dream of perfect communication. They emphasize the extent to which language, in its figural or rhetorical dimension, tends always to complicate the dialogue between poem and reader, to the point where no degree of hermeneutic tact can offer an assurance of right understanding.[8] Hartman never goes quite so far in this direction as others like J. Hillis Miller, whose progress from a phenomenological 'criticism of consciousness' to a thoroughgoing deconstructionist rhetoric of tropes provides the most striking example of this symptomatic shift of allegiance.[9] But he does show clearly what Gasché has in mind when he traces the emergence of 'literary' deconstruction to a certain thematics of reflexivity deriving from Kant, Hegel and the German metaphysical–idealist tradition. Transposed into the context of Romantic nature-poetry, this leads to a stress on those moments of intense visionary pathos where language comes up against the paradoxes inherent in all such reflection on time, memory and inward self-knowledge. Despite the shift toward a more rhetorical register, deconstruction in this mode remains closely tied to its origins in phenomenological criticism and, beyond that, in the line of reflexive or speculative thinking that feeds from German idealist philosophy into English Romanticism. It is still, in this sense, a 'criticism of consciousness', whatever the obstacles that language is seen to place in the way of any pure, unimpeded communion of minds.

Gasché considers this a false idea of what deconstruction is properly about. 'False', that is to say, in the sense that it ignores the most radical implications of Derrida's work, although Gasché can hardly deny that this is the form, however misconceived or 'vulgarized', in which deconstruction has so far made its chief institutional mark. Nevertheless he is determined to locate the erroneous premises upon which this widespread misunderstanding rests. They begin, he argues, with the move to assimilate deconstruction to that line of idealist-speculative thought which takes the antinomies of mind, meaning and subjective experience as its thematic starting-point. 'Reflection and reflexivity . . . are precisely what will not fit in Derrida's work — not because he would wish to refute or reject them in favour of a dream of immediacy, but because his work questions reflection's unthought, and thus the limits of its possibility' (Gasché, p. 6). Hence the decidedly cryptic title of Gasché's book, where the 'tain' of the mirror (from French *étain*) refers to the 'tinfoil, the silver lining, the lusterless back' in the absence of which no reflection could occur, but which itself lacks any kind of mirroring or reflective quality. And so it is with deconstruction, an activity whose real interest is in that which lies behind, beyond or beneath the paradoxes of self-conscious speculative thought. Thus Derrida's philosophy is engaged in exploring systematically that 'dull surface' which enables reflection to take place, but which cannot itself take part in 'reflection's scintillating play'.

What distinguishes *echt*-deconstruction from these other, less rigorous literary analogues is precisely its refusal to dwell at the point where consciousness willingly enters the labyrinths of speculative thought. Thus Gasché perceives a clear link between the kinds of aesthetic speculation that followed from various misreadings of Kant and the current celebrations of rhetorical 'freeplay' that likewise think to find warrant in Derrida's philosophy. These result from the failure to perceive that Derrida is engaged in a quite different enterprise, one that belongs squarely within the Kantian-Hegelian lineage, despite raising questions that press far beyond the more familiar (reflexive or speculative) terms of that tradition. It would therefore be a great mistake, Gasché argues, 'to conclude that because deconstruction is critical of the discourse of metaphysics and its concept of method . . . it would, in total disregard of all levels, indulge in uncontrollable free play' (Gasché, p. 123). The 'levels' in question are those established by the Kantian critique of knowledge and representation, a critique whose terms Derrida subjects to a rigorous deconstructive reading, but which cannot be simply wished away (as Rorty would have it) by an appeal to some undifferentiating rhetoric of tropes. What is required is a patient and meticulous thinking-through of the problems that emerge as Kant's philosophy is criticized by subsequent thinkers in the same tradition — Fichte, Schelling and Hegel — to the point where its ultimate presuppositions are thrown into sharp relief. It is here, according to Gasché, that Derrida's project can claim to represent both the legitimate continuation and the most radical, far-reaching critique of Kantian idealist thought.

This involves him in some lengthy and elaborate passages of argument, conducted in a prose style that makes few concessions to the non-specialized reader. For the reviewer to pick out occasional chunks of summary statement is of course to run the risk of simplifying and distorting Gasché's hard-won position. All the same one can gain some idea of his project in its broadest outlines from the following synoptic statement, where Gasché lays out both the main issues and the various geneaological stages through which they have arisen:

> Fichte's, Schelling's, and Hegel's philosophies develop the speculative and dialectical elements in Kant, promising that the gap opened up between thinking and being, sensibility and understanding, theory and praxis, and so on which Kant's philosophy appears unable to overcome might be bridged. This impossibility of coming to grips with dualism characterizes Kant's philosophy as a philosophy of reflection; consequently, any attempt to ground thinking in the speculative germs of Kant's enterprise must be viewed as a critique of reflexivity. [Gasché, p. 25]

This passage more or less sets the terms for Gasché's ambitious undertaking. It involves, firstly, a detailed account of how Fichte and Schelling pressed the dualities of Kantian thought toward the twin extremes of subjective and objective idealism. These putative 'systems' were in turn criticized by Hegel, who expressly identified with Schelling's (objective) dialectics of nature, but whose main argumentative drift was to demand that thinking overcome such bad antinomies in the passage to a higher stage of truly dialectical synthesis. Thus in Hegel's mature philosophy 'being and thinking are one, only moments in the objective process of self-developing thought'. But Hegel also sees that this wished-for outcome is dependent on a prior assumption, namely that concepts and sensuous intuitions must at some point coincide in what Kant had termed the 'transcendental unity of apperception'. Otherwise there could be no firm guarantee that the world of experience as construed by the knowing subject corresponded with anything actually 'there' in the world of external objects and events.

This doctrine of 'intuitive intellect' is for Kant an absolute necessity, since it offers the only available bridge between the mind's a priori forms of cognition and the realm of empirical self-evidence or commonsense knowledge. His philosophy therefore rests on the twofold axiomatic claim that 'intuitions without concepts are blind' and 'concepts without intuitions are empty'. But this remains a matter of juridical fiat, rather than lending itself to any kind of rigorous transcendental deduction. It thus gives rise to that oscillating movement between idealism in its 'subjective' and 'objective' modes that characterized the post-Kantian history of thought. And so it was left to Hegel to draw out the full problematical entailments of Kantian thinking. 'Hegel's argument demonstrates that Kant's attempts to mediate apparently irreconcilable opposites falls prey to his philosophy of reflection' (Gasché, p. 31). For it became evident that all such speculative systems — all philosophies aimed toward resolving or transcending the dialectic of subject and object — necessarily partake of a circular logic which allows of no escape from the antinomies of pure reason. 'Since the opposition that remains is that between self-consciousness and empirical or objective consciousness, the unsolved problem arises from turning the original unity of apperception into mere formal self-reflection' (Gasché, p. 32). What Hegel brings out — and what is also, according to Gasché, brought out by deconstruction in its rigorous, Derridean form — is the fact that no form of speculative reason can hope to articulate the 'unthought' background of assumptions from which its own dialectical strategies take rise. The 'tain of the mirror' is both the precondition of this endless reflexive self-scrutiny and that which cannot itself be included in the play of specular representations.

In developing this argument, Gasché writes at length on the cardinal role of aesthetic judgement in the overall scheme of Kantian critique. It is by means of this appeal to art as *par excellence* the domain of reconciled antinomies — of 'a nondiscursive intellect, linking things as heterogeneous as the intellect and the intuitions' — that

Kant is able to predicate the ultimate unity of subject and object, mind and world. The aesthetic thus becomes, under various names (including that of 'productive imagination') the principle that bridges the otherwise disparate realms of conceptual and sensuous knowledge. But again, this principle can only be invoked by an act of *de jure* stipulation, an act which answers to the deepest requirements of Kantian critique but which cannot be shown to follow necessarily from anything established elsewhere in the logic of that critique. Gasché cites a passage of Hegel (from *Faith and Knowledge*) which makes this point and strikingly anticipates much of what the current deconstructors', among them Paul de Man, will have to say on the topic of Kantian aesthetics.[10] 'We must not', Hegel writes,

> take the faculty of productive imagination as the middle term that gets inserted between an existing absolute subject and an absolute existing world. The productive imagination must rather be recognized as what is primary and original, as that out of which subjective Ego and objective world first sunder themselves into the necessarily bipartite appearance and product, and as the sole In-itself. [Gasché, p. 31]

It is from this starting-point in Hegel's critique of speculative metaphysics that Gasché derives the authentic, the rigorous form of deconstructive thinking. It aims to uncover those grounding assumptions that underlie the speculative project at every stage — that make up its very conditions of possibility — yet which cannot be articulated within the logic or constitutive terms of that project. 'In a strange way, "arche-writing" is at once both more and less transcendental than the Kantian transcendental originary syntheses' (Gasché, p. 276). Deconstruction is therefore unthinkable outside the post-Kantian tradition of thought, but also (in a sense which Gasché seeks to elucidate) strictly unthinkable on the conditions laid down by that same tradition.

This leads him to describe the central terms of Derridean critique as 'quasi-transcendentals', figures of thought adopted in the knowledge that they cannot provide any ultimate account of their own genesis or structure, but deployed none the less with a view to explaining just how and why such necessities arise. For it is, Gasché argues, impossible to avoid that requirement of method or system which has always been a part of the philosophic project, even where reason turns back upon itself in the form of reflective auto-critique. What deconstruction brings out with maximum force, notably in Derrida's readings of Hegel, is the presence of heterogeneous elements that cannot be finally subsumed or transcended through the powers of dialectical or totalizing thought.[11] Gasché devotes a large portion of his argument to showing just how these elements work to disrupt any philosophy supposedly grounded in pure, self-identical concepts. But he also maintains that thinking cannot begin to criticize its own preconceptions without at some point yielding to the need for system and method. Deconstruction acknowledges this need while at the same time resisting the desire to treat it as a source of ultimate conceptual truths. Hence the various Derridean techniques for using terms whose philosophic import is strategically conserved yet placed 'under erasure' by means of typographic or other devices. It is at this stage — where philosophy comes up against the limits of its own conceptualization — that Gasché locates the real pertinence and force of deconstructive critique. What remains of the Kantian project is a principled scepticism as regards its more dogmatic or 'totalizing' claims, but also the knowledge that those claims cannot be criticized without the most rigorous account of their necessity within the Kantian system.

'Differance', 'arche-writing', 'supplementarity' and other such Derridean key-terms are various names for that which exceeds philosophical reflection in its quest for legitimizing principles or grounds. They should be seen, Gasché suggests, as so many quasi-transcendentals or 'infrastructures', paradoxically marking both the limits of conceptual critique and (in an eminently Kantian sense) its conditions of possibility. Thus he lists a whole series of Derrida's strategic neologisms in a paragraph (Gasché, pp. 223–4) which spells out precisely their unsettling effect upon the logic, ontology and grounding assumptions of philosophic discourse. In a subsequent passage he takes up the point that this critique can only claim any kind of philosophical warrant in so far as it works through and beyond the terms established by other, more traditional forms of thinking.

> Focusing on an analysis of those heterogeneous instances that are the 'true' conditions of possibility of reflection and speculation without being susceptible to accommodation by the intended totality, Derrida's philosophy reinscribes, in the strict meaning of this word, reflection and speculation into what exceeds it: the play of the infrastructures. [Gasché, p. 239]

Rather than merely dispose of reflexivity ('the surest way for it to reenter through the backdoor'), deconstruction sets out to think the limits of speculative reason and to show where it encounters irreducible problems in the nature of its own enterprise. One should not be misled, therefore, when Gasché uses the word 'play' to describe that perpetual slippage or undecidability which governs the working of these 'infrastructural' predicates. Such play has nothing whatsoever to do with the attitude of free-for-all interpretative licence which is commonly ascribed to deconstruction by literary critics (who welcome its advent) and by mainstream analytical philosophers (who reject it as merely a species of last-ditch rhetorical sophistry). It should rather be conceived by analogy with a piece of precision machinery where the 'play' between parts, for instance in a bearing, is a matter of fine tolerance and essential to the machine's proper functioning.

This is what makes it so hard for philosophy to think beyond the limiting conditions laid down by an essentially reflective or speculative notion of its own project. Gasché here refers to one of Derrida's essays on Hegel ('From Restricted to General Economy'), where the issue is posed once again in terms of a generalized 'writing' whose effects exceed and frustrate the grasp of any purely dialectical account.

> Total reflection is a limited play, not because of some defect owing to its finitude — as Hegel has shown, it is a *truly* infinite play — but because of the structurally limitless play of the undecidables that make it possible, which the mirror's play cannot accommodate without at the same time relinquishing the telos of its operation: the actuality of the unity of all that is reasonable.' [Gasché, p. 238]

It is in this sense that Derrida's work must be seen as at once intensely philosophical and yet as surpassing the conceptual limits of hitherto existing philosophies. Deconstruction is concerned with 'a naïvete unthought by philosophy in general, a blindness constitutive of philosophical thought, Hegel's speculative system included' (Gasché, p. 125). But this blindness or naïvety cannot be counted as one more sign of philosophy's chronic obsolescence, of its not having grasped (as Rorty would say) the current 'conversational' rules of the game, a game that would demote philosophy to just another 'kind of writing' and effectively substitute rhetoric for reason. Such moves are beside the point, Gasché contends, since they ignore the complex philosophical genealogy of all those terms and distinctions which they blithely, uncritically continue to use. Thus 'the logical and the rhetorical are, precisely, corresponding intraphilosophical norms of the cohesion and coherence of the discourse whose unthought is being focused upon here' (Gasché, p. 126). To pass straight over these obstacles is to fall back upon an attitude of pre-critical dogmatism that ignores not only the rigours of Derridean thought but the whole history of conceptual debate carried on by philosophers from Plato and Aristotle to the present.

It is one great virtue of Gasché's book that it dispels so many of these false or conveniently simplified ideas. This is not to deny that there are problems with his way of distinguishing sharply between genuine ('philosophical') deconstruction and its hybrid, vulgarized or 'literary' forms. As other critics have remarked, notably Suzanne Gearhart, in a penetrating essay for the journal *Diacritics*, Gasché's distinction appears to be premised on a kind of generic essentialism (philosophy versus literature) which scarcely stands up to deconstructive scrutiny.[12] It encounters resistance in the work of Paul de Man, where clearly there is something more going on — something more 'philosophical', less concerned with matters of localized thematic or interpretative interest — than in the writings of, say, Geoffrey Hartman or J. Hillis Miller. Yet de Man constantly denied any involvement with 'philosophy' as such; thought of himself as first and foremost a close-reader of literary texts; and often came out in marked opposition to Gasché's line of argument by claiming that 'literature' was the most rhetorically self-conscious, hence the least mystified form of discourse, and that therefore the delusive truth-claims of philosophy were best deconstructed by way of a 'literary' reading.[13] Furthermore, Gearhart argues, there is no getting around this awkward series of facts by constructing (as Gasché does) a partially redemptive version of de Man which would have his main emphasis conveniently shift from the 'literary' interests of *Blindness and Insight* to the more 'philosophical' position developed in *Allegories of Reading*. What this version has to ignore is the evidence that de Man continued to promote literature above philosophy, to the point of stating — in a much-quoted passage from *Allegories* — that philosophy may at last turn out to be 'an endless reflection on its own destruction at the hands of literature'.[14] Gearhart is furthermore able to show that de Man persisted in equating deconstruction with a certain thematics of reflexivity, despite what Gasché is disposed to view as his progress beyond such a limiting approach.

In *The Tain of the Mirror* Gasché has little to say about de Man, understandably perhaps in a book that has its work cut out establishing Derrida's philosophical credentials. In fact his one passing reference appears to concede the major points of Gearhart's critique, stressing as it does the very marked 'discrepancy' between Derrida's and de Man's projects, and assimilating the latter to a species of literary–critical practice whose real antecedents should be sought not in philosophy but in a certain tradition of 'American-bred literary scholarship' (p. 3). The question then remains as to how far Derrida's work permits of such a rigorous and confident beating of the bounds between philosophical and non-philosophical discourse. On the one hand Gasché argues that philosophy has always in some sense pre-empted such distinctions; that 'literature speaks the voice of philosophy . . . it is a mere proxy, stillborn . . . there has hardly ever been any literature, if literature is supposed to mean something other than philosophy' (Gasché, p. 256). The same would apply to those characteristic features (like metaphor) whose presence has traditionally been thought to signal the difference between literature and other kinds of language.[15] On the contrary, says Gasché: 'owing to the particular status of this quasitranscendental, determined by the very specific philosophical problems to which it responds, Derrida's theory of metaphoricity cannot be of any *immediate* concern to literary theory' (Gasché, p. 318). But if literature — and presumably literary theory — is in any case part and parcel of philosophy, there would seem to be no real purpose in arguing against the kinds of appropriative reading that deconstruction has allegedly suffered at the hands of literary critics.

Gasché of course thinks otherwise and states categorically that 'Derrida's marked interest in literature . . . has never in his thinking led to anything remotely resembling literary criticism or to a valorization of what literary critics agree to call literature' (Gasché, p. 255). His reasons for this are equally clear: the belief that deconstruction has been kidnapped and deprived of its critical force through the current *mésalliance* with literary theory. It is important that this case should be made, especially in view of the routine dismissal of Derrida by philosophers who take the presumed tie between deconstruction and literary theory as a pretext for simply failing to read him with anything like the requisite care and attention. Still there is a problem for Gasché in the fact that Derrida's writings have encouraged, even actively solicited, such treatment by literary critics. And this is not merely (though it is in large part) an accidental feature of the process of transmission into a different cultural context. It also has to do with what Gasché himself acknowledges: the way that 'arche-writing essentially communicates with the vulgar concept of writing', so that deconstruction lends itself as it were naturally to the purposes of textual criticism. In this respect it is worth noting that Derrida has maintained a certain studious reserve on the topic of so-called 'American deconstruction'. His response when questioned is usually to remark that the word has taken on a life of its own, a whole set of independent meanings and fortunes for which he can scarcely be held accountable.[16] Some of these developments are no doubt strikingly remote from anything that Derrida would wish to recognize as germane to his own enterprise. But he is clearly just as anxious not to suggest that they have somehow missed the whole point, or that they represent a mere falling-away from the philosophic rigour of *echt*-deconstruction.

This puts Gasché in the odd position of claiming to know more surely than Derrida what should or should not be accounted a proper, philosophically warranted use of Derrida's work. It results, I think, from Gasché's extreme determination to banish those elements of literary interest — thematic, self-reflexive or whatever — which strike him as a mere distraction from Derrida's most important work. However, this position is hard to maintain if one considers, for instance how, 'writing' functions in the chapters on Rousseau in *Of Grammatology*, or (again) how Derrida's essays on Freud complicate the relation between life, writing and fantasy-investment to a point where such distinctions must appear grossly misconceived.[17] Gasché is certainly right to insist that these texts cannot be reduced to just one more, ultra-sophisticated variant of old-style thematic criticism. Thus 'writing' as it figures in Rousseau's corpus is a term whose unsettling chain of effects goes far beyond anything that could ever be pinned down or treated as a straightforward literary 'theme'. Gasché might then seem fully justified in his claim that 'writing, a concept that has been so easily accommodated by so-called deconstructionist criticism, has little or nothing to do with the (anthropological, subjective, and so on) act of writing, with the psychological pleasures and displeasures to which it gives rise . . .' (Gasché, p. 274). Nevertheless, such statements must appear unduly restrictive when set alongside Derrida's reading of Rousseau. For there is simply no way of drawing such a firm, juridical line between 'writing' as the quasi-transcendental term which governs the elusive economy of Rousseau's discourse and 'writing' as the theme, activity or focus of obsessional fear and desire which effectively provides the *mise-en-scène* of Derrida's reading. And the same applies to all those other deconstructive key-terms which Gasché would likewise restore to a condition of philosophic purity and rigour.

These problems should in no way be taken as detracting from the

fine achievement of Gasché's book. Along with recent publications by
Irene Harvey and John Llewelyn, it marks the emergence of a serious,
intellectually demanding response to Derrida's work among the more
acute Anglo-American commentators.[18] In the end there is no denying Gasché's central claim: that Derrida is a thinker of the highest
philosophical importance whose writings both require and repay such
scrupulous analytic treatment.

References

1. See especially Geoffrey Hartman, *Saving the Text: literature/Derrida/
   philosophy*, Baltimore, Johns Hopkins University Press, (1981).
2. See Hartman, *Criticism in the Wilderness: the study of literature today*, New
   Haven, Yale University Press, (1980).
3. Jacques Derrida, 'Signature Event Context', *Glyph*, Vol. I (1977), pp. 172–
   97; John R. Searle, 'Reiterating the Differences', *Glyph*, Vol. I, pp. 198–
   208; Derrida. 'Limited Inc. abc.', *Glyph*, Vol. II (1977), pp. 162–254.
4. See Richard Rorty, 'Philosophy as a Kind of Writing', in *Consequences of
   Pragmatism*, Minneapolis, University of Minnesota Press, (1982), pp.
   89–109.
5. This argument is further developed by Rorty in his essay 'Deconstruction
   and Circumvention', *Critical Inquiry*, Vol. XI, (1984), pp. 1–23.
6. Jacques Derrida, 'White Mythology: metaphor in the text of philosophy',
   in *Margins of Philosophy*, Alan Bass (trans.), Chicago, University of
   Chicago Press, (1982), pp. 207–71.
7. Geoffrey Hartman, *Wordsworth's Poetry, 1787–1814*, 3rd edn, New Haven,
   Yale University Press, (1971).
8. See for instance Hartman, 'Diction and Defense in Wordsworth', in
   Joseph H. Smith (ed.), *The Literary Freud*, New Haven, Yale University
   Press, (1980), pp. 205–15; 'A Touching Compulsion: Wordsworth and the
   Problem of Literary Representation', *The Georgia Review*, Vol. XXXI (1977),
   pp. 345–61, and 'Words, Wish, Worth: Wordsworth', in H. Bloom *et al*
   (eds), *Deconstruction and Criticism*, New York, Seabury, (1980), pp.
   177–216.
9. See J. Hillis Miller, 'The Geneva School', *Critical Quarterly*, Vol. VIII
   (1966), pp. 307–21, and representing his more recent work, *Fiction and
   Repetition: seven English novels*, Oxford, Basil Blackwell, (1982) and *The
   Linguistic Moment: Wordsworth to Stevens*, Princeton NJ, Princeton
   University Press, (1985).
10. Paul de Man, 'Phenomenality and Materiality in Kant', in Gary Shapiro
    and Alan Sica (eds), *Hermeneutics: questions and prospects*, Amherst,
    University of Massachusetts Press, (1984), pp. 121–44.
11. Derrida, 'From Restricted to General Economy: a Hegelianism without
    reserve', in *Writing and Difference*, Alan Bass (trans.), London, Routledge
    and Kegan Paul, (1978), pp. 251–77.
12. Suzanne Gearhart, 'Philosophy *Before* Literature: deconstruction,
    historicity and the work of Paul de Man', *Diacritics*, Vol. VIII, Winter,
    (1983), pp. 63–81.
13. See especially the essays collected in de Man's posthumous volume, *The
    Resistance to Theory*, Minneapolis, University of Minnesota Press,
    (1986).
14. Paul de Man, *Allegories of Reading: figural language in Rousseau, Nietzsche,
    Rilke, and Proust*, New Haven, Yale University Press, (1979), p. 172.

15. On this topic see Derrida, 'White Mythology' (op. cit) and 'The *Retrait* of Metaphor', *Enclitic*, Vol. II, No. 2 (1978), pp. 5–33.
16. See for instance his remarks on 'American deconstruction' in Richard Kearney (ed.), *Dialogues with Contemporary Continental Philosophers*, Manchester, Manchester University Press, (1984), pp. 83–105.
17. See Derrida, *Of Grammatology*, Gayatri C. Spivak (trans.), Baltimore, Johns Hopkins University Press, (1977); 'Freud and the Scene of Writing', in *Writing and Difference* (op. cit.), pp. 196–231; 'Coming into One's Own', in Geoffrey Hartman (ed.), *Psychoanalysis and the Question of the Text*, Baltimore, Johns Hopkins University Press, (1978), pp. 114–48; and 'Speculating: on Freud', *Oxford Literary Review*, No. 3 (1978), pp. 78–97.
18. John Llewelyn, *Derrida on the Threshold of Sense*, London, Macmillan, (1985); Irene Harvey, *Derrida and the Economy of Differance*, Bloomington, Indiana University Press, (1986).

10 What's in a name? Derrida's 'Signsponge'

There are many possible ways to describe this text, none of them adequate but some (at least) less misleading than others. One can begin on safe ground, surely, by saying that *Signsponge* is 'about' the French poet Francis Ponge; that it involves a sustained and intricate meditation on the status of proper names and signatures in general; that it takes up themes from Derrida's previous writing, notably from *Limited Inc*, his exchange with John Searle on the topic (supposedly) of speech-act philosophy; and that *Signsponge* is perhaps his most extravagant text to date, judged by all the normal, reputable standards of literary–critical practice. So much by way of brief introduction. But having said all this one has really done no more than mark off a space in the (by now) quite familiar ongoing project known as Derridean deconstruction. And if there is one thing that *Signsponge* sets out to undermine it is the placid confidence that gathering texts under an author's proper name is enough to ensure the substantial unity of a work, a corpus, an *oeuvre*. Derrida signs on, so to speak, at the point where most interpretation signs off: with the idea that putting one's name to a text can ever be a simple gesture of containment, a claim to authorial copyright. What *Signsponge* calls into question is 'the link (be it natural or contractual) between a given text, a given so-called author, and his name designated as proper' (p. 24). This it does by a species of massive and wilful impropriety, discounting the rule that would commonly regard wordplay on an author's name as the merest of impertinent jokes.

Poets have traditionally been rather less touchy than critics in this respect. Shakespeare's sonnets — like much Renaissance poetry — often make elaborate play on his own and other proper names. There is also the series of punning refrains in Donne's penitential 'A Hymn to God the Father' ('When thou hast done, Thou hast not done, For I have more'). Interpreters mostly rest content with noting such *jeux d'esprit* as a habit rather strange to modern (post-romantic) ideas of poetical dignity and truth, but otherwise a fairly harmless indulgence.

Jacques Derrida, *Signéponge/Signsponge*, Richard Rand (trans.), New York, Columbia University Press, (1985) (French/English parallel text). All page references are to this book.

Even so, they would be hard put to countenance what Derrida does with the name 'Francis Ponge'. He disregards the elementary protocol which assumes that an author's proper name is a signature placed *outside* the text by way of establishing the simple fact of authorship, and therefore in no sense a *part* of the text, open to interpretation or speculative reading. 'It is therefore in the abyss of the proper that we are going to try to recognize the impossible idiom of a signature' (p. 28). This reading will conduct itself (so Derrida promises) without overstepping the line very properly laid down between life and work, biography and textual inscription. In so far as Ponge is here to be discovered as a 'presence' in his own writing, it is not — most assuredly — the same Francis Ponge who has his own life to lead and objects very much to critics who ignore that courteous distinction. In fact, as Richard Rand informs us in his Preface, Ponge was present at the colloquium in Cérisy-la-Salle where Derrida first delivered portions of his text, so we are not to expect any clumsy intrusions of unlicensed biographical fancy. In taking 'Francis Ponge' as the name of his topic — or in addressing the topic of his name — Derrida is by no means out to blur the line between life and work. Rather, he is insisting that we re-think the entire structure of assumptions by which an author's proper name is thought to belong exclusively to him, the individual (living or dead) whose right to it includes the subsidiary right to append it to his texts without thereby making textual material of it. Nothing could be further from Derrida's design than to break down the barriers of studious detachment that Ponge has erected around his literary production. What he sets out to demonstrate, on the contrary, is the way that Ponge's *name* is taken up into a play of textual inscription that finally confounds all standard ideas of 'proper' (or propriety) naming.

Derrida's point can be made clearly enough in terms borrowed from Mill, Russell and modern 'analytic' philosophy. (Indeed, a good deal of his recent thinking has been prompted by ideas from that tradition, a fact unremarked by Anglo-American opponents who assume that no Frenchman ever paid attention to a self-respecting 'logical' argument.)[1] In this case the operative concept is that which distinguishes 'proper' from 'common' names, the former marked out by the fact that they refer directly to some unique individual (person, object or event). With common names, on the other hand, any act of reference — any use of the word to pick out some particular thing — will depend upon one's first having grasped its meaning, i.e. the criteria that determine whether the word has been correctly or intelligibly used. It remained for certain modern philosophers, notably Russell and Frege, to complicate the picture by pointing out that proper names were also subject to a sense-making logic of semantic implication. Thus in Fregean terms, if one were asked the question 'Who is Derrida?', it would not be an adequate response (for most purposes) simply to point to the bearer of that name. One would need to reply that Derrida was, among other things, a French philosopher, author of *Of Grammatology* and a leading proponent of (so-called) 'deconstruction'. Simply to point him out, Derrida *ipse*, would be to mistake the enquirer's meaning if he or she wanted to know who 'Derrida' was. Using the name 'properly' in most contexts of discussion would involve knowing something about Derrida's texts, their strategies of argument and also what they signify in terms of current philosophical debate. Thus 'sense determines reference', as Frege puts it, even in the case of proper names, at least where those names are not used in a purely ostensive fashion but indicate a grasp of certain pertinent facts on the speaker's part.[2]

The presence of Ponge in Derrida's audience gives rise to some inevitable play with the conventions of polite academic address. His being there in person is occasion for homage, but also for a series of distancing gestures which rapidly establish a very different relation between speaker and subject. At one level the use of his name may be taken as a straightforward apostrophe or tribute, a 'greeting addressed to him'. Such naming serves to summon up a presence which is then sustained simply by the communal knowledge that Ponge is *there*. It is an 'indisputable reference', Derrida writes, 'one which my language will never have a chance to close on, and one which it will never have a risk to run with' (p. 2). And there is a second kind of reference, also off-limits for Derrida's purpose, which consists in a straightforward designative naming, an act of ostensive definition, utterly devoid of semantic content. ('Here is Francis Ponge, it is him that I name as a third person while pointing my finger.')

But it is the third modality of naming that fascinates Derrida and that opens the way, in *Signsponge*, to a range of extraordinary speculative flights which are yet constrained by a scrupulous adherence to the letter of Ponge's texts. Here it is a case of names that overrun all the limits of unique or determinate reference, effectively confounding the 'proper' with the 'common' through an open-ended play of textual inscription. 'Not him, and not with a deictic manifestation, but his name, which can always do without him . . . "Francis Ponge" is the name of his name. One can always say this' (p. 2). The argument applies not only to individual names but also to sentences (like the above) which can always be placed within quotation-marks and treated as a kind of compound nominal string. Here, once again, Derrida is drawing on Russell and the theory of logical 'types' or levels of discourse, adopted to avoid the various problems and paradoxes created by self-referring statements. It can hardly be claimed that Derrida's main object is to rescue language from unnecessary traps and confusions. The point he is making here — that meaning is never wholly determined by context; that sentences may always have been cited, parodied or otherwise deprived of their 'obvious', first-order sense — is the same gambit that enabled him, in *Limited Inc*, to run rings around the stoutly commonsensical John Searle.[3] Clearly it is a ruse which opens up hitherto undreamt-of opportunities for textual play. But it is also (though this fact most often goes unrecognized, by Derrida's admirers and detractors alike) a position arrived at through arguments akin to those of Frege and Russell.

Where Derrida decisively breaks with this tradition is in pressing the semantic potential of names beyond all the limits of commonplace acceptability. There is a powerful convention that dictates, as he writes, how 'the proper name, in its aleatoriness, should have no meaning and should spend itself in immediate reference' (p. 118). Analytical philosophers may question this simplified picture, but they still take it for granted that a more refined theory, in so far as it clarifies the semantic economy of reference, must finally guarantee the 'proper' status of names. It is this assurance that Derrida chiefly calls into question. He insists on paying the most scrupulous attention to the ways in which proper names *signify*, or take on attributes of (seemingly improper) sense. Expressed in terms of his favorite distinction, it may be the case that proper names are *de jure* protected from semantic drift, but this protection is undermined by the evident (*de facto*) possibility of proving otherwise. If one can demonstrate the effects of textual dissemination — no matter how repugnant to normal ideas of interpretative tact and propriety — then those effects can scarcely be denied by appealing to some abstract regulative law. Hence what Derrida calls the 'aleatory' potential, 'the chance or the misery of its arbitrary character', contained within every proper name (p. 118). This risk attaches to the fact that its inscription in language 'always affects it with a potential for meaning, and for no longer being proper once it has a meaning'. To broach this possibility is also to see how arbitrary are the rules that conventionally govern the ascription both of meaning to texts and authority to names.

So much for what might be called (though ineptly) the philosophical underpinning of Derrida's text. But why Francis Ponge, and why this obsessive fastening on his name in particular? It is not just a case of both elements possessing a vague penumbra of associative hints and suggestions. ('Francis' = 'frank', 'French'; 'Ponge' = 'sponge', 'spongiosity' etc.) More revealing, Derrida argues, is the effect of these names taken together, treated as a compound signifying term. In the play of sense opened up by this chance conjunction of names we are able to read 'the syntax, the fabulous story and the rich possibilities of syntactical articulation between the two lexical elements' (p. 118). What Derrida brings to light is not some 'deep' unconscious thematics or image–repertoire there to be discovered 'in' or 'behind' Ponge's writing. Rather, it is the constantly repeated sign of a slippage from naming to signification, a process let loose within language by the mere fact that names cannot always be prevented from taking on lexical attributes. Derrida makes the point by alluding once again to Bertrand Russell and the 'theory of descriptions', according to which any genuine proper name (i.e. one that succeeds in referrring to someone or something) can be analysed in terms that spell out its operative truth-conditions.[4] In Ponge, as Derrida reads him, this theory is subjected to a kind of systematic *reductio ad absurdum* because the poet 'disguises every proper name as a description and every description as a proper name' (p. 118). The upshot is a generalized undecidability that affects all the commonplace assumptions bound up with the referential structure of language. It is by way of this 'ruse', Derrida suggests, 'that such a possibility, always an open one, is constitutive of writing, to the extent that literature works it over on all sides'.

So 'literature' is precisely that kind of writing, or that effect of textual displacement, which works to erase all the marks and tokens of propriety in language. And *Signsponge* is a text expressly devoted to showing how far, and with what strange results, this process of erasure can be carried into practice. For sponges or sponge-like things and attributes figure insistently in Ponge's writing. They are objects of mixed fascination and disgust, 'ignoble' in so far as the sponge absorbs all manner of contaminating fluid, but possessed of a cleansing or hygienic power that oddly contradicts such impressions. Thus 'sponge' becomes, improbably enough, the very name and locus of that undecidability which Derrida finds everywhere at work in language. It signifies the deconstruction of limits, the dissolving of clearly marked concepts and categories into a generalized porosity of substance and idea where boundaries no longer apply. The sponge gathers up all those basic antinomies (proper/improper, self/other, nature/culture, presence/absence) that organize the discourse of classical reason. Itself a substance of physically dubious character — solid or liquid? organic or synthetic? — the sponge occupies a fantasmatic zone of tangled crossings and confusions. It thus comes to stand metonymically for everything that tends to disrupt or subvert the proper economy of reference.

On the one hand, Derrida writes, the sponge is that which 'expunges the proper name . . . effaces it and loses it, soils it as well in order to make it into a common name' (p. 64). Thus it figures as a pitiful, contemptible object, one whose very nature or mode of existence is to sponge incessantly on everything around it. At the same time this all-absorbing material has a curious power to transform and preserve that which it soaks up into itself. Here Derrida touches once again on that typical Renaissance trope wherein names are monumentalized — saved from the process of natural attrition — by thus becoming part of a larger textual system. 'Ignoble as it may be, . . . poor in its genealogical extraction, and unable to choose between the proper and the improper, the economy of the sponge is nonetheless better able to resist the oppressor — *its ignoble labor enfranchises it*' (p. 66; Derrida's italics). What the proper name loses in this transfer of attributes — its identity, individual value, 'title of ownership over the text' — it more than makes up for in the gain of rhetorical interest and complexity. The sponge, most debased and amorphous of materials, always in the end 'recovers its composure', reverts to the condition of 'a free and frank object' untouched by impurity or change. Here, of course, Derrida is alluding pointedly to that other dimension of semantic possibility contained in the name 'Francis Ponge'. What redeems the sponge from its ignoble status is the 'frankness', the 'freedom' and the sheer resilience by which it habitually loses and regains its textural (or textual) composure. Hence its absurd but incomparable aptness as a figure that denominates the potential for meaning concealed within proper names.

It is clear enough by now that Derrida's interest in 'Francis Ponge' has nothing to do with biography or matters of express authorial intent. But it does suggest a certain toning down of the hard-line veto placed upon such interests by the zealots of post-structuralist theory. Thus Derrida writes (somewhat guardedly) that the style of textual commentary broached in *Signsponge* 'is not inconsistent with that death or omission of the author of which, as is certainly the case, too much of a case has been made' (p. 22). What he is proposing here is clearly no return to an author-based or intentionalist mode of criticism merely purged of its more naïve assumptions. Indeed, one of Derrida's chief complaints about the way that critics have hitherto read Francis Ponge is their habit of smuggling such assumptions back under cover of various refined methodologies. Thus one finds them debating (for example) whether Ponge is a genuine *chosiste*, returning incessantly to 'things in themselves', or whether he is not more aptly described as a phenomenologist, exploring the states of consciousness evoked by those things. To Derrida, such discussions seem largely beside the point, a mere exchange of abstract priorities which ceaselessly 'turn in the same rut'. He notes in passing that Ponge has refused to go along with either interpretation, maintaining a strategic silence in the face of these competing critical views. There is a parallel here with Derrida's project, impelled as it was, from his earliest writings, by a refusal to decide between the twin temptations of a 'purely' structuralist and a 'purely' phenomenological point of departure. Structuralism tended to pre-empt the issue by conceiving of language as a closed, self-sufficient system that found no room for consciousness, intentionality or other such subjectivist notions. But equally suspect, so Derrida argued, was the move by which Husserlian phenomenology sought to establish a pure ground of reason, equated with the acts of lucid self-knowledge attained by the transcendental ego. Deconstruction brings a vigilant critique to bear on both these forms of pre-emptive philosophical closure. What it needs to maintain (as Derrida writes in his essay 'Genesis and Structure') is 'the principled, essential, and structural impossibility of closing a structural phenomenology'.[5] This resistance is directed in part against that structuralist desire to expunge 'the author' — or at any rate, as *Signsponge* would have it, the author's *name* — as a locus of meaning or textual productivity.

In a sense, as Derrida more than once implies, this issue comes down to the 'difference' between philosophy and literature. It is a mark of the literary text (or, more to the point, of texts that can be so read) that writing tends to overrun any clear demarcation between text and signature, work and name. Philosophers typically tend to suppose that their works have a certain self-evident coherence and autonomy, such that the act of appending their name merely goes to confirm the author's full control over how his or her text shall be read. That names should be exposed to the dangerous contingencies of textual inscription is a thought scarcely thinkable within this eminently proper domain. 'Every philosopher denies the idiom of his name, of his language, of his circumstance, speaking in concepts and generalities that are improper' (p. 32) — 'improper' in the sense that they covertly deny, repress or ignore the kind of textual activity that gives their writing whatever genuine interest it possesses. No 'philosopher', in short, 'will have signed his text, resolutely and singularly, will have spoken in his own name, accepting all the risks involved in doing so'.

In bringing this charge against 'philosophy' Derrida is not, as might appear, attacking a whole preconstituted discipline of ideas and knowledge. Rather, he is aiming to call that discipline into question in so far as it resists a certain kind of 'literary' reading that would problematize some of its key concepts and categories. Thus Derrida has continued to read philosophical texts, but to read them in ways which have, sure enough, been perceived as highly unorthodox, not to say scandalous, by many professional workers in the field. One major cause of this outraged response has been precisely Derrida's refusal — his 'perverse' disregard — of this protocol that keeps an author's signature firmly at the foot of his or her text. This question of statutory limits and border-lines is taken up most strikingly in 'Economimesis', an essay on the discourse of Kantian aesthetics.[6] Here the proper name ('Kant' = 'edge' or 'boundary') enters into a play of structured oppositions which, as Derrida reads them, fail to work out according to plan. The whole conceptual edifice of Kantian philosophy rests upon certain crucial ideas developed in the *Critique of Judgement*. The doctrine of aesthetic 'disinterest' — and its corollary, the autonomous or self-sufficient character of artworks — is chief among these cardinal axioms. But it is also (Derrida argues) subject to various unsettling doubts and indecisions. It requires a strict (*de jure*) demarcation of conceptual bounds which are actually (*de facto*) subverted in the course of Kant's detailed argument. One way to track these unruly effects is to notice how 'Kant' insistently foregrounds this entire supressed problematic by metamorphosing, as it were, from a 'mere' proper name to an element of textual signification.

Of course Derrida has to place his own name at risk when he asks what is involved in this business of authorized signatures. Elsewhere — notably in *Limited Inc* and *Glas* — he allows the name 'Derrida' to penetrate his text through a range of associative hints and allusions that open up manifold possibilities of meaning. Above all, as he writes in *Signsponge*, 'I must refuse to be the philosopher that, in the light of some appearances, I am thought to be . . . and to do this, I have to have it out with the signature, with his, with mine, perhaps, and with the other's . . .' (p. 32). For philosophy is all too prone to 'wash its hands' of the signature, or the whole risky enterprise of speaking in its own (or in the other's) name. Thus Derrida sides with Ponge in his dislike for those 'grand metaphysicolicians' who erect a fine edifice of theory in order to avoid such contaminating influence. At the same time he is anxious to dispel this suspicion, to refuse the name 'philosopher' and engage with Ponge's texts through a different, more 'singular' practice of reading. To do this, he writes, it is necessary to 'make a scene in which I oblige him not to wash his hands any more of the things I say here, be they proper or improper' (p. 32). So the end of all Derrida's apostrophizing play is to break down those well-prepared textual defences that Ponge puts up against the adepts of system and theory. 'Will I myself have caught the whole drift of his work from the accident of his name?' The idea is so absurd, so unthinkable, that it falls beyond range of Ponge's objections.

Despite Derrida's contemptuous remarks about 'philosophy', this text has a certain rigour in its waywardness that may well be ignored by critics all too willing to take those remarks at face value. For *Signsponge* is not, as such readers would have it, just a species of extravagant textual 'freeplay', totally unconcerned with issues of relevance or truth. Certainly Derrida strains these requirements to the limit, and this by way of showing how narrowly — or according to what dogmatic assumptions — they are commonly applied. But there is a widespread reading of Derrida ('American deconstruction', in convenient shorthand) which fastens on his more exciting pronouncements and simply takes for granted the extensive work of analysis from which those pronouncements derive. This is one reason for sounding a cautionary note while otherwise welcoming Richard Rand's admirably sensitive and idiomatic translation. *Signsponge* is, of all Derrida's writings, the text most amenable to domestication on terms laid down by literary critics. What is apt to drop out in this transaction is any real sense of the detailed arguments, including the 'philosophical' pertinence, of Derrida's texts.

So it is well to insist (though at risk of playing the philosopher as straight-man or dupe) that *Signsponge* is a work of considerable analytic power, and one that touches on numerous questions in the province of modern linguistic philosophy. Nor should it come as any great shock to readers, say, of Austin or Ryle that *Signsponge* raises these questions in a mode of calculated hyperbolic fancy. Thus Derrida asks at one point: 'If he (Ponge) had had another name, and if by some incredible hypothesis he could still have been the same person, would he have written *the same thing*?' (p. 116). Outlandish though it seems, this counterfactual scenario is similar to those often conjured up by contemporary philosophers, especially when discussing how names and identities translate between the various 'possible worlds' of logical conjecture.[7] Derek Parfitt's book *Reasons and Persons* — by far the most stimulating recent work of British moral philosophy — has constant resort to such far-fetched hypotheses in testing ideas of our accountability for past and future events.[8] There may seem a world of difference between Derrida's exorbitant 'textualist' style and the clarifying aims of this British analytical tradition. But the difference begins to look less clear-cut as one recalls to what lengths of counterfactual invention philosophers have gone in pursuing the logic of their arguments.

With Ponge, Derrida writes, 'you never know whether he names or describes, nor whether the thing he describes–names is the thing or the name, the common name or proper name' (p. 118). Such remarks can lead off in a number of different directions. One — the most obvious — points toward Frege, Russell and the 'theory of descriptions'.

Another (as I have argued) suggests certain parallels with current ways of thinking in ethics and moral philosophy. And of course there is the use to which this text will surely be put in the interests of a literary-critical drive to free interpretation from the irksome restraints of 'proper', responsible reading. Indeed there are many passages in *Signsponge* that would seem to warrant such claims. 'Once the tyrant has been dethroned, his unique and proper name becomes a common one. The law reveals itself as prostitution' (p. 142). But again, such passages need to be read in the context of Derrida's close and continuing engagement with 'the law' in its manifold aspects, from generic constraints upon writing to the exercise of state power through teaching and other institutions.[9]

For *Signsponge* is as much 'about' the politics of reading as any of Derrida's recent texts. It is in working through the question of juridical border-lines and limits that the sponge, most ambivalent of objects, takes on its peculiar role. This 'thing', Derrida writes, 'is not just something conforming to laws that I discuss objectively (adequately) or, on the contrary, subjectively (anthropomorphically)' (p. 12). Such seeming alternatives — the stock-in-trade of Ponge criticism — are here shown up as delusive oppositions masking a deeper metaphysical complicity. 'Beforehand, the thing is the other, the entirely other which dictates or which writes the law . . .' Only a scrupulously *literal* reading of Ponge can muster the degree of resistance required to grasp that law in all its alien forms and effects. This is the kind of reading that Derrida offers in *Signsponge*. Its force will most likely be lost upon those who approach it — for whatever institutional reasons — in the spirit of anarchic hedonist 'freeplay' that isolated passages seem to invite.

References

1. See especially the references to Russell, Ryle and other 'analytical' philosophers in Derrida, *La Carte Postale de Socrate à Freud et au-delà*, Paris, Flammarion, (1980).
2. See Gottlob Frege, 'On Sense and Reference', in *Translations from the Philosophical Writings of Gottlob Frege*, Max Black and P.T. Geach (eds), Oxford, Basil Blackwell, (1970).
3. For the exchange with Searle, see Derrida, 'Signature Event Context', *Glyph*, Vol. I, Baltimore, Johns Hopkins University Press, (1977), pp. 172–97; Searle, 'Reiterating the Differences', *Glyph*, Vol. I, pp. 198–208; and Derrida, 'Limited Inc abc', *Glyph*, Vol. II, (1977), pp. 162–254.
4. See Bertrand Russell, *An Enquiry into Meaning and Truth*, London, Allen and Unwin, (1948).
5. Derrida, 'Genesis and Structure', in *Writing and Difference*, Alan Bass (trans.), London, Routledge and Kegan Paul, (1978), pp. 154–168.
6. Derrida, 'Economimesis', *Diacritics*, Vol. II, No. 2 (1981), pp. 3–25.
7. For a discussion of naming and the logical problems of 'trans-world' identity, see Saul Kripke, *Naming and Necessity*, Oxford, Blackwell, (1980).
8. Derek Parfitt, *Reasons and Persons*, Oxford, Clarendon Press, (1984).
9. See for instance Derrida, 'The Law of Genre', *Glyph*, Vol. VII, (1980), pp. 202–29; also 'Devant La Loi', in A. Phillips Griffiths (ed.), *Philosophy and Literature*, Cambridge, Cambridge University Press, (1984), pp. 173–88.

11 Textual theory at the bar of reason

This book is by far the most sustained and intelligent critique of post-structuralist theory yet published in Britain or America. It is argued from an adversary stance, but with a vigour and an intellectual passion all too rare among opponents of 'theory' in whatever threatening shape or guise. According to Rose, it is the fault of post-structuralism, not that it has become too much embroiled in theoretical issues, but that it has failed to think through the problems bequeathed by philosophers in the critical tradition descending from Kant. That tradition she sees as having set the main terms for a debate whose categories are centrally those of *jurisprudence*, or the individual subject and his or her standing before the law. Post-Kantian philosophy is heir to certain problems in the nature of its own grounding concepts which cannot be simply pushed aside in the name of some radical break with 'Western metaphysics'. Such gestures are a species of intellectual nihilism, a refusal to engage with hegemonic structures of reason, legality and ethical discourse alike. Taking issue with Foucault and Derrida especially, Rose argues that post-structuralism has not come out, as its proponents would claim, on the far side of those problems and antinomies that dominate classical reason. Rather, it has attempted to exclude them *de jure* from its own more 'radical' or liberated discourse, only to reveal how far it is in thrall to those same (unrecognized) critical motifs. In short, these thinkers have opted for a rhetoric of militant unreason, thereby depriving thought of any power to criticize its own regulative concepts and categories.

The starting-point of Rose's argument is a series of highly persuasive analogies between the Kantian tribunal of philosophic reason and the process of law as administered in court. In each case there is a subject ('natural consciousness'), placed in the position of an unreliable witness whose claims are to be duly cross-questioned and judged by some higher, self-validating discourse of truth. But reflection on the status of the court-room officials suggests that this

Dialectic of Nihilism: post-structuralism and law, Gillian Rose, Oxford, Basil Blackwell, (1984).

authority of law (or reason) may be subject to further complications. To enquire whence derives the ultimate verdict — the *quaestio quid juris* of legal philosophy — is also to ask what grounds exist for the Kantian distinction between 'natural' and 'critical' consciousness. 'For cross-examination reveals the purportedly impersonal authority of Reason to be an ensemble of the three fictitious persons of the law: the judge, the witness and the clerk of the court' (Rose, p. 6). Reason is forced back onto a series of antinomies wherein these roles are seen as perpetually shifting in relation to some ultimate verdict of truth.

Hence Rose's claim that philosophy in the critical (post-Kantian) tradition has developed in close and productive exchange with the discourse of jurisprudence. Philosophy makes trial of 'natural' (pre-reflective) consciousness from the standpoint of a higher, more rational or self-legitimating discourse of knowledge. Legal justice likewise rests its claims upon a careful separation of the courtroom roles of witness, clerk and judge. But there remains the problem of preserving this authority of Law or Reason in face of the conflicting testimonies on offer and the practical business of courtroom administration. The status of the civil subject 'before the law' can thus be compared to the role of natural consciousness when required by Kant to give rational account of its own unexamined presuppositions. The *quaestio quid juris* has the same effect in each case: to reveal yet further antinomies of reason and judgement which admit to final, authoritative verdict.

Rose sees no escape from these antinomies, at least so long as theory acknowledges the fact of its involvement with forms of civil and juridical reason, and hence with institutions of power. Her objection to post-structuralism is that it thinks to place itself beyond them, either by declaring (with Foucault) that power and knowledge are so closely intertwined as henceforth to discredit every form of rational critique, or by heralding (like Derrida) a new dispensation where 'writing' comprehends — and renders undecidable — all the claims of justice and truth. The result in each instance is to yield up the powers of dialectical reason to a spurious radicalism devoid of any genuinely critical content or grasp. In Derrida, she writes, 'this license is employed to undermine, not metaphysics, but political and social theory' (Rose, p. 141). In Foucault, a monolithic concept of 'power', identified at root with the system of monarchical government, gives rise to a straightforward conflation of power and knowledge that in turn underwrites the Nietzschean drive toward a nihilist abandonment of reason itself. 'Once power is made prior to justification, whether legal or philosophical and scientific, the history of law and the history of knowledge are treated as a single process of "epistemologico-juridical" formation' (Rose, p. 174). In this way Foucault collapses a number of crucial distinctions, as between the state and civil society, monarchical government and the rule of law, the interests of power and those of enlightened critique. In calling for a generalized 'political economy of the will to knowledge' he reduces the terms of any such analysis to 'the circulation of pre-political resources, a natural law of power'. Thus Foucault effectively elides the stages of progressive self-understanding inscribed in the tradition of critical thought from Kant, through Hegel to the Frankfurt School. The 'dialectic of nihilism' stigmatized in Rose's title is therefore very much a modern French phenomenon, for all that it finds an elective pre-history in Nietzsche's swerve from the rigours of Kantian critique.

What we are offered in place of this dead-end modernity is a scrupulous thinking-back through the problems thrown up by critical reason in its 'litigious' or legal-interrogative aspect. Here as in earlier books on Hegel and Adorno,[1] Rose takes the path of an immanent critique in which the strategies of argument themselves reproduce the antinomies and blind-spots encountered in the texts she reads. That such obstacles cannot be avoided — unless by falling back on a spurious, self-deceiving rhetoric — is the burden of her case against those who would reject this labour of negative dialectics. The only way forward is to re-think tradition in the light of those set-piece juridical 'scenes' where reason brings experience to the bar of critical reflection.

> Willing to acknowledge that science appeals in the guise of the clerk to the two other legal personae, witness and judge — compacted as that familiar, ungainly 'we' of science — 'we' will seek to re-experience our scientific development without that innocence which unquestioningly accepts the normal, litigious personae and procedures of science, but also without claiming a new, spurious post-legal authority: the aim is simply to be fully alert, to know the score, when faced with the prospect of a newly insinuated law dissembled as a nihilistic break with knowledge and law, with tradition in general. [Rose, p. 7]

This passage brings out both the unremitting argumentative drive and, inseparable from that, the extreme stylistic density of Rose's writing. She has evidently taken Adorno's lesson to heart: that the rigours of immanent critique go along with a sternly self-denying ordinance in point of stylistic appeal.

To take full stock of Rose's arguments would require nothing less than a book-length commentary. Let me at least summarize her main objections to post-structuralist theory, since they amount to a cogent and principled critique which warrants detailed attention. Post-structuralism takes it as a well-established fact that thought is always and everywhere governed by the systems of linguistic representation that make up a given discourse of knowledge. This position is arrived at, to put it very briefly, by a joint application of Saussure's insistence on the 'arbitrary' nature of the sign and a Nietzschean critique of philosophic truth-claims as mere by-products of the will-to-power vested in figural language. The result is a thoroughgoing relativist stance that acknowledges no basis for the claims of truth or reason aside from their role in some particular cultural 'discourse'. Rose sets out to challenge this consensus in the name of an alternative (post-Kantian) tradition that resists the drift toward an all-embracing moral and epistemological scepticism. Even in appropriating Nietzsche, she argues, contemporary theorists have had to disregard his residual 'conscience of method' — or critical thrust — in order to reduce his arguments to the play of ungrounded figural representation. This they have achieved only by ignoring the extent to which Nietzsche's ultimate scepticism came of his engagement with those same central problems that characterized Kantian thought. In retrospect it may seem that reason was 'crippled' by Nietzsche's willingness to press these problems to the point where philosophy relinquished all claim to discriminate truth and error. But the modern recasting of Nietzschean rhetoric embraces his nihilist conclusions while failing to grasp the structured genealogy of concepts that lay behind it. 'Concentrating on Nietzschean perspectivism, on truth as rhetorical value, Foucault would blind us to the truth both of Nietzsche's and of his own rhetoric' (Rose, p. 210). Post-structuralism is deluded if it thinks to arrive at this position 'beyond' metaphysics — or beyond the regime of truth and error — without working through the complex pre-history that led up to Nietzsche's symptomatic crisis of reason.

It is on these grounds that Rose takes issue with the nihilistic strain in current critical theory. Such thinking adopts the 'linguistic turn', or the privilege accorded to rhetoric over reason, as a pretext for ignoring crucial problems in the way of enlightened social critique. Post-structuralism never questions the idea that our concepts and categories are entirely determined by the various signifying codes and systems that make up a given 'discourse'. Yet, as Rose points out, 'the claim that representation is a matter of linguistic convention, not a synthesis of concept and intuition, presupposes both the concept of language and the concept of convention' (Rose, p. 210). It substitutes a suasive rhetoric, a language devoid of philosophic rigour, for the Kantian tradition of hard-pressed argument on and around the categories of knowledge. Hence the main object of Rose's book: to recount the various stages of a long debate in which reason has constantly defended its role as arbiter of truth and justice. Hence also her two-pronged line of attack, on the one hand dealing with post-Kantian philosophers from Hegel to Heidegger and Derrida, while on the other raising issues in the sphere of juridical precept and practice.

In particular she fastens on the differences of view between theorists of the Marburg and Heidelberg schools who produced some sharply conflicting versions of Kantian legal philosophy. Here again, their debate takes the customary form of a civil courtroom proceeding, with the plaintiffs called upon to justify their case and the reader standing in (for theoretical reason) as judge of their competing claims. Under four main headings — 'the concept of law, the categories of law, the persons of law, and natural law' — reason sets out to adjudicate the rival arguments and thereby confirm its own status of impartial authority. But the upshot is always to question that authority, in so far as it rests on a division of roles (within law and reason alike) whose categorical judgements are indefinitely open to appeal. Any verdict handed down by juridical fiat can always be challenged by disputing the grounds of its rational or legislative power.

Thus law, like philosophy, constantly runs up against the problem of establishing its own claims-to-truth on the ground of impartial reason. Decisions of the court are repeatedly quashed and the case reopened for further cross-examination. But these attacks on the system from beyond its immediate jurisdiction always fail in their attempt to shift the debate onto a radically different terrain.

New claimants to the heritage keep appearing, brandishing their own special right, and intent on compounding the matter — on settling out of court. Yet each attempt to fight consciousness and its possessions on non-litigious terrain does not dissolve but reinforces the antinomy of law, the battle over jurisdiction, and ends up back in court. [Rose, p. 25]

In the same way, a thinker like Foucault claims to have broken with the age-old antinomies of philosophic reason, only to leave his texts in thrall to a cruder, undifferentiated notion of ubiquitous power/knowledge. With Derrida also, as Rose reads him, the extension of 'writing' to cover every instance of socio-cultural inscription results in a failure to grasp the antinomies of law and juridical reason. 'Derrida would have us perish without knowing why, for he leaves the law as unknowable as it was before he raised the question of the *graphein*' (Rose, p. 168). This gives rise to a discourse whose 'radical' credentials are underwritten only by a Nietzschean rhetoric of out-and-out epistemological scepticism.

The Kantian antinomies of pure and practical reason — played out between the parties in successive juridical scenes — may admit of no final arbitrating judgement. But they do at least keep open the critical court of appeal, in so far as they allow reason to grasp the constitutive process that has engendered the individual subject and his or her standing before the law. Post-structuralism mystifies this process by dissolving the antinomies and recognizing only a Hobbesian contest of wills between rival claimants to power. 'Critique has turned into discourse as the court of theoretical reason has turned into the court of practical reason' (Rose, p. 173). Such is the consequence of Foucault's equating all forms of knowledge with the exercise of a power whose effects may be located in discourse but whose authority is subject to no kind of rational account. The original 'court of knowledge' whose procedures are established in Kant's *Critique of Pure Reason* has by now become a 'post-critical tribunal', concerned only to expound and classify the various arbitrary dictates of power. Thus in Foucault, according to Rose, 'the internal construction of knowledge changes to conform to the successive epochs of law which it serves' (Rose, p. 173). Any attempt to think through the antinomies of law and, with them, the conflicts of critical reason is henceforth abandoned in the name of a scarcely yet conceivable break with all past and present forms of knowledge.

This apocalyptic strain finds an image in the figure of Nietzsche's Zarathustra, bringing down his new dispensation from the mountain-top but lacking the disciples to convey or interpret his message. 'Behold, here is a new law table; but where are my brethren who will carry it with me into the valley and into the hearts of flesh?'[2] For Rose, the radical injunction contained in this Nietzschean 'transvaluation of values' has lost all its force through being assimilated to a rhetoric that is merely indifferent as regards the truth-claims of law and reason alike. Foucault's genealogy of the will-to-power reverts to a stage of civil society anterior to everything established in the court of juridical reason. This regression is signalled by its falling back upon a language of military tactics and strategies, a discourse sustained by feudal metaphors of warfare and direct coercion. The result is to sever all connection between law and reason as joint representatives of bourgeois society in search of an ultimate legitimizing ground. In Foucault's work, as Rose describes it,

> the intrinsic but unacknowledged connection in the critique of theoretical reason between technical terms of law and the conditions of legitimate knowledge is exposed from the perspective of the era of the post-critical tribunal. [Rose, p. 173]

Thus thought is deprived of any critical purchase on the forms of administrative reason and justice whose evolving relationship Foucault does little to explain.

Rose can also demonstrate convincingly that post-structuralism ignores the legal and historical implications of its own favoured metaphors and tropes. What is truth? asks Nietzsche, and responds with a series of illustrative figures often cited by his contemporary disciples. Truth is 'a mobile, marching army of metaphors, metonyms and anthropomorphisms . . . which after long use seem firm, canonical and obligatory to a people . . . coins which have lost their insignia and now matter only as metals, no longer as coins'.[3] The passage is commonly taken as a pure deconstructive allegory of reading, a reminder that 'truths' are merely another, more persuasive variety of error, and that reason always comes down in the end to a species of rhetorical imposition. But this is to ignore what Rose very acutely remarks: that Nietzsche's language involves a number of specifically *civil* and *economic* metaphors, images whose force goes largely unnoticed on the standard post-structuralist reading. The figure of 'truth' as a currency or coinage should remind us not only that rhetoric pervades the discourse of reason, but also that reason is inescapably bound up with those relations of exchange and control that constitute a given social order. Deconstructionists regularly interpret this passage as an allegory enforcing the *undecidability* of 'literal' versus 'figurative' meaning, and hence — by a barely legitimate extension — of 'truth' versus 'error'. To Rose this account seems the merest of sophistical evasions. What the metaphor should tell us is 'something about the power and weakness of rhetoric and illusion themselves' (Rose, p. 110). The effacement of identifying marks on a coin may be taken more pointedly as signalling the way in which regulative concepts maintain their power despite our forgetting whence they derive. What we should therefore be alert to in Nietzsche's metaphor is 'something we may have forgotten, even though all our exchanges and contracts ('human relations') depend on memory: that the standard or law we implicitly rely on may have lost its authority but nevertheless continues to mediate our innumerable, immediate exchanges' (Rose, p. 110). Thus Rose turns back the post-structuralist reading at precisely the point where it thinks to capitalize on Nietzsche's suggestive metaphor.

The image of truth as a 'mobile, marching army' of rhetorical figures can likewise be read in a diagnostic light very different from the usual post-structuralist gloss. To interpret it wholly in linguistic terms is to imagine, as Rose suggests, an army 'settled in to permanent occupation', since reason would then be powerless to transform the conditions of its own subject status. What is required is the effort to demystify this powerful irrationalist strain in modern thinking in order to demonstrate the motives at work in the turn toward language (or rhetoric) as an ultimate ground of explanation. Post-structuralism fails to meet this requirement, since it always discovers the same baffling end-point to rational thought: the idea that knowledge is everywhere subject to rhetorical forces beyond its power to grasp or effectively criticize. And this last-ditch scepticism goes along with a regressive tendency to bypass the antinomies of critical reason as they bear upon the discourses of law and politics. Hence, as Rose argues, the incapacity of post-structuralist reason to think its way beyond the terms and conditions of a 'feudal', pre-critical order. 'Does it make injustice more tangible, and thereby transformable to locate it in the civil form itself — in the "army", the "coinage", in language itself?' (Rose, p. 109). The literalization of Nietzsche's metaphor can therefore be seen as a reflex symptom of the drive to incapacitate critical reflection by reducing all knowledge to an epiphenomenon of power.

I have perhaps said enough to give some idea of this book's impressive range of reference and sheer intellectual vigour. Certainly Rose's arguments will have to be reckoned with by anyone concerned to gauge the political implications of post-structuralist theory. One reason for Foucault's widespread following at present is the perceived failure of Althusserian Marxism to make good its claims for a 'scientific' discourse of ideological critique.[4] As those claims began to look increasingly dubious — not least under the pressure of deconstructive reading — so theorists turned to another, less vulnerable source of ideas, one that preserved its radical credentials while yielding no hostages to 'science'. What Foucault seemed to promise was a means of demystifying the relationship between power and knowledge without thereby setting up his own discourse as an ultimate (or 'meta-linguistic') source of authority and truth. However, this move has turned out to have disturbing consequences. With Foucault as with Nietzsche, the adoption of a stance supposedly beyond truth and error has lent itself to a great variety of uses, all of them in some sense 'radical' but otherwise spanning the political range from New-Right reaction to ultra-left activist rhetoric. And this ambivalence can be seen as the result of abandoning that tradition of enlightened critique which has characterized not only Marxist thinking but every attempt to separate truth from ideological illusion. Without at least an operative grasp of what it means to uphold this distinction, thinking is thrown back into a relativist position where, quite simply, truth is up for grabs in the medley of competing discourses.

Post-structuralism needs to address these issues more seriously if its political claims are to carry much weight. One possible line of enquiry — as I have argued elsewhere[5] — would bring it into contact with modern analytical philosophy, in particular those developments in truth-conditional semantics that point a way beyond relativist notions of meaning and reference.[6] Another is precisely the path marked out by Gillian Rose in her patient dialectical reconstruction of philosophy in the court of critical reason. This approach has the further significant effect of exposing post-structuralism to the kind of immanent critique practised by Adorno, Habermas and other proponents of Frankfurt-style Critical Theory. It thus provides a point of dialectical leverage for uncovering deep-laid assumptions and problems invisible from within the post-structuralist perspective. In part this amounts to a critique of that perspective from the standpoint of a rival sociology of knowledge derived from the German tradition. But there is also the argument, taken up from Rose's earlier book, *Hegel Contra Sociology*, that critical reason cannot be reduced to a mere reflex product of its own social interests and conditioning. 'It may be', she writes here, 'that we have become so accustomed to thinking that law blinds us to the social that we overlook how socio-logic blinds us to law' (p. 211).

So reason has to steer a critical path between these two opposing temptations. On the one hand it needs to resist the allure of a scepticism rooted in the fetishized notion of a language that everywhere exceeds and disables the power of reason itself. On the other, it must hold out against any reductive sociology of knowledge that would seek to 'explain' such movements of thought entirely in terms of their socio-historical provenance. In short, there is no substitute for the kind of properly dialectical critique that thinks its way through the determinate stages of a certain intellectual history, without thereby abandoning reflection to the 'socio-logic' of relativist fashion. And this means returning to the 'unanswered question' of Kantian philosophy, the *quaestio quid juris* that still, according to Rose, conditions our most basic yet problematic categories: 'metaphysics and science; theory and practice; freedom and necessity; history and form' (Rose, p. 212). There is no thinking 'beyond' these categories while ignoring the antinomies of legislative reason inscribed within them. Such projects may announce themselves as an end to metaphysics or a break with the old, repressive regime of univocal truth and authority. What in fact they reveal, as Rose would argue, is 'in each case a speculative jurisprudence: a story of the identity and non-identity of law and metaphysics retold by the *rhetor* in the mask of the *histor*' (Rose, p. 208).

Rose's case against Foucault has an argumentative force and precision which fully bear out its dialectical claims. I am less convinced by what she has to say about Derrida, partly because she tends to pass over those texts and those aspects of his writing which do precisely engage with the antinomies of civil and legislative reason. This connection is made quite explicitly in a number of recent essays where Derrida deconstructs (for want of a better, less prejudicial term) the historical relation between forms of knowledge and structures of 'juridico–discursive' power.[7] Elsewhere he addresses the Kantian antinomies in just such a way as to bring out their bearing on the civil institutions of law and an emergent bourgeois public sphere.[8] To some extent, no doubt, these texts reflect a growing unease on Derrida's part concerning the charges of political quietism levelled against deconstruction. But his writing has always been politically engaged in the sense of revealing those mythologies and systems of premature totalization which reduce all history to so many episodes in the course of some grand teleological Idea.

Predictably, it is Derrida's reading of Hegel that provokes Gillian Rose's most hostile commentary.[9] 'History for Derrida becomes the repetitive story of a "closed field of metaphysics" which he himself has closed, and within which his "indefinite exchange of Rousseauist and Hegelian positions . . . obeys the laws inscribed within all the concepts that he has just recalled"' (Rose, p. 147). It takes a careful scrutiny (attending to the quote-marks) to notice that Rose is here citing Derrida back against himself in order to suggest that *he*, and not Hegel, is guilty of such mystifying tactics. But a simple *tu quoque*, however neatly turned, is not sufficient to discountenance the extreme critical rigour that Derrida brings to his reading of Hegel. Since Rose lines up (to put it crudely) very much on the side of Hegelian dialectic, she fails to take the force of Derrida's argument, preferring to treat it as just another species of 'textualist' mystification. But this is to ignore both the textual specificity and the critical thrust of Derrida's reading: namely, that the marked political ambivalence of Hegel's discourse comes of its residual Idealist attachment to a myth of universal history.

Deconstruction is not just one more variety of a generalized 'poststructuralist' discourse. What is lacking in Rose's otherwise admirably cogent critique is any sense of the distinction between Foucault's thoroughly relativist equation of power and knowledge and Derrida's more rigorous thinking-through of its problematic textual consequences. What is more, this rigour is by no means confined to epistemological subtleties, but extends into regions of political and (in Rose's own terms) of legal–administrative reason. Derrida's recent texts provide some striking examples of how this project may be carried through in the form of a deconstructive close-reading of philosophic arguments. And there are others — notably Paul de Man — whose writings can likewise be enlisted on behalf of a rigorous socio-political critique. De Man's chapters on Rousseau (in *Allegories of Reading*) are centrally concerned with issues in the province of law and constitutional theory. His essay on *The Social Contract*[10] is perhaps the most scrupulous and hard-pressed reading to date of how politics enters the discourse of reason through effects of a legislative rhetoric none the less powerful for its lack of any ultimate epistemological authority. Yet the upshot of de Man's reading — to summarize, again very crudely — is that no genuine understanding is possible unless one presses the textual critique to a point where theory begins to grasp the antinomies of law and reason.[11]

At the limit he finds that Rousseau's statements in the *Contract* are caught up in the strictly 'undecidable' play of its own textual constitution. Thus:

> the tension between figural and grammatical language is duplicated in the differentiation between the State as a defined entity (État) and the State as a principle of action (Souverain) or, in linguistic terms, between the constative and the performative aspect of language.[12]

On a cursory reading it might seem that de Man is embracing a typecast 'Nietzschean' scepticism which would treat all issues of politics and knowledge as products of an arbitrary will-to-power within language. But this reading — like similar accounts of Derrida's work — must needs pass over the radical implications of thinking through the antinomies of law inscribed in the founding texts of Western tradition. Gillian Rose tends to ignore this aspect of the deconstructive enterprise in her will to prove that it finally rejoins the 'dialectic of nihilism' whose history runs, in symptomatic stages, from Nietzsche to Foucault. I would argue, on the contrary, that deconstruction is more properly aligned with that other tradition of enlightened critique where Rose locates the main sources of resistance to the latter-day powers of unreason.

This is not to quarrel with her broader diagnosis of the post-structuralist condition. Here she has argued a powerful case for doubting the self-styled 'radical' effects of a discourse that seemingly renounces all claim to adjudicate in matters of reason and truth. Her book should stimulate widespread discussion among critics, philosophers and, more particularly, theorists of a post-structuralist persuasion.

References

1. See Gillian Rose, *Hegel Contra Sociology*, London, Athlone, (1981) and *The Melancholy Science: an introduction to the thought of Theodor W. Adorno*, London, Macmillan, (1978).
2. Quoted by Derrida in *Writing and Difference*, Alan Bass (trans.), London, Routledge and Kegan Paul, (1978), p. 30.
3. Nietzsche, 'On Truth and Falsehood in an Ultra-Moral Sense', in *The Portable Nietzsche*, Walter Kaufmann (trans.), New York, Viking, pp. 46–7.
4. See for instance Paul Hirst, 'Althusser's Theory of Ideology', *Economy and Society* 5 (1976), pp. 385–412.
5. In *The Contest of Faculties: philosophy and theory after deconstruction*, London, Methuen, (1985).
6. See especially Donald Davidson, *Inquiries into Truth and Interpretation*, London, Oxford University Press, (1984).
7. See for instance Derrida, 'Où commence et comment finit un corps enseignant', in Dominique Crisoni (ed.), *Politiques de la philosophie*, Paris,

Grasset, (1976), pp. 55–97. Also his essay 'On an Apocalyptic Tone Recently Adopted in Philosophy', John P. Leavey (trans.), *The Oxford Literary Review*, Vol. VI (1984), pp. 3–37.

8. Derrida, 'Economimesis', translated in *Diacritics*, Vol. XI, (1981), pp. 3–25.

9. Derrida, 'From Restricted to General Economy', in *Writing and Difference*, Alan Bass (trans.), London, Routledge and Kegan Paul, (1978), pp. 251–77.

10. Paul de Man, 'Promises (*Social Contract*)', in *Allegories of Reading: figural language in Rousseau, Nietzsche, Rilke, and Proust*, New Haven, Yale University Press, (1979), pp. 246–77.

11. De Man's later essays are very much concerned with the politics of deconstruction, or — more precisely — the ideological motives bound up with the widespread 'resistance to theory'. See for instance de Man, 'Hegel On The Sublime', in Mark Krupnick (ed.), *Displacement: Derrida and after*, Bloomington, Indiana University Press, (1983), pp. 139–53; also 'The Resistance to Theory', in Barbara Johnson (ed.), *The Pedagogical Imperative, Yale French Studies*, Vol. LXIII, (1982), pp. 3–20.

Index of Names

McAuslan, P. 28
McClary, S. 57
McIntyre, A. 166–7, 185–6
Mendelssohn, Felix 31
Michaels, W.B. 82, 154
Mill, J.S. 228
Miller, J. Hillis 27, 162, 165–8, 172,
    179, 182–3, 185, 198, 217, 222, 225
Milton, John 27, 90, 122
Mitchell, W.J.T. 27, 154
Mizumura, M. 186
Mozart, Wolfgang A. 43, 49
Murphy, W.T. 154

Nabokov, V. 208
Nietzsche, Friedrich 12, 16, 31, 36–7,
    55–6, 65, 95–6, 107, 112–13, 124,
    128, 148–9, 155, 157, 180–1, 187–98,
    213–14, 237–42, 245
Norton, R. 57
Novalis 161
Nuttall, A.D. 212

Olsen, Regine 172
Ong, W. 155
Owen, Robert 29

Parfitt, D. 234–5
Paulin, T. 212
Plato 10, 12, 35, 109, 124, 148, 191,
    216, 222
Ponge, Francis 227–35
Pope, Alexander 9, 39, 84–108, 125,
    186
Poulet, G. 162–3
Pradhan, S. 79–81, 83
Price, M. 96–8
Protagoras 136
Proust, Marcel 173, 183–4
Pythagoras 45

Quine, W.V. 60–2, 66–9, 71, 73–4,
    82
Quintilian 150

Rabinow, P. 153
Rameau, Jean-Philippe 50
Ramus 155
Rand, R. 227–8, 234
Ransom, John Crowe 85, 107
Rawls, John 128, 133–4, 154
Richards, I.A. 201
Ricks, C. 211–12
Rorty, R. 9–10, 12–13, 26–7, 66–83,
    194–5, 198, 214–5, 222, 225
Rose, Gillian 28, 236–46
Rosen, C. 56
Rousseau, J.-J. 18, 20, 39, 49–53, 57,
    136–9, 143–5, 162, 172–3, 183–4,
    224, 244–5

Russell, Bertrand 228–30, 234–5
Ryle, Gilbert 234–5

Saint-Simon 29
Salusinszki, I. 198
Sapir, E. 62
Saussure, F. de 37, 64, 66, 82, 120,
    149, 238
Schelling, F.W.J. 35, 164, 175, 214,
    218–19
Schiller, J.C.F. 46, 141, 205–6
Schlegel, Friedrich 156–62, 163, 168–9,
    177–9, 183–5
Schoenberg, Arnold 41–2, 45–7, 56
Schopenhauer, A. 31–3, 36–7, 40–1,
    53–5
Searle, John R. 80, 83, 133–4, 154,
    189, 198, 214, 225, 227, 229,
    235
Sellars, W. 71
Shakespeare, William 9, 86, 96,
    109–25, 212, 227
Shaw, G.B. 117
Shelley, P.B. 122, 176, 186
Sidney, Sir Philip 102
Simpson, D. 107
Singer, J.W. 153
Socrates 36, 95, 113, 136, 177–8, 181,
    188
Solger, K. 161, 177
Spenser, Edmund 102
Sprinker, M. 40, 56, 205–6,
    209–12
Stalin, Josef 34
Starobinski, J. 163, 169
Stevens, Wallace 159, 208, 225
Stick, J. 154
Strawson, P. 194
Subotnik, Rose R. 57
Swift, Jonathan 169, 185–6
Szondi, P. 163, 169

Tarski, A. 61–2
Tate, Allen 84–5, 107
Taylor, M.C. 186
Thébaud, J.-L. 198
Thompson, Josiah 186
Tolstoy, Leo 117
Trollope, A. 166
Trubek, D. 153
Truffaut, F. 204
Tushnet, M. 153

Unger, R.M. 27, 146, 153, 155

Wagner, Richard 36, 41–3, 54–5
Warminski, A. 184
Weber, Max 47, 57
White, Hayden 13, 16, 25, 27
Whorf, B.L. 62–4, 66, 73